FINDING THE END OF THE WORLD

By Ron Braley

xulon PRESS

FINDING THE END OF THE WORLD
by Ron Braley

Printed in the United States of America

ISBN 9781613791448

www.xulonpress.com

TABLE OF CONTENTS

Table of Graphics

ACKNOWLEDGMENTS

I'm eternally grateful to God and His Spirit for patience, mercy, and guidance during the many years this project has spanned. Nothing matters more to me than pleasing God and His Christ, so I'm humbled to have been allowed to write this study guide and teach such a controversial but important topic.

Many of my fellow human beings have also been instrumental in the creation and development of this wonderful product. It would've been difficult if not impossible to do without several key participants. I'd like to thank them personally. Most significantly, I'd like to acknowledge Christopher Sellers and the part he played in birthing this book. I'm convinced my family would never have realized the benefit of having me as the spiritual leader of our household had he not challenged my lack of biblical understanding and faith. This study guide certainly would have never materialized, and I would have remained lost! Christopher: Thank you! My prayer is that you'll always be blessed for changing my life and potentially the lives of whoever reads this text.

Next, my heart bursts with affection and gratitude for Joanne, my beautiful bride of 27 years. Her love, patience, support, and feedback have paved the way for God to do this work through me. Had it not been for her gentle nudges and encouragement, I'm sure I would've given up on this difficult undertaking long ago. What a blessing she has been! Joanne: I love you and am looking forward to whatever God has next for us!

I'd also like to thank my children, who've had to listen to what probably seemed like a million hours of my ramblings on this subject over the years. Most significantly, I'm very grateful to my daughter Tiffany, who did a wonderful job of tackling this project from the perspective of a devoted student. Her input and feedback have proven invaluable to fine-tuning this teaching tool. And spending time with her in working on this was fun!

My father, Dennis Braley, has been helpful in identifying specific technical issues related to the publication. I also greatly appreciate the projector he gave me as an aid in conducting group study sessions. Larry Herzog, one of my best friends for the last 15 years, has been a cornerstone in this project since just after its inception. Among other things, he established sites (like e-fellowship.net) for early Internet studies of this topic. I've appreciated his encouragement and his input from a student's standpoint.

A very special thank you goes to my friend and pastor, Mr. Ron Almberg. There's absolutely no way this writing could have succeeded without him. I can't imagine the countless hours he spent editing this document and providing feedback and accountability. Ron: Thank you for your selfless contribution in helping me in this endeavor. I'm sure God will greatly reward your efforts!

Finally, I'd like to thank Rick Meyers, creator of E-Sword, for his wonderful donation-based study tool. I'm sure he's gone through great efforts to produce this powerful Scripture toolbox, building something that can turn seemingly impossible and time-consuming tasks into simple jobs that can be done in seconds. I suspect I'd still be working on Chapter Four if not for his wonderful gift to the world.

FOREWORD

Our world as we know it will end suddenly one day. But God's incredibly destructive wrath and a gathering of those faithful to Christ will come first. You and I will be in one of two groups if this happens in our lifetime: those gathered before the destruction begins, or the rest who'll suffer the wrath of God and eternal torment. No other options exist. Following a misguided church tradition and believing in false doctrine can cause a lack of faith based on a misunderstanding of the gospel, placing one in the latter group. Also, being ignorant of what God has already told us about the end of time by not exposing ourselves to gospel teaching about it can result in the same outcome.

The objective of this study is to help you avoid the destruction and torment mentioned above by accomplishing several goals:

- Guide you through as much Scripture as possible dealing with Christ's return so that you can make your own informed decision about what it teaches.
- Offer insight into existing end-times theories to examine where they may get it right or wrong.
- Teach you how to study Scripture so that you'll have a basic foundation for reading and studying it on your own.

Additional rewards I hope you'll gain from going through this study:

- Increased knowledge of Christ's return. This will reduce confusion and help keep you from being vulnerable to false doctrine.
- Motivation to become a spiritual leader in your home or community.
- Able to study God's Word more effectively.
- Stronger faith through learning the gospel.

While I don't intend to push a particular end-times view, the circumstances surrounding Christ's return – and certainly His actual coming – will become clearer and relatively easy to understand. Of course, whether this happens as advertised will depend on your approach to studying the topic and related Scripture. If you're like I was in my earlier spiritual journey, you may have already adopted your church's end-times doctrine (probably without question). In my experience, a pre-tribulation rapture position seems to be most prevalent – at least with evangelical churches in the United States. This is what I believed. Again, it's what my church doctrine reflected. My desire is to share with you my subsequent discoveries in the Scripture, and to provide you with the tools to do your own study and build your own faith.

Why am I so passionate about this topic? Until 1998, I was a statistic – one of 95% of Christians who don't read God's Word on a regular basis. Most of my biblical knowledge had come only from others. I was playing scriptural "Russian roulette," taking what some pastors and a few other well-meaning souls said as "gospel" in regards to end-times events. This was a great mistake and very dangerous. Why? What I learned later through my own study of Scripture was that much of what I believed concerning the end times resulted from misinterpretations, misunderstandings, personal or hidden agendas, or incomplete Scripture references taken out of context. But what did I know? I had no idea of what I *didn't* know, so I was very content.

There's danger in being scripturally illiterate. The Bible makes it very clear that our faith is strengthened from hearing the gospel, which is the good news of Jesus Christ's accomplishments in His first coming and the promise of His second coming. However, if what we know or believe is contrary to it, then our faith can be false or nonexistent. According to Scripture, we know there'll be a falling away from the faith and great deception of believers in the last days (cf. 1 Timothy 4:1, for instance). The lack of faith – or a faulty foundation built on false teaching – will open the door to allow this to happen. Conversely, I strongly believe that those who study Scripture and history carefully, while asking for God's Holy Spirit to give them wisdom, will have a strong faith and won't easily be tricked or confused.

So there I was in 1998 – full of bliss and of little faith until I started studying God's Word after being challenged by a friend. In this particular case, he revealed my misunderstandings about Christ's return, which was based on partial verses such as "*Pray to be found worthy to escape,*" or "*Jesus will come back like a thief.*" Angered at first (no one likes being wrong!) I told him I'd prove the end-of-the-world theory I believed. After all, there had to be a good reason why so many people believed as I did.

After about 90 days of extensive Internet research, bugging pastors about why they believed what they believed, and sporadic Bible searches, I had to go back to my friend empty-handed and admit there was a problem and that I needed to become more knowledgeable. This humbling experience changed my life forever. I became the spiritual leader in my home and began daily devotions with my family. I also began building and strengthening my faith through regular study of God's Word and was relentless in my pursuit of the truth regarding Christ's return.

During this time, I found that no one could (or would) present a valid defense of their end-times belief based upon Scripture. Out of frustration, some people (including pastors) would say, "It doesn't matter what you believe about the rapture anyway as long as you're saved." I accepted this at first. However, I understood it to be a false sentiment after learning more about the signs surrounding Christ's return to earth and the subsequent gathering.

God's Word teaches us there'll be a falling away from the faith and a great deception of believers in the last days. We're also taught that the "chosen of God" will undergo persecution and possibly death during a period of extreme trouble. If you're having difficulty with these ideas, I encourage you to be patient and follow along in this study. I believe you'll come to the same conclusion despite what you think you may already know about "the falling away," "the great deception," "the time of extreme trouble," "the rapture," or "the chosen of God." And even if you don't, you'll have the personal satisfaction of knowing you studied it for yourself and came to your own conclusions.

Passionate about teaching others to read and understand Scripture and learn the truth about many false church teachings (like several current end-times theories), I created a pamphlet, which turned into a larger document, which then turned into an Internet study, which . . . well, you get the idea. This project has grown considerably and been met with open arms by people just like me who for many years were ignorant of God's Word and had little faith. Since 1998, I've devoted well over 3,000 hours to researching, reading about, writing, thinking about, discussing, and teaching this very important topic. It's my pleasure to share the results with you.

Here's a brief overview of what we'll study together:

End-of-the-age prophecies: Preview of what the Bible has to say about the end of our world as we know it.

How to study Scripture: Important preparation for your study! Yes, there's more to understanding God's Word than just reading it.

History of the Jews: From the time of Abraham to the present. It also includes the end-of-the world visions of prophets like Daniel and Ezekiel.

End-times terminology: Common end-of-the-age terms and supporting Scripture.

The big picture: Beginning with a review of prophecy and a look at what Jesus, Peter, and Paul had to say about this subject. You'll also do an in-depth study of the Revelation given to John by Jesus.

End-times theories: Insight into existing views related to Christ's return.

Please review the Study Plan in APPENDIX A if you're interested in establishing an individual structured plan or if you'll be leading a group study. You're welcome, and encouraged, to take all the time you need to go through the course comfortably – the plan and templates are only loose guidelines and certainly not binding. Head to the *Introduction* afterward for basic tips that will help you make the most of your end-of-the-world education.

My sincere wish is that your life (and that of others around you) will be forever changed in a positive way, just as mine was, after going through this study.

With heartfelt gratitude and best wishes,

Ron Braley
endoftheworld@FindingRevelation.com
www.findingrevelation.com

Introduction

Before embarking on your new adventure, I'd like to talk about a couple of fundamental concepts related to this study and offer a few tips that will help you make the most of your time and make it more enjoyable.

First and foremost, there's nothing more important than the hope and expectation of Christ's return and the salvation that awaits those who are His. He will return as promised despite the fact that we don't always agree on the timing or sequence of events surrounding His second coming. If you don't know Christ or haven't yet accepted Him as the way to God, I encourage you to take what you'll learn in Chapter Seven of this guide to heart. Accepting the gift of Christ will change your life forever. TRUE

Second, since the title of this guide is *Finding the End of the World*, I guess we should define what *world,* or *age*, is and when it will end.

The Greek word for *age* or *world* is *aiōn* (ahee-ohn') and it represents an era. Most verses in our study related to *age* or *world* use that Greek word to depict the *current* era. We're in the last days as evidenced by the writings of Jesus and Paul, but the end of the current era/world/age won't occur until after the following events have passed: appearance of the Antichrist, three-and-a-half-year Great Tribulation, God's wrath, Christ's kingdom, and the great judgment. We'll certainly delve deeper into these things in the coming chapters. You may also want to preview the index of end-times terminology in Appendix B.

On the subject of the actual study, you may be asking yourself, "Which Bible translation should I use when reading the references?" I encourage the use of the King James Bible or NASB (New American Standard Bible) and discourage use of the NIV (New International Version) Bible. All Scripture quoted in this book came from the

NASB unless otherwise noted, and is presented in italicized text. Boldfacing in Scripture quotes was applied solely by me for the purpose of highlighting.

Use what you feel comfortable with, but please know there are differences between translations; the NIV, in my opinion, contains significant omissions and modifications that could negatively affect your study. Here's one source of many you can query if you're curious about NIV challenges: trinitarianbiblesociety.com/site/articles/NIV.asp. I tend to compare Scripture through multiple translations when researching important issues. You may wish to do the same. I can't imagine the agony translators must experience when trying to convert writings into equivalent meanings in other languages! Cross-examining English texts can give a person a better understanding of what the source is trying to communicate.

We'll take a literal approach to studying the Scriptures. We'll also consider Scripture references in context and take them at face value whenever possible, allowing the use of symbolism only where the interpretation is obvious. We'll also make sure we search and compare all Scripture and history (where known) to ensure we assign accurate meaning to those symbols.

I need to stress at this point that Jesus was very clear about the need to keep His Revelation to John intact, unchanged, and heeded by believers. I'm passionate about helping you do just that through this study. Toward that end, I've divided key areas into sections, or themes, and supported those themes through detail provided in section chapters.

- **PART ONE**: Setting the Stage. This section provides insight into why this topic is so important to learn – and learn correctly. It also includes a summary of what Scripture has to say about the sequence of the end of the world to help stimulate and keep your interest in this program.

- **PART TWO**: Faith & Foundation - How to Study Effectively.

Discover the true meaning of faith and how to obtain and keep it through effective study of the Word of God. Much of this section deals with study tools and proper methods of scriptural interpretation.

- **PART THREE**: The Cast, Crew, & Props. By far the longest and most intense theme, this portion of the program goes to great lengths to help you find out as much about end-of-the-world players as possible. You'll learn about the Antichrist, False Prophet, Harlot Babylon, those who will be beheaded for their faith, and much more through an exhaustive study of Scripture.

- **PART FOUR**: Revelation & Insight. This section offers something of a guided tour through apocalyptic literature written by Old Testament prophets like Daniel and Ezekiel, New Testament apostles such as Peter and Paul, and our Lord Jesus Christ. We'll cover the biblical books of Daniel and the Revelation in addition to highlighting what Jesus, Peter, Paul, and others had to say about the end of the world. You'll have seen many of these Scripture references by now. However, this particular theme will help you build a complete and accurate picture of what the end will look like through an unveiling of what each writer had to say on the subject. You'll be amazed at how the prophecies and apocalyptic writings corroborated and supported each other even though they were written tens or hundreds of years apart.

- **PART FIVE**: Putting It All Together. Compare and contrast different end-times viewpoints. By this time you should have gained considerable knowledge and insight into this subject and therefore should be able to look at what others think about this subject objectively. Finally, firm up what we've learned together by reviewing all previous sections.

Each part is broken down into chapters and subtopics. Chapters provide the background and support for section themes. I've bulleted headings and topics to make it easier to follow the points and find Scripture references. Guidance with regard to chapter components:

RECOMMENDED READING: You'll find them at the beginning of some of the topics (within Chapter Twelve, for instance). Please read or review them before continuing with the study.

SUPPLEMENTAL READING: These are related to chapter topics and will provide a lot more background and proof texts than the narrative alone. Not every chapter will have SUPPLEMENTAL READING, but you'll find them at the end of the chapter for those that do.

✓ **Quick Reference**: I've often broken up topics into smaller units and put supporting Scripture into a Quick Reference that follows. You'll also find them at the beginning of topics in some cases. Please read them to enhance your study session.

CHECKUP QUESTIONS: These are meant to check your understanding of what was covered in the chapter and provoke additional thoughts and questions to elevate your learning to a higher level.

May you be blessed as you begin your study with PART ONE – Setting the Stage.

PART ONE

Setting the Stage

Chapter One

Why Worry About This?

Being uninformed is never a good thing and can be dangerous – especially if it leads to ignorance of things related to Christ – past, present, or future. Getting some biblical things wrong or ignoring certain spiritual truths altogether can be deadly. Stiff penalties and great judgment can await those who allow themselves to be misled through false teaching. Will it matter that they're just taking in what they've been taught (e.g. through church tradition)? No! Ignorance is no excuse. Those who aren't confirming what they're being told risk taking in false teaching, which could open the door to spiritual destruction.

For instance, in the Revelation given to the apostle John we're told that those taking the mark or name of a dreadful worldwide ruler (you'll learn later that this is the Antichrist) during his reign of terror will be blotted from the Book of Life and suffer God's wrath. I've heard at least one person claim they'll take that mark because God will understand the need for them to feed their families since those NOT taking this mark will have a tough time buying or selling goods during the Great Tribulation. Apparently this individual is ignorant of the warning against taking the mark and of the consequences mentioned in Scripture. Also, we're told true believers during that terrible time won't "*love their lives so much as to shrink from death*" (Revelation 12:11). Those who truly love Christ and follow Him will love Him more than earthly treasures or even their own lives.

Another unfortunate side-effect to scriptural ignorance is inability or difficulty in preaching the gospel to others. Christ admonished us to "*make disciples of all nations.*" Doing this will be hard if not impossible if we don't know what we believe or why.

But why is learning what the Bible has to say about the end times important? The topic of the end of the world is discussed extensively in Old and New Testament Scriptures. Most of the Old Testament prophets revealed end-times information. Jesus and several New Testament apostles did too (Appendix B contains most related Scripture references). Apparently, God feels it should be important to us! As such, the Bible contains plenty of clues and signs to teach us about the end-times sequence of events.

Jesus gave us signs to watch for in advance of His return. The apostle Paul reiterated a couple of those when he reminded Jew and Gentile Christians in Thessalonica that Christ wouldn't appear and gather believers to Himself until after a falling away from the faith and after the Antichrist enters the temple and exalts himself above God. Other signs that will precede Christ's return include an increase in false messiahs, violence, famines, and earthquakes.

You're probably saying to yourself, "Alright already! Answer the question: Why is this end-times stuff so important?" I hope that by reading the above scenarios, you've begun to understand that having the wrong answer to the right question or not knowing anything at all can be spiritually risky. In the case of the end of the world, it can be downright deadly. Not knowing what to expect with regard to the time of the end could cause:

1. Confusion, hatred of God, and falling away from the faith by those who erroneously believe they'll be removed from earth before the Great Tribulation (wrath of the Antichrist).
2. Suffering God's wrath. Again, accepting this "mark" of the Antichrist to save ourselves will result in a loss of salvation and the suffering of God's wrath, which will be poured out on the rest of the world after true believers have been gathered.
3. Inability to witness effectively before or during that time (how can we preach what we don't know?).

While doing research for this study guide, I've heard many lighthearted responses such as, "I'm a pan-tribber – it will all pan out in the end." Or, "It doesn't matter what you believe about the return of Christ as long as you're saved." Let's be clear: this scriptural teaching matters and things WON'T just pan out in the end! As stated above, there'll be a falling away from the faith and deception in the end – most likely made possible by shaky faith built from false doctrine and a lack of knowledge of God's Word. It's important to note here that false doctrine and lack of knowledge, and the shaky faith that follows, will result in a misunderstanding of other doctrines of the faith as well, not just eschatology (study of end-times events).

Some have discouraged Christians from studying the writings of biblical prophets like Daniel and Ezekiel or the Revelation given by Jesus. Why? In my experience, it's because they believe Christians will already be in heaven before events portrayed within those prophecies or the Revelation begin. As a result, they're sure none of it will apply to them anyway. There's no biblical support for this point of view. What will proponents of that end-times position feel after believing they'll be whisked off the earth before the events foretold by Jesus unfold, but things don't work out that way? Perhaps betrayed or abandoned. Or they may believe there's no God since things didn't work out the way they thought they would and that no good God would let people suffer the way they will during the Great Tribulation. Again, this certainly opens the door to a possibility of falling away from faith in Christ and the hope we place in Him.

Confusion. Deception. Walking away from the faith. Spiritual and physical death. All of these are possible outcomes of not knowing God's Word – the end-of-the-world Scripture, in our case. Let's avoid destruction and confusion by digging in and becoming more knowledgeable of what God, His prophets, and His Son had to say about this extremely important topic.

In the next chapter, we'll whet your appetite by previewing the end-of-the-world picture you'll study in great detail later.

SUPPLEMENTAL READING (Either the KJV or NASB version of the Bible is recommended; read at least three verses before and after scriptural references to understand the context better):

1. Falling away from the faith in the last days:
    a. Matthew 24:10
    b. 2 Thessalonians 2:3
    c. 1 Timothy 4:1
2. Being deceived:
    a. Matthew 24:4, 5, 11, & 24
    b. Mark 13:5 & 6
    c. Luke 21:8
    d. 2 Timothy 3:13 – 17
3. Consequences of false teaching:
    a. Jeremiah 14:14 & 15
    b. Jeremiah 23:32 – 34
    c. Zechariah 10:2
    d. Matthew 7:15-19
    e. 2 Peter 2:1 – 10
    f. Revelation 2:20 – 22
4. Warned to be watchful for Christ's return:
    a. Matthew 24:37-51
    b. Mark 13:32-37
    c. Luke 12:35-46; 17:26 & 27; 21:28-36
    d. 1 Thessalonians 5:2-23
    e. 2 Timothy 4:1-4 and 3:1-3
    f. 2 Peter 3:10-18
    g. Revelation 3:3; 16:15
5. Consequences of taking the "mark of the beast": Revelation 13:16; 14:9 & 11; 16:2; 19:20
6. Revelation – for the church: Revelation 1:1; 22:9 & 16

CHAPTER TWO

A GLIMPSE OF THE END

It would be really boring to make you wait until you've learned study tools, terminology, history, etc., before getting to the meat – the end-of-the-world Scripture. So, to build and keep your interest, we'll spend some time previewing what Scripture has to say about the times of the end. But please allow me to present a brief disclaimer first.

There are several end-times views and differences of opinion within each major view. All have some valid points. It's unlikely a reader will agree on every statement made in this guide or anywhere else for that matter. So let's agree to play nicely and remain open to instruction and correction from God's Word. Please read the entire text carefully along with all related Scripture, even if you hold to a view that isn't in alignment with this study.

So what is the "end"? According to Jesus, it will be the conclusion of this current age with the great judgment preceding the creation of a new heaven and earth. According to the apostle Paul, we're already in the "last days" leading up to the very end. The following is a preview of the end times in a nutshell along with a brief description of each major section it comprises. I promise we'll cover these subjects in greater detail. Everything addressed will be based on Scripture and historical evidence.

- End (or last) days:
  - Began with Christ's ascension into heaven.
  - Includes signs such as increasing violence and earthquakes.
  - Will climax with a three-and-a-half-year time of great trouble, gathering of believers, wrath of God against the rest of the world (destruction), and reign of Christ on earth.

- End of the world (age): Conclusion of this age at the great judgment preceding the creation of a new heaven and earth.

The diagram and explanations below will shed more light on these landmark events.

2.1 Abbreviated Timeline

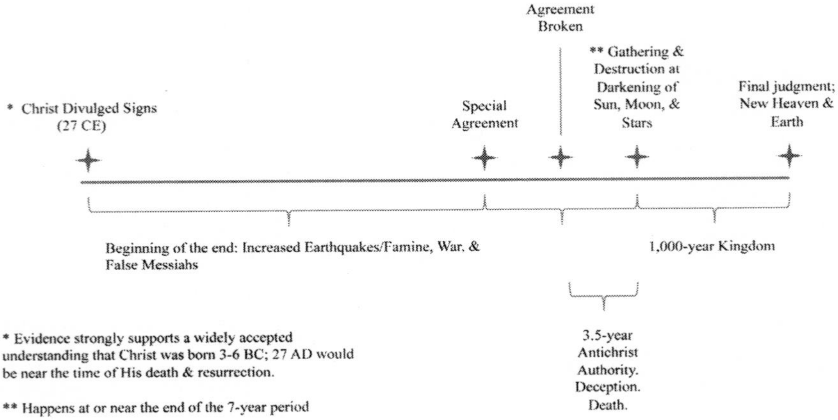

Beginning of the end: Christ forewarned that symptoms of the end such as false messiahs, wars, and earthquakes and famine will occur with greater intensity and frequency as the end draws near. As a result, He called them "birth pangs," but they wouldn't necessarily indicate the very end had arrived. According to the Old Testament prophet Daniel, a seven-year period (or a week of years) remains to usher in Christ's kingdom, end sin, and bring everlasting righteousness. An "agreement" between Israel and others will start that seven-year period. Again, this will happen just before the end when there'll be an increase in violence, earthquakes, and deception. We know nothing about how the first three and a half years of the seven-year timeframe will go, but the Bible has plenty to say about the last half as you'll learn later.

✓ **Quick reference:**
- False messiahs: Matthew 24:5 & Revelation 6:2

    - NOTE: Righteousness is suggested, but Christ's weapon is the sword, not bow. We'll discuss this further in Chapter Sixteen.
- War/violence: Matthew 24:6 & Revelation 6:4
- Famine/earthquake: Matthew 24:7 & Revelation 6:5-6
- Seven-year period: Daniel 9:27 (one week of years)

Change of heart: After the first three and a half years, the authority we call the Antichrist will break the agreement and begin a three-and-a-half-year reign of terror, or great tribulation, against God's chosen – Jew and Christian alike. Jesus quoted Daniel's prophecy about this when discussing the end of the world with His disciples. This period won't come as a surprise to those of us who are aware of the signs and warnings. Please note that the "time, times, and dividing of time" in Daniel 7:25 (listed below) represents 1 year + multiple (2) + half for a total of 3.5 years. This will be corroborated by other scriptural references and explained further in our study, but I've listed the reference here for your edification.

✓ **Quick reference**:
- Broken agreement: Daniel 9:27; Matthew 24:15
- Three-and-a-half-year authority: Daniel 7:25
- Great Tribulation: Matthew 24:9 & 21; Revelation 7:9-14

Signs of the times: According to Daniel, Jesus, and the apostle Paul, the timeframe to include the Antichrist's wrath, the gathering of believers, and God's wrath will be accompanied by signs. Here are a few you'll learn about:

- The Antichrist coming to authority in a particular way.
- A broken agreement with negative consequences to Israel and all true believers of Jesus.
- The creation of a "mark" needed to buy and sell.
- Great tribulation/persecution of God's chosen (up to three and a half years).
- Darkening of the sun, moon, and stars to usher in Christ's return and our gathering by His angels.

✓ **Quick reference:**
- The mark: Revelation 13:16-18; 14:9-11; 15:2; 16:2; 19:20; 20:4
- Darkening of the sun, moon, and stars: Matthew 24:29; Revelation 6:12-13

Gathering of the good: Jesus will appear with His angels and gather believers – those who've died and those still alive in Christ – at some point during the second half of this three-and-a-half-year period. His appearing and the gathering will be preceded by a complete darkening of the sun, moon, and stars. Please note there may be some disagreement as to whether this will happen just before the end or exactly at the end of this time period. Regardless, nothing in Scripture, history, or prophecy suggests the gathering – or *rapture* – will happen any sooner.

✓ **Quick reference:**
- Gathering of believers: Matthew 13:30 & 24:30-31; 2 Thessalonians 2:1; Revelation 14:15-16

Wrath of God: Those left on the earth will suffer incredible destruction as God's angels deploy His wrath, which will be represented by 14 judgments or events. These will begin after a half-hour of silence in heaven once believers have been gathered. Christ will set up His kingdom in Jerusalem at the end of that time. Satan will be bound until Jesus' 1,000-year reign on earth is nearly over.

✓ **Quick reference:**
- Warning/signs of God's wrath: Revelation 6:15-17 & 14:18-20; 1 Thessalonians 5:1-4; Matthew 13:39-43 & 49-50; Matthew 24:30
- Half-hour of silence before God's wrath: Revelation 8:1
- Sequence of God's wrath: Revelation 8:2-13; 9:1-21; 15:1-8; 16:1-21

1,000 years of peace: Christ and others, like those martyred for their faith during the time of the Great Tribulation, will reign for

1,000 years in Jerusalem. Toward the end of this reign, Satan, loosed for a short time, will war unsuccessfully against God.

- ✓ **Quick reference:**
    - 1,000-year reign of Christ: Revelation 20:1-10

Final judgment: Following his final defeat, Satan will be destroyed and all who were not gathered before Christ's 1,000-year reign will be judged by their actions/works. This group includes all who had lived and died before Christ. Those not in God's Books of Life will be destroyed along with Satan by being thrown into the "lake of fire."

- ✓ **Quick reference:**
    - Great judgment of God: Revelation 20:11-15

New heaven and earth: God will establish a final, everlasting kingdom after His great judgment. This is where the "*righteous will shine like the sun forever*" as indicated by Daniel and Jesus.

- ✓ **Quick reference:**
    - New heaven and earth: Revelation 21:1-27 & 22:1-5
    - Righteous shine like the sun forever: Matthew 13:43 & Daniel 12:2-3

Here's a review of what we've learned so far:

1. There'll be an increase in false messiahs, war, and earthquakes as the end times approach.
2. An evil authority we call the Antichrist will enter into an agreement with Israel, kicking off a seven-year period.
3. That Antichrist will break the agreement after three and a half years and begin a three-and-a-half-year reign of terror.
4. The time of this wicked authority will end with Christ's appearing, the gathering of believers, and the wrath of God against the rest of the world.
5. The 1,000-year reign of Christ will follow.
6. Destruction of Satan and final judgment will occur at the end

of Christ's reign.

7. God's new heaven and earth will begin afterward and will never end.

Okay! You've had a sneak preview of the end times and what we'll be studying. Now we really should get down to business and learn a few tools necessary for any biblical study. Let's proceed to PART TWO where we'll discuss faith and its connection to learning the gospel, and then explore good study tools you'll need for PARTS THREE – SIX of this Bible study guide.

SUPPLEMENTAL READING (Either the KJV or NASB version of the Bible is recommended; read at least three verses before and after scriptural references to understand the context better; the following is just a sampling of the myriad of supporting Scripture we'll explore later):

1. Please read all the Quick Reference verses listed above if you haven't already done so
2. Daniel's preview of the end: Daniel chapter 7
3. Jesus' introduction to the end: Matthew 13:24-30 & 36-43 & 49-50
4. Jesus' detailed vision of the end: Matthew 24:1-51
5. Paul's confirmation (in part): 1 Thessalonians 1:10; 2 Thessalonians 2:1-12

CHECKUP
CHAPTERS ONE & TWO

The following questions are meant to check your understanding of what we've covered so far and provoke additional thoughts and questions to elevate your learning to a higher level. You don't *have* to answer *Private Challenge/Discussion* questions (or share the answers publicly if you do). They're just for your own consideration or group discussion.

Possible answers to all questions can be found in Appendix D.

1. Why is the end-of-the-world topic so important?

2. According to Christ, what will be some of the signs leading up to the seven-year period at the end?

3. How long, according to Daniel, will the entity we call the Antichrist be in authority and persecute God's chosen?

4. What sign will precede Christ's appearing in the clouds and our subsequent gathering?

5. Who or what will gather all true believers in Christ at His appearing?

6. *Private Challenge / Discussion*: What's your understanding regarding this Bible subject? What had you read, heard, or been taught regarding it before reading Chapters One and Two? What have you done to research, validate, or confirm that information?

PART TWO

Faith & Foundation
How to Study Effectively

Chapter Three

Faith – Truth or Consequences

It's important to understand what faith is. Why? Jesus said, and Paul reiterated, that believers will fall away from it in the end. In part it comes from learning the truth from Scripture. The writer of the New Testament letter to Hebrew believers said it's the *assurance* of things hoped for (cf. Hebrews 11:1). You'll learn that faith is the belief in what we can't see. But that faith has to be based on truth – there must be a reason for believing in the things we can't see. Otherwise we could believe in anything that sounds good. After all, why shouldn't I believe fairies exist by believing hard enough? I could easily say I have faith in those things if I incorrectly believe that faith is a "feeling" that something is true, or I believe in a thing just because it sounds attractive.

Here's a good case-in-point: I was seated next to a young woman during a return trip from Vancouver, BC, in 1998. She had with her a kit containing a variety of wooden tuning forks and crystals. Her belief was that the articles could heal someone through frequency vibration. I asked her why she believed this, and her response was, "I don't know – I just do because it sounds right." She became irritable when I pressed her for any kind of evidence or testimony that would help support her belief. We talked about God, and even after sharing personal testimonies and fulfilled prophecies, she remained unwilling to accept the concept of Him or of His Son as Savior. This was despite those things that offered assurance and lent credibility to what we discussed. I asked, "Why are you willing to believe in something that sounds good and has no support, and unwilling to believe in God and His Son despite the support and testimonies?" That pretty much ended the conversation.

Faith assured through knowing the gospel keeps us believing in the right things for the right reasons. Without faith built on truth, we may easily choose the wrong direction when faced with adversity.

You'll learn, as we continue through the course, that not knowing the right answer can prove deadly. In other words, being scripturally ignorant leaves us with little if any faith, which can be physically or spiritually dangerous. That topic is coming next in our study.

So how do Webster's dictionary and the Bible define faith? According to Webster, faith is firm belief in something for which there is no proof; complete trust; something that is believed especially with strong conviction. This is what normally comes to mind when people think of having faith in something (or someone) like God.

You'll find that the original Greek word used for faith in the context of our lesson is *pistis*. *Strong's Concordance* labels this as G4102 and defines it as: *persuasion, that is, credence; moral conviction (of religious truth, or the truthfulness of God or a religious teacher), especially reliance upon Christ for salvation; abstract constancy in such profession; by extension the system of religious (Gospel) truth itself: - assurance, belief, believe, faith, fidelity.*

Now, consider the following verse I referred to in the first paragraph of this section: "*Now faith is the assurance of things hoped for, the conviction of things not seen.*" —Hebrews 11:1.

Does that mean we should just blindly believe in something we can't see? No! Where do the assurance and conviction the writer spoke of come from? They come from hearing the gospel, which is the good news of what God accomplished through Jesus Christ for humankind: "*So faith comes from hearing, and hearing by the* ***word*** *of Christ.*" —Romans 10:17.

That "word" – and God's Word in general – provides testimony that lends credibility to what we believe by showing us the results of fulfilled prophecy and answered prayer. Without obtaining that assurance, there can be no real faith. Should God expect us to believe in something without any kind of testimony – eyewitness accounts, corroborating history, or confirmed miracles? We have to know what we believe and why; this comes from learning.

The SUPPLEMENTAL READING will expose you to additional Scripture references that strongly support the claim that faith is based on testimony and learning.

Besides being something we have (or believe we have), faith is also something with which we associate. For instance, I'm a part of the Christian faith – an association related to what I *believe*. I'm of the Christian faith, and my faith in Christ should be based on confidence gained from reading the Scriptures and related testimonies. It's popular in some circles to believe that once you are saved, you're saved forever. I wish it were that simple. We won't debate the "once saved, always saved" (Calvinism) doctrine here, but you should know there's a distinct risk in having little or no faith. The important basic truths from Scripture concerning our faith are:

- Faith is built on hearing the gospel and responding.
- A lack of faith from having no exposure to the gospel opens the door for deception.
- A lack of faith and subsequent deception allows wicked doctrine based on man's wisdom to take root and keep some from *the* faith.
- Being scripturally ignorant can be deadly.

Being scripturally ignorant can definitely be deadly. We could suffer God's wrath because of making bad choices due to not knowing His Word. This can even apply to those of us who believe we're *saved*. Remember the churchgoer I mentioned in Chapter One – the one who stated he'd take the mark of the beast and that God would understand? Well, God won't understand. Here's what Jesus told John about this particular situation:

> *Then another angel, a third one, followed them, saying with a loud voice, "**If anyone worships the beast and his image, and receives a mark on his forehead or on his hand, he also will drink of the wine of the wrath of God**, which is mixed in full strength in the cup of His anger; and he will be tormented with fire and brimstone in the presence of the holy angels and in the*

> *presence of the Lamb. And the smoke of their torment goes up forever and ever; they have no rest day and night, those who worship the beast and his image, and whoever receives the mark of his name."* —Revelation 14:9-11.

This is confirmed during a description of the second half of God's wrath (vial judgments):

> *So the first angel went and poured out his bowl on the earth; and it became a loathsome and malignant sore on the people who had the mark of the beast and who worshiped his image.* —Revelation 16:2.

As you can see, anyone taking the mark of the beast will suffer God's wrath and be removed from the Lamb's Book of Life. But how is it possible to get to such a state and perhaps fall from the Christian faith or suffer God's wrath?

As stated before, there will be great deceit and a falling away from the faith in the last days. If faith comes from hearing the gospel, then the more we hear or learn, the stronger our faith and the less likely we'll be to fall away from the fellowship of believers or be deceived. Conversely, less hearing means less faith and more possibility of deceit. Paul wrote to Timothy that some would fall away from the faith later. Consider this: "*But the Spirit explicitly says that in later times some will fall away from the faith, paying attention to deceitful spirits and doctrines of demons . . .*" —1 Timothy 4:1. Paul also told Timothy that "*. . . who have gone astray from the truth saying that the resurrection has already taken place, and they upset the faith of some.*" —2 Timothy 2:18.

And Jesus said, "*At that time many will fall away and will betray one another and hate one another. Many false prophets will arise and will mislead many. Because lawlessness is increased, most people's love will grow cold. But the one who endures to the end, he will be saved.*" —Matthew 24:10-13.

In summary, faith is the assurance of what we can't see. We gain that assurance and therefore faith by learning the truth – God's Word. Build your faith by continually learning that truth. Otherwise you may not be adequately prepared when faced with difficult or potentially deadly choices. Increase your faith by reading God's Word daily and through regular fellowship with other likeminded believers to avoid being deceived. In the next section, we'll give you the tools to do that effectively.

SUPPLEMENTAL READING (Either the KJV or NASB version of the Bible is recommended; read at least three verses before and after scriptural references to understand the context better)

1. Mentoring for the purpose of (increasing) faith: Philippians 1:25
2. Faith grounded in hearing the gospel: Colossians 1:23
3. Faith *taught*; warning not to be spoiled by man's philosophy (strong faith will keep this from taking place): Colossians 2:7-8
4. Word of the Lord to keep us from going the way of wicked men without faith: 2 Thessalonians 3:1-2
5. Faith and good doctrine are related: 1 Timothy 4:6-7
6. Learning the Scriptures to become wise unto salvation through faith (and all Scripture is inspired by God): 2 Timothy 3:14-16
7. Sound in faith to avoid fables and commandments of men who turn from the truth: Titus 1:13-14

Chapter Four

How to Study...or Not!

We now know faith is based on our exposure to, and understanding of, God's Word. How we interpret it is vital to ensuring we "get it right." Remember that getting it wrong could have devastating consequences. Those who mislead others will be judged accordingly. Ignorance could lead to experiencing God's wrath, disappointment, deception, a falling away from the Christian faith, etc., as we learned in the previous chapter.

The goal of this portion of our study is to help you avoid the above consequences and introduce you to tools and concepts you can use to accurately understand Scripture. This section isn't a comprehensive study of hermeneutics (Bible interpretation). It only focuses on what I consider to be the most important concepts and principles. But it should encourage you to do your own Scripture studies and give you a good start in the right direction.

Before we begin, I'd like to give credit where it's due by letting you know how beneficial the Global University's Introduction to Hermeneutics course[1] was to preparing this instruction. Many of the technical points you'll read about in this chapter came directly from the course. I highly recommend it to anyone interested in learning more about how to study Scripture. You'll find more information about the reference material in Appendix C.

Rule number one of Bible interpretation: do everything possible to determine the writer's original intent. Rule number two of Bible interpretation: see rule number one. Figuring out what the text writer meant to say to the intended audience should be your primary focus. The next goal of Scripture interpretation should be to find out how the message applies to us today. A good understanding of grammatical principles and attention to format and message context will help ensure your success. Please take a moment to familiarize yourself with the following terms before continuing to the next paragraph where we'll begin exploring proper grammar and sentence structure.

TERMS – SENTENCE STRUCTURE/GRAMMAR

Antecedent: The noun or pronoun to which a pronoun refers. Examples: referring to Jesus in a subsequent sentence as "He," or several apostles as "they" to make the sentence shorter and simpler.

Conjunction: A word that connects or otherwise establishes a relationship between two or more words, phrases, or clauses. Examples include *but, and*, *nor*, *neither*, and *because*.

Connecting adverb: A word that serves roughly the same function as a conjunction. Examples include *therefore* and *nevertheless*. Paul used "therefore" regularly to continue from one idea to another related idea; *therefore* means "for that reason."

TERMS – FORMAT

Allegory: A short story or teaching that contains few details but many points of comparison.

Apocalyptic writing: Specific revelations addressed to future generations that usually include symbols and specific outcomes. The Revelation given to John by Christ is a great example of this type of "unveiling."

Figurative language: Describes language that uses symbols. Figures of speech use words for more than their literal meanings. Figurative language can enhance meaning by making comparisons and connections that draw on one idea or image to explain another.

Literal: Plain, direct common speech that doesn't use symbols. Approach Scripture interpretation from this angle whenever possible! Literal language is direct and factual – straight to the point.

Parable: A brief, succinct story that illustrates a moral lesson by comparing at least two subjects or concepts.

Prophecies: Oracles concerning the future given directly by God to man.

Types: A foreshadow of things to come. These can be many Old Testament events, ideas, objects, and people as patterns or symbols of something future. The New Testament often fulfilled what the Old Testament "types" pointed to.

TERMS – INTERPRETIVE CONCEPTS AND TOOLS

Allegorize: Searching for hidden meaning in Scripture. This generally results in a departure from the writer's original intent.

Concordance: Alphabetical listing of words with scriptural references of where the words can be found in the Bible. Some are "exhaustive" and some are "condensed."

Dictionaries: Help us to understand words better, but be careful – the definitions are based on opinion and man's wisdom. Also, context determines which of several possible meanings applies in a particular text or Scripture.

Eisegesis: Inserting meaning INTO one's interpretation of the Word of God. Searching for, or focusing on, pieces of Scripture to support a personal belief by imposing one's views or beliefs upon scriptural interpretation.

Exegesis: Taking meaning OUT of the Word of God. Gleaning what God intended to communicate through the author's language, literary structure, culture, and history.

Law of context: The true meaning of any verse or even a single word is the meaning it has in its literary context.

Study Bible: A Bible that provides introductions to books, maps, articles, explanations, etc. Be aware that study Bibles are often produced by authors or denominations that have a particular theological viewpoint or method of interpreting Scripture.

Translation comparison: Using multiple Bible translations for biblical harmony.

SENTENCE STRUCTURE & GRAMMAR

Understanding basic concepts related to sentence structure and grammar is vital to Bible interpretation. You've most likely attended several English courses by now, so I won't bore you by discussing the basics. However, we'll need to focus on the following, which are directly related to understanding a writer's original intent: antecedents, pronouns, conjunctions, similes, and metaphors. Let's start by discussing antecedents and pronouns, mostly in the context of end-times writings.

Antecedents and pronouns: An antecedent is the noun(s) or pronoun(s) to which a pronoun refers. Their use makes sentences simpler and shorter. For instance, we can select from pronouns like *they* to represent a variety of people or *those* to refer to a multitude of things you wouldn't want to list individually. We must be able to associate antecedents with their pronouns to ensure we're focused on the right people, places, or things. Why is this important? Relating a pronoun to its noun will help you keep focused on the correct players in scriptural context. One good example we'll revisit later:

> *. . . and the people of the* ***prince*** *who is to come will destroy the city and the sanctuary. . . . And* ***he*** *will make a firm covenant with the many for one week, but in the middle of the week* ***he*** *will put a stop to sacrifice and grain offering ...* —Daniel 9:26-27.

In this example, it would be possible to miss the association between those who eventually destroyed Jerusalem and the temple in 70 CE (Common Era) and the end-times Antichrist without recognizing the antecedent of "*prince*" and related pronoun of "*he*." Unfortunately, some disregard this association to support a view that Jesus is the *prince* who has already made a spiritual agreement and ended the need for sacrifice. Even if you miss the association between the prince and coming Antichrist, the context of the verse within the chapter and Jesus' later acknowledgment of this prophecy (cf. Matthew 24:15) support that association: "*When therefore ye see the abomination of desolation, which was spoken of through Daniel the prophet, standing in the holy place . . .*"

You'll find it's important to compare Scripture with Scripture to discover relationships like this. Let's look at other examples of antecedents and pronouns.

Example 1:

> *Now we request you, brethren, with regard to the coming of our* ***Lord Jesus Christ*** *and our gathering together to* ***Him*** *. . .* —2 Thessalonians 2:1. Here, Jesus Christ is the antecedent referred to later in the sentence as "Him."

Example 2:

> *For you yourselves know full well that the day of the Lord will come just like a thief in the night. While they are saying, "Peace and safety!" then destruction will come upon them suddenly like labor pains upon a woman with child, and they will not escape. But you, brethren, are not in darkness, that the day would overtake you like a thief. . .* —1 Thessalonians 5:2-4.

- "*yourselves*" represents those Paul was talking to. In context, you'll see they are the "*brethren*" also described as those "*not in darkness*."
- "*they*" are the opposite of those Paul was talking to. You can glean from this that he's referring to people who aren't exhibiting the same pattern of behavior as the brethren (believers).
- "*that day*" is tied to the "*day of the Lord*" in the beginning

of the verses.

Example 3: The phrase *"these things"* below refers to the heavens, the elements, and the earth and all it contains. You've probably suspected by this time that the Day of the Lord will include the destruction of the wicked – those who aren't holy as Peter goes on to describe.

> *But the day of the Lord will come like a thief, in which the heavens will pass away with a roar and the elements will be destroyed with intense heat, and the earth and its works will be burned up. Since all these things are to be destroyed in this way,* ***what sort of people ought you to be in holy conduct and godliness*** . . . —2 Peter 3:10-11.

Conjunctions and connecting adverbs: These components join or show the relationship between two or more words, phrases, or clauses. Original Scripture writers didn't use verses, chapters, or books to divide their writings. So this portion of our instruction is very important to understanding the relationship and flow between major points. You may find that many concepts and primary message points span multiple chapters because of where early translators placed the divisions. This won't be a problem as long as you look for complete ideas when interpreting the Bible. Being able to spot words or phrases that connect verses and chapters to complete the writer's message will make this easier to do.

Conjunctions include *but*, *because*, *either*, and connecting adverbs like *therefore* and *furthermore*. Consider the following examples:

> *You will be hearing of wars and rumors of wars. See that you are not frightened, for those things must take place,* **but** *that is not yet the end.* —Matthew 24:6. There'll be an increase in war as the end approaches, although the increase in itself won't indicate the end.

. . . that you not be quickly shaken from your composure ***or*** *be disturbed* ***either*** *by a spirit or a message* ***or*** *a letter as if from us, to the effect that the day of the Lord has come.* —2 Thessalonians 2:2. Paul is telling believers of his time not to erroneously believe that the Day of Christ (appearing and gathering) had happened.

And they overcame him by the blood of the Lamb, and by the word of their testimony; and they loved not their lives unto the death. ***Therefore*** *rejoice, ye heavens, and ye that dwell in them.* —Revelation 12:11-12 (KJV). Because they'll overcome the Antichrist through faith in the end, believers should rejoice.

To the end he may stablish your hearts unblameable in holiness before God, even our Father, at the coming of our Lord Jesus Christ with all his saints. ***Furthermore*** *then we beseech you, brethren, and exhort you by the Lord Jesus, that as ye have received of us how ye ought to walk and to please God, so ye would abound more and more.* —1 Thessalonians 3:13-4:1 (KJV). We must remain pure until the end when Christ returns with His angels by behaving and pleasing God as the apostle taught us through his admonishment to the church at Thessalonica.

Simile and metaphor: Simile makes a comparison between two things by using the word *like*: "*The kingdom of heaven is like a mustard seed . . .*" —Matthew 13:31. A metaphor, just like simile, is a comparison between two things, but instead of words such as *like*, you'll find direct comparisons by using *is* or *am*. Examples of metaphors used by Jesus to make a point: "*I* ***am*** *the Light of the world . . .*" —John 8:12 or "*You* ***are*** *the salt of the earth . . .*" —Matthew 5:13.

I encourage you to refresh your understanding of English grammar and mechanics as necessary to make your biblical studies more accurate and enjoyable. You might also wish to take a course in Bible interpretation (hermeneutics) like the Global University course I mentioned at the beginning of this chapter. Now that we've covered details and mechanics related to sentence structure, let's discuss different literary formats used in the Bible. Knowing of these formats and tips for understanding them will further enhance your study.

FORMAT

Parable: A parable is a brief, succinct story that illustrates a moral lesson – usually by comparing multiple subjects or concepts. Because of the multiple comparisons, which use words such as *like*, a parable therefore uses simile. Key points to remember when interpreting parables:

- Examine the setting (time, reason for the parable, and application)
- Look for an explanation at the end of the parable
- Analyze the parable by identifying:
    - the characters
    - points of comparison
    - the main and any lesser lessons
- Avoid assigning hidden meaning to meaningless details

Jesus' parable of the Wheat and Tares and built-in explanation can help illustrate these points:

> The parable: *Jesus presented another parable to them, saying, "The kingdom of heaven may be compared to a man who sowed good seed in his field. But while his men were sleeping, his enemy came and sowed tares among the wheat, and went away. But when the wheat sprouted and bore grain, then the tares became evident also. The slaves of the landowner came and said to him, 'Sir, did you not sow good seed in your field? How then does it have tares?' And he said to them, 'An enemy has done this!' The slaves said to him, 'Do you want us, then, to go and gather them up?' But he said, 'No; for while you are gathering up the tares, you may uproot the wheat with them. 'Allow both to grow together until the harvest; and in the time of the harvest I will*

say to the reapers, "First gather up the tares and bind them in bundles to burn them up; but gather the wheat into my barn." — Matthew 13:24-30.

The explanation: *Then He left the crowds and went into the house. And His disciples came to Him and said, "Explain to us the parable of the tares of the field." And He said, "The one who sows the good seed is the Son of Man, and the field is the world; and as for the good seed, these are the sons of the kingdom; and the tares are the sons of the evil one; and the enemy who sowed them is the devil, and the harvest is the end of the age; and the reapers are angels. So just as the tares are gathered up and burned with fire, so shall it be at the end of the age. The Son of Man will send forth His angels, and they will gather out of His kingdom all stumbling blocks, and those who commit lawlessness, and will throw them into the furnace of fire; in that place there will be weeping and gnashing of teeth. Then THE RIGHTEOUS WILL SHINE FORTH AS THE SUN in the kingdom of their Father. He who has ears, let him hear.* —Matthew 13:36-43.

Analysis of the Wheat and Tares parable:

- Examine the setting (time, reason for the parable, and application): In Matthew 13, Jesus was speaking to a multitude in the form of several parables. The theme of this parable appears to be sowing and reaping for the kingdom of heaven, the relationship between *hearing* and *understanding* the gospel, and letting it take root to resist evil. The farming theme is significant because Jesus was speaking to a farming community. He was conveying His message in terms they would most likely relate to.
- Look for an explanation at the end of the parable: In this case, Matthew 13:36-43 explains the meaning of the parable. This explanation helps us to understand and analyze it.
- Analyze the parable by identifying:

- The characters:
  - Christ
  - The world
  - Believers/the righteous
  - Unbelievers
  - Satan (the devil)
  - Reapers
- Points of comparison
  - Christ and the sower
  - Field and the world
  - Good seed and believers/the righteous
  - Bad seed and tares (weeds)/unbelievers
  - Enemy sowing weeds and Satan
  - Angels and reapers
  - Harvest and end of the world
- The main and any lesser lessons: Most importantly, this parable warns that there will be a gathering of the righteous and destruction of the wicked at the end.

• <u>Avoid assigning hidden meaning to meaningless details</u>: While it may be tempting to assign hidden meaning to parts of a parable – especially if we see some personal significance – we need to avoid this practice, which is called *allegorizing*. For instance, someone could allegorize that "*. . . he went his way . . .*" in Matthew 13:25 referred to Satan's hold over planet earth as its *prince*, or that the servants mentioned in verse 28 were really indicative of anyone who evangelizes or serves in the body of Christ. If we don't take Scripture at face value wherever possible, we'll run the risk of missing or masking the writer's message. You'll find that most symbols or comparisons (like this parable) are explained for us within Scripture.

Allegory: An allegory is a short story or teaching containing few details but many points of comparison. It's a message full of metaphors to make a point. One very good example is Paul's allegory comparing bodily and spiritual armor.

Therefore, take up the full ***armor*** *of God, so that you will be able to resist in the evil day, and having done everything, to stand firm. Stand firm therefore, HAVING* ***GIRDED*** *YOUR LOINS WITH* ***TRUTH****, and HAVING PUT ON THE* ***BREASTPLATE OF RIGHTEOUSNESS****, and having shod YOUR* ***FEET WITH THE PREPARATION OF THE GOSPEL*** *OF PEACE; in addition to all, taking up the* ***shield of faith*** *with which you will be able to extinguish all the flaming arrows of the evil one. And take THE* ***HELMET OF SALVATION****, and the sword of the Spirit, which is the word of God. . . .* —Ephesians 6:13-17.

Allegories can be good teaching tools as long as the storyteller makes clear that their comparisons of Scripture to elements in their allegory are just metaphors and not direct interpretations of hidden meaning from Scripture. Not doing so can mislead the reader into believing they're reading proper translations. This results in *allegorizing* – a practice that is generally bad because the reader is reading into the Scripture what they imagine (eisegesis). Doing that is poor hermeneutics and doesn't bring out the original message. We'll discuss this very poor method of biblical interpretation in the next section.

Types: These are typically prophecies of future events and include people, events, actions, objects, and ceremonies. In Scripture, the Old Testament types are referred to as *shadows* (or foreshadows) of things to come. Understanding what a type is will help you during the interpretation of prophetic Scripture by making it easier to recognize relationships between Old Testament prophecies and future fulfillment. Examples include: the Passover lamb as an Old Testament type fulfilled by Jesus in the New Testament; the Most Holy Place in the tabernacle fulfilled by God's presence in heaven; Jewish feasts and festivals fulfilled by Christ's life, death, resurrection, and future appearing. Let's consider these in more detail.

The Passover lamb was a type of the sacrifice Christ would ultimately become for everyone: "*He was oppressed and He was afflicted, Yet He did not open His mouth; Like a lamb that is led to slaughter, And like a sheep that is silent before its shearers, So He did not open His mouth.*" —Isaiah 53:7 and also "*Clean out the old leaven so that you may be a new lump, just as you are in fact unleavened. For* ***Christ our Passover also has been sacrificed.***" —1 Corinthians 5:7.

The tabernacle in the Old Testament was a type of the tabernacle in heaven: "*For Christ did not enter a holy place made with hands, a mere copy of the true one, but into heaven itself, now to appear in the presence of God for us; nor was it that He would offer Himself often, as the high priest enters the holy place year by year with blood that is not his own.*" —Hebrews 9:24-25 and also "*Therefore, brethren, since we have confidence to enter the holy place by the blood of Jesus, by a new and living way which He inaugurated for us through the veil, that is, His flesh . . .*" —Hebrews 10:19-20.

Jewish feasts and festivals are types of the future events filled, or to be fulfilled, by Christ: *Therefore no one is to act as your judge in regard to food or drink or in respect to a festival or a new moon or a Sabbath day -- things which are a mere* ***shadow*** *of what is to come; but the substance belongs to Christ.* —Colossians 2:16-17.

Be careful to limit comparison of the type and fulfillment to the points the Bible makes. In other words, don't read anything more into the text. Otherwise, when it comes to end-times scriptural warnings, you'll most likely miss the writer's point or the events to watch for if the type hasn't already been fulfilled. As with allegorizing, this is dangerous! Doing so leads people to see a "type" in everything and attempt to find a New Testament parallel for everything in the Old Testament. Or they find an end-times meaning where it isn't intended. Be very careful to limit types to only those the Bible uses!

Prophetic: Old Testament prophecies were oracles given to man by God. They sometimes reflected a clear idea of the prediction with an easy-to-understand fulfillment. For instance, Christ's birth, ministry, and crucifixion fulfilled over 100 direct Old Testament prophecies. The following are but two:

> Jesus born in Bethlehem: "*But as for you, Bethlehem Ephrathah, Too little to be among the clans of Judah, From you One will go forth for Me to be ruler in Israel. His goings forth are from long ago, From the days of eternity.*" —Micah 5:2.

> Isaiah's prophecy about His being born of a virgin: "*Therefore the Lord Himself will give you a sign: Behold, a virgin will be with child and bear a son, and she will call His name Immanuel.*" —Isaiah 7:14.

Additionally, oracles often presented choices for the Jews – sort of an if/then scenario like those passed on by the prophet Jeremiah:

> *As a well keeps its waters fresh, So she keeps fresh her wickedness. Violence and destruction are heard in her; Sickness and wounds are ever before Me.* ***Be warned, O Jerusalem, Or I shall be alienated from you, And make you a desolation****, A land not inhabited.* —Jeremiah 6:7-8.

Or by the prophet Isaiah:

> *Learn to do good; Seek justice, Reprove the ruthless, Defend the orphan, Plead for the widow. Come now, and let us reason together," Says the LORD, "Though your sins are as scarlet, They will be as white as snow; Though they are red like crimson, They will be like wool.* ***If you consent and obey, You will eat the best of the land; But if you refuse and rebel, You will be devoured by the sword.***" *Truly, the mouth of the LORD has spoken.* — Isaiah 1:17-20.

We've introduced two types of prophetic fulfillments so far – direct or specific fulfillment (e.g. non-negotiable details about Christ), and not-so-direct (e.g. oracles where the Jews could change future consequences of their actions by turning back to God as their first love).

A third type of prophetic fulfillment, also non-specific, is a "telescopic" fulfillment. You'll see this type often in Old Testament prophecies that contain both near-term and far-term or end-times apocalyptic events. We call them near-far oracles fulfilled in stages over a long period of time.

Prophets like Isaiah and Joel predicted the imminent captivity and destruction of the Jews as consequences of their adulterous behavior, but in the same writing they often gave a glimpse of redemption in the last days. The purpose was to give Israel hope by letting them know that despite the imminent judgment of the day, God will keep His promise to Abraham and David and abide with them in the end. Jesus also gave near-far apocalyptic glimpses to His disciples on the Mount of Olives when answering their questions about when the temple would be destroyed, the signs of the end, and of His return. Let's take a look at Joel 2:25-32 to give you a better understanding of their construction:

> Part One – *imminent* prophecy of the restoration of Israel (verses 25-27): "*Then I will make up to you for the years That the swarming locust has eaten, The creeping locust, the stripping locust and the gnawing locust, My great army which I sent among you. You will have plenty to eat and be satisfied And praise the name of the LORD your God, Who has dealt wondrously with you; Then My people will never be put to shame. Thus you will know that I am in the midst of Israel, And that I am the LORD your God, And there is no other; And My people will never be put to shame.*" —Joel 2:25-27.
>
> Part Two (*already* happened in the first century AD):
>
> - Last-days prophecy of the pouring out of God's Spirit on all people (verses 28-29): "*It will come about after this That I will pour out My Spirit on all mankind; And your sons and daughters will prophesy, Your old men will dream dreams, Your young men will see visions. Even on the male and female servants I will pour out My Spirit in those days.*" —Joel 2:28-29.

- Confirmation of fulfillment by Luke on the day of Pentecost: "*but this is what was spoken of through the prophet Joel: AND IT SHALL BE IN THE LAST DAYS,' God says, 'THAT I WILL POUR FORTH OF MY SPIRIT ON ALL MANKIND; AND YOUR SONS AND YOUR DAUGHTERS SHALL PROPHESY, AND YOUR YOUNG MEN SHALL SEE VISIONS, AND YOUR OLD MEN SHALL DREAM DREAMS; Act 2:18 EVEN ON MY BONDSLAVES, BOTH MEN AND WOMEN, I WILL IN THOSE DAYS POUR FORTH OF MY SPIRIT And they shall prophesy.*" —Acts 2:16-18.

Part Three *(will happen near the end of time)*:

- Darkening of the sun, moon, and stars in the last days just before the end (verses 31- 32*)*: "*I will display wonders in the sky and on the earth, Blood, fire and columns of smoke. The sun will be turned into darkness And the moon into blood Before the great and awesome day of the LORD comes.*" —Joel 2:31-32.
    - Reiteration of this "far" prophecy by Jesus: *But immediately after the tribulation of those days THE SUN WILL BE DARKENED, AND THE MOON WILL NOT GIVE ITS LIGHT, AND THE STARS WILL FALL from the sky, and the powers of the heavens will be shaken. And then the sign of the Son of Man will appear in the sky, and then all the tribes of the earth will mourn, and they will see the SON OF MAN COMING ON THE CLOUDS OF THE SKY with power and great glory.*" — Matthew 24:29-30

Paying attention to historical context and parallel lines of text in the prophecies themselves is important to interpreting these messages effectively. For instance, it's good to know that the kingdom of Israel was divided in the time of Joel and that Joel's prophecy was directed at Judah – one of the kingdom halves.

The following are Old Testament books that are primarily **prophetic**:

- By major prophets:
  Isaiah Jeremiah Ezekiel Daniel
- By minor prophets:

Hosea	Joel	Amos
Obadiah	Jonah	Micah
Nahum	Habakkuk	Zephaniah
Haggai	Zechariah	Malachi

Historical: The purpose of this type of writing is to describe events or behaviors as they occurred. Many books of the Old Testament fall into this category. Here's a listing of Old Testament books that are primarily **historical**:

Joshua	Judges	Ruth
1 & 2 Samuel	1 & 2 Kings	1 & 2 Chronicles
Ezra	Nehemiah	Esther
1, 2, 3, & 4 Maccabees*		

*(very important historical documentation found in the biblical Intertestamental Apocrypha)

Historical accounts, which often document fulfillment of prophecy, can be important to lending credibility to the prophecies themselves and often reveal the end of the story. For instance, fulfillment of Daniel's prophecies related to the first type of Antichrist as seen in chapter 8 of his writings were fulfilled as reported by Judah Maccabeus – a Jewish priest. His historical accounts are contained within the biblical Apocrypha.

In this case, Daniel foretold of an evil character of Greek descent that would persecute the Jews and greatly defile the temple. He went on to prophesy that the individual would be defeated and the temple cleansed and rededicated. Daniel was referring to Antiochus Epiphanes, defeated by Judah Maccabeus and his army over 300 years later during a revolt beginning in 167 BCE (Before the Common Era). The temple was cleansed and rededicated afterward as Daniel had prophesied. The miraculous way this happened brought about the annual Jewish celebration of Hanukkah.

Other prophecies and fulfillment, which include conquest by the Assyrians and captivity by the Babylonians, can be seen in most of the Old Testament historical and prophetic books. Other historical documentation invaluable to interpretation includes the writings of historians like Flavius Josephus and early church fathers such as Polycarp and Irenaeus.

We've introduced parables, allegories, types/shadows, prophecy, and historical writing as different literary formats from which you'll extract meaning as you interpret the Bible. Let's look at one last format you'll see often as we continue our study: apocalyptic literature.

Apocalyptic literature: Revealing – or unveiling – future events (from the perspective of the writer). While prophetic writings were usually addressed to the current population, apocalyptic prophecy was addressed to future generations. Examples of Old Testament unveiling of the end of our world can be found in Isaiah 24-27, Daniel 7-12, Ezekiel 1, 8-10, and Zechariah 9-14. Apocalyptic revelation in the New Testament came primarily from Jesus. For the most part, it is contained in His Mount of Olives responses to His disciples (Matthew 24, Mark 13, and Luke 21) and in the book of Revelation.

Prophecies conveyed in apocalyptic literature were often presented in the form of dreams or visions. The word-painted pictures often contained symbols, which made the prophecy easier to convey and perhaps remember. As you'll discover, they're almost always explained immediately in Scripture or gleaned from the context or by comparing Scripture references. Good examples can be found in Daniel's visions and throughout the Revelation:

- Daniel 7:3
  - Symbol: *And **four great beasts** were coming up from the sea, different from one another.*
  - Explanation: Four kingdoms that would come to power from the Babylonian kingdom until the end: Babylonian, Mede/Persian, Greek, and Roman (cf. Daniel 2:38-40 & 8:20-21)

- Daniel 7:4
  - Symbols: *The first was **like a lion and had the wings of an eagle**. I kept looking until its wings were plucked, and it was lifted up from the ground and made to stand on two feet like a man; a human mind also was given to it.*
  - Explanation: This represented the Babylonian kingdom led by Nebuchadnezzar (also represented by the statue's gold head in Daniel 2:37-38).

- Daniel 7:5
  - Symbol: *And behold, another beast, a second one, resembling a **bear**. And it was raised up on one side, and three ribs were in its mouth between its teeth; and thus they said to it, 'Arise, devour much meat!'*
  - Explanation: This represented the coming Mede/ Persian Empire. Persia was the stronger of the two collaborating entities, and the three ribs most likely represented the three Persian rulers between Cyrus II and Xerxes (cf. Daniel 2:39 & 8:20).

- Daniel 7:6
  - Symbols: *After this I kept looking, and behold, another one, like a **leopard**, which had on its back **four wings of a bird**; the beast also had four heads, and dominion was given to it.*
  - Explanation: This represented the Greek kingdom, led by Alexander the Great, that would defeat the Persians. It was split into four divisions upon

Alexander's death (cf. Daniel 2:39 & 8:21).

We'll discuss how to interpret this type of writing in our next section: *Interpretive Concepts & Tools*.

Interpretive Concepts & Tools

There's no point interpreting Scripture unless you plan to do it correctly. As we've already discussed, polluting ourselves with false messages through poor interpretation is bad enough, but feeding the corrupted information to others is much worse. Remember, there'll be consequences for those who mislead others. So we need principles to guide us to ensure we discover biblical meaning correctly and don't mislead anyone. These principles have been around for hundreds of years and address the difficulties we face during interpretation of Scripture. These difficulties include:

- **Time**: Biblical writings can be thousands of years old. Time introduces a variety of changes and challenges to include differences in philosophy, ways of life, and language. Using Bible dictionaries and encyclopedias, and examining the writings of others who lived near or at the same time, would be helpful here.
- **History and Culture**: Translating Scripture can be tough if we try to do it without considering the historical era or culture the author and audiences lived in at the time of the writing. Most of the prophetic texts were generated during troublesome times such as the Assyrian, Babylonian, and Persian conquests, occupations, and captivities. Apocalyptic literature in the New Testament was created throughout the Roman occupation, which enveloped the life, death, and resurrection of Christ. The timeframe also included the destruction of Jerusalem and dispersion of the Jews as foretold by Jesus.
- **Language**: Because Scripture may have been written in Hebrew, Aramaic (Babylonian), or Greek, and then translated, you'll want the ability to go back to the original words or

phrases to truly understand them. A good concordance or Bible dictionary can help.

Early Jewish rabbis like Hillel offered reminders and rules of interpretation that help address the challenges listed above. Six of them are as follows:

1. Understand the word in its sentence and the sentence in context.
2. Compare Scripture on similar topics (compare all references to a topic in Scripture; try to identify complete thoughts rather than segments; comparing multiple parallel passages can give a balanced view and show "both sides of the coin").
3. Prefer a clear passage to a difficult one (look for clear, explicit text to clarify or support difficult parallel writing).
4. Pay attention to grammar, spelling, and figures of speech.
5. Determine whether to apply the text to areas in life not mentioned directly by Scripture.
6. God has revealed Himself through the tongues of men.

Let's focus on a few golden rules of interpretation that include some of the points made above before going through a list of interpretive activities to do (or not). Remember the primary goal of interpretation is to extract the writer's message. So, although a verse may have multiple applications, **it can have only one meaning**. Here are some tips to help you understand the writer's intent:

- Be prepared to study through guidance by God's Spirit, having a teachable spirit and a good attitude, etc.
- Take Scripture literally whenever possible and accept the simplest meaning first.
- Consider the author.
- Understand the recipient(s).
- Analyze the context.
- Consider historical/cultural background first.
- Compare translations.
- Consider apocalyptic symbols.
- Use study tools and aids whenever possible.

~ Do ~

Be prepared. Several qualities adopted in advance of our studies are essential to accurate interpretation. For instance, we must be *born again spiritually* to effectively study Scripture. Why? Christ said the Holy Spirit would guide us and give us wisdom. The Holy Spirit that Jesus promised to believers is absent in anyone who isn't a *born again* believer. So while an unbeliever may understand sentence structure and context and therefore glean the writer's intent in many cases, they may not be able to accurately interpret much of what the Bible has to tell us or receive the complete meaning in all cases. Pray regularly for guidance by God's Spirit before beginning your studies.

We also must be teachable. Unfortunately, being closed-minded and practicing eisegesis (reading *into* Scripture what we imagine) is commonplace. In Chapter Seventeen of this study, we'll compare and contrast different end-times theories. It will become very clear that some give in to a temptation to pick and choose pieces of Scripture to support a particular theory instead of considering all Scripture and then forming a belief or doctrine. Believers who are unteachable risk blocking guidance from the Holy Spirit, thereby missing the point of the writer in the same way an unbeliever would.

✓ **Quick reference:**
- He that has ears let him hear (cf. Mark 4:9)
- Be swift to hear (cf. James 1:19)
- Jesus' promise to heal those who'll hear with their ears and see with their eyes (cf. Matthew 13:15)

Take Scripture literally whenever possible. Taking text literally, unless there's good reason to believe it's meant to be figurative, will reduce the risk of finding unintentional hidden meaning. John used figurative language often. Old Testament prophets did as well to describe their visions. So you'll see symbols and figurative language, but their use is the exception and usually defined. Here are some steps you can take to decide whether the text should be taken literally or figuratively:

1. Take the text literally if it makes sense as is. The simplest meaning in context is most often *the* meaning.
2. If the text doesn't make sense as is, look for explanations within the context or in other books as necessary.
3. Look for symbols or hidden meanings (in context first) if all else fails.

Consider the author. It will be much easier to determine the writer's message if you know something about the individual. Five questions you should answer about the author:

1. Who was he?
2. When did he write the book?
3. What setting was he in?
4. What relationship did he have with those to whom he wrote?
5. What was his purpose?

Get to know the recipient(s). Improve your chances of figuring out the writer's intent by understanding who he was writing *to*. Four questions you should answer about the recipients:

1. Who were they?
2. What was their city or town like?
3. What was their social status?
4. What were their shared history, religious experiences, and myths and legends?

Analyze the context. Words make up sentences and sentences make up paragraphs. Biblical chapters are composed of paragraphs and all work together to convey a message or *theme*. A theme may span multiple chapters. So look at the chapter before and after the one you're interpreting. Never try to interpret a verse alone – consider it within the paragraph (smallest circle of context for a sentence or verse). Interpret a passage by its context in a larger theme of the book (may encompass many chapters).

4.1 Analyzing Context

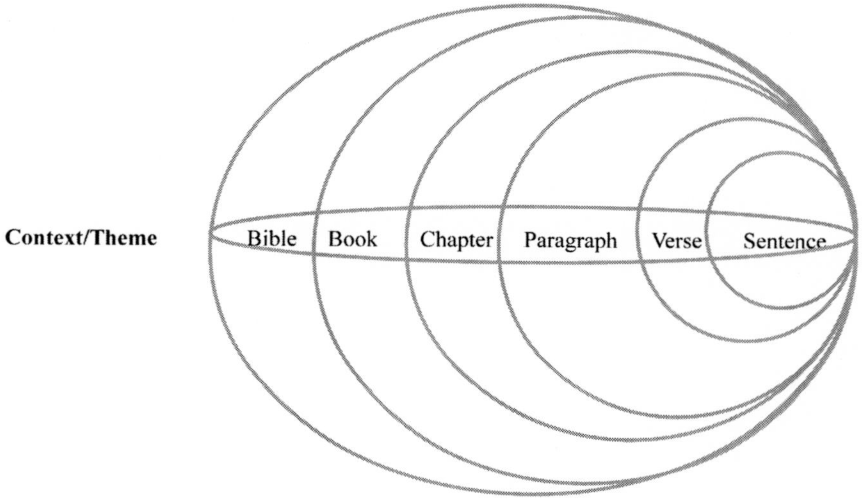

Not considering Scripture in context opens the door to incomplete or false interpretation. And, as we've discussed, this introduces the risk of false teaching, which carries negative consequences. A couple of very good, but unfortunate, examples of taking text out of context:

- In Revelation 4:1, John is summoned in the spirit to heaven so he can watch and record the end-times events Jesus is about to show him: "*. . . and the first voice which I had heard, like the sound of a trumpet speaking with me, said, "Come up here, and I will show you what must take place after these things . . .*" Some take this sentence out of context and isolate it to support a claim that it represents the coming rapture/ gathering, and that since John "went up hither" before the events were displayed, this is symbolic of a pre-tribulation rapture.
- One popular means of supporting an imminent, any-moment pre-tribulation rapture theory is to claim that Jesus will "*come back like a thief.*" This is based on partial Scripture such as 1 Thessalonians 5:2 and 2 Peter 3:10. However, you'll find

that when taken in context, the Scripture is a warning to the unsaved about the coming Day of the Lord destruction.

✓ **Quick reference:**
- John's invitation to heaven for a vision of the end (cf. Revelation 4:1-11).
- Day of the Lord destruction as a "thief in the night" for those in darkness (cf. 1 Thessalonians 5:2-6).
- Day of the Lord destruction as a "thief in the night" for the unsaved; looking forward to the new heaven and earth that follows (cf. 2 Peter 3:13).

Consider historical/cultural background. As with time, historical eras bring about adjustments in culture and language. Also, it can be difficult to understand the context of a particular piece of literature and therefore accurately extract the message if the historical setting isn't known. Using historical and archaeological books along with the Old Testament to interpret the New Testament can help you overcome this hurdle.

Understanding the culture of the people you're reading about in Scripture can help you determine the rationale for certain actions or identify common figures of speech. For instance, Jesus used a figure of speech also referred to by Job hundreds of years previously (compare Matthew 24:28 to Job 39:27-30 below). If we didn't know this, we might be tempted (as some have been) to allegorize Christ's reference and believe it's symbolic of the Roman destruction of Jerusalem in 70 CE. This allows them to then say this is proof that Christ returned at that time (common in a post-millennial end-times theory we'll discuss later). They believe the eagle in the saying is symbolic of the eagle attached to the top of poles carried by Roman soldiers, and that the carcass is symbolic of the dead bodies left behind in the city by Roman soldiers during the destruction. Let's compare/contrast the references by Job and Christ:

- Matthew 24:28 (KJV): *For **wheresoever the carcase is, there will the eagles** be gathered together.*

- Job 39:27-30 (KJV): "*Doth the* ***eagle*** *mount up at thy command, and make her nest on high? She dwelleth and abideth on the rock, upon the crag of the rock, and the strong place. From thence she seeketh the prey, and her eyes behold afar off. Her young ones also suck up blood:* ***and where the slain are, there is she***."

What's the point of the above saying in context? Basically, "When you see *this*, you'll then see *that*." There's no mystery here – Jesus was giving signs to watch for and was just making a point. He makes the same point later in the paragraph by comparing springtime and a budding fig tree (cf. Matthew 24:32-33).

Answer these questions to help discover the historical/cultural background of a specific passage:

1. How does the specific passage relate to the author's purpose?
2. Are there any specific historical details to explain?
3. Are there any specific cultural details to explain? Examples:
    a. Social roles, values, or customs
    b. Economic concerns
    c. Political matters
    d. Religious beliefs or practices

Compare translations. This can be very important to interpreting difficult or critical passages. Take advantage of the strength of different translations and recognize weaknesses. For instance, the King James Bible is scripturally strict and very accurate, but it's difficult to read. This can lead to misinterpretation despite the accuracy of the text. On the other hand, modern translations such as the NIV are easier to read but not as scripturally accurate. I've found the NASB to be very accurate and easy to read. But I'll often compare particular verses from multiple translations while also looking back at the original Hebrew or Greek root to help me understand the writer's intent. You can do this easily and quickly through the use of computer tools like e-Sword (www.e-sword.net). This is one of the best I've seen. It's free of charge, although donations are encouraged and accepted.

Consider apocalyptic symbols. Remember to take Scripture literally unless it becomes obvious it's figurative in nature because of the use of symbols. But follow these guidelines if you need to interpret symbols in apocalyptic literature:

1. Look for meaning in the context. Many if not most symbols are explained within the paragraph, chapter, or book.
2. Look for meaning in the history or culture of the writer as discussed previously.
3. Look for meaning in previous apocalyptic literature by comparing Scripture to Scripture. For instance, compare the beast in Daniel's vision (chapter 7) to the abomination/beast mentioned by Jesus and Paul. Another example: symbols used in Revelation to represent churches, multitudes, kingdoms, etc., are explained in previous books as you'll discover later in our study.

Use study tools and aids whenever possible. Attempting to interpret Scripture without keeping it within context or considering the historical/cultural background would be foolish. Likewise, not utilizing tools to help with accurate interpretation is equally silly and risky. We have the means to easily and quickly compare Scripture to parallel Bible references and other supporting text. We can also discover the root or original meaning of a particular word, find all references to a word or phrase, or consider the interpretations of early church fathers that knew Christ's disciples (or at least associated with others who did). Using these resources improves our chances of accurately interpreting Scripture. Here's a list of possible tools and resources you should have at your disposal:

- <u>Study Bible</u>: In addition to containing Scripture, these will also host a variety of other resources such as maps, commentaries, a concordance, and charts. They're written by humans and are therefore fallible. So use them wisely. You'll find many examples in hard copy and in electronic format. A free, downloadable study Bible is available at e-Sword.net. Modules offering multiple translations, commentaries, and dictionaries can also be downloaded from this site.

- Concordance: A good concordance will contain an alphabetical listing of words used to create translations such as the King James Bible. Use it to find the root of a word or its origin whether Hebrew or Greek. *Strong's Exhaustive Concordance* is very popular and comes embedded into some study Bibles. Two possible sources of electronic Bible concordances are www.abibleconcordance.com and e-Sword.net Bible modules.
- Commentaries: These can help with the study of Scripture by providing subjective explanations and interpretation of biblical text. While commentaries can be helpful, you must remember they contain the opinions and wisdom of men and particular theological stances that will interpret Scripture a particular way. To use a commentary wisely, you should know the theological tradition of the author or series. That way, one can read them with eyes wide open. Access commentaries online at www.biblestudytools.com/commentaries.
- Bible dictionaries: These define terms and names and are also based on man's wisdom and theological points of view. You can find one online at www.biblestudytools.com/dictionaries or download a Bible dictionary as an e-Sword module (e-Sword.net).
- Electronic tools: Portable, electronic Bibles can make referring to Scripture easier when you're away from the family computer. The Internet offers great search and reference capabilities. You'll find many online Bibles and Bible study portals. E-Sword.net, www.biblestudytools.com, and www.biblegateway.com are but several choices out of many.

~ Don't ~

Allegorizing Scripture by assigning hidden meaning where it doesn't exist and taking Scripture out of context hide the true meaning and writer's intent. We're intelligent creatures and often see complex relationships within our realm of understanding. So the temptation to find multiple meanings will exist. Just be careful not to claim the manipulated Scripture as "gospel."

As we've discussed, allegorizing Scripture changes its meaning. When this takes place, literal writing can suddenly become figurative in the reader's mind. Various end-times theorists do this because a literal interpretation doesn't fit the doctrine they subscribe to. In my research, I've found this to be most pervasive in the pre-tribulation rapture theory I used to believe in many years ago. Let's look at a couple of examples to drive this point home.

> ***Allegory***: *The budding of the fig tree as mentioned by Jesus in Luke 21:29-30 is symbolic of Israel becoming a nation.*
> ***Literal meaning***: Just as with the eagle and carcass example we covered earlier, Jesus is simply reminding the disciples that "when you see this, you'll then see that." He's giving the signs that will precede His coming and then goes on to discuss His subsequent appearing. It's true that the Jews needed to come back to their homeland before the end as foretold by Old Testament prophets, but this saying has nothing to do with that event.
>
> ***Allegory***: *The letters from John to the churches in Revelation 2 and 3 represent church ages.*
> ***Literal meaning***: God admonished seven real, historical churches – all in Asia Minor and within John's realm of influence. Sinful behavior has looked the same throughout the centuries, so God's warnings and reassurances echoed in the letters can benefit us today too. However, it would be dangerous to read anything more into it – especially if doing so leads to the creation of a church doctrine about various dispensations from God and symbolic church ages.

This practice is nothing new. Augustine and others like Clement of Alexandria, Clement of Rome, Maximus the Confessor, and Origen did this throughout the early church period. Origen taught that each biblical text had three levels of meaning: body, soul, and spirit. And Augustine is famous for his allegorical interpretations. One good example is the allegory that he turned the Good Samaritan parable into. The following is the original parable and allegorical components he created from the parable.[2]

The parable: *Jesus replied and said, "A* ***man*** *was going down from Jerusalem to* ***Jericho****, and fell among robbers, and they stripped him and beat him, and went away* ***leaving him half dead****. And by chance a priest was going down on that road, and when he saw him, he passed by on the other side. Likewise a Levite also, when he came to the place and saw him, passed by on the other side. But a Samaritan, who was on a journey, came upon him; and when he saw him, he felt compassion, and came to him and bandaged up his wounds, pouring* ***oil*** *and wine on them; and he put him on his own* ***beast****, and brought him to an* ***inn*** *and took care of him."* — Luke 10:30-34.

Some of Augustine's allegories:

- "A certain man went down from Jerusalem to Jericho" represents Adam.
- "Jericho" means the moon and signifies Adam's mortality.
- "Leaving him half dead" means that as a man Adam lives, but he died spiritually; therefore he is half dead.
- "Oil" represents comfort of good hope.
- "Beast" means the flesh of Christ's incarnation.
- "Inn" signifies the church.

Other practices that can hide the true meaning of Scripture: taking it out of its context or focusing on just bits and pieces while disregarding the context altogether. Doing either makes it harder to take Scripture literally, which can lead to misinterpreting the biblical text. We've already discussed the example regarding a "thief in the night," but here's another:

Statement taken out of context: Some people assert that "Jesus can return at any moment since the Bible says no one knows when Christ will return." This is based on Matthew 24:36: "*But of that day and hour no one knows, not even the angels of heaven, nor the Son, but the Father alone.*"
Literal meaning in context: This is probably the worst case I've seen with regard to taking last-day Scripture out of context. Read Matthew 24, Mark 13, Luke 21, and 2 Thessalonians 2 among others and you'll quickly understand in the whole biblical context that a sequence of events and signs will precede Christ's return. So while it's true we won't know the exact time of His appearing, we'll know the season by being watchful as Christ admonished us to do.

In summary, take Scripture literally whenever possible. Also, keep it within the context of the verse, then the passage, then the book, and then the whole of Scripture. Compare Scripture with Scripture (parallel lines within a theme or similar Scripture in multiple books). Use study tools, most of which you can find free of charge (or by donation) to increase your chances of producing accurate and timely interpretations.

Now that we know how to (and how *not* to) study Scripture, let's apply what we've learned beginning with the next section: PART THREE - The Cast, Crew, & Props. But first, please answer the Checkup questions for Chapters Three and Four on the following page to check your understanding of what we've just covered.

Checkup

Chapters Three & Four

The following questions are meant to check your understanding of what we've covered so far and provoke additional thoughts and questions to elevate your learning to a higher level. You don't have to answer Private Challenge/Discussion questions (or share the answers publicly if you do). They're just for your own consideration or group discussion.

Possible answers to all questions can be found in Appendix D.

1. Why is it important to understand what an antecedent is and to be able to identify them?

2. How should you first approach Scripture interpretation – literally or figuratively? Why?

3. A ________________ is the smallest circle of context for a sentence or verse.

4. What resource(s) should you consult to discover the root or meaning of certain words in Scripture?

5. Why is allegorizing Scripture so dangerous?

6. *Private Challenge / Discussion*: What are some possible biblical allegories you've heard? Would you take the time to validate them through Scripture research and comparison?

PART THREE

The Cast, Crew, & Props

Chapter Five

Brief History of Israel & the Temple of God

"What was going on in the world when Daniel foretold of the future "type" of Antichrist that would come before the real and final Antichrist?" "And when did that Antichrist wannabe show up anyway?" "The Bible talks about the temple – past and future." "Where do the different versions of it fit into prophecy and history?"

Whoa, Nelly! These are all good questions related to biblical history and prophecy. My purpose in giving you this section – especially just before digging into the apocalyptic literature – is to help develop perspective through relationships. What relationships? Those found in Bible prophecies, events surrounding those messages, and their fulfillment as shown throughout the centuries. But this won't be a comprehensive, detailed lesson in Jewish history.

Many books have been written about the history of Israel. For instance, *A History of Israel* by John Bright is a very comprehensive historical publication. And *The Stones Cry Out* by Randall Price is an excellent resource for learning about archeological discoveries that corroborate biblical events and give us a better understanding of the history of Israel. Study Bibles like *Every Man's Bible* (New Living Translation) often contain timelines to help provide background for scriptural studies. The Bible itself contains much historical literature (see the list of the historical books of the Bible in the previous chapter). Flavius Josephus wrote extensively about the history of the Jews including details of the Jewish wars. These sources have been invaluable to preparing this brief historical summary. In fact, many dates and timelines have come directly from chapter introductions in *Every Man's Bible* and the Study Aids, Notes, and Indices section of *The Stones Cry Out*.

There's no way I could provide similar detail to what those books do in a single chapter. Instead, I'd like to summarize and chronicle historical data pertinent to prophetic and apocalyptic literature addressed throughout our study. Israel and its people, the Jews, have undergone incredible persecution and oppression throughout the centuries at the hands of several kingdoms. These kingdoms and associated eras were foretold in advance by the likes of Ezekiel and Daniel, and they sequentially take Israel from its beginnings to the very end of the world.

So I've decided to present the historical summary in timelines associated with these major eras as follows:

- Birth of a Nation: Abraham to Egypt (1945 - 1660 BCE).
- Egypt, the Exodus, and Beyond (1660 – 722 BCE).
- Assyrian Rule: Assyrian domination up to the Babylonian invasion (722 – 605 BCE).
- Babylonian Rule: Through the Babylonian era (605 - 539 BCE).
- Mede-Persian Rule: From the end of the Babylonians until the Greeks (539 – 331 BCE).
- Greek Rule: Time of the Greek occupation and persecution until the Romans (331 - 63 BCE).
- Roman Rule: After the Greeks and through the dispersion (63 BCE – 1948 CE).
- Homecoming: Israel becoming a nation again until the present (1948 CE - Present).
- The Temple: A history of the temple from the time of David and its significance (966 BCE - ??).

NOTE: There may be slight variations in dates when comparing this summary to other resources. These should be infrequent and result in differences of no more than a year or two past the Exodus from Egypt. A possible cause for minor variations may be the use of different calendars or dating systems by those assigning timeframes to events. The biggest discrepancy (the time of Abraham through the stay in Egypt) is due to differences of opinion regarding how long the Israelites actually stayed in Egypt. Common thought is that the Israelites were in Egypt for 430 years. However, we understand from Galatians 3:17 that the 430 years was the total timeframe from the promise by God to Abram till receipt of the Law (Ten Commandments) on Mount Sinai by Moses in 1445 BCE. This is the approach I took in determining dates for events and births/deaths during this time period. Unfortunately, the difference is about 215 years. Regardless, any differences will be insignificant since this chapter is primarily meant to give perspective by relating events to biblical prophecy. The next page introduces the history of Israel and begins with the era of the *Birth of a Nation.*

5.1 Timeline of the History of Israel

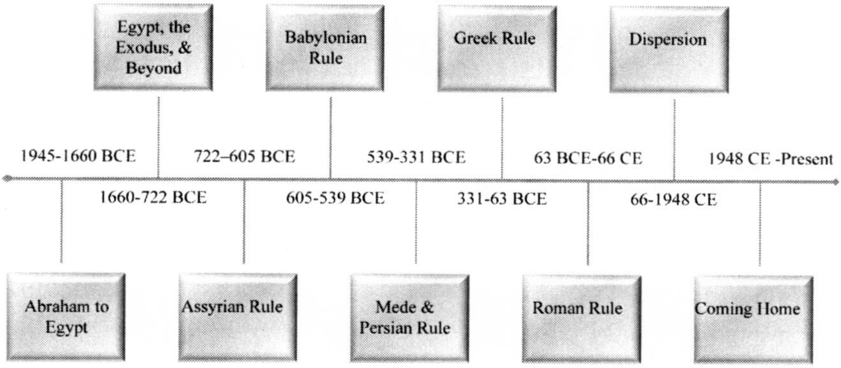

BIRTH OF A NATION (1945 - 1660 BCE)

The year is roughly 1875 BCE, and the great flood had come and gone about 360 years before. God found favor in Abram, the son of Terah, who until this time lived at the home of his father in Ur. Provided you can get into the property, you can still see the ruins of Terah's home and of the Ziggurat (an ancient Chaldean temple), which are located next to Tallil Air Base in southern Iraq.

God's promise of blessing to Abram in part: "*And I will make you a great nation, And I will bless you, And make your name great; And so you shall be a blessing.*" —Genesis 12:2. Abram was 70 years old at this time, which was just before he left the home of his father. In a vision, Abram is told by God that his descendants will be great in number like the stars in the heavens (Genesis 15:5).

God goes on to tell Abram in a different vision that his descendants will serve as sojourners and slaves for 400 years (beginning from the birth of Isaac) (cf. Genesis 15:13). There would be a total of 430 years from the promise made to Abram (cf. Genesis 12:1-3 & Galatians 3:17) until the Law is given to Moses. God also told Abram that the fourth generation of his people would come back to where he'd lived in the land of Canaan. The Lord made a covenant at the same time to establish the lands of Abram's descendants (cf. Genesis 15:18-21).

Wanting to force the issue and help God keep His promise (apparently things weren't moving fast enough for him), Abram had intercourse with his wife's servant to produce an heir. So, at 86 years old, Abram had his first son. He named him Ishmael. This is the father of the Arab nations, and Genesis 16:12 records, "*He will be a wild donkey of a man, His hand will be against everyone, And everyone's hand will be against him; And he will live to the east of all his brothers.*" Ishmael and his descendants have inhabited the lands from Egypt to Assyria ever since. Although God did bless Ishmael and made him the father of 12 princes just as Isaac became the father of 12 tribal leaders, His covenant remains with Abraham and his people (cf. Genesis 17:19-21).

Keeping His promise, God then established a covenant with Abram and his descendants when he was 99 years old (approximately 1846 BCE - Genesis 17). In this encounter, God changed Abram's name to Abraham, which meant "father of a multitude." Ishmael was 13 years old by then. Abraham's second son Isaac, the heir of God's covenant, was born a year later when Abraham was 100 years old.

Isaac took a wife from the land of his father Abraham at the age of 40. His bride's name was Rebekah. When Isaac was 60 years old, Rebekah gave birth to twins in roughly 1785 BCE: Esau and Jacob. Esau lost his birthright and his father's blessing through

Jacob's trickery (cf. Genesis 25:29-34). Esau's curse was that his descendants would serve those of his younger brother, Jacob. Jacob fled to escape Esau's wrath, had his name changed to *Israel* by an angel, and married two wives in the process – Leah and Rachel. Both wives and their servants gave him a total of 12 sons; these became the leaders of the 12 tribes of Israel. One of the sons was named Joseph.

Joseph was Jacob's favorite, and Jacob gave his son a colorful coat to prove it. In addition, Joseph had prophetic dreams revealing a scenario where his brothers would bow down to him. He wasted no time in telling them. Finally, they'd had enough and sold Joseph to slave traders, telling their father he'd been killed by a lion. Joseph was 17 and the year was roughly 1660 BCE – five years after his grandfather, Isaac, had died. The traders took Joseph to Egypt where he was sold into slavery.

5.2 Timeline from Abraham to the Exodus from Egypt
Years are Before the Common Era (BCE)

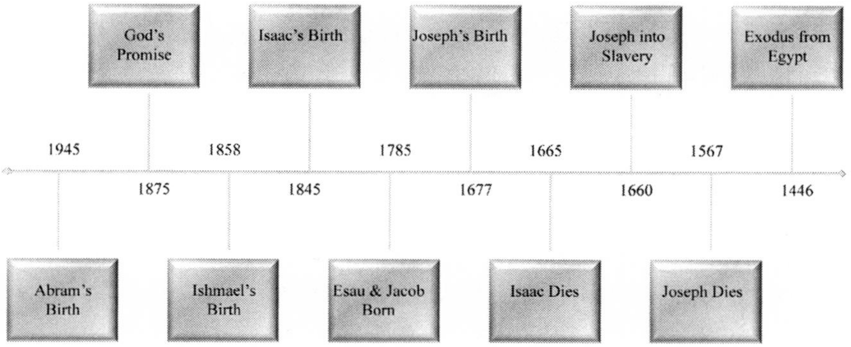

Egypt, the Exodus, & Beyond (1660 – 722 BCE)

The Lord favored Joseph and so did Egypt's ruler after Joseph accurately interpreted the Pharaoh's dream about coming times of feast and famine. The Pharaoh made Joseph second-in-command over the entire country. Joseph's family came to Egypt looking for food during the famine and became reunited with Joseph, who forgave his brothers for their treachery. The people of Israel moved to Egypt and enjoyed great wealth and protection until Joseph died at the age of 110 (1567 BCE) and the Egyptians forgot his legacy. Egypt would become the first of a total of eight kingdoms highlighted by the prophet Daniel and the apostle John. The Israelites remained in Egypt for another 128 years until the great exodus in 1446 BCE. It seemed they were doomed to a life of servitude. But God saved His people once again – through Moses this time.

Moses was born in 1526 BCE, a single generation after the death of Joseph, at a time when the Egyptians began oppressing the Israelites out of fear because of their increasing numbers. Slaves were given heavier burdens and harder work, and the Pharaoh ordered the slaughter of all newborn Israelite boys to maintain control. Moses' mother saved him by placing the baby in a basket and hiding him in the reeds of the Nile River. Ironically, one of Pharaoh's daughters found the basket, rescued Moses, and asked the baby's mother to nurse him. Moses was then raised in Pharaoh's court. His time there was cut short when Moses killed an Egyptian taskmaster who was beating one of his fellow Hebrews. Out of fear, he fled to an area called Midian near Mount Sinai.

God appeared to Moses (when he was 80 years old) in the form of a burning bush that "*didn't burn up*" and asked him to go back to Egypt to secure the freedom of his fellow Hebrews. Through Moses, God performed miracles and invoked several plagues in an attempt to convince the Pharaoh to free His people. The final plague that brought death to the firstborn of all Egyptians – human and animal alike – did the trick. A celebration of Passover has occurred annually ever since in remembrance of God's angel of death "passing over" the Israelites.

The Israelites collected their belongings (and some donated Egyptian belongings as well) and headed quickly out of Egypt. God led them through the mountains to what is most likely the Gulf of Aqaba where they camped between the mountains and water. (NOTE: You should consider looking into this. Like me, you'll probably be impressed and reassured by the accuracy of geography compared to Scripture, and by the chariot wheels and other evidence discovered in the bay at Aqaba.) Pharaoh had a change in heart and chased the Israelites to their campsite by the sea. Through Moses, God parted the water so the people could cross and escape the clutch of their adversary. Thousands of pursuing Egyptians (to include Pharaoh) and their chariots were swallowed up by the water after God's people had crossed safely.

Two months after leaving Egypt, God gave Moses the first part of the Law in the form of ten commandments. The total number of years from the time God gave Abram His promise at the age of 70 until the Hebrews received the Law in 1445 BCE after leaving Egypt was 430 (400 from the birth of his first descendant). This is confirmed in Galatians 3:15-17. The group wandered in the desert for 40 years waiting to cross into the land God had promised their ancestor Abraham. While Moses could see the land, he was not allowed to enter it as a consequence of a sinful act. During the wilderness sojourn, judges were established over groups of 1,160 people to maintain the peace and help Moses keep his sanity (cf. Exodus 18:21). Moses died in 1406 – the same year Joshua led the conquest of Jericho upon entering Canaan (the Promised Land).

After Moses' death and the occupation of Canaan by the Israelites, the tribes split into two groups: the northern portion (Israel/Samaria) and the southern portion (Judah), which contained Jerusalem. The tribes were governed by judges for several hundred years from roughly 1389 – 1050 BCE until the period of kingly rule began. Saul was the first; he was succeeded by David as the king of Judah in 1010. David went on to become king of Israel in 1003 and captured Jerusalem in 1000. David died in 970 BCE and was succeeded by his son Solomon, but not before he'd joined the northern and southern kingdoms into a unified Israel and brought back the ark of the covenant. Solomon transformed the home of the ark into a splendid temple, which he completed in 959 after seven years of construction. This was definitely a golden age for Israel, but it wouldn't last long.

Israel split into two parts again in 930 BCE – one year after Solomon's death. Each had its kings: Hoshea was Israel's last (732-712) and Zedekiah was Judah's final king (597-586). Here's a list of each group's kings from the reign of Solomon:

5.3 Israel and Judah's Kings

JUDAH (Southern Kingdom)		ISRAEL (Northern Kingdom)	
Solomon	**970-931**	**Solomon**	**970-931**
Rehoboam	931-913	Jeroboam I	931-910
Abijah	913-911	Nadab	910-909
Asa	911-870	Baasha	909-886
Jehoshaphat	870-848	Elah	886-885
Jehoram	848-841	Zimri	885
Ahaziah	841	Omri	885-874
Athaliah	841-835	Ahab	874-853
Joash	835-796	Ahaziah	853-852
Amaziah	796-767	Joram	852-841
Uzziah	767-740	Jehu	841-814
Jotham	740-732	Jehoahaz	814-798
Ahaz	732-716	Jehoash	798-782
Hezekiah	716-687	Jeroboam II	782-753
Manasseh	687-642	Zechariah	753-752
Amon	642-640	Shallum	752
Josiah	640-608	Menahem	752-742
Jehoahaz	608	Pekahiah	742-740
Jehoiakim	608-597	Pekah	740-732
Jehoiachin	597	**Hoshea**	**732-712**
Zedekiah	**597-586**		

As you'll learn in the next section, the northern kingdom of Israel fell in 722 BCE to the Assyrians, who'd begun to harass Israel in about 743 BCE with the invasion led by Tiglath-Pileser III. The southern kingdom of Judah persevered until the Babylonian conquest in 605 BCE.

God spoke to the kingdoms through prophets like Joel and Elijah. Their messages usually contained admonishments and warnings that weren't generally well-received by the kings. Joel, Isaiah, Daniel, Ezekiel, and Jeremiah also revealed future apocalyptic events.

The following table shows at a glance which prophets served which kings. Dates in this and subsequent tables are approximate. I cross-referenced several resources to document what I believed to be the most accurate dates or date ranges. In addition to the resources already listed, I also used the Babylonian timelines listed at www.bible-history.com to help in the comparisons. You'll find this table ends by 722 BCE, which is when the Assyrians took control of the northern kingdom. I'll include similar tables to continue the trend in the next several sections, which address the Assyrian, Babylonian, Mede-Persian, Greek, and Roman eras.

5.4 Prophets and Their Kings (before the reign of Assyria)

Prophet	Timeframe	King(s)	Biblical References
Elisha	Late 800s	Israel-Omri; Ahab	1 Kings 19:16-19 2 Kings 2-8 & 13
Elijah	892-832	Israel- Baasha, Elah, Zimri, Omri, Ahab, Ahaziah, Joram, & Jehu	1 Kings 17-19 & 21:17-28 2 Kings 1 & 2, 3:11, 9:36, 10:10, & 10:17 2 Chronicles 21:12 Ezra 10:21
Joel	850	Jehoshaphat	Joel
Jonah	770	Israel-Jeroboam II	2 Kings 14:25 & Jonah
Amos	760	Israel-Jeroboam II	Amos
Hosea	760-730	Israel-Jeroboam II, Zechariah, Shallum, Menahem, Pekahiah, Pekah, & Hoshea	Hosea
Isaiah	740-700	Judah-Jotham, Ahaz, & Hezekiah	2 Kings 19 & 20 2 Chronicles 26:22, 32:20, & 32:32 Isaiah
Micah	736-690	Judah- Jotham, Ahaz, & Hezekiah	Micah

5.5 Timeline from Egypt to the Assyrian Period

Years are Before the Common Era (BCE)

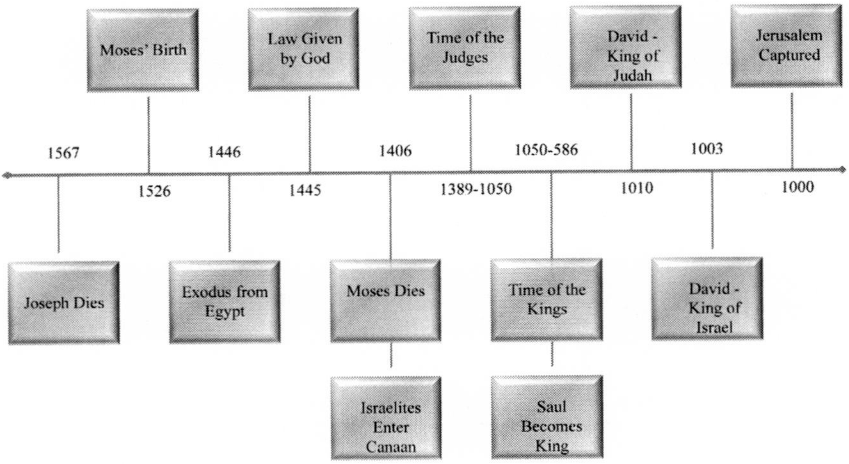

5.6 Timeline from Egypt to the Assyrian Period (Cont.)

Years are Before the Common Era (BCE)

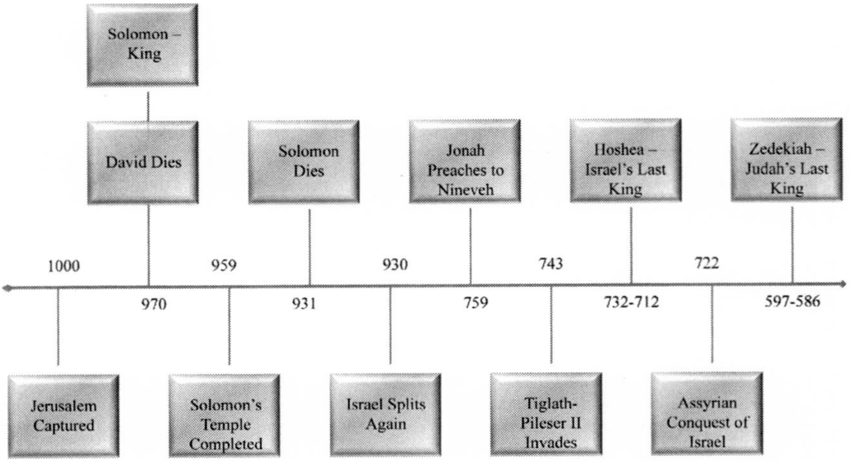

Assyrian Rule (722 – 605 BCE)

Assyria was the second of five pre-Roman kingdoms to have authority over the Jews (Egypt was the first). It was quite large, encompassing Egypt, Babylon, Persia, Syria (Damascus), and Nineveh. Susa in modern-day Iran was to the east, and Ur (the home of Abraham's father) was to the extreme south. Nineveh lay to the extreme north of the empire. The language of the day was Aramaic. Although the empire had been around for a while, our summary will focus on the time of persecution, captivity, and oppression of the Jewish people starting with the invasion of Israel by Tiglath-Pileser III in 743 BCE.

Tiglath-Pileser III became king of Assyria in 745 – two years before invading the northern kingdom of Israel. Their cultural center was Nineveh, the great city Jonah prophesied to over 100 years earlier. During his reign, Tiglath invaded Israel and exiled many of the people to Assyria. He left Judah alone after being paid off by its king, Ahaz. Unfortunately, the payment was made with gold and other articles taken from the temple, indicating to future conquerors the wealth that awaited them. Tiglath-Pileser was succeeded by Shalmaneser V.

Shalmaneser V returned and captured Samaria, the capital of Israel, in 722 BCE after defeating King Hoshea in the ninth year of his reign. The siege of Samaria lasted three years. Israel's remaining population was deported to Assyria afterward. Judah's King Hezekiah had been in power for seven years by the end of the siege in Israel. Shalmaneser V was replaced as king of Assyria by Sargon II in the same year, and he in turn was succeeded by Sennacherib in 704 BCE.

In the 14th year of Judah's King Hezekiah (approximately 702 BCE), Sennacherib surrounded Jerusalem and attempted to take control. God admonished him, and His angel of death killed 13,000 Assyrian men that night. Sennacherib returned to Nineveh and was later killed by his sons in 681. Esarhaddon then became king of Assyria in 680 BCE.

Esarhaddon, in turn, was replaced by Ashurbanipal in 668 BCE. During his reign, the prophet Nahum predicted the fall of Nineveh. The city did indeed fall to Babylon in 612 BCE during the rule of Ashur-Uballit II. He was to be the last king of the Assyrian empire.

Babylon's King Nebuchadnezzar besieged Jerusalem in the third year of the reign of Judah's King Jehoiakim. The year was 605 BCE. (Continued in the next section.)

5.7 Assyrian Kings (during the reign over Israel)

Assyrian King	Timeframe	Significant Events	Biblical References
Tiglath-Pileser III	745-727	First invasion and captivity of Israel (King Pekah); paid off by Ahaz for Judah	2 Kings 15:29 & 16:7-10 1 Chronicles 5:6 & :26 2 Chronicles 28:20
Shalmaneser V	726-722	Captured Samaria (capital of Israel); King Hoshea defeated; deported Israelites to Assyria	2 Kings 17:3 & 18:9
Sargon II	721-705		
Sennacherib	704-681	Taunted Hezekiah by surrounding Jerusalem; killed by his sons	2 Kings 19 2 Chronicles 32 Isaiah 36:1 & 37:17,21, & 37
Esarhaddon	680-669	Replaced Sennacherib	2 Kings 19:37 Ezra 4:2 Isaiah 37:38
Ashurbanipal	668-627	Nahum predicted the fall of Nineveh	
Ashu-Etel-Ilani	627-624		
Sin-Shar-Ishkun	623-612		
Ashur-Uballit II	612	Nineveh fell to Babylon	

5.8 Prophets and Their Kings (during the reign of Assyria)

Prophet	Timeframe	King(s)	Biblical References
Isaiah	740-700	Judah-Jotham, Ahaz, & Hezekiah	2 Kings 19 & 20 2 Chronicles 26:22, 32:20, & 32:32 Isaiah
Micah	736-690	Judah- Jotham, Ahaz, & Hezekiah	Micah
Nahum	648	Judah-Manasseh	Nahum
Zephaniah	640-621	Judah-Josiah & Amon	2 Kings 25:18 1 Chronicles 6:36 Jeremiah 29:25 & :29, 37:3, & 52:24 Zechariah 6:10 & :14
Habakkuk	630-588	Judah-Josiah, Jehoahaz, Jehoiakim, Jehoiachin, & Zedekiah	Habakkuk
Jeremiah	627-580	Judah-Josiah, Jehoahaz, Jehoiakim, Jehoiachin, & Zedekiah	2 Chronicles 35:25, 36:12, 36:21-22 Ezra 1:1 Nehemiah 10:2,12 Jeremiah Daniel 9:2
Daniel	605-530	Judah-Jehoahaz, Jehoiakim, Jehoiachin, & Zedekiah	Daniel
Ezekiel	593-570	Judah-Zedekiah	Ezekiel

5.9 Timeline from the Assyrian to Babylonian Periods
Years are Before the Common Era (BCE)

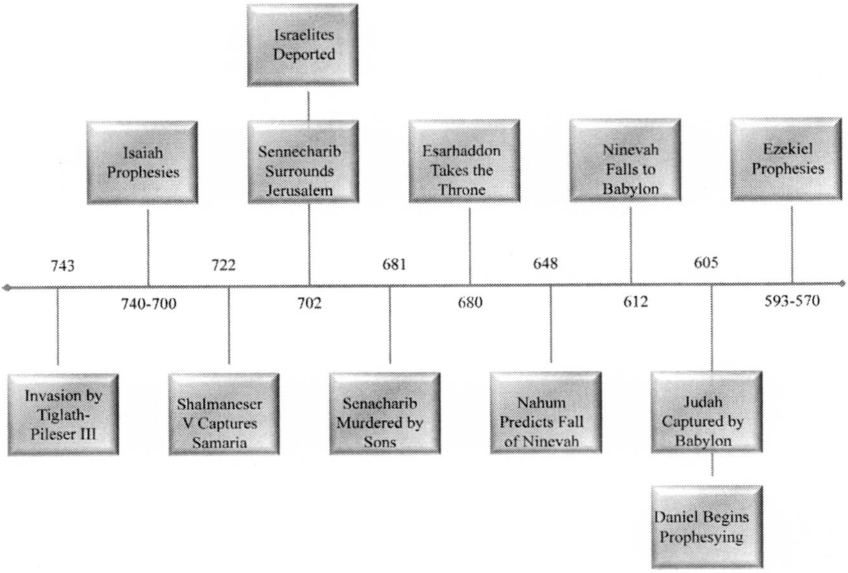

BABYLONIAN RULE (605 - 539 BCE)

Nebuchadnezzar became king of the Babylonian Empire in 605 BCE (the third year of reign of Judah's King Jehoiakim). He captured Judah by besieging Jerusalem and deporting the king and some of the most intelligent citizens to Babylon at that time. One of those deported was Daniel, who was about 18 years old (cf. Daniel 1:1-6).

Much of what we know of biblical Babylon during the Babylonian rule comes from the writings of the prophet Daniel. Knowing the interpretations of Nebuchadnezzar's dreams and Daniel's own visions is important to our study. So we'll defer regularly to what he wrote during this summary of the Babylonian era. I found Stephen R. Miller's book *An Exegetical and Theological Exposition of Holy Scripture – Daniel* to be extremely valuable to creating this and the next portion of our historical summary. Many dates and explanations have come from this resource in addition to others noted earlier in this chapter. Let's begin with a brief look at the main biblical players from this time period: Daniel, Nebuchadnezzar, and Belshazzar.

Daniel: Upon his deportation to Babylon from Jerusalem, this youngster's name was changed to Belteshazzar, which meant "Bel will protect." He earned great fame and wealth in the king's court through his God-given wisdom and ability to interpret the king's dreams. Two of the king's dreams and their interpretations can be found in the second and fourth chapters of the book of Daniel. In addition to interpreting prophetic dreams, Daniel also received several visions. Most of the dreams and visions occurred during the time of Babylonian authority:

- Chapter 2: Nebuchadnezzar's statue dream (603 BCE).
- Chapter 4: Nebuchadnezzar's tree dream.
- Chapter 5: Interpreted handwriting on the wall the night before the Persian/Mede invasion (539 BCE).
- Chapter 7: First year of Belshazzar – vision of the Antichrist and of the end (553 BCE).
- Chapter 8: Third year of Belshazzar - vision of the initial Antichrist type (Greek ruler Antiochus Epiphanes) (551 BCE).

Nebuchadnezzar: He was the first of several kings to rule the Babylonian empire during the exile of the Jews. As you'll see from the second, third, and fourth chapters of the book of Daniel, this king had trouble remembering that he was in authority only because God allowed him to be. He finally recognized God as the source of his kingdom after a seven-year bout of insanity as prophesied by Daniel. You can read about this in the king's letter contained in Daniel 4. King Nebuchadnezzar's grandson, Belshazzar, became the regent of Babylon in 553 BCE. Nabonidos was the last king of the Babylonian Empire.

Belshazzar: He was the spoiled grandson of King Nebuchadnezzar who became the regent of Babylon in 553 BCE. In 539 BCE, on the night the combined force of Medes and Persians invaded Babylon, he was drinking wine out of the gold and silver vessels taken from God's temple in 605 BCE. Handwriting from God appeared on the wall, and Daniel interpreted the meaning as, "*God has numbered your kingdom and put an end to it. You have been weighed on the scales and found deficient. Your kingdom has been divided and given over to the Medes and Persians.*" —Daniel 5:26-28. The Mede-Persian army slipped under the city walls after diverting the Euphrates River and overtook the city within hours of this revelation.

Also worth mentioning are three other deportees: Hannaniah, Mishael, and Azariah. They were of the same caliber as Daniel and had great faith in God. As with Daniel, their names were changed as follows:

Hebrew Name	Babylonian Name	Meaning
Hannaniah	Shadrach	"Inspired of Aku"
Mishael	Meshach	"Belonging to Aku"
Azariah	Abed-nego	"Servant of Nego"

As recorded in Daniel 3, these men were thrown into a fiery furnace – a consequence of not worshipping the king (remember that he kept forgetting who the *real* boss was!). God saved these men from the fire,and Nebuchadnezzar once again gave glory to Him for a short time. Now that we've met the main characters of our discussion, let's resume a chronological approach to looking at the Babylonian era.

Events portrayed in Daniel 1-3 probably occurred within the first several years after his deportation and that of Hannaniah, Mishael, Azariah, and King Jehoiakim to Babylon from Jerusalem. We certainly know the events of chapters 1 and 2 did. The ordeal of the fiery furnace climaxed with a promotion for Hannaniah, Mishael, and Azariah.

During this time (603 BCE), the king asked Daniel to interpret a dream in which he saw a large statue composed of different metals. You'll learn more about the statue in Chapter Twelve of this study. Basically, each metal represented a significant authority over the Jews from the Babylonian Empire to the final kingdom at the time of Christ's return as follows:

- Head of **gold** - *Babylon* (cf. Daniel 2:32 & 2:38).
- Breast/arms of **silver** – *Mede-Persia* (cf. Daniel 2:32).
- Belly/thighs of **bronze** – *Greece* (cf. Daniel 2:32 & 2:39).
- Legs of **iron** – *Rome* (cf. Daniel 2:33 & 2:40).
- Feet of **iron and clay mixed** – *kingdom/authority defeated by Christ in the end* (cf. Daniel 2:34 & 2:41-45).

Afterward, in 586 BCE, Babylon again invaded Jerusalem and destroyed the city and temple. Most of the remaining population of Judah was deported except for a smattering of farmers. Most likely, Babylon was ensuring that no one who could create weapons or wage war remained behind. King Zedekiah, the last king of Judah, was also taken to Babylon at this time.

King Nebuchadnezzar had another dream interpreted by Daniel. It and the interpretation are relayed in the king's own words as part of a letter he wrote during his reign. It's difficult to say when the letter was written, but it was probably produced after the destruction of Jerusalem in 586 but before the end of the king's reign in 562 BCE. Daniel included the letter in his writings (chapter 4). After the interpretation came true (for not giving God the glory for his wealth and authority), the king came to his senses.

Belshazzar (Nebuchadnezzar's grandson) became the regent of Babylon in 553. This was three years before Cyrus I became king of Persia in 550 BCE. Babylon fell to the Mede-Persian army, headed by Darius the Mede, in 539 BCE. This change of authority brought to an end a 70-year exile and introduced a new era for the Jews. They were about to be allowed to return home to Jerusalem and eventually rebuild the city, walls, and temple.

5.10 Babylonian Rulers (during the reign over Israel)

Babylonian Ruler	Timeframe	Significant Events	Biblical References
Nabopolasser (King)	626-605		
Nebuchadnezzar II (King)	605-562	Invaded Jerusalem in 605 BCE and deported Daniel & others; destroyed Jerusalem & temple in 586 BCE and deported most of the rest	2 Kings 25:22 1 Chronicles 6:15 2 Chronicles 36 Ezra 1:7; 2:1; 5:12 & 5:14; 6:5 Nehemiah 7:6 Jeremiah 21:2 & 21:7; 22:25; 24:1; 25:1; 25:9; 27; 28; 29; 32; 34; 35; 37:1; 39; 43:10; 44:30; 46; 49; 50:17; 51:34; 52 Ezekiel 26, 29, & 30 Daniel 1-5
Amel-Marduk (King)	562-560		
Neriglissar (King)	560-556		
Labashi-Marduk (King)	556		
Nabonidus (King)	556-539		
Belshazzar (Regent)	553-539	Regent of Babylon; received a message from God the night of the Mede-Persian invasion	Daniel 5; 7:1; 8:1

5.11 Prophets and Their Kings (during the Babylonian Empire)

Prophet	Timeframe	King(s)	Biblical References
Habakkuk	630-588	Josiah, Jehoahaz, Jehoiakim, Jehoiachin, & Zedekiah	Habakkuk
Jeremiah	627-580	Judah- Josiah, Jehoahaz, Jehoiakim, Jehoiachin, & Zedekiah	2 Chronicles 35:25, 36:12, 36:21-22 Ezra 1:1 Nehemiah 10:2,12 Jeremiah Daniel 9:2
Daniel	605-530	Judah-Jehoahaz, Jehoiakim, Jehoiachin, & Zedekiah	Daniel
Ezekiel	593-570	Judah-Zedekiah	Ezekiel
Obadiah	580	N/A	Obadiah

5.12 Timeline from the Babylonian to Mede-Persian Periods

Years are Before the Common Era (BCE)

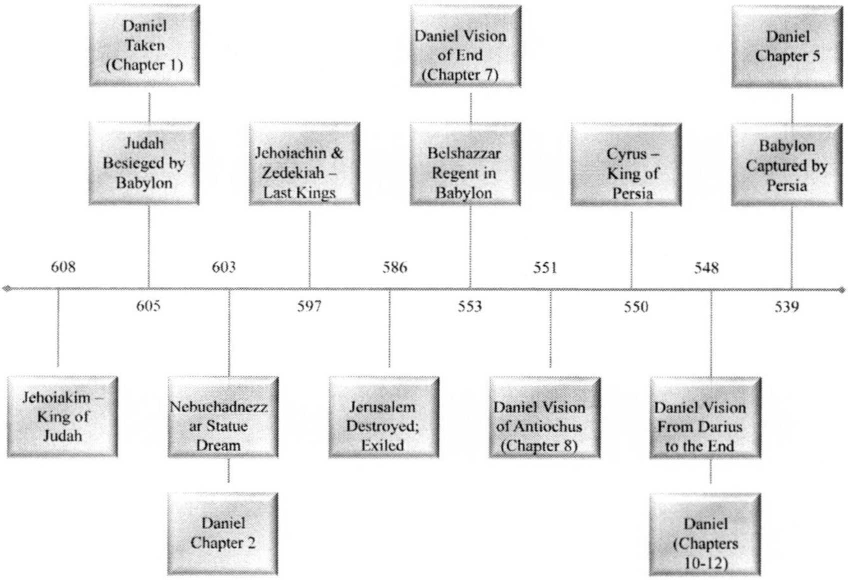

MEDE-PERSIAN RULE (539 – 331 BCE)

Identified in Daniel 2:32 as the "*breastplate and arms of silver*," Darius the Mede and his Mede-Persian army cleverly overtook Babylon in 539 BCE. They did this by diverting the Euphrates River and entering the city from beneath its walls where the river had been. But Babylonian Regent Belshazzar had advance warning from God. As you learned in the previous section, God penned a wall-born message for the king. Daniel interpreted the handwriting, which told Belshazzar the kingdom would be divided between the Medes and Persians that very night. Other visions and interpretations by Daniel during the Mede-Persian rule included:

- Chapter 9: First year of Darius in 539 BCE – a vision of the 490-year redemption period (483 years to Christ, then seven years at the very end before Christ's return to earth).
- Chapters 10-12: Third year of Cyrus of Persia in 537 BCE – a vision of the world from the time of the Persian Empire until the end.

Darius the Mede was the new king of Babylon and leader of the smaller of two kingdoms that had collaborated in the defeat of the Babylonian Empire. Upon gaining ownership of Babylon, he divided his new kingdom into 120 provinces. Meanwhile, Cyrus II (the Persian king) issued a decree allowing the Jews to return to their homeland and rebuild the city and temple in 538 BCE. Priest Zerubbabel and Joshua went back to Palestine at that time to begin the work. Many of those exiled to Babylon in the late sixth century returned to Jerusalem in 537 BCE and began rebuilding the temple in 536. The project was completed in 516 BCE and the temple dedicated in 515. This was the second temple; Solomon's was the first.

Persia was the stronger of the two collaborating kingdoms. The fact that the one was stronger than the other is made clear in Daniel 7:5, 8:3, and 8:20.Three of these Persian rulers (between Cyrus II and Xerxes) are represented by the three ribs in the "bear with three ribs" of Daniel 7:5 (cf. 11:1-2). For the most part, the Persians were good to the Jews – at least until the time of Queen Esther.

The year is 484 BCE and Persian King Xerxes (Ahasuerus) is having trouble with his wife, Vashti. She refuses to present herself to the king during a feast. He has her removed from his palace and exiled as a result. The new problem: he needs a queen to replace Vashti. After a kingdom-wide review of the existing virgins, he chooses Esther as Persia's newest queen. But who is she?

Esther was a Jew. Her Hebrew name was Hadassah, but her uncle Mordecai changed it to Esther to hide her true identity. Beautiful, wise, and well-educated, she found favor with King Xerxes, who chose her to be his bride sometime between 483-478 BCE. Things went well until a wicked Agagite named Haman tried to have her uncle Mordecai hanged and the Jews exterminated.

The Agagites (from King Agag of the Amalekites) were enemies of the Jews. Haman hated them, and while he didn't know yet that Esther was a Hebrew, he knew that Mordecai was indeed Jewish (Mordecai had been exiled from Jerusalem in 586 BCE). King Xerxes promoted Haman to a position second only to his, and Haman abused his power by demanding everyone at the gate bow to him as he passed by. Mordecai refused, invoking Haman's wrath. He plotted to have Mordecai hanged and convinced Xerxes to sign a decree authorizing the extermination of the Jews living in the 127 Persian provinces. This happened in the 12th year of King Xerxes' reign (475 BCE).

Esther and the other Jews in Persia were distraught as they anticipated their slaughter. Under the threat of death (because of the laws of the time) Esther approached her husband and exposed Haman's wicked plans. The king reversed the order, allowing the Jews to instead slaughter those who had plotted the Hebrew exterminations. He also had Haman hanged on the same gallows Haman erected to kill Mordecai. The Jewish people created the annual Feast of Purim in 473 BCE to commemorate their escape from death (the Pur was the lot cast during the planning of the Jewish extermination). The feast continues to this day.

Yearning to return home, Ezra took a small contingent of Jews back to Palestine in 458 BCE after a decree from the king. Nehemiah did the same in 445 after another decree. Ezra and Nehemiah both resumed the reading of Scripture to the Jews in 443 BCE. The Jewish people enjoyed a relative time of peace and safety until the Greeks came onto the scene beginning in 331 BCE.

5.13 Mede and Persian Kings (from the defeat of Babylon)

Mede-Persian King	Timeframe	Significant Events	Biblical References
Cyrus I (Persia)	550		
Darius (Mede) (son of Ahasuerus) /Cyrus II (Persia)	539-529	Decree permitting the return to Palestine & rebuilding of the temple; Judah split into 120 provinces; second temple construction begins (536 BCE); 70-year exile prophecy by Jeremiah ends; Daniel's vision of 490 years; Daniel's near-far vision of the end	2 Chronicles 36:22-23 Ezra 1:1, 2,7, & 8; 3:7; 4:3 & 5; 5:13, 14, & 17; 6:3 & 14 Isaiah: 44:28 & 45:1 Jeremiah: 25:11-12 & 29:10 Daniel 1:21; 6:28; & chapters 9-12
Cambyses (Persia)	530		
Smerdis (Persia)	521		
Darius I Hystapses (Persia)	521	Second temple halted in 520, but completed in sixth year of Darius' reign (516 BCE); second temple dedicated in 515 BCE	Ezra 4:5 & 24; 5:5-7; 6:1 & 12-15 Nehemiah 12:22 Daniel 5:31; 6:1, 9, 25, & 28; 11:1 Haggai 1:1 & 15; 2:10 Zechariah 1:1 & 7; 7:1
Xerxes (Ahasuerus) (Persia)	486	Esther (queen of Persia) saves the Jewish people; Feast of Purim started; fourth Persian king in Daniel's vision	Esther Ezra 4:6 Daniel 11:2

Mede-Persian King	Timeframe	Significant Events	Biblical References
Artaxerxes I (Persia)	464	Decree to Ezra allowing Jews to return & resume temple activities (458 BCE); decree to Nehemiah to rebuild wall of Jerusalem in 20th year of his reign (445 BCE)	Ezra 4:6-7, 8, 11, & 23; 6:14; 7:1, 7, 11, 12, & 21; 8:1 Nehemiah 2; 5:14; 13:6 Daniel 9:25
Darius II (Persia)	423		
Artaxerxes II (Persia)	404		
Artaxerxes III (Persia)	359		
Darius III (Persia)	331	Defeated by Alexander's armies	Daniel 11:2

5.14 Prophets (during the reign of Persia)

Prophet	Timeframe	King(s)	Biblical References
Haggai	520	N/A	Ezra 5:1 & 6:14 Haggai
Zechariah	520-518	N/A	Ezra 5:1 & 6:14 Nehemiah 12:16
Malachi	430	N/A	Malachi

5.15 Timeline from the Mede-Persian to Greek Periods
Years are Before the Common Era (BCE)

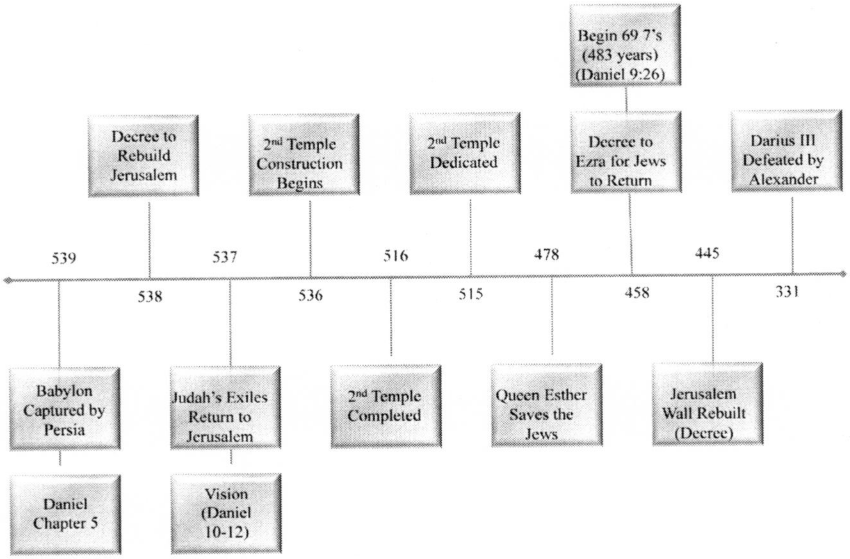

GREEK RULE (331 - 63 BCE)

From Alexander the Great, who became king of Greece in 336 BCE, to Antiochus IV Epiphanes, this era – the fifth of five pre-Roman empires – is very significant to biblical history as well as prophetic and apocalyptic literature. Daniel referred to the Greek kingdom as:

- Thighs of bronze (cf. Daniel 2:32 & 2:39) (605 BCE)
- Leopard (cf. Daniel 7:6) (553 BCE)
- Goat (cf. Daniel 8:5-8) (551 BCE)

In 331 BCE, Alexander the Great defeated Darius III and took Babylon captive as prophesied by Daniel (cf. 11:3). He died only eight years later in that city in 323 BCE at the age of 32. Upon his death, Alexander's empire was divided into four kingdoms just as Daniel also prophesied (cf. Daniel 8:8; 11:4): Macedonia (Greece), Ptolemaic (Egypt), Seleucid (Syria), and Pergamum (northwest Asia

Minor in modern-day Turkey). Our summary of the Greek Empire will focus on the Seleucid kingdom, which had the greatest impact upon the Jews during this era.

In the second century BCE, the Seleucid kingdom was the largest division of Alexander's empire. The extensive area included Syria, Palestine, Persia, and Susa. As it lay north of Jerusalem, it is identified as the *king of the north* mentioned repeatedly by Daniel in chapter 11. Egypt is south of Jerusalem. So the Ptolemaic kingdom was the *king of the south* as denoted by Daniel in his chapter 11 prophecy. Unfortunately, Palestine was sandwiched between these two "kings" who fought and reconciled several times during the second century. Egypt to the south wasn't the only challenge the Seleucid rulers faced though.

Rome was expanding its empire to the east, giving Antiochus III, the Seleucid ruler at that time, something else to worry about besides the rival Ptolemaic kingdom. The Syrians were defeated by Rome at Thermopylae in 191 BCE. Antiochus III signed a treaty with the Romans several years later in 188 – roughly 13 years before the wicked Antiochus IV came to power. The conflict with the Romans and subsequent treaty were foreseen by Daniel and recorded cryptically in chapter 11 verse 18. The stage was now set for the one who would become a *type* of the Antichrist to come at the end of time.

Daniel prophesied about a precursor to the future Antichrist ruler he spoke of in chapter 7. He couldn't have known he was foretelling of a Syrian leader within the Greek kingdom: Antiochus IV Epiphanes. He came to power in 175 BCE and is identified in Daniel 8:5-25 and 11:21-35. Like the future Antichrist revealed to John in about 90 CE, this evil ruler was labeled as one who would magnify himself above God, deceive through a peace agreement, and end daily sacrifice.

Antiochus IV Epiphanes entered into an agreement with Hellenized Jews, who supported him in Jerusalem. Not everyone followed suit though, and rebellion broke out. Antiochus was furious, and after losing another bout with Egypt, he stopped at Jerusalem on his way home and vented his anger. He broke the peace agreement, quelled the rebellion, and sated his violent appetite by killing roughly 80,000 men, women, and children in 167 BCE. Furthermore, he stopped the faithful Jews from following the Law. He ended daily sacrifices in the temple and desecrated the holy place by sacrificing a pig on the altar and erecting a statue of Zeus. Judah Maccabeus and a number of followers revolted because of this and corruption in the priesthood. They quickly regained control of Jerusalem and the temple despite their small force and overwhelming odds.

The Maccabean revolt lasted about four years. In 164 BCE, Maccabeus and the priests of the Lord cleansed the temple and rededicated it. This in itself was a miracle because there was only a one-day supply of pure, virgin olive oil – not nearly enough for the eight-day rededication of the temple. However, the Lord provided a miracle and the oil burned for the entire rededication period. The Jews remember this amazing work of the Lord through the annual celebration of Hanukkah.

True to the Word of God given through Daniel (cf. 8:25), Antiochus IV Epiphanes died in 163 BCE of a nasty bowel disease ("*broken without hand*"). The Roman Empire worked its way eastward and took control of Palestine in 63 BCE.

5.16 Macedonian Rulers

Macedonian Ruler	Timeframe	Significant Events	Biblical References
Alexander III (the Great)	336–323	Defeated Persia; kingdom split four ways upon death in July 323 BCE	Daniel 2:32 & 39; 7:6; 8:5-8
Philip III Arrhidaios	323–317	Macedonian ruler after Alexander	
Perseus	179–168	Last Macedonian ruler	

5.17 Ptolemaic Rulers

Ptolemaic Ruler	Timeframe	Significant Events	Biblical References
Ptolemy I Soter	323–285		
Ptolemy II Philadelphos	285–246		
Ptolemy III Euergetes	246–222		
Ptolemy IV Philopator	222–204		
Ptolemy V Epiphanes	210–180		
Cleopatra I	180–177		
Ptolemy VI Philometor	180–145		
Cleopatra II	170–115		
Ptolemy VIII	170–163		

5.18 Seleucid Rulers

Seleucid Ruler	Timeframe	Significant Events	Biblical References
Seleukos I Nikator	323-281		
Antiochos I Soter	281–261		
Antiochos II Theos	261–246		
Seleukos II Kallinikos	246–225		
Seleukos III	225–223		
Antiochos III Megas	223–187		
Seleukos IV Philopator	187–175		
Antiochus IV Epiphanes	175–163	Broke an agreement with the Jews and slaughtered many; defiled temple and altar in 167 BCE; died of bowel disease	Daniel 8:5-25; 11:21-35 Maccabeus books

5.19 Pergamum Rulers

Pergamum Ruler	Timeframe	Significant Events	Biblical References
Philetairos	323–263	First ruler of the Pergamum division of Alexander's kingdom	
Eumenes II Soter	197–158	Pergamum ruler during the Maccabean revolts in 167-164	

5.20 Timeline from the Greek to Roman Periods

Years are Before the Common Era (BCE)

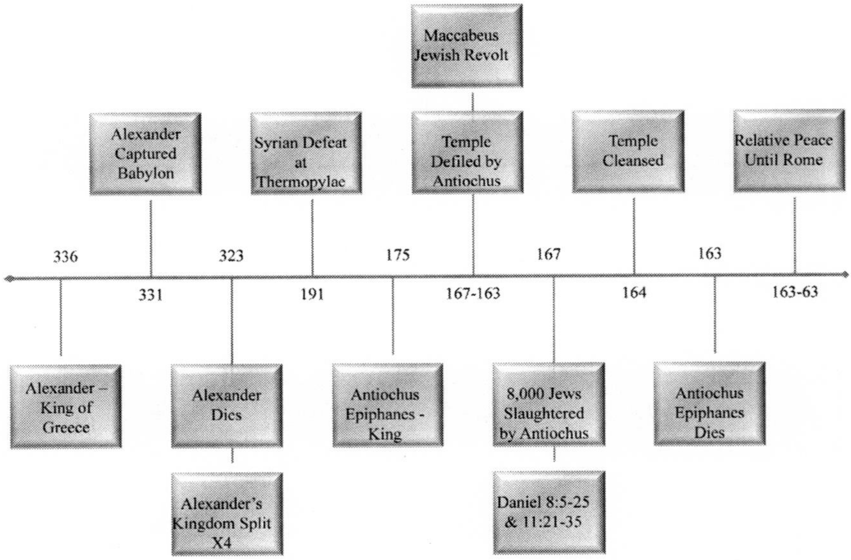

Roman Rule & Dispersion (63 BCE – 1948 CE)

And they are seven kings; five have fallen, **one is**, *the other has not yet come; and when he comes, he must remain a little while. The beast which was and is not, is himself also an eighth and is one of the seven, and he goes to destruction.* —Revelation 17:10-11.

As we've already learned, the five fallen kingdoms mentioned in the Revelation to John (above) were Egypt, Assyria, Babylon, Mede-Persia, and Greece. The Roman Empire is the kingdom that "is" at the time of Christ's revelation to John. Roman ruler Pompeus captured Jerusalem in 63 BCE and annexed Palestine to Rome at that time. The empire, which consisted of a western half with Rome as its capital and an eastern side with Constantinople as an eventual capital, lasted for hundreds of years. However, we'll focus on the time from 63 BCE when Jerusalem was captured by Rome until the end of the third Jewish war in 138 CE.

Daniel saw the Roman Empire as "*legs of iron*" on the statue in Nebuchadnezzar's dream (cf. Daniel 2:40) and the "*dreadful and terrifying beast*" of Daniel 7:7. Rome allowed Palestine to retain its own kings for a time; we'll begin with Herod the Great, who became king in about 37 BCE.

Herod the Great had four wives, and his bloodline produced the likes of Herodias, who married two of her uncles (Herod Philip II and Herod Antipas), and Herod Agrippa, who ruled during the time of the apostle Paul. He spearheaded a massive overhaul of the second temple from 19 BCE – 22 CE and was king during the census taken at the time of Jesus' birth in 5 or 6 BCE. He was also the King Herod who attempted to kill Jesus by having all boys two years old or younger slaughtered. An angel warned Joseph of this in a dream, and he, Mary, and the baby went to Egypt until the death of Herod the Great. They returned to Palestine afterward when Jesus was roughly two years old.

When Herod the Great died in 4 BCE, his area of authority was divided into regions given to his sons. Herod Antipas became ruler of Galilee, which would become the stomping grounds of Jesus and His disciples about 30 years later. Herod Antipas ruled until 39 CE and took part in the judgment and crucifixion of Christ after also having John the Baptist beheaded at the request of his wife, Herodias. Herod Agrippa, Herodias' brother, became the king of Israel upon Herod Antipas' death.

The beheading of John the Baptist and crucifixion of Christ occurred in close proximity of the year 28 CE. Luke records this and lists some of the main players in the third chapter of his epistle:

> *Now in the fifteenth year of the reign of Tiberius Caesar, when Pontius Pilate was governor of Judea, and Herod was tetrarch of Galilee, and his brother Philip was tetrarch of the region of Ituraea and Trachonitis, and Lysanias was tetrarch of Abilene, in the high priesthood of Annas and Caiaphas, the word of God came to John, the son of Zacharias, in the wilderness.* —Luke 3:1-2.

Luke 23:7-8 shows a bit of Herod's involvement in Jesus' crucifixion (most likely in 28 or 29 BCE), which also concludes the first 483 years of Daniel's 490-year prophecy:

> *Then after the sixty-two weeks [of years] the Messiah will be cut off and have nothing. . . .* —Daniel 9:26.

Please note that I've added comments in brackets to help with your understanding of the passage. Don't worry; we'll cover this in much more detail later in Chapter Twelve.

The next 40 or so years until the destruction of the temple in 70 CE witnessed the infilling of God's Spirit into Christ's followers starting at Pentecost. His ascension and the creation of the New Testament Gospels and letters to the church followed. Stephen and Paul were two of many martyred for their faith during this time (35 and 67 CE respectively). You've probably already discovered that Paul's letters are an integral part of solving the end-times mystery. Here's a partial listing of them:

- 50 CE: 1 Thessalonians while in Corinth
- 51 CE: 2 Thessalonians
- 65 CE: 1 Timothy
- 66 CE: 2 Timothy

Fed up with Roman rule, the Jews began a four-year revolt in 66 CE. Rome squashed the revolt in 70 CE after General Titus' soldiers destroyed the temple as Jesus had predicted (e.g. Matthew 24:2). Daniel also saw this coming as part of a vision recorded in chapter 9 verse 26: ". . . *and the people of the prince who is to come will destroy the city and the sanctuary* . . . ."

General Titus was the son of Roman Emperor Vespasian. Sent by Rome to quell the uprising in 70 CE, he instructed his soldiers to avoid destruction of the temple. Unfortunately, ambitious soldiers set the structure on fire while trying to smoke out a large group of Jews who had barricaded themselves inside. The temple had been covered in gold, which melted and ran into the crevices of the stones during the fire. To reclaim the precious metal, the soldiers overturned every stone, which they then discarded into the Kidron Valley. Jesus' prediction that no stone would be left upon another was fulfilled at this time:

> *Jesus came out from the temple and was going away when His disciples came up to point out the temple buildings to Him. And He said to them, "Do you not see all these things? Truly I say to you, not one stone here will be left upon another, which will not be torn down."* —Matthew 24:1-2.

Many Jews had been driven out of Jerusalem from the start of the first revolt, which culminated in the destruction of the temple. Those dispersed would be in one of three primary groups:

- Ashkenaz (Germany/central Europe)
- Sephardic (Spain/Portugal)
- Mizrahim (North Africa, Middle East, and Central Asia)

One deportee was the apostle John, who wrote three letters to the church in 85 CE and recorded the Revelation given to him by Christ in about 90 CE while exiled to the Isle of Patmos near Greece. John most likely mentored several churches in Asia Minor as you'll learn later. While he's the last apostle we hear from in the New Testament, key players like his disciple Polycarp and Polycarp's disciple Irenaeus continued to propel the church forward.

God's chosen people made two more attempts to overcome Roman rule: Kito's war from 115-117 CE and Kokhba's revolt from 132-135 CE. However, the Romans prevailed and the Jews were removed from Palestine. It wasn't long before none remained and Rome had put its own face on much of Jerusalem. This condition wouldn't be permanent, and Palestine would change hands again before the people of Israel would be permitted back into their homeland after a 1,880-year separation.

Islamic occupation of the Temple Mount and Jerusalem began in 638 CE after the Caliph Omar entered Jerusalem riding a white camel. Caliph Abdel-Malik commissioned the building of the Dome of the Rock in 691 CE. The following excerpt from the Temple Mount group provides insight into the back-and-forth transfer of Mount Moriah between Muslims and Christians in the 11th and 12th centuries CE (www.templemount.org/allah.html):

> On July 15, 1099 Jerusalem was taken from the Muslims by the Crusaders from Europe. The Crusaders slaughtered the inhabitants of Jerusalem in an unjustified carnage. The Dome of the Rock was converted into a Christian Church called the Templum Domini – "Temple of our Lord." The Crusaders then began to use the Al-Aksa Mosque as headquarters for the Knights of the Templar who officiated the Temple Compound. A remnant of the Crusader occupation still exists today, the tombs of the assassins of Thomas Beckett the Archbishop of Canterbury (1118-1170). After murdering Beckett the assassins traveled to Jerusalem and took up with the Templar Knights. Their tombs are situated near the main entrance. The Western

world rejoiced that Jerusalem was in the hands of "Christians." The victory, however, caused Muslims to immediately launch campaigns to regain the city and the Dome from the Christian infidels. The Crusader occupation was relatively short-lived. The Muslim leader Saladin (Salah al-Din) proclaimed a jihad, or holy war, to retake the land of Palestine. After ninety years of Crusader control, Jerusalem surrendered to Saladin's army on October 2, 1187. In contrast to the brutality of the Crusaders, Saladin treated the defeated Crusaders with kindness and mercy. The golden cross that was placed on the Dome of the Rock was torn down. Saladin rededicated the Templar's headquarters as a mosque. The Dome was covered with beautiful mosaics and a prayer niche facing Mecca was added. Jerusalem was back in the hands of the Muslims and Europe was ready to avenge the defeat. A Third Crusade was undertaken (1189-1192) to free Jerusalem from the armies of Saladin. Richard the Lion-hearted led England and other Crusaders in a fruitless attempt to retake the city. To this day, the Temple Mount remains in Muslim control.

The eastern half of the Roman Empire persevered as the eventual Christian Byzantine kingdom but dwindled until late into the 15th century CE – well after the Muslim occupation of Mount Moriah had begun and the Crusades had ended. One major upset and sign of the end of the empire was the conquest of its capital of Constantinople by the Turks in 1453. The Ottoman Empire, founded by Osman Gazi in 1299, would go on to control Palestine from 1515-1918 CE. Earlier in our discussion of Roman biblical history, we learned that Rome was the sixth kingdom in a series as revealed to John by Christ. He also stated that a seventh kingdom would come for a short time before the eighth and final kingdom – that of the Antichrist. Some believe the seventh kingdom was the Ottoman Empire since it had control of Palestine in the same manner that Babylon, Persia, Greece, and Rome had. The only thing left to do at this point was for God to bring His people home in the last days as promised long ago through prophets such as Jeremiah and Ezekiel:

Say to them, 'Thus says the Lord GOD, "Behold, I will take the sons of Israel from among the nations where they have gone, and I will gather them from every side and bring them into their own land" —Ezekiel 37:21.

And He will lift up a standard for the nations And assemble the banished ones of Israel, And will gather the dispersed of Judah From the four corners of the earth. —Isaiah 11:12.

Then I Myself will gather the remnant of My flock out of all the countries where I have driven them and bring them back to their pasture, and they will be fruitful and multiply. —Jeremiah 23:3.

Next: The *Homecoming*

5.21 Roman Emperors (during the reign over Israel)

Roman Emperor	Timeframe	Significant Events	Biblical References
Augustus	27 BCE –14	Census at time of Christ's birth; Mary, Joseph, and Jesus flee to Egypt to escape death decree	Luke 2:1 Acts 21:21 Acts 25:21 & 25
Tiberius	14–37	Christ's life, death, and resurrection	Luke 3:1
Gaius Germanicus (Caligula)	37–41	Friend of Herod Agrippa	
Claudius	41–54		Acts 11:28
Nero	54–68	Paul martyred in Rome; Jewish revolt	2 Timothy 4:22
Galba	68–69	Jewish revolt	
Otho	69	Jewish revolt	
Vitellius	69	Jewish revolt	
Vespasian	69–79	Son Titus' soldiers burned and dismantled the temple; Jewish revolt	
Titus	79–81		
Domitian	81–96	The Revelation given by Christ to John	
Nerva	96–98		
Trajan	98–117	Second Jewish revolt	
Hadrian	117–138	Third Jewish revolt	

5.22 Key Jewish Leaders during Rome's Rule

Years are in the Common Era (CE) unless otherwise noted

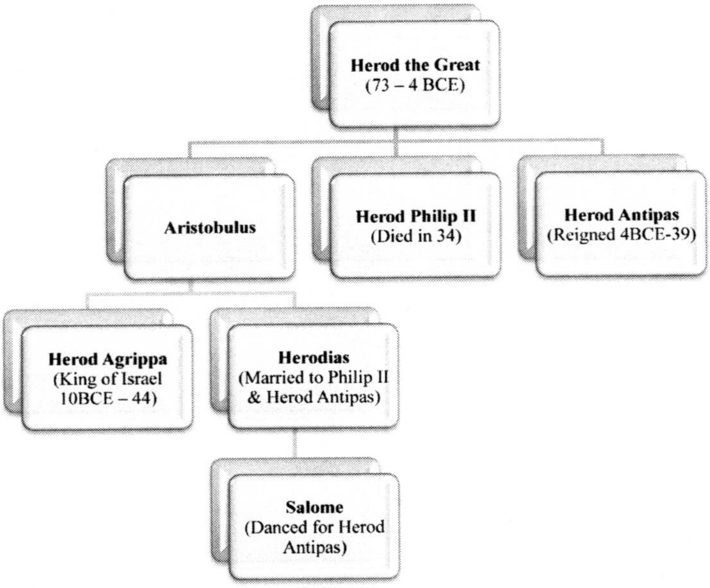

5.23 Timeline from the Biblical Roman Period through the Jewish Wars

Years are Before the Common Era (BCE) or in the Common Era (CE)

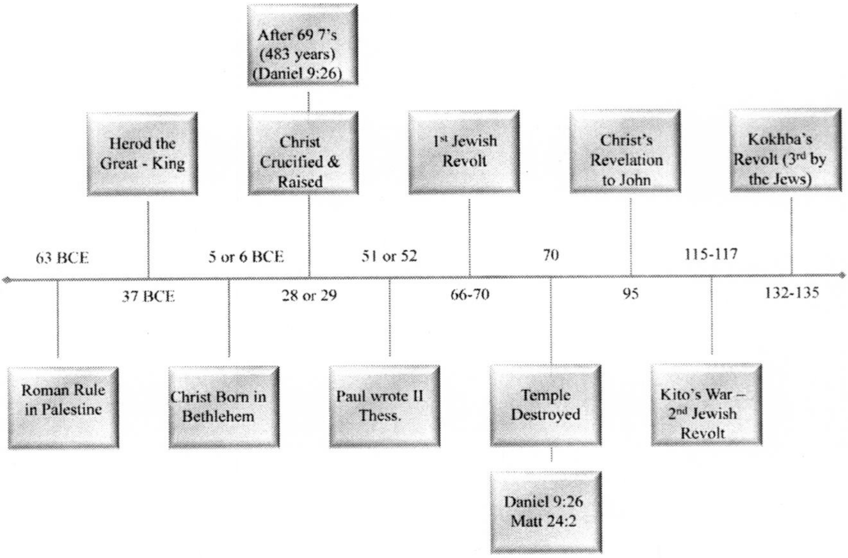

Homecoming (1948 CE - Present)

God gave the Jews hope by promising to bring them back to their homeland in the last days (e.g. Isaiah 11:11-12 and Jeremiah 23:3). This promise was finally realized on May 15, 1948, when Israel once again became a nation after 1882 years of Diaspora (dispersion). Unfortunately, they immediately had to defend their homeland during a 19-month war with neighboring Arab countries. This became known as the Israeli War of Independence.

Nineteen years later, in 1967, Israel once again had to defend the land given to them by God so many centuries ago in what has been called the Six-day War (June 5-10). Egypt, Jordan, and Syria came against Israel from nearly every side. At the time, these three Arab nations ruled the following areas in Palestine:

- Egypt – Gaza
- Jordan – West Bank
- Syria – Golan Heights

Israel took control of the Sinai Peninsula (to the Suez Canal) and these regions after defeating the Egyptian, Jordanian, and Syrian forces. What was the significance of the Suez Canal? It connects the Mediterranean and Indian Oceans, eliminating the need to navigate around Africa to transport cargo between Europe and Asia. They also took control of the Temple Mount and Dome of the Rock, which are sacred to Muslims around the world. Within hours, General Moshe Dayan transferred control to the Muslim Waqf (religious trust), temporarily squashing any hopes of moving the Dome to Mecca and constructing the third temple in its place. Israel's conquest and resulting relative peace would last for only six years until the next conflict.

Egypt and Syria again attacked Israel on October 6, 1973, during the Jewish Holiday of Yom Kippur (also during the Islamic Ramadan) in yet another Arab-Israeli war. This one lasted until October 26. Egypt attacked the Suez Canal, now occupied by Israel, and Syria attacked Golan Heights. Early Arab victories may have suggested the Israelis were in for defeat. However, they prevailed and were nearly within striking distance of Cairo in Egypt and Damascus in Syria when a ceasefire was signed.

Although Arab-Israeli peace continued to be elusive, one significant milestone in the Middle East peace process was the Oslo Peace Accord signed in Washington, D.C., on September 13, 1993. The intent was to provide a framework for future negotiations and relations between the Israeli and Palestinian governments. Peace didn't happen as hoped though. For instance, more than 6,500 people had been killed by the conclusion of the Al-Aqsa Intifada, which began in late September 2000. The violence occurred on the Temple Mount near the Dome of the Rock. Hamas, rising to power in 2006 (well after the 1993 peace agreement had been signed), doesn't recognize the Oslo Peace Accord and aggressions continue to this day. Most recently, the Temple Mount and Land of Israel Faithful Movement groups reported these aggressive acts:

> On Thursday, June 10, 2010, Rosh Chodesh Tammuz, while thousands of Israelis were planning to surround the Temple Mount, as we do every Rosh Chodesh following the biblical tradition at the beginning of each new month, we were shocked to see the Turkish flag being raised over the Temple Mount as a follow-up to the Gaza flotilla clash.
>
> On the 7th of June, the Iranians declared that they are going to send to Gaza another flotilla of terror that will be followed by Iranian-armed soldiers. This is the Iran that has stated again and again during the last couple of years that her goal is to remove Israel from the map of the world. We can be sure that Israel will not allow this terror provocation and attack against Israel to come to Gaza in order to further arm the Hamas terror organization that continues to attack Israel with rockets and missiles.

The latter report refers to statements made by Iran that they plan to remove Israel from the map of the world. This may have been what the psalmist saw and reflected in Psalm 83:

For behold, Your enemies make an uproar, And those who hate You have exalted themselves. They make shrewd plans against Your people, And conspire together against Your treasured ones. They have said, "Come, and let us wipe them out as a nation, That the name of Israel be remembered no more." —Psalm 83:2-4.

So what about Israel's future? We know from prophecies made by Ezekiel, Joel, and Daniel that a covenant will indeed be made with Israel in the last days and then broken before another great war breaks out against her:

- The covenant will be made and then broken after three and a half years: "*And he will make a firm covenant with the many for one week, but in the middle of the week he will put a stop to sacrifice and grain offering . . .*" —Daniel 9:27.
- The war of Gog and Magog against Israel and the coming judgment of the nations at the end of God's wrath: Ezekiel 38 & 39 and Zechariah 12 & 14 (to name a few of many references that describe the Day of the Lord judgment).

In a nutshell, here are the future events that still need to happen before the very end:

1. Building of the third temple for the sake of God's relationship with His chosen people, the Jews.
2. Agreement/covenant (see references to Isaiah and Daniel's prophecies above).
3. Agreement dishonored after three and a half years (again, see above).
4. A great war between the Jews and others (you'll learn later that this is referred to as Armageddon).

You can view and download up-to-date information about current hostilities against Israel among other topics at the Israeli Ministry of Foreign Affairs website (www.mfa.gov.il/MFA).

5.24 Timeline from the Homecoming to Present
Years are in the Common Era (CE)

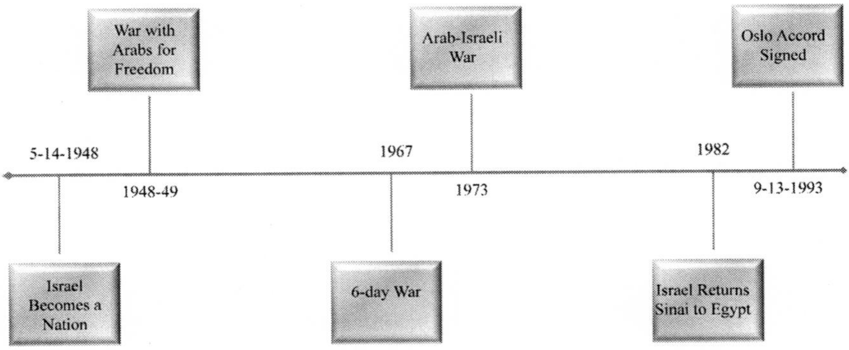

THE TEMPLE (966 BCE - ???)

Learning about the temple and the requirement for a third earthly version is important to understanding end-of-the-world Scripture. A temple will exist in Jerusalem in the last days, and its construction and desecration by the Antichrist are integral parts of the end-times sequence of events. Daniel, Jesus, Paul, and John all attested to this.

From the time God led His people out of Egypt, He has desired to reside with those faithful to Him. The first dwelling place was a *tabernacle* in the form of a tent. God gave Moses strict guidelines with which to construct it and the articles to be used in worship, including the priests' garments. King David resumed worship of God upon the capture and reoccupation of Jerusalem, and his son Solomon built the Lord a proper place to dwell among the Jews later. The temple has been rebuilt once and improved once as well. Both versions of the temple have been destroyed, but a third temple will again provide a place for God to reside with those who love and worship Him. It will be different from the temple of the Holy Spirit (us) and the heavenly temple, of which the earthly temple is a type.

Some people believe the third temple mentioned in Scripture is symbolic and not a physical structure. A component of this false teaching is that the biblical third temple is actually representative of every Christian. While it's true that believers in Christ are called the temple of the Holy Spirit (cf. Ephesians 2:21 and 1 Corinthians 3:16-17 & 6:19), there's no reason to believe the third temple itself will be anything other than what the Bible says it will be: a temple of the Lord built for God by the Jews, and desecrated by the Antichrist. Believing anything else regarding the temple will make it difficult to keep on track in our study of the end of the world. God's Holy Spirit does reside in and with Christian believers, negating the need for *us* to have a temple, but apocalyptic literature in the Bible has revealed that the Jews will build one in fulfillment of end-times prophecy. Let's take a more in-depth look at the history of God's temple.

After the Exodus of 1446 BCE, God renewed an everlasting covenant with the Hebrews (e.g. Exodus 34:10). He gave them guidelines to live by and instructions for building a tabernacle – a place where He could dwell with them:

> *Let them construct a sanctuary for Me, that I may dwell among them. According to all that I am going to show you, as the pattern of the tabernacle and the pattern of all its furniture, just so you shall construct it.* —Exodus 25:8-9.

The tabernacle of the Lord housed the ark of the covenant created by Moses according to God's specification during his trek in the desert. Unfortunately, the Philistines captured the ark sometime before King David united the northern and southern kingdoms. After David took control of Jerusalem, the Philistines sent the ark back to Palestine to get rid of it. According to the Bible, Philistine people suffered plagues and destruction everywhere they sent the ark within their own lands. David eventually transported the ark to Jerusalem where he set it up inside the tent tabernacle. But this would be a temporary resting place.

God nudged David to build a permanent dwelling place:

> *Go and say to My servant David, Thus says the LORD, "Are you the one who should build Me a house to dwell in? For I have not dwelt in a house since the day I brought up the sons of Israel from Egypt, even to this day; but I have been moving about in a tent, even in a tabernacle."* —2 Samuel 7:5-6.

David's son Solomon honored God's request for a more permanent structure and began building the first temple in 966 BCE:

> *Now it came about in the four hundred and eightieth year after the sons of Israel came out of the land of Egypt, in the fourth year of Solomon's reign over Israel, in the month of Ziv which is the second month, that he began to build the house of the LORD. As for the house which King Solomon built for the LORD, its length was sixty cubits and its width twenty cubits and its height thirty cubits.* —1 Kings 6:1-2.

He finished the job in 959 BCE after employing many foreign laborers to cut stone and work metal – things the Israelites didn't have much experience with yet. Additionally, he imported cedar beams from Lebanon and enjoyed a close relationship with the Queen of Sheba during this period. You can read more about the construction of the temple in 1 Kings 6 and 7. Nearly 370 years would pass before being destroyed by the Babylonians.

In 586 BCE, the Babylonian army under leadership of King Nebuchadnezzar destroyed the temple and took the articles contained within it to Babylon along with thousands of Jewish deportees. This was in addition to the articles and people taken during the original raid in 605 BCE (when Daniel and some of his friends were taken captive). The temple and city of Jerusalem lay in ruins until 70 years had passed and rebuilding began.

The year 536 BCE witnessed a rebirth of sorts with the return of some Jews to Jerusalem and the blessing from Cyrus, king of Persia, to rebuild the temple and city. After a temporary work stoppage, temple construction resumed in 520 and was completed in 516 BCE. Jewish priest Zerubbabel dedicated it a year later in 515 BCE. The second temple stayed erect until it was destroyed by the Romans in 70 CE, but it had undergone desecration and a facelift before then.

One character that will continually surface during our study is Antiochus IV Epiphanes – the Syrian Seleucid ruler of Daniel's vision (see Daniel 8 and others already covered). This wicked king established a covenant with Jews unfaithful to God, but broke the agreement and abolished temple sacrifice and observance of God's laws. He killed roughly 80,000 men, women, and children and desecrated the temple by slaughtering a pig on the altar and erecting on it a statue of Zeus. Antiochus and his forces were repelled by faithful Jews headed by Judah Maccabeus in 167 BCE. They reclaimed the temple and purified it in 164 BCE after 1,150 days (2,300 evenings and mornings) as prophesied by Daniel:

> *It even magnified itself to be equal with the Commander of the host; and it removed the regular sacrifice from Him, and the place of His sanctuary was thrown down. And on account of transgression the host will be given over to the horn along with the regular sacrifice; and it will fling truth to the ground and perform its will and prosper. Then I heard a holy one speaking, and another holy one said to that particular one who was speaking, "How long will the vision about the regular sacrifice apply, while the transgression causes horror, so as to allow both the holy place and the host to be trampled?" He said to me, "For 2,300 evenings and mornings; then the holy place will be properly restored."* —Daniel 8:11-14.

In 19 BCE, Herod the Great started a 40-year project to give the second temple a facelift. He also added considerably to the Temple Mount, which is where the temple sat atop of Mount Moriah. Jesus' disciples commented on the magnificent structures one day when they were on their way to the Mount of Olives. He responded by telling them of the future destruction that would happen in 70 CE:

> *Jesus came out from the temple and was going away when His disciples came up to point out the temple buildings to Him. And He said to them, "Do you not see all these things? Truly I say to you, not one stone here will be left upon another, which will not be torn down."* —Matthew 24:1-2.

Two down, one earthly temple to go. Jesus showed John in 90 CE (25 years after the destruction of the second temple) a vision of the third temple in Jerusalem:

> *Then there was given me a measuring rod like a staff; and someone said, "Get up and measure the temple of God and the altar, and those who worship in it. Leave out the court which is outside the temple and do not measure it, for it has been given to the nations; and they will tread underfoot the holy city for forty-two months."* —Revelation 11:1-2.

We shouldn't be surprised because Paul reminded the believers in Thessalonica that the Antichrist would enter the temple and exalt himself above God, referring to events that must happen *before* Christ's appearance and our gathering:

> *Let no one in any way deceive you, for it will not come unless the apostasy comes first, and the man of lawlessness is revealed, the son of destruction, who opposes and exalts himself above every so-called god or object of worship, so that he takes his seat in the temple of God, displaying himself as being God.* —2 Thessalonians 2:3-4.

But Daniel was the first to tell us this when recounting his vision of the end. He initially revealed that the Antichrist would enter the temple and abolish sacrifice midway through a seven-year agreement in these two statements from 9:27 and 12:11:

> *And he will make a firm covenant with the many for one week [of years], but in the middle of the week [of years] he will put a stop to sacrifice and grain offering . . .* —Daniel 9:27.

From the time that the regular sacrifice is abolished and the abomination of desolation is set up, there will be 1,290 days. —Daniel 12:11.

A few have questioned the authenticity of Daniel's visions (perhaps to rationalize a personal end-times position). That wouldn't be a good thing to do since Jesus gave credibility to Daniel's visions of the end by stating: "*Therefore when you see the ABOMINATION OF DESOLATION which was spoken of through Daniel the prophet, standing in the holy place (let the reader understand)*" —Matthew 24:15. The Greek words the translation of "*holy place*" came from in Matthew 24:15 are *hagios* and *topos*, which together define a "ceremonially consecrated location" – not a figurative temple of the Holy Spirit.

So is anyone serious about building the third temple? You bet! Many Jews have looked forward to this since June 1967 when the Israelis once again controlled the Temple Mount and Dome of the Rock (where they believe the Holy of Holies and ark of the covenant had been in Solomon's days). The control only lasted for a few hours, but many Israelis still hope to one day obtain permission to rebuild the temple. Several significant sources raise funds, create temple articles, or educate the public on the topic of the Temple Mount and temple: Temple Institute (www.templeinstitute.org), Temple Mount Faithful (templemountfaithful.org) and Temple Mount resource compilation (www.templemount.org).

The first site reflects efforts to build the new temple while the latter seems to be a good source of information related to Islam, Judaism, Christianity, and the Temple Mount. Some of the preparations already made for the third temple include:

1. Reestablishment of the Jewish Sanhedrin.
2. Creation of cornerstones in 1989 (attempts made annually to place these have been unsuccessful thus far).
3. Attempting to determine the exact location of where the temple should go (the location may be several hundred feet

from the Dome of the Rock, allowing it and the new temple to exist simultaneously and peacefully).

4. Seeking the Red Heifer (the ashes of which are necessary for the process of temple purification).
5. Creation of various temple vessels to include the menorah and temple utensils.

5.25 Timeline of Temple Eras

Years are Before the Common Era (BCE) or in the Common Era (CE)

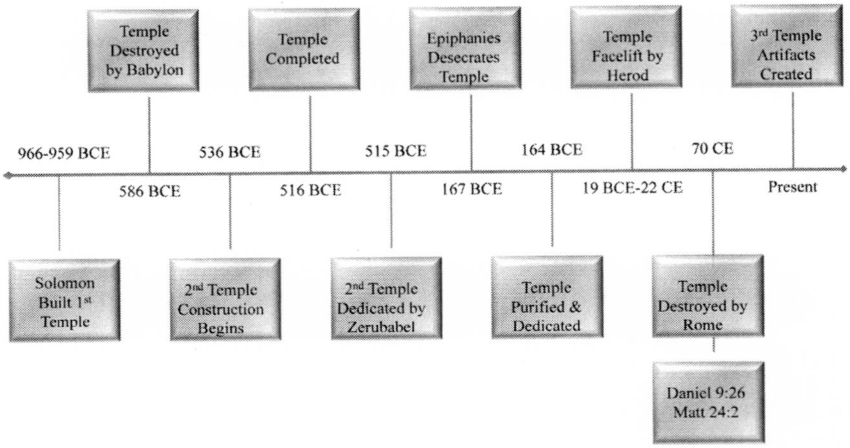

Chapter Six

Key End-times Players

As I mentioned at the beginning of this study guide, we'll be in one of two groups at Christ's appearing: those gathered as the Elect Bride of Christ or those who will remain on earth during God's wrath. These two groups will be broken down into their respective components and defined in the next several chapters. End-times players we'll explore:

- *Remnant of Israel*: Jews from the 12 tribes God promised to bring home at the end.
- *144,000 from the 12 tribes*: First-fruits of God's chosen kept safe during His wrath.
- *Two witnesses*: Two heavenly hosts who will preach during the three-and-a-half-year Antichrist reign (the Great Tribulation).
- *Beheaded*: Those martyred for their faith during the Great Tribulation and resurrected to reign with Christ for 1,000 years.

My desire in presenting these end-times players is to strengthen your foundation in apocalyptic Scripture, which will:

1. Aid in your end-times study.
2. Help you discern and disregard false teaching.

Manifestations of the key players above can be difficult to understand. Getting the best grasp possible requires comparing Scripture to Scripture, often looking at Old and New Testament texts together in their individual contexts and considering original language. Otherwise, a risk of misunderstanding them exists. For instance, Hal Lindsey and others have stated that the 144,000 of the Revelation will be *Jews for Jesus evangelizing the world.* Certain denominations claim that number is symbolic and represents their particular faith. And the Revelation 11 topic of two witnesses has prompted several theories about who they are, what they'll do on earth, and how long they'll be here for.

So what's a student of apocalyptic Scripture to do? Remember that some issues are secondary and not critical to keeping your salvation. There isn't always a lot of information to go on, so we'll do our best to glean what we can and move on. Let's focus on what we know and refrain from creating theology out of what we can only guess at.

✓ **Quick reference:**

- *Remnant of Israel*: Jeremiah 30:3, Joel 2:32, Jeremiah 23:3-6, Ezekiel 37:21-25, Isaiah 1:9, Romans 9:27-29, & Matthew 24:21
- *144,000 from the 12 tribes*: Revelation 7:3-8 & 9:4, & Revelation 14:1-5
- *Two witnesses*: Revelation 11
- *Beheaded*: Revelation 6:7-11 (seals 4 and 5) and Revelation 20:4-6

REMNANT OF ISRAEL

The people of Israel have suffered mass genocide by several empires and, most recently, at the hands of the Germans in World War II. To add insult to injury, they were kept out of the land God gave them for nearly 1,900 years. Despite all odds and great calamity, God has kept the Jews – His original chosen people – from being exterminated from the face of the earth. He also promised to bring His people back home to Israel as the end approaches. The door was finally opened in May 1948 when Israel again became a nation and the land's rightful owners were allowed to come back to the place given to them by God nearly 3,400 years ago.

This returning group is at least part of the remnant prophets like Jeremiah and Ezekiel foretold of so long ago. What do we know about them and their context at the end? (Please refer back to *Format* in Chapter Four for a refresher in near-far prophecy and apocalyptic literature if necessary.)

God will gather the Jews from where they've been dispersed and bring them back to their homeland, and Christ will reign over them. Daniel saw this as coming at the completion of the 490-year period (Daniel 9:24-27 & 12:7). The timeframe will come to a close and Christ's kingdom will begin at the seventh trumpet judgment (cf. Revelation 11:15).

> *Then I Myself will* ***gather the remnant of My flock out of all the countries*** *where I have driven them and bring them back to their pasture, and they will be fruitful and multiply. I will also raise up shepherds over them and they will tend them; and they will not be afraid any longer, nor be terrified, nor will any be missing, declares the LORD. 'Behold, the days are coming', declares the LORD, '****When I will raise up for David a righteous Branch; And He will reign as king and act wisely*** *And do justice and righteousness in the land. In His days Judah will be saved, And Israel will dwell securely; And this is His name by which He will be called, 'The LORD our righteousness'.* —Jeremiah 23:3-6.

> *'Say to them', Thus says the Lord GOD, 'Behold,* ***I will take the sons of Israel from among the nations where they have gone, and I will gather them from every side and bring them into their own land****; and I will make them one nation in the land, on the mountains of Israel; and one king will be king for all of them; and they will no longer be two nations and no longer be divided into two kingdoms. They will no longer defile themselves with their idols, or with their detestable things, or with any of their transgressions; but I will deliver them from all their dwelling places in which they have sinned, and will cleanse them. And they will be My people, and I will be their God.* ***My servant David will be king over them, and they will all have one shepherd****; and they will walk in My ordinances and keep My statutes and observe them. They will live on the land that I gave to Jacob My servant, in which your fathers lived; and they will live on it, they, and their sons and their*

sons' sons, forever; and David My servant will be their prince forever'. —Ezekiel 37:21-25.

God's chosen will be caught up in the greatest time of trouble ever seen, which God will cut short to ensure they (and Christian believers) aren't completely wiped out:

Unless the LORD of hosts had left us a ***few survivors, we would be like Sodom, we would be like Gomorrah****.* —Isaiah 1:9.

For then there will be a great tribulation, such as has not occurred since the beginning of the world until now, nor ever will. ***Unless those days had been cut short, no life would have been saved****; but for the sake of the elect those days will be cut short.* —Matthew 24:21-22.

This remnant will consist of Jews from the two tribes of the southern kingdom of Judah dispersed at the Babylonian captivity and again at the hands of the Romans. It will also contain members of the ten "lost" tribes of the northern kingdom of Israel dispersed by the Assyrians in roughly 722 BCE. These northern tribes are considered lost because of the lack of accountability and known whereabouts from the time they were dispersed by the Assyrians (see Chapter Five for additional information). Regardless, this remnant from all 12 tribes will be in Israel at the time of Christ's kingdom (cf. Revelation 11:13-15).

There may also be another component of the remnant of Israel: the 144,000 Jews identified in Revelation 7. We'll cover this group next.

144,000 FROM THE 12 TRIBES OF ISRAEL

And I saw another angel ascending from the rising of the sun, having the seal of the living God; and he cried out with a loud voice to the four angels to whom it was granted to harm the earth and the sea, saying, "Do not harm the earth or the sea or the trees until *we have sealed the bond-servants of our God on their foreheads". **And I heard the number of those who were sealed, one hundred and forty-four thousand sealed from every tribe of the sons of Israel...***—Revelation 7:2-4.

Just who will be the members of this group? Apparently they'll be special representatives of Israel in the form of 12,000 from each of the 12 tribes as follows:

- Judah
- Rueben
- Gad
- Asher
- Naphtali
- Manasseh (Joseph's son; replaced Dan)
- Simeon
- Levi
- Issachar
- Zebulon
- Joseph
- Benjamin

Note that one of the original tribal leaders, Dan, was later replaced by Joseph's son Manasseh after Dan's clan was disowned (most likely because of idolatry). This is important, as some denominations claim that because the list of tribes is different from the original found in the Old Testament, the group is symbolic of their particular denomination and not Jews as stated by Christ. This allegorizing of Scripture is done to pave the way for at least two unscriptural theories:

1. Seventh-Day Adventists: to support a belief that true believers will still be on earth during the time of God's wrath and therefore will need the seal of God for protection (Shepherd's Rod Message - www.shepherds-rod-message.org/outlines/144000.pdf). But as the apostle Paul pointed out, we who believe aren't destined for God's wrath.

2. Jehovah's Witnesses: to support a belief that the group of 144,000 represents their denomination as the only Christian sect that will be taken to heaven upon Jesus' return (www.newworldencyclopedia.org/entry/144,000).

Little is known about this group that's *redeemed from among men* (cf. Revelation 14:14), but God will clearly set them apart and protect them during the time of His wrath. Again, this is most likely part of the remnant God promised to save in the last days; they'll be in Jerusalem with Christ at the onset of His kingdom. A belief that they'll be "Jews for Jesus" spreading the gospel to the entire world during the tribulation (e.g. as Hal Lindsey states in chapter 7 of *There's a New World Coming*) is scripturally unfounded.

The following are key points regarding the 144,000:

- Sealed for protection against God's impending wrath (cf. Revelation 7:3-8 & 9:4).
- Seen with Christ on Mount Zion during the time of God's wrath, but before the seventh trumpet when Christ will gain His kingdom and enter Jerusalem. They "*follow Him wherever He goes*" (cf. Revelation 14:1).
- There'll be a new song in heaven that no man can learn but the 144,000 redeemed from the earth (cf. Revelation 14:2-3).
- Redeemed from among men, being the first-fruits unto God and to the Lamb (cf. Revelation 14:4).
- They'll be virgins and without fault (cf. Revelation 14:4-5).

Most intriguing is the fact that they'll be redeemed from among men and from the earth, and will be first-fruits unto God and Christ (cf. Revelation 14:2-4). The origin of *redeemed* is the Greek word *agorazo*, which means "to purchase" in the way Christ purchased us at a price. In the same way, they'll be purchased from the earth/mankind as seen by the use of the Greek words *ghay* for the *earth* and *anthropos* for *mankind*. Why does the Bible say they'll be "first-fruits" unto God and Christ? Christ was crucified and then resurrected, becoming the first-fruits to God as Paul reminded us:

> *For as in Adam all die, so also in Christ all will be made alive. But each in his own order: Christ* ***the first fruits****, after that those who are Christ's at His coming, then comes the end, when He hands over the kingdom to the God and Father, when He has abolished all rule and all authority and power.* —1 Corinthians 15:22-24.

Qualities of the 144,000:

- Redeemed from among men, being the first-fruits unto God and to the Lamb (cf. Revelation 14:4).
- They will be virgins and without fault (cf. Revelation 14:4-5).
- "*And in their mouth was found no guile: for they are without fault before the throne of God*" (Revelation 14:5).

What will be the role of this group? Nothing in Scripture tells us for sure. Regardless, they'll be one of three groups of people in Jerusalem at the time Christ becomes king:

- Anyone left standing after the Great Tribulation and God's seven trumpet judgments (cf. Revelation 11:13-15).
- The 144,000 seen with Christ (cf. Revelation 14:1).
- Those beheaded for their faith during the three-and-a-half-year reign of the Antichrist (cf. Revelation 20:4).

Finally, Scripture also says this about the 144,000: "*And no lie was found in their mouth; they are blameless.*" —Revelation 14:5. Compare this to Zephaniah 3:13-15:

> ***The remnant of Israel will do no wrong And tell no lies****, Nor will a deceitful tongue Be found in their mouths; For they will feed and lie down With no one to make them tremble. Shout for joy, O daughter of Zion! Shout in triumph, O Israel! Rejoice and exult with all your heart, O daughter of Jerusalem! The LORD has taken away His judgments against you, He has cleared away your enemies. The King of Israel, the LORD, is in your midst; You will fear disaster no more.*

The following timeline will help you see at a glance where the group most likely fits into the end-times sequence.

6.1 Context of the 144,000

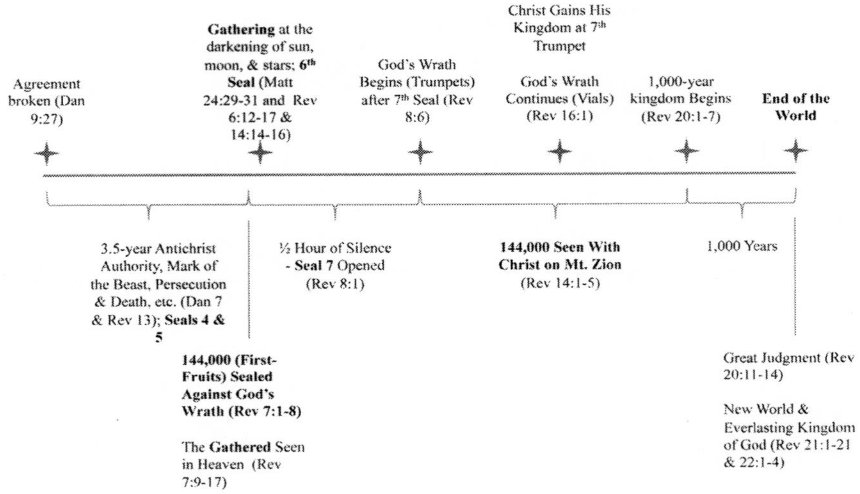

In summary, let's look at what we know and don't know and what is untrue about the 144,000 of Revelation:

What we *know*:

1. The group will be 144,000 Jews who'll be first-fruits unto Christ.
2. They'll be protected against God's wrath (e.g. the sixth trumpet judgment in Revelation 9:4). They'll also be seen with Christ during the time of God's wrath and will be with Him as He gains His kingdom at the seventh trumpet.

What we *don't know*:

1. Where the ten lost tribes of the kingdom of Israel are

today, although there's much speculation on the subject. However, God has promised Israel to bring all the tribes back together at the end and protect a remnant.

2. Specifically, why Christ will select them—unless their purpose is to reign with Him in Jerusalem.

Unscriptural:

1. The 144,000 will be Jews for Jesus evangelizing the world.
2. The 144,000 won't be Jews but special evangelizing Christians.
3. The 144,000 are symbolic and represent particular Christian denominations.

Next we'll take a look at the *two witnesses* outlined in Revelation 11.

TWO WITNESSES

Who will these apocalyptic preachers be? According to Scripture, they'll be two heavenly hosts sent to earth to prophesy and witness for three and a half years during the time of the Antichrist. But exactly *who* will they be? Are there any references to them besides those in Revelation 11? Let's start by answering the latter after looking at where these two may fit into the end-times sequence of events.

Jesus gave an end-times sequence of events to His disciples on the Mount of Olives (cf. Matthew 24, Mark 13, and Luke 21). Because He was answering questions concerning the destruction of Jerusalem (near-term) and His return at the end of the world (far-term), the list contains near and far events as follows (taken from Matthew 24):

1. False messiahs, violence, and ecological calamity that will increase in frequency and intensity as the end draws near ("birth pangs," as Jesus put it). These signs correspond to

seals 1-3 in Revelation 6.

2. **The gospel will be preached to all nations and then the end will come** (compare with Revelation 14:6-7).
3. Persecution and death until the end (see seals 4-5 in Revelation 6). The destruction of Jerusalem and the temple in 70 CE and subsequent dispersion was prophesied here as was the death and persecution at the end. Again, this is a near-far prophecy and verses 9-13 most likely relate to the near-term while 14-34 apply directly to the end and Christ's return.
4. Great tribulation by the Antichrist *at the end* (see seals 4-5 in Revelation 6).
5. Darkening of the sun, moon, and stars; tribes of the earth mourn (compare with the sixth seal in Revelation 6).

Scripture mentions a specific and future preaching of the gospel only twice (on the Mount of Olives in Matthew 24 and again in Revelation 14). Because the two witnesses will be put here to preach the gospel, they may be the ones who'll carry out this preaching before the gathering and wrath of God as indicated in Matthew 24 and Revelation 14. Whether this will be the case is a secondary issue; I make the point only for consideration. There's no direct mention of them outside Revelation 11. Now let's explore the really controversial topic of their identity.

The two witnesses are identified as the *two olive trees and two candlesticks that stand before God*. You'll find references to the two olive trees that stand before God in Revelation 11:4 and Zechariah 4:11-14:

> *Then I said to him, "What are these* ***two olive trees*** *on the right of the lampstand and on its left?" And I answered the second time and said to him, "What are the two olive branches which are beside the two golden pipes, which empty the golden oil from themselves?" So he answered me, saying, "Do you not know what these are?" And I said, "No, my lord." Then he said, "****These are the two anointed ones who are standing by the Lord of the whole earth****."* —Zechariah 4:11-14.

These are the two olive trees and the ***two lampstands that stand before the Lord of the earth****.* —Revelation 11:4.

Zechariah's wording in 4:14 shows us that the two olive trees are *anointed ones* through the use of the Hebrew words labeled under Strong's H112 and H3323 as follows:

H1121 bên (bane) - a **son** (as a builder of the family name), in the widest sense (of literal and figurative relationship, including grandson, subject, nation, quality or condition, etc.

H3323 yitshâr (yits-hawr') **oil (as producing light); figuratively anointing**: - + anointed, oil.

We can only guess at who these two witnesses will be. Some believe they'll be Enoch and Elijah because they were taken to heaven by God without suffering physical death. Others believe they'll be Moses and Elijah because they were the ones who appeared on the mountain with Jesus and Peter (cf. Matthew 17:1-3) and because the miracles of the witnesses mirror those performed by Moses and Elijah. Hal Lindsey rationalized that the witnesses will be Moses and Elijah in *There's a New World Coming* because neither had the chance to complete their ministries and will therefore be given the chance to come back and do so.

Another belief, expressed by Ellis Skolfield in his book *The False Prophet*, is that the two witnesses are symbolic of the Jews and the Christian church. Ellis believes the two olive trees represent Israel and the two candlesticks represent the church. This is partially based on Revelation 1:20 where "*seven candlesticks*" represent seven churches of Asia Minor. He claims the time of the Jewish and Christian witnesses started in 688 CE with Muslim control of Jerusalem and ended 1,260 years later in 1948 when Israel became a nation. The concept of turning 1,260 days of ministry into 1,260 years is intriguing because the timeframe does fit between 688 and 1948 CE – both significant dates. However, this is likely to be just a coincidence since nothing else fits the scriptural description of these two witnesses and their role as outlined in Revelation.

What we do know is that the two witnesses will prophesy for three and a half years and will have the supernatural ability to control the rain, turn water to blood, and smite the earth with plagues (this sounds a lot like what happened in Egypt during the exodus). The Antichrist, empowered by Satan, will kill these two. Their bodies will lie in the streets of Jerusalem for three days while many people rejoice because of their deaths. After three days, they'll be resurrected and taken to heaven just before a great earthquake shakes Jerusalem and Christ gains His kingdom as stated below:

> *And they heard a loud voice from heaven saying to them, "Come up here." Then they went up into heaven in the cloud, and their enemies watched them. And in that hour there was a great earthquake, and a tenth of the city fell; seven thousand people were killed in the earthquake, and the rest were terrified and gave glory to the God of heaven. The second woe is past; behold, the third woe is coming quickly. Then the seventh angel sounded; and there were loud voices in heaven, saying, "The kingdom of the world has become the kingdom of our Lord and of His Christ; and He will reign forever and ever."* — Revelation 11:12-15

The time of their three-and-a-half-year witness will be finished at the end of Daniel's seven-year period when Christ gains His kingdom. Therefore, we can place the arrival of the two witnesses on earth at the time the Antichrist enters the temple, stops daily sacrifice, and begins his reign of terror. This will be midway through Daniel's seven-year period. The following timeline will help visualize this.

6.2 Context of the Two Witnesses

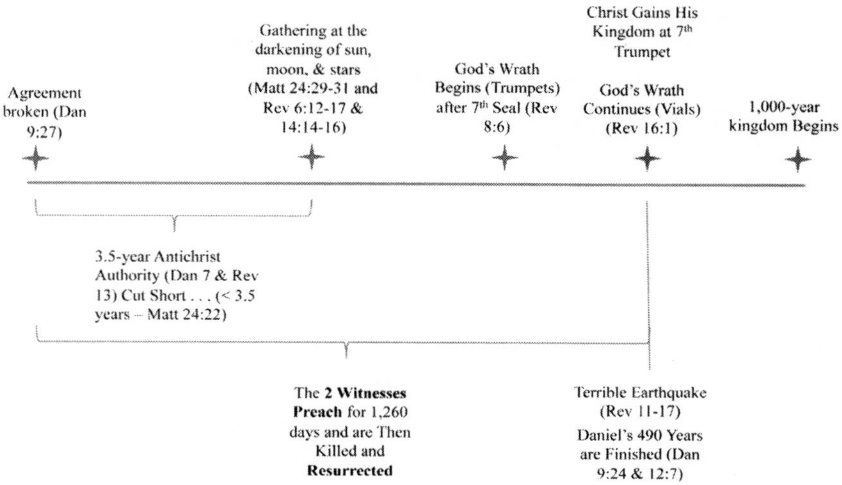

The next section will introduce those who'll be beheaded for their faith and for refusing to take the mark of the Antichrist's kingdom during the Great Tribulation.

BEHEADED

At first glance, it would seem there isn't much we can say about this group of end-times martyrs. But certain circumstantial evidence can be gleaned from what little Scripture there is on this subject. Direct evidence and other helpful hints can be combined to help us understand more about these faithful believers. Let's build a foundation based on the facts and then consider other helpful hints to paint an accurate portrait.

As previously discussed, the seals broken in Revelation 6 reiterate what Jesus shared with His disciples on the Mount of Olives (cf. Matthew 24, Mark 13, and Luke 21). Seals 1-3 were broken to reveal birth pangs of false messiahs, war, and earthquakes/famine that will increase in intensity and frequency as the end draws near.

Compare the following Scripture references:

- Seal #1: Matthew 24:5 & Revelation 6:2
- Seal #2: Matthew 24:6 & Revelation 6:4
- Seal #3: Matthew 24:7 & Revelation 6:5-6

Seals 4-5 were broken to reveal martyrdom and persecution that will happen during the reign of the Antichrist. There are several good reasons to believe this:

1. The position of the fourth and fifth seals places the persecution of Antichrist after the events revealed by the breaking of seals 1-3, and before the darkening of the sun, moon, and stars at Christ's appearing (seal 6).
2. The context of the events of the fourth and fifth seals strongly suggests death of certain saints just before the end. Compare Matthew 24:15-26 and Revelation 6:9-11.
3. The Greek word used to represent **beasts** in Revelation 6:8 is *therion* – the only word used to represent the Antichrist or his kingdom in Revelation.

Here's the Scripture reference for seal #4:

> *When the Lamb broke the fourth seal, I heard the voice of the fourth living creature saying, "Come." I looked, and behold, an ashen horse; and he who sat on it had the name Death; and Hades was following with him. Authority was given to them over a fourth of the earth, to kill with sword and with famine and with pestilence and by the wild* ***beasts*** *of the earth.* —Revelation 6:7-8.

Consider Revelation 13:15, which provides more insight regarding the false prophet of the Antichrist and the death he'll be able to facilitate:

> *And it was given to him to give breath to the image of the beast, so that the image of the beast would even speak and cause as many as do not worship the image of the beast to be*

killed. —Revelation 13:15.

While seal 4 text revealed martyrdom, seal 5 was broken to reveal some very interesting facts about those being killed in the events of seal 4:

1. They'll be slain for the Word of God and their testimony (cf. Revelation 6:9).
2. Their souls will be waiting for certain conclusion: God's wrath and vengeance, which we know will come after the gathering of believers at the darkening of the sun, moon, and stars (Revelation 6:10).
3. They'll be waiting for a certain number of fellow martyrs to be met (cf. Revelation 6:11).

Here's Revelation 6:9-11 in its entirety:

When the Lamb broke the fifth seal, I saw underneath the altar the souls of those who had been ***slain because of the word of God, and because of the testimony*** *which they had maintained; and they cried out with a loud voice, saying, "How long, O Lord, holy and true, will You refrain from judging and* ***avenging our blood*** *on those who dwell on the earth?" And there was given to each of them a white robe; and they were told that they should rest for a little while longer,* ***until the number of their fellow servants and their brethren who were to be killed even as they had been, would be completed also****.* —Revelation 6:9-11.

Jesus had told His disciples this martyrdom would happen and that things will get really bad once the Antichrist takes up residence in the temple. As already discussed, broken seals 4-5 in the Revelation reflect this time of trouble. But then what? Scripture tells us these martyrs will be resurrected in what will be the first resurrection and reign with Christ for 1,000 years as outlined below in Revelation 20:4-6:

Then I saw thrones, and they sat on them, and judgment was given to them. And ***I saw the souls of those who had been***

> ***beheaded because of their testimony of Jesus and because of the word of God, and those who had not worshiped the beast or his image, and had not received the mark on their forehead and on their hand; and they came to life and reigned with Christ for a thousand years.*** *The rest of the dead did not come to life until the thousand years were completed.* ***This is the first resurrection.*** *Blessed and holy is the one who has a part in the first resurrection; over these the second death has no power, but they will be priests of God and of Christ and will reign with Him for a thousand years.* — Revelation 20:4-6.

Before we move on to the next chapter, let's review what we know about this group:

- They'll be beheaded for their testimony of Jesus and for not taking the mark of the Antichrist during the Great Tribulation.
- They'll be waiting for God's vengeance to begin (the wrath of God that will follow the gathering of the "wheat" at the cutting short of the Great Tribulation).
- They're told to wait until a specific number of those martyred in the same way has been met.
- They'll be resurrected after the Great Tribulation in what's referred to by Jesus as the first resurrection.
- They'll reign with Christ during His 1,000-year reign.

6.3 Context of the Beheaded

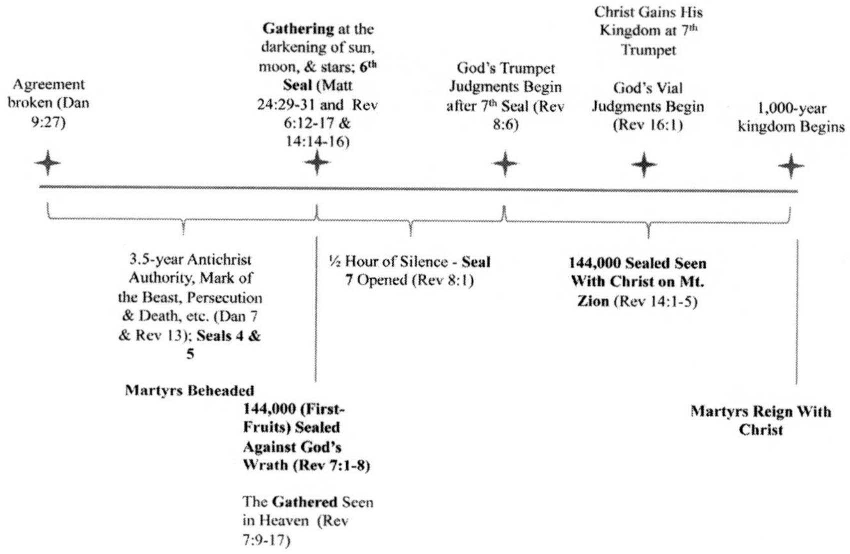

CHAPTER SEVEN

THE ELECT BRIDE

The next two topics (*The Elect* and *The Bride*) will address the New Testament chosen (elect) – everyone who has given (or will give) themselves to Christ and remained His since the time of His death and resurrection. Although the term *elect* also includes Old Testament Jews who died before Christ's ministry, we won't discuss them here since their resurrection will come at *the* Great "White Throne" Judgment concluding the 1,000-year reign of Christ and this age (world).

- The elect: God's chosen in the context of those who'll be gathered by Christ at His return (see "the bride").
- The bride: The church gathered (raptured) and taken to the marriage supper of Christ.

✓ **Quick reference:**

- The elect: wheat, woman, & offspring:
  - Jew and Gentile elect: Colossians 3:11-12
  - Wheat harvested: Matthew 13:24-39
  - Grapes harvested: Revelation 14:13-16
  - Elect gathered (harvested): Matthew 24:29-31
  - The *woman*: Revelation 12

✓ **Quick reference:**

- The bride:
  - Betrothal – Gentiles also as the chosen: Romans 11:24-25
  - Betrothal – Purchased by Christ's sacrifice, not with silver and gold: 1 Peter 1:3-5 & 18-23
  - Betrothal – How to accept and enter into the covenant: John 3:16, Romans 10:9-10, & Acts 2:38
  - Betrothal – Covenant, sealed with wine: Matthew 26:27-29
  - Betrothal – Spiritual cleansing: Ephesians 5:25-27, 1 Corinthians 6:10-11, & Revelation 7:13-14

- Betrothal – Bride's vow: 1 Corinthians 6:20
- Betrothal – Groom leaves/separation: Matthew 9:14-15
- Betrothal – Father prepares home: John 14:2
- Betrothal – No one but Father knows the ceremony day and hour: Mark 13:26-32
- Wedding ceremony – Announcement by shout and trumpet: Matthew 24:30-31 & 1 Thessalonians 4:16-17
- Wedding ceremony – Wedding feast: Revelation 19:7-9
- Afterward: Revelation 21:1-2 & 9-10

THE ELECT: WHEAT, WOMAN, & OFFSPRING

The *elect* are God's chosen – faithful Old Testament Jews and New Testament Christians alike. The Old Testament word used to describe the Jews as God's chosen is *bâchıyr*, meaning *chosen one* (cf. Isaiah 45:4 and 65:9; see also Strong's H972 and Appendix B). The New Testament uses the Greek word *eklektos* (see Strong's G1588) to refer to those who are Christ's. For instance, it's used to label those who'll be gathered (raptured) in Matthew 24. The same New Testament Greek word is used for *elect* and *chosen*, and both depict followers of Christ. Examples include:

- **Elect**: "*And He will send forth His angels with A GREAT TRUMPET and THEY WILL GATHER TOGETHER His* ***elect*** *from the four winds, from one end of the sky to the other.*" —Matthew 24:31.
- **Chosen**: *For many are called, but few are* ***chosen***. —Matthew 22:14. Also, "*a renewal in which there is* ***no distinction between Greek and Jew****, circumcised and uncircumcised, barbarian, Scythian, slave and freeman, but Christ is all, and in all. So, as those who have been* ***chosen*** *of God, holy and beloved, put on a heart of compassion, kindness, humility, gentleness and patience*" — Colossians 3:11-12.

Why is understanding who the elect are important? Since it's one of the main themes of apocalyptic Scriptures, knowing this will help you follow them as you move from Old Testament visions to New Testament revelation. As mentioned above, there are two elect groups: faithful Jews before Christ and everyone alive and dead in Him since His death and resurrection. Each group will be redeemed and gathered uniquely:

- Elect Jews *before* Christ: will be raised and judged at the great judgment at the end of Christ's 1,000-year reign.
- Elect believers in Jesus (Jew or Gentile, dead or alive) – Christ's bride: gathered for the wedding feast at His appearing, which will occur at the end of the Great Tribulation.

The New Testament gathering of the bride of Christ is compared to a harvest of wheat and of grapes in Scripture. But that won't be the only harvest after Christ's appearing. Jesus' parable of the Wheat and Tares reflected in Matthew 13 helps us understand that there'll be two harvests at the end of the age: that of the wheat (the elect, the children of the kingdom) and of the tares (children of the wicked one (Satan). The parable is shown here in part:

> *Jesus presented another parable to them, saying, "The kingdom of heaven may be compared to a man who sowed good seed in his field. But while his men were sleeping, his enemy came and sowed* ***tares*** *among the* ***wheat****, and went away . . . Allow both to grow together until the harvest; and in the time of the harvest I will say to the reapers, "First gather up the tares and bind them in bundles to burn them up; but* ***gather the wheat*** *into my barn."* —Matthew 13:24-30.

Jesus Himself gave us the meaning of the symbols: ". . . *and the field is the world; and as for the good seed, these are the sons of the kingdom; and the tares are the sons of the evil one; and the enemy who sowed them is the devil, and the harvest is the end of the age; and the reapers are angels."* —Matthew 13:38-39.

These two harvests at the end of the age (world) are also reflected in Matthew 24, John 5:28, and Revelation 14. First, the harvest of the *children of the kingdom* at the end of great tribulation:

> *But immediately after the tribulation of those days THE SUN WILL BE DARKENED, AND THE MOON WILL NOT GIVE ITS LIGHT, AND THE STARS WILL FALL from the sky, and the powers of the heavens will be shaken. And then the sign of the Son of Man will appear in the sky, and then all the tribes of the earth will mourn, and they will see the SON OF MAN COMING ON THE CLOUDS OF THE SKY with power and great glory. And He will send forth His angels with A GREAT TRUMPET and THEY WILL GATHER TOGETHER His elect from the four winds, from one end of the sky to the other.* —Matthew 24:29-31.

> *And I heard a voice from heaven, saying, "Write, 'Blessed are the dead who die in the Lord from now on!' "Yes," says the Spirit, "so that they may rest from their labors, for their deeds follow with them." Then I looked, and behold, a white cloud, and sitting on the cloud was one like a son of man, having a golden crown on His head and a sharp sickle in His hand. And another angel came out of the temple, crying out with a loud voice to Him who sat on the cloud, 'Put in your sickle and reap, for the hour to reap has come, because the harvest of the earth is ripe'. Then He who sat on the cloud swung His sickle over the earth, and the earth was reaped.* —Revelation 14:13-16.

And then God's wrath against the rest:

> *And another angel came out of the temple which is in heaven, and he also had a sharp sickle. Then another angel, the one who has power over fire, came out from the altar; and he called with a loud voice to him who had the sharp sickle, saying, 'Put in your sharp sickle and gather the clusters from the vine of the earth, because her grapes are ripe'. So the angel swung his sickle to the earth and gathered the clusters from the vine of the earth, and threw them into the great wine press of the wrath of God. And the wine press was trodden outside the city, and blood came out from the wine press, up to the horses' bridles, for a distance of two hundred miles.* —Revelation 14:17-20.

So who will be the *woman* and *offspring* mentioned in the title of this study section, and why is their reference important? We'll discuss the topic in greater detail during our study of the Revelation (12:1-2 and 12:5), but know that the woman represents a remnant of Israel at the end – possibly the 144,000. We can say this with confidence, as you'll learn, because of the 12 stars and their representation of the 12 tribes, and the reference to Christ as the offspring. The important thing to understand is that she'll be protected by God in the wilderness for three and a half years and that her *offspring – those who hold to the testimony of Jesus Christ* – will also be subjected to the wrath of Satan (most likely the Antichrist's Great Tribulation) during that time:

- Israel as the *woman*:

A great sign appeared in heaven: a ***woman*** *clothed with the sun, and the moon under her feet, and on her head a crown of twelve stars; and she was with child; and she cried out, being in labor and in pain to give birth . . . And she gave birth to a son, a male child, who is to rule all the nations with a rod of iron; and her child was caught up to God and to His throne.* —Revelation 12:1-5.

- Israel kept safe during the three-and-a-half-year wrath of Satan/Antichrist once he's cast to earth, and the wrath (again, most likely the three-and-a-half-year Great Tribulation) extended to Christian believers:

For this reason, rejoice, O heavens and you who dwell in them. ***Woe to the earth and the sea, because the devil has come down to you, having great wrath, knowing that he has only a short time. And when the dragon saw that he was thrown down to the earth, he persecuted the woman who gave birth to the male child****. But the two wings of the great eagle were given to the woman, so that she could fly into the wilderness to her place, where she was* ***nourished for a time and times and half a time****, from the presence of the serpent. And the serpent poured water like a river out of his mouth after the woman, so that he might* *cause her to be swept away with the flood. But the earth helped the woman, and the earth opened its mouth and drank up the river which the dragon poured out of his mouth. So the dragon was enraged with the woman, and went off to* ***make war with the rest of her children, who keep the commandments of God and hold to the testimony of Jesus****.* —Revelation 12:12-17.

In summary, the New Testament *elect* primarily refers to the bride of Christ as evidenced by the use of *eklektos* mostly in the context of the Christian and as a reference in apocalyptic literature. The woman in Revelation 12 refers to a portion of Israel and is significant for at least two reasons:

1. She – the remnant of Israel – is important to God, as He'll protect her during the time of Satan's wrath at the end.
2. Her offspring (made possible by God's covenant with Israel extended to gentiles) – those who hold to the testimony of Christ – will suffer during the wrath of Satan. This corroborates other Scripture indicating Christian believers will be subjected to the Antichrist's wrath during his three-and-a-half-year authority, which will be cut short with Christ's appearing and our gathering (cf. Matthew 24:21-22 and 29-31).

The Bride

I, Jesus, have sent My angel to testify to you these things for the churches. I am the root and the descendant of David, the bright morning star. The Spirit and the bride say, "Come." And let the one who hears say, "Come." And let the one who is thirsty come; let the one who wishes take the water of life without cost. —Revelation 22:16-17.

This is undoubtedly the most important section in the entire study. If you're a true believer betrothed to Christ, then your sincerest hope and longing is for His return to take you to the marriage ceremony in heaven. Otherwise, there's no point in finishing this study unless you're just interested in knowing what certain destruction and final judgment will look like. If you haven't already accepted Christ's saving grace, I beg you to have a change of heart and enter into an everlasting covenant with Him while you can. We'll discuss exactly what that means in the following paragraphs.

Who is the *bride of Christ*? Originally, Israel was the bride of God (e.g. Hosea 2:19-20). But in His mercy, He extended the invitation to the rest of the world (gentiles) through a "grafting" into the original vine as the apostle Paul addressed here:

> *For if you were cut off from what is by nature a wild olive tree, and were grafted contrary to nature into a cultivated olive tree, how much more will these who are the natural branches be grafted into their own olive tree? For I do not want you, brethren, to be uninformed of this mystery--so that you will not be wise in your own estimation--that a partial hardening has happened to Israel until the fullness of the Gentiles has come in;* —Romans 11:24-25.

> *For I am jealous for you with a godly jealousy; for I* ***betrothed you to one husband, so that to Christ I might present you as a pure virgin.*** —2 Corinthians 11:2.

The process of betrothal to Christ and the subsequent marriage of the church to Him follow ancient Hebrew marriage traditions. Like the Jewish spring feasts that were shadows of events fulfilled by Christ at His death and resurrection, the marriage process was (and still is) also a shadow and type of union with Him. There are two major parts to a typical Jewish wedding: the betrothal and the wedding ceremony. Jesus and the church have been fulfilling the betrothal steps since the night before His death and will continue to do so until His return. Let's explore each phase starting with the betrothal – the *eyrusin*.

~ Betrothal ~

Several pre-betrothal events take place before the actual betrothal period, which is one of separation during which the bride and groom prepare for marriage. The *first* step in the pre-betrothal process is the *shiddukhin* where the father of the groom-to-be selects a wife for his son. God has chosen all of us as possible brides for Christ since the beginning of time as indicated by Paul:

> *Blessed be the God and Father of our Lord Jesus Christ, who has blessed us with every spiritual blessing in the heavenly places in Christ, just as* ***He chose us in Him before the foundation of the world****, that we would be holy and blameless before Him. In love He predestined us to adoption as sons through Jesus Christ to Himself, according to the kind intention of His will* —Ephesians 1:3-5.

Afterward, a legal contract (covenant) called a *ketubah* is established between the future bride and groom. The groom will then pay a price – a *mohar* – for his future bride. Before Christ, God's bride (Israel) paid the dowry in the form of sacrifices. Since Christ's death and resurrection, no sacrifices are needed as He bought us at quite a high price by becoming the ultimate sacrifice Himself. He redeemed us not with gold and silver, but with His blood. Here's what Peter had to say on this subject:

> *. . . knowing that you* ***were not redeemed with perishable things like silver or gold*** *from your futile way of life inherited from your forefathers,* ***but with precious blood, as of a lamb unblemished and spotless, the blood of Christ****. For He was foreknown before the foundation of the world, but has appeared in these last times for the sake of you who through Him are believers in God, who raised Him from the dead and gave Him glory, so that your faith and hope are in God. Since you have in obedience to the truth purified your souls for a sincere love of the brethren, fervently love one another from the heart, for you have* ***been born again*** *not of seed which is perishable but imperishable, that is,* ***through the living and enduring word of God****.* —1 Peter 1:18-23.

The agreement is sealed by sharing a cup of wine (the cup of *ketubah*). Jesus Christ established a new covenant during the last supper He enjoyed with His disciples, and He enters into it with anyone who will believe He's God's Son and repent of their sinful ways. In keeping with the ceremony, Jesus presented the wine of the new covenant and reminded the others that He wouldn't partake of it again until the marriage ceremony of which the second cup of wine is an integral part:

> *And when He had taken a cup and given thanks, He gave it to them, saying, "Drink from it, all of you; for this is* ***My blood of the covenant****, which is poured out for many for forgiveness of sins. But I say to you,* ***I will not drink of this fruit of the vine from now on until that day when I drink it new with you in My Father's kingdom.****"* —Matthew 26:27-29.

We who have willingly entered into this agreement likewise seal it and remember Christ and the covenant by taking communion with other believers. We're not just remembering the sacrifice Christ made for us, but confirming the marriage contract. Don't take this lightly.

The contracted bride and groom then undergo a *mikveh* – a ceremonial cleansing – before exchanging vows (promises). Christ did this with water through the baptism by John, who preached baptism of repentance for the remission of sins (e.g. Luke 3:3-4). But we who are betrothed to Christ have been "cleansed" and sanctified through Christ's sacrifice and the indwelling of God's Spirit. This is in addition to the water baptism done as a sign of our repentance of sin. Both *mikvehs* are as follows:

> Mikveh-Groom (Christ): "*Then Jesus arrived from Galilee at the Jordan coming to John, to be baptized by him. But John tried to prevent Him, saying, "I have need to be baptized by You, and do You come to me?" But Jesus answering said to him, "Permit it at this time; for in this way it is fitting for us to fulfill all righteousness." Then he permitted Him. After being*

baptized, Jesus came up immediately from the water; and behold, the heavens were opened, and he saw the Spirit of God descending as a dove and lighting on Him, and behold, a voice out of the heavens said, "This is My beloved Son, in whom I am well-pleased." —Matthew 3: 13-17.

Mikveh-Bride (believers):

- Physically by water at the repentance of sin: *Peter said to them, "Repent, and each of you be baptized in the name of Jesus Christ for the forgiveness of your sins; and you will receive the gift of the Holy Spirit."* —Acts 2:38.
- Through spiritual sanctification:
  - By the Word of Christ: *Husbands, love your wives, just as Christ also loved the church and gave Himself up for her, so that He might sanctify her,* ***having cleansed her by the washing of water with the word,*** *that He might present to Himself the church in all her glory, having no spot or wrinkle or any such thing; but that she would be holy and blameless.* —Ephesians 5:25-27.
  - Washed, justified, and sanctified in the name of the Lord Jesus and by the Spirit: . . . *nor thieves, nor the covetous, nor drunkards, nor revilers, nor swindlers, will inherit the kingdom of God. Such were some of you;* ***but you were washed, but you were sanctified, but you were justified in the name of the Lord Jesus Christ and in the Spirit of our God.*** —1 Corinthians 6:10-11).
  - In the blood of the Lamb (Christ): *Then one of the elders answered, saying to me, "These who are clothed in the white robes, who are they, and where have they come from?" I said to him, "My lord, you know." And he said to me, "****These are the ones who come out of the great tribulation, and they have washed their robes and made them white in the blood of the Lamb.****"* —Revelation 7:13-14.

Vows are promises the future bride and groom make to each other. In our case, Christ has promised us everlasting life and a place in heaven. As our vow and dowry, we must in return promise to glorify God in our body and spirit as outlined by Paul:

> *For you have been bought with a price: therefore glorify God in your body.* —1 Corinthians 6:20.

Finally, the groom will give the bride-to-be a gift before the betrothal separation. Christ has given His bride gifts of the Holy Spirit and righteousness in fulfillment of this marriage requirement:

> *All the circumcised believers who came with Peter were amazed, because the **gift of the Holy Spirit had been poured out on the Gentiles also**.* —Acts 10:45.

> *. . . or if by the transgression of the one, death reigned through the one, much more those who receive the abundance of grace and of the **gift of righteousness** will reign in life through the One, Jesus Christ.* —Romans 5:17.

Actual betrothal is also called *kiddushim*, which means to be "set apart." Selection, contract, cleansing, vows, and gifts are done and now it's time to separate and prepare for the wedding. The betrothal period (typically one year for Jewish couples) is a time of preparation that may include buying or building a home, making a dress, etc. The couple is considered married during this time although they won't see each other again until the wedding ceremony. Jesus' statements below connect the Jewish tradition of this time of separation to our relationship with Him:

> **The need for the groom to temporarily leave the bride**: "*Then the disciples of John came to Him, asking, 'Why do we and the Pharisees fast, but Your disciples do not fast?' And Jesus said to them, 'The attendants of the bridegroom cannot mourn as long as the bridegroom is with them, can they? But the days will come when the **bridegroom is taken away from them**, and then they will fast.*'" —Matthew 9:14-15.

> **Building of the couple's new home**: "*In My* ***Father's house are many dwelling places****; if it were not so, I would have told you; for I go to* ***prepare a place for you****.*" —John 14:2.

When will our betrothal period end? It will end when Christ returns to gather His elect for the marriage supper. He told His disciples that no one would know the time or the hour except the Father. This is in keeping with Jewish marriage tradition. The groom's father would often build the new home and determine when the marriage ceremony would take place. Neither the bride nor groom would know the exact time of the ceremony. This facet of the wedding process is reflected in Jesus' comment to His disciples on the Mount of Olives:

> *Then they will see THE SON OF MAN COMING IN CLOUDS with great power and glory . . . But of that day or hour no one knows, not even the angels in heaven, nor the Son, but the Father alone. Take heed, keep on the alert; for you do not know when the appointed time will come.* —Mark 13:26-33.

Then, at the precise day and time predetermined by the groom's father, one of the groomsmen will shout and blow a trumpet to announce the start of the marriage ceremony. We'll study the announcement in greater detail later in this section.

Knowing about the relationship with Christ and the upcoming marriage is good, but how can we partake of the salvation Jesus promised the church? What's necessary for becoming saved from God's wrath to come and lake of fire judgment? Simple:

1. **Believe** with all your heart that Christ is the Son of God sent as the ultimate sacrifice for our sinful nature. **Confess** this.
    a. <u>Believe</u>: *For God so loved the world that He gave His only begotten Son, that whoever believes in Him shall not perish, but have eternal life.*" —John 3:16.
    b. <u>. . . and confess</u>: "*. . . that if you confess with your mouth Jesus as Lord, and believe in your heart that*

God raised Him from the dead, you will be saved; for with the heart a person believes, resulting in righteousness, and with the mouth he confesses, resulting in salvation." —Romans 10:9-10.

2. **Repent** of any sinful behavior and cease the practice of sin. By its nature, repentance is a change of heart that brings about a change in behavior. We all commit sins, but those who practice sinful behavior will remain outside God's kingdom in the age to come.
    a. <u>Repent</u>: *Peter said to them, "Repent, and each of you be* ***baptized*** *in the name of Jesus Christ for the forgiveness of your sins; and you will receive the gift of the Holy Spirit.*" —Acts 2:38.
    b. <u>Don't practice sin</u>: . . . *and walk in love, just as Christ also loved you and gave Himself up for us, an offering and a sacrifice to God as a fragrant aroma. But immorality or any impurity or greed must not even be named among you, as is proper among saints; and there must be no filthiness and silly talk, or coarse jesting, which are not fitting, but rather giving of thanks. For this you know with certainty, that no immoral or impure person or covetous man, who is an idolater, has an inheritance in the kingdom of Christ and God. Let no one deceive you with empty words, for because of these things the wrath of God comes upon the sons of disobedience.* —Ephesians 5:2-6.
3. **Be baptized** as an outward expression of your faith in God and Christ, symbolic also of the *mikveh* we mentioned earlier.
4. **Keep your vow** to the groom – Christ.

Accepting Christ and the gift of His righteousness is akin to being born again spiritually – something Jesus said needs to happen before we can enter God's kingdom in heaven:

Jesus answered and said to him, "Truly, truly, I say to you,

> *unless one is born again he cannot see the kingdom of God." Nicodemus said to Him, "How can a man be born when he is old? He cannot enter a second time into his mother's womb and be born, can he?" Jesus answered, "Truly, truly, I say to you,* ***unless one is born of water and the Spirit he cannot enter into the kingdom of God****. That which is born of the flesh is flesh, and that which is born of the Spirit is spirit."* —John 3:3-6.

Also, we know that flesh can't enter the kingdom of God. A *reborn* spirit is necessary to entering heaven as Jesus told Nicodemus (above), but our physical self will also be transformed when Christ comes to get us for the marriage:

> *Behold, I tell you a mystery; we will not all sleep, but* ***we will all be changed, in a moment, in the twinkling of an eye****, at the last trumpet; for the trumpet will sound, and the dead will be raised imperishable, and* ***we will be changed****. For this perishable must put on the imperishable, and this mortal must put on immortality.* —1 Corinthians 15:51-53.

Let's review before we proceed to a discussion of the marriage ceremony by looking at a list of events related to our betrothal to Christ:

1. *Shiddukhin* (bride selection by the father)
2. Legal contract (*ketubah* – new covenant) confirmed by the cup of wine (communion)
3. *Mohar* (price Christ paid for us through crucifixion)
4. *Mikveh* (ceremonial cleansing of body and spirit in our case)
5. Vows and dowry paid (our promise to honor God with body and spirit)

~ Marriage ~

The bride and groom will appear at the day and hour determined by the groom's father to complete the wedding, attend the marriage supper, and receive the *Sheva Berachos* (seven blessings). Known as the *Nissuin*, this second half of the marriage process will begin with a shout by a groomsman and trumpet blast calling for the marriage to take place. Jesus taught us about the upcoming announcement of our wedding ceremony as follows:

> *And then the sign of the Son of Man will appear in the sky, and then all the tribes of the earth will mourn, and they will see the SON OF MAN COMING ON THE CLOUDS OF THE SKY with power and great glory.* ***And He will send forth His angels with A GREAT TRUMPET and THEY WILL GATHER TOGETHER His elect from the four winds, from one end of the sky to the other***. —Matthew 24:30-31.

> *For the Lord Himself will* ***descend from heaven with a shout, with the voice of the archangel and with the trumpet of God****, and the dead in Christ will rise first. Then we who are alive and remain will be caught up together with them in the clouds to meet the Lord in the air, and so we shall always be with the Lord.* —1 Thessalonians 4:16-17.

The marriage ceremony itself consists of the wedding feast (*Seudas Mitzvah*), seven blessings (*Sheva Berachos*), and a final confirmation over a cup of wine. All guests participate in the wedding feast to celebrate with the bride and groom. Everyone enjoys dancing to show support for the newlyweds. The bride is then "carried away" by the groom. We've seen Scripture detailing the marriage announcement, but is there any shedding of light on the marriage supper and what will follow? Yes. Consider what Jesus revealed to John about the marriage supper, which will occur in heaven just before Christ and His heavenly army defeat the Antichrist at Armageddon (cf. Revelation 16:16-18:24 and 19:11-21):

Let us rejoice and be glad and give the glory to Him, for the marriage of the Lamb has come and His bride has made herself ready. It was given to her to clothe herself in fine linen, bright and clean; for the fine linen is the righteous acts of the saints. Then he said to me, "Write, 'Blessed are those who are invited to the marriage supper of the Lamb.'" And he said to me, "These are true words of God." —Revelation 19:7-9.

~ SUMMARY ~

The bride is the church, made up of those who've entered into the new covenant and live accordingly. Christ will return with a shout and trumpet call to take His bride to the wedding ceremony in heaven. The righteous you've learned about in this chapter are in sharp contrast to the children of wrath and disobedience. You'll learn about this group and their *father* in the next chapter: *Satan & the Antichrist*.

Additional resources I found very helpful in the creation of this section:

- messianicfellowship.50webs.com/wedding.html (Messianic Pastor Glenn Kay)
- www.jewish-history.com/minhag.htm
- www.myjewishlearning.com/life/Relationships/Spouses_and_Partners/About_Marriage/Ancient_Jewish_Marriage.shtml

CHECKUP

CHAPTERS SIX & SEVEN

The following questions are meant to check your understanding of what we've covered so far and provoke additional thoughts and questions to elevate your learning to a higher level. You don't have to answer *Private Challenge/Discussion* questions (or share the answers publicly if you do). They're just for your own consideration or group discussion.

Possible answers to all questions can be found in Appendix D.

1. What two major events are identified in Jeremiah 23:3-6 and Ezekiel 37:21-25?

2. The 144,000 will be __________ unto Christ.

3. The 144,000 will be sealed against what?

4. Why isn't the tribe of Dan mentioned in the list of the 12 tribes to be sealed? Which tribe/leader replaced it?

5. What will happen to the elect/chosen when Christ appears (according to Matthew 24:31)?

6. When will everyone who died before Christ's new covenant, or who refused to enter into Christ's covenant, be judged?

7. Which two harvests are identified in Matthew 13, John 5:28, and Revelation 14?

8. How long will the two witnesses preach?

9. What will happen to the two witnesses at the end of their ministry?

10. Which seals in the Revelation pertain to persecution and death at the hands of the Antichrist?

11. What will happen to those beheaded for their faith during the Antichrist's reign?

12. Christ's bride (the church) regularly seals the marriage contract in accordance with which part of a traditional Jewish wedding?

13. List at least one gift Christ as a groom gave the church upon leaving for the betrothal period.

14. Which events will directly precede the gathering of the chosen/elect for the marriage supper?

15. *Private Challenge / Discussion*: What have you been told in the past regarding the identity of the 144,000 Jews? The two witnesses? Do you believe Jews who accept Jesus and enter into the marriage covenant are called and gathered for the marriage supper at the same time as all other believers who've given their lives to Christ?

CHAPTER EIGHT

SATAN & THE ANTICHRIST

According to the Scriptures below, anyone not of Christ's chosen is by default one of the *sons of disobedience*. This group is spiritually fathered by Satan and destined for wrath, judgment, and the lake of fire.

> *For this you know with certainty, that no immoral or impure person or covetous man, who is an idolater, has an inheritance in the kingdom of Christ and God. Let no one deceive you with empty words, for because of these things the* ***wrath of God comes upon the sons of disobedience****.* —Ephesians 5:5-6.

> *Then death and Hades were thrown into the lake of fire. This is the second death, the lake of fire.* ***And if anyone's name was not found written in the book of life, he was thrown into the lake of fire****.* —Revelation 20:14-15.

To fully understand end-times events, we need to know about characters who'll oppose Christ and God during the last several years preceding Christ's kingdom. We'll explore two of these players in great detail throughout this chapter:

- *The Dragon – Satan*: As prince of this world and the great deceiver, he'll once again attempt to annihilate God's people through the Antichrist and his false prophet.
- *The Antichrist*: The great military and religious leader who will rule the earth for roughly three and a half years while empowered by Satan.

Because Satan, the great deceiver and father of lies, is at the root of all this end-of-the-age evil, we'll start with a discussion of him, his influence, and his representation as a dragon in Revelation.

✓ **Quick reference:**

- The Dragon – Satan: Isaiah 14:1-27; Revelation 12
- The Antichrist: Isaiah 28:1-19; Ezekiel 38; Daniel 7:7-25, 9:25-27; 2 Thessalonians 2:1-10; Matthew 24:15-26

The Dragon - Satan

And he laid hold of the dragon, the serpent of old, who is the devil and Satan, and bound him for a thousand years; and he threw him into the abyss, and shut it and sealed it over him, so that he would not deceive the nations any longer, until the thousand years were completed; after these things he must be released for a short time. —Revelation 20:2-3.

Satan has been represented in Scripture as a serpent, the most subtle of God's creatures (Genesis 3:1). He was able to trick Eve into disobeying God and has been deceiving mankind ever since. Not content with just causing us to disobey God, he then "tattles" and makes our sin known to Him. This deceiver is the archangel Lucifer labeled also as the devil, Satan, and the dragon in Christ's Revelation to John. The terms are officially defined here (courtesy of *Strong's Exhaustive Concordance*):

- **Dragon**: G1404 drakōn (drak'-own) a fabulous kind of serpent (perhaps as supposed to fascinate): - dragon.
- **Devil**: G1228 Diabolos (diabolos) slanderous, accusing falsely: - devil, malicious gossips.
- **Satan**: G4567 Satanas (sat-an-as') the accuser, that is, the devil: - Satan.

Isaiah prophesied about the fall of Satan and of Christ's kingdom at the end of this age as reflected in Isaiah 14. John saw much of the same in what he penned in Revelation 12:

How you have fallen from heaven, O star of the morning, son of the dawn! You have been cut down to the earth, You who have

> *weakened the nations! But you said in your heart, 'I will ascend to heaven; I will raise my throne above the stars of God, And I will sit on the mount of assembly in the recesses of the north. 'I will ascend above the heights of the clouds; I will make myself like the Most High.' Nevertheless you will be thrust down to Sheol, To the recesses of the pit.* —Isaiah 14:12-15.

> *And the great dragon was thrown down, the serpent of old who is called the devil and Satan, who deceives the whole world; he was thrown down to the earth, and his angels were thrown down with him. Then I heard a loud voice in heaven, saying, "Now the salvation, and the power, and the kingdom of our God and the authority of His Christ have come, for the accuser of our brethren has been thrown down, he who accuses them before our God day and night. . ."* —Revelation 12:9-10.

He also recorded that Satan is the *father of lies* and *ruler of this world* (cf. John 8:44, 12:31, 14:30, and 16:11). Paul also calls him the *prince of the power of the air* in Ephesians 2:2.

> *You are of your* ***father the devil****, and you want to do the desires of your father. He was a murderer from the beginning, and does not stand in the truth because there is no truth in him. Whenever he speaks a lie, he speaks from his own nature, for* ***he is a liar and the father of lies****.* —John 8:44.

> *Now judgment is upon this world; now the* ***ruler of this world*** *will be cast out.* —John 12:31.

> *I will not speak much more with you, for the* ***ruler of the world*** *is coming, and he has nothing in Me . . .* —John 14:30.

> *. . . in which you formerly walked according to the course of this world, according to the* ***prince of the power of the air****, of the spirit that is now working in the sons of disobedience.* —Ephesians 2:2.

Satan is a spiritual principality – one that empowered Herod to try to kill Christ after His birth (remembered in Revelation 12:3-5) and that will influence the Antichrist (cf. Ezekiel 28, 2 Thessalonians 2:9, Revelation 13:2). The apostle Paul taught us to put on the spiritual armor of God to protect ourselves against the influence of the father of lies and the deceitful nature of this angel of light lest we become one of the many who'll be deceived at the end of the age.

Plot to kill the Christ child remembered: "*And the dragon stood before the woman who was about to give birth, so that when she gave birth he might devour her child. And she gave birth to a son, a male child, who is to rule all the nations with a rod of iron; and her child was caught up to God and to His throne.*" —Revelation 12:4-5.

Satan's influence on the Antichrist:

- *. . . the one whose coming is in accord with the activity of Satan, with all power and signs and false wonders* —2 Thessalonians 2:9.
- *Then another sign appeared in heaven: and behold, a great red dragon having seven heads and ten horns, and on his heads were seven diadems.* —Revelation 12:3.
- All of Ezekiel 28 is devoted to an apocalyptic view of the Antichrist (labeled as the *King of Tyrus* in this case) and Satan who influences him.

Satan as an angel of light: "*No wonder, for even Satan disguises himself as an angel of light. Therefore it is not surprising if his servants also disguise themselves as servants of righteousness, whose end will be according to their deeds.*" —2 Corinthians 11:14-15.

Armor of God as protection against Satan: "*Put on the full armor of God, so that you will be able to stand firm against the schemes of the devil. For our struggle is not against flesh and blood, but against the rulers, against the powers, against the world forces of this darkness, against the spiritual forces of*

> *wickedness in the heavenly places. Therefore, take up the full armor of God, so that you will be able to resist in the evil day, and having done everything, to stand firm.*" —Ephesians 6:11-13.

Again, Satan is the great deceiver who trips us up and then "tattles" on us to God. Christ reminds us through John that he accuses us before God constantly (cf. Revelation 12:10). We first learned of Satan's continued access to God and ability to accuse through the account of Job's testing and triumph. Satan challenged God to allow him to torment Job, claiming that Job's faith wouldn't be strong enough to keep him faithful under duress. Satan was wrong: Job kept his faith despite great calamity and God rewarded him accordingly. One thing this text reveals though is the fact that Satan had (and still has) access to God and heaven despite a popular belief that he was thrown out of heaven at the beginning of time. Here's the opening Scripture depicting Satan in heaven and his challenge to God:

> *Now there was a day when the sons of God came to present themselves before the LORD, and **Satan also came among them**. The LORD said to Satan, "From where do you come?" Then Satan answered the LORD and said, "From roaming about on the earth and walking around on it." The LORD said to Satan, "Have you considered My servant Job? For there is no one like him on the earth, a blameless and upright man, fearing God and turning away from evil." Then Satan answered the LORD, "Does Job fear God for nothing? Have You not made a hedge about him and his house and all that he has, on every side? You have blessed the work of his hands, and his possessions have increased in the land. **But put forth Your hand now and touch all that he has; he will surely curse You to Your face**."* —Job 1:6-11.

So when *will* Satan be kicked out of heaven? Isaiah offered an apocalyptic view of his involuntary exodus from heaven and his destruction near the end of time (this is the context of Isaiah 14). Jesus showed John that it will happen following war in heaven midway through Daniel's seven-year period (about three and a half years before Christ's return). This makes sense since we now also know that Satan will empower the Antichrist and initiate great wrath (tribulation) against God's chosen – both unbelieving Jews and all believers in Christ – once he's cast to the earth. Consider these futuristic excerpts from Scripture:

> *How you have fallen from heaven, O star of the morning, son of the dawn! You have been cut down to the earth, You who have weakened the nations! But you said in your heart, 'I will ascend to heaven; I will raise my throne above the stars of God, And I will sit on the mount of assembly In the recesses of the north. 'I will ascend above the heights of the clouds; I will make myself like the Most High.' Nevertheless you will be thrust down to Sheol, To the recesses of the pit.* —Isaiah 14:12-15.

> *And there was* ***war in heaven****, Michael and his angels waging war with the dragon. The dragon and his angels waged war, and they were not strong enough, and there was* ***no longer a place found for them in heaven****. And the* ***great dragon was thrown down****, the serpent of old who is called the devil and Satan, who deceives the whole world; he was thrown down to the earth, and his angels were thrown down with him. Then I heard a loud voice in heaven, saying, Now the salvation, and the power, and the kingdom of our God and the authority of His Christ have come, for the accuser of our brethren has been thrown down, he who accuses them before our God day and night. And they overcame him because of the blood of the Lamb and because of the word of their testimony, and they did not love their life even when faced with death. For this reason, rejoice, O heavens and you who dwell in them.* ***Woe to the earth and the sea, because the devil has come down to you, having great wrath, knowing that he has only a short time****. And when the dragon saw that he was thrown down to the earth, he persecuted the woman who gave birth to the male child.* —Revelation 12:7-13.

Satan still has access to God and heaven and will continue to until he's removed from there and cast to the earth roughly three and a half years before Christ's return. What then? We understand from

Scripture that God will bind Satan and keep him in the abyss for nearly the entire 1,000-year reign of Christ. Then he'll be released for a short time before being thrown into the lake of fire.

> *And he laid hold of the dragon, the serpent of old, who is the devil and Satan, and bound him for a thousand years; and he threw him into the abyss, and shut it and sealed it over him, so that he would not deceive the nations any longer,* ***until the thousand years were completed****; after these things he must be released for a short time.* —Revelation 20:2-3.

> *Nevertheless you will be thrust down to Sheol, To the recesses of the pit.* —Isaiah 14:15.

> *Then He will also say to those on His left, 'Depart from Me, accursed ones, into the eternal fire which has been prepared for the devil and his angels . . . '*—Matthew 25:41.

> ***When the thousand years are completed****, Satan will be released from his prison, and will come out to deceive the nations which are in the four corners of the earth, Gog and Magog, to gather them together for the war; the number of them is like the sand of the seashore. And they came up on the broad plain of the earth and surrounded the camp of the saints and the beloved city, and fire came down from heaven and devoured them. And the devil who deceived them was* ***thrown into the lake of fire and brimstone, where the beast and the false prophet are also****; and they will be tormented day and night forever and ever.* —Revelation 20:7-10.

Although it's beyond the scope of this study to thoroughly discuss where our souls go when we die, I thought I'd offer a quick introduction to several relative terms and differentiate between them: hell – gehenna, hell – Hades, the abyss (bottomless pit), and the lake of fire. Gehenna and the lake of fire appear to be synonymous, as do Hades and the bottomless pit, also known as the abyss. Gehenna and the lake of fire will be the final destination for anyone not listed in the Book of Life (including Satan and his angels), but Hades (aka the bottomless pit) is a *temporary* repository for the souls of dead humans and Satan. The following lists each term, Strong's reference, and supporting Scripture:

- **Hell – Gehenna**: Equivalent to the lake of fire, this is where evil/tares will be burned up at the very end of this age at the great judgment. (See G1067 gehenna (gheh'-en-nah) valley of (the son of) Hinnom; gehenna (or Ge-Hinnom), a valley of Jerusalem, used (figuratively) as a name for the place (or state) of everlasting punishment: - hell.) cf. Matthew 5:22-30; Matthew 10:28; Matthew 18:9; Matthew 23:15; Matthew 23:33; Mark 9:43, 45, & 47; Luke 12:5; James 3:6.
- **Lake of Fire**: Where anyone not found in the Book of Life at the great judgment will be thrown. Also thrown there for eternal torment will be the devil and his angels, the Antichrist, the Antichrist's false prophet, death, and Hades (no more use for a holding place for souls). cf. Revelation 19:20; Revelation 20:10, 14-15; Revelation 21:8.
- **Hell – Hades**: Appears to be a place where souls go after death while awaiting resurrection or judgment. This may be synonymous with the **bottomless pit**. (See G86 hadēs (hah'-dace) properly unseen, that is, "Hades" or the place (state) of departed souls: - grave, hell.) cf. Matthew 11:23; Matthew 16:18; Luke 10:15; Luke 16:23; Acts 2:27; Acts 2:31; 1 Corinthians 15:55 (grave); Revelation 1:18; Revelation 6:8; Revelation 20:13; Revelation 20:14.
- **Bottomless Pit/Abyss**: This is where Satan will be, at least after being thrown to earth after war in heaven three and a half years before the end. The Beast (Antichrist) empowered by Satan comes from this location as do the locusts of God's wrath. Satan – Apollyon/Abaddon – is labeled as their king. He'll be bound and kept here during the 1,000-year reign of Christ. (See G12 abussos (ab'-us-sos) depthless, that is, (specifically), (infernal) "abyss": - deep, (bottomless) pit.) cf. Luke 8:31; Romans 10:7; Revelation 9:1-2 & 11; Revelation 11:7; Revelation 17:8; Revelation 20:1 & 3.

- **Cast into the Abyss**: (See G5020 tartaroō (tar-tar-o'-o) From Τάρταρος Tartaros (the deepest abyss of Hades); to incarcerate in eternal torment: - cast down to hell.) cf. 2 Peter 2:4.

To summarize, the dragon is Satan—the principality who'll influence the Antichrist. Meanwhile, he continues to deceive and accuse Christians. While God is the Father of children of righteousness, Satan is the father of lies and of the children of disobedience. Certain wrath and destruction awaits him and those who refuse to follow Christ. Next we'll look at what Scripture has to say about the Antichrist.

THE ANTICHRIST

I can't imagine a more controversial entity shrouded in so much mystery as the Antichrist. Speculation as to his or its identity has ranged from the Soviet Union's President Mikhail Gorbachev (because of the unique birthmark on his head) to the Prince of Wales (because his crest includes a unicorn). Included in the endless list is President George W. Bush, who's apparently unlucky enough to have the numbered letters in his name add up to 666. Still others believe it's not a *he* but the World Bank. Of course, today's pick is President Barack Obama. We can safely say that none of these choices is correct based on Scripture.

So who or what will be the Antichrist? It will be a wicked principality that deceives God's people into entering into an agreement with his kingdom roughly seven years before Christ's second coming. Midway through the timeframe, he'll dishonor the agreement, establish residence in the third temple, and begin a three-and-a-half-year reign of terror. The coming Antichrist will be empowered by Satan and is called the *Mystery of Iniquity* by Paul and *Abomination of Desolation* by Christ.

You may be hoping to discover his identity after studying this portion of our study. While you won't get *that*, you *will* receive a better understanding of identifying traits of the Antichrist and his kingdom. Why is this important? Daniel and Jesus have shown us that the saints – Jews and all believers in Christ – will be subject to a time of tribulation like never seen before (or again). This terrible time of persecution and death will be instigated by the Antichrist. Therefore, we must know what's coming to avoid being deceived. Discussing in detail what Scripture reveals about the Antichrist will help us accomplish that. This section is divided into the following related subtopics:

- *Distinguishing Features*: Characteristics revealed through Scripture.
- *Rise to Power*: The journey from being unknown to becoming the leader of an eight-member coalition.
- *Covenant of Death*: Agreement foretold by Daniel, confirmed by Isaiah, and mentioned by Christ on the Mount of Olives.
- *Term of Office*: Term of persecution and death as revealed by Daniel and confirmed by Christ in the Revelation. This time will begin with the *covenant of death.*
- *Sealing Followers – the Mark*: Exploring and debunking the myths surrounding what will imitate the mark (or seal) of God.
- *Tribulation & Beheading*: Consequences of the *covenant of death* – the making of martyrs.
- *War to End All Wars*: Wrapping up God's wrath at the battle of Armageddon and disposing of the unholy trinity of the Antichrist, his false prophet, and Satan.
- *Summary*: A recap of what was covered in this section.

~ DISTINGUISHING FEATURES ~

Children, it is the last hour; and just as you heard that antichrist is coming, even now many antichrists have appeared; from this we know that it is the last hour. . . Who is the liar but the one who denies that Jesus is the Christ? This is the antichrist, the one who denies the Father and the Son. . . . And every spirit that does not confess Jesus is not from God; this is the spirit of the antichrist, of which you have heard that it is coming, and now it is already in the world. —1 John 2:18-22 & 4:3.

As John pointed out (above), a *spirit* of antichrist is at work to deny God and Christ, but Ezekiel, Daniel, Isaiah, Jesus, Paul, and John described the coming Antichrist in several ways and by many names. Through them, we understand that he'll be empowered by Satan and will exalt himself above God in an attempt to be worshipped as God. This and the fact that the Jews will enter into an agreement (*covenant of death* as Isaiah put it) with him is sobering since it reveals just how deceptive the Antichrist will be.

The following are several characteristics of the Antichrist along with events to watch for:

- Different names for the Antichrist:
    - Moab (or ruler of Moab)
      (Isaiah 16 & 25:10; Jeremiah 48)
    - Cruel master and mighty king
      (Isaiah 19:14)
    - Assyrian
      (Isaiah 31:8-9; Micah 5:5-6)
    - Destroyer
      (Isaiah 33:1)
    - King of Tyre
      (Ezekiel 26-28)
    - Gog – chief ruler of Magog
      (Ezekiel 38:2 & 16; 39:1 & 11)
    - Little horn (ruler)
      (Daniel 7:8)
    - Prince who is to come
      (Daniel 9:26)
    - One who makes desolate
      (Daniel 9:27)
    - Abomination of Desolation
      (Daniel 9:27; Matthew 24:15; Mark 13:14)

    - Son of Destruction
      (2 Thessalonians 2:3)
    - Man of Lawlessness
      (2 Thessalonians 2:3)
    - Lawless One
      (2 Thessalonians 2:8)
- Influenced and empowered by Satan:
    - Influenced by Satan
      (Ezekiel 26-28)
    - Empowered by Satan
      (2 Thessalonians 2:9; Revelation 13:2)
- Enters into a seven-year covenant of death (see *Covenant of Death*)
- Exalts himself as God and speaks against the true God (cf. Daniel 7.25; 2 Thessalonians 2:4; Revelation 13:5-6)
- Rules the "beast" kingdom (see *Rise to Power*)
- Requires a mark for commerce (see *Sealing Followers – the Mark*)
- Creates great trouble for God's people for nearly three and a half years (see *Tribulation & Beheading*)

~ Rise to Power ~

Horns, heads, and mountains were symbols of powers and authorities in prophecy and apocalyptic literature. And the term *beast* was used to denote kingdoms. Daniel saw the coming Antichrist as a "*little horn*" – or minor authority – that will arise and subdue three of ten other rulers as he becomes a world leader. That kingdom of eight primary rulers will have authority to persecute God's people for three and a half years (although it will be cut short by Christ's coming). While you'll learn more about the *beast* kingdom during our study of the book of Daniel, it is helpful to know that it will be made up of the areas that constituted the four empires of Daniel's visions: Babylon, Mede/Persia, Greece, and Rome (I've placed the names in [ ] below for your benefit):

*And four great beasts were coming up from the sea, different from one another. The first was like a lion and had the wings of an eagle [**Babylonian**]. I kept looking until its wings were plucked, and it was lifted up from the ground and made to stand on two feet like a man; a human mind also was given to it. And behold, another beast, a second one, resembling a bear [**Mede/Persian**]. And it was raised up on one side, and three ribs were in its mouth between its teeth; and thus they said to it, 'Arise, devour much meat!' After this I kept looking, and behold, another one, like a leopard, which had on its back four wings of a bird; the beast also had four heads, and dominion was given to it [**Greek**]. After this I kept looking in the night visions, and behold, a fourth beast, dreadful and terrifying and extremely strong; and it had large iron teeth [**Roman**].* —Daniel 7:3-7.

*It devoured and crushed and trampled down the remainder with its feet; and it was different from all the beasts that were before it, and it had **ten horns [future and final beast kingdom that comes from part of the old Roman Empire**]. While I was contemplating the horns, behold, **another horn**, a **little one**, came up among them, **and three of the first horns were pulled out** by the roots before it; and behold, this horn possessed eyes like the eyes of a man and a mouth uttering great boasts.* —Daniel 7:7-8.

*Thus he said: 'The fourth beast will be a fourth kingdom on the earth, which will be different from all the other kingdoms and will devour the whole earth and tread it down and crush it. As for the ten horns, out of this kingdom ten kings will arise; and another will arise after them, and **he will be different from the previous ones and will subdue three kings. He will speak out against the Most High and wear down the saints of the Highest One**, and he will intend to make alterations in times and in law; and they will be given into his hand for a time, times, and half a time.* —Daniel 7:23-25.

Jesus showed John the same thing – a future kingdom made up of empires and countries that had been part of four kingdoms Daniel prophesied about:

> *And the dragon stood on the sand of the seashore. Then I saw a beast coming up out of the sea, having* ***ten horns*** *and seven heads, and on his horns were ten diadems, and on his heads were* ***blasphemous*** *names. And the beast which I saw was like a* ***leopard****, and his feet were like those of a* ***bear****, and his mouth like the mouth of a* ***lion****. And the dragon gave him his power and his throne and great authority.* —Revelation 13:1-2.

We've learned from Daniel 7:23-25 above that what will begin as a collection of ten leaders will be reduced to seven after the Antichrist "*subdues*" three. Seven remaining leaders plus the Antichrist will make **eight final rulers** that come together to support the Antichrist's cause. What cause? The destruction of Israel and God's people, as you'll learn from the subtopic *Tribulation & Beheading* in this section, and subsequent sections *Sealing Followers – the Mark* and *Babylon: Past, Present, & Future*. At any rate, there should be no doubt as to the Antichrist's agenda according to this passage: "*They have said, 'Come, and let us wipe them out as a nation, that the name of Israel be remembered no more.*'" —Psalm 83:4.

Which area will the Antichrist come from? Which seven countries/authorities will make up the final list of the Antichrist's cohorts? Ezekiel gave us a complete list in chapter 38.

> *Son of man, set your face toward Gog of the land of* ***Magog****, the prince of Rosh,* ***Meshech*** *and* ***Tubal****, and prophesy against him and say, 'Thus says the Lord GOD, "Behold, I am against you, O Gog, prince of Rosh, Meshech and Tubal. I will turn you about and put hooks into your jaws, and I will bring you out, and all your army, horses and horsemen, all of them splendidly attired, a great company with buckler and shield, all of them wielding swords;* ***Persia****,* ***Ethiopia*** *and* ***Put*** *with them, all of them with shield and helmet;* ***Gomer*** *with all its troops;* ***Beth-togarmah*** *from the remote parts of the north with all its troops--many peoples with you.*" —Ezekiel 38:2-6.

The *prince of Rosh* in verse 2 (above) should be translated as "the head of." The Hebrew word *Roshe* translates to "head" and is the root of other phrases such as *Rosh Hashanah*, which means "Head of the Year" or *Rosh Chodesh*, which means "Head of the Month." So **Gog** (another name for the **Antichrist) will come from Magog**, the head of Meshech and Tubal.

This is important to understand because many like Hal Lindsey have associated Roshe, Meshech, and Tubal with Russia, Moscow, and Tobolsk in Siberia because the names sound similar. This makes it easier to rationalize a European Antichrist and paves the way for cold-war hype regarding Russia and nuclear war. But this approach can result in a confusing departure from Scripture. Further support for a more southern, non-Russian Meshech and Tubal can be found in Ezekiel 27:2 & 13 where we learn that these two regions were trading partners with Tyre (modern-day Lebanon).

Magog, Meshech, Tubal, Put, Gomer, and Beth-togarmah probably don't sound familiar to you as they're the names of Noah's grandsons responsible for migrating and populating various Middle-Eastern and Asian areas after the great flood. Let's take a look at the regions they represent, along with the others that will make up the Antichrist's kingdom:

8.1 Antichrist's Kingdom Makeup

Name in Ezekiel 38	Region/Country
Magog (Antichrist's origin)	Scythians; Southern Russia; north of Iran; Eastern Turkey; probably includes Republics of Kazakhstan, Kyrgyzstan, Uzbekistan, Turkmenistan, Tajikistan, and perhaps northern parts of modern Afghanistan
Meshech	Near Phrygia (biblical region) in central and western Asia Minor (north of Cyprus in central Turkey)
Tubal	Eastern Asia Minor (around Georgia)
Persia	Iran

Name in Ezekiel 38	Region/Country
Ethiopia	Originally Cush, most likely Sudan instead of Ethiopia
Put	Libya (west of Egypt)
Gomer	Central Turkey (Cappadocia of biblical times)
Beth-togarmah	Southeastern Turkey near the Syrian border

8.2 Map of the Middle East

(Map obtained under the GPL from Wikimedia Commons)

At this point, we need to address the Antichrist's origin and a misconception that he'll be a blue-eyed, fair-haired authority figure from Europe. For centuries, many have believed the Antichrist will be European and may even be the pope. This is understandable considering the history of bloodshed and corruption at the hands of the Roman Empire and later the Catholic Church. Hatred for the Catholic Church ran deep, perpetuating this theory of a pope Antichrist from before Martin Luther and the Reformation of the church until now. In 2003, I attended a prophecy seminar hosted by a particular denomination; the speaker staunchly supported this position despite Scripture and clues to the contrary.

Why do some people believe that the end-times beast kingdom will be a revived Roman Empire with a European or pope Antichrist?

1. The Antichrist's kingdom will comprise components of the old Roman Empire. This is from Daniel's interpretation of Nebuchadnezzar's dream, which featured a statue. Its legs were of iron (known to be the Roman Empire) and the feet represented the future Antichrist kingdom. They were made of iron and clay mixed, suggesting the Antichrist's kingdom will be partially made up of components from the old Roman Empire.
2. Daniel's vision of the 70 weeks of years and the destruction of Jerusalem revealed that the Antichrist will come from the people who destroyed Jerusalem in 70 CE (cf. Daniel 9:26). However, the "people" were from part of the Roman Empire that was made up of Middle Eastern forces.

Here are the Scripture references for the statue's legs and feet, suggesting the final beast empire will contain components of the original Roman Empire that will be crushed by Christ (see reason #1 above):

> *. . . legs of iron, its **feet partly of iron** and partly of clay. You continued looking until a stone was cut out without hands, and it struck the statue on its feet of iron and clay and crushed them.* —Daniel 2:33-34

As the toes of the feet were partly of iron and partly of pottery, so some of the kingdom will be strong and part of it will be brittle. And in that you saw the iron mixed with common clay, they will combine with one another in the seed of men; but they will not adhere to one another, even as iron does not combine with pottery. In the days of those kings the God of heaven will set up a kingdom which will never be destroyed, and that kingdom will not be left for another people; it will crush and put an end to all these kingdoms, but it will itself endure forever. —Daniel 2:42-44.

Here's the reference for reason #2 (the people who destroyed the temple in 70 CE were under Roman leadership, causing some to believe the Antichrist's kingdom will be Italian):

. . . there will be seven weeks[of years] and sixty-two weeks [of years]; it will be built again, with plaza and moat, even in times of distress. Then after the sixty-two weeks the Messiah will be cut off and have nothing, and the ***people of the prince who is to come*** *will destroy the city and the sanctuary . . .* —Daniel 9:25-26.

Daniel is telling us that by the time 483 years (69 weeks of years) had passed from the decree to rebuild Jerusalem, the Messiah would be crucified. Afterward, the temple would be destroyed by the "*people of the prince to come*." In context, the *prince* to come will be the Antichrist. Therefore, there must be some kind of relationship to the *prince* and his people who came in 70 CE to destroy the temple. Don't worry – we'll cover these visions of Daniel in great detail later in our study!

So what components of old Rome will make up the Antichrist's kingdom? Who were the "*people*" of the *prince* (Antichrist) to come? We already know from our study in this subtopic that the countries making up the Antichrist's kingdom will be Middle-Eastern, not European. This is fine and works with Daniel's vision of a partially Roman Antichrist kingdom.

One needs to understand that the Roman Empire stretched

from Europe into the Middle East and Asia and actually had two capitals: Rome in the western half of the empire, and Constantinople (modern-day Istanbul) in the eastern portion. The empire was vast, and Italian Romans would have often been the minority – especially in the eastern half. Many of the soldiers were Arabs, Assyrians, and Greeks (among others) led by officers from Rome. Jewish historian Flavius Josephus corroborates this by reporting the following in his accounts in *The Jewish Wars*:[3]

- Book 3, Chapter 1, paragraph 3:
  - "*. . . came by land into* ***Syria****, where he gathered together the Roman forces, with a* ***considerable number of reinforcements from the kings in that neighborhood****.*"
- Book 3, Chapter 4, paragraph 2:
  - "*There were also a considerable number of reinforcements got together, that came* ***from the kings Antiochus, and Agrippa, and Sohemus, each of them contributing one thousand footmen that were archers, and a thousand horsemen****.*"
  - "*Malchus also, the* ***king of Arabia, sent a thousand horsemen, besides five thousand footmen****, the greatest part of which were archers; so that the whole army, including the reinforcements sent by the kings, as well horsemen and footmen, when all were united together, amounted to sixty thousand . . .*"

Additional resources related to this section:

- Scythians, members of a nomadic people of Iranian stock who migrated from their Iranian homeland in Central Asia to southern Russia in the 8th - 7th centuries BCE from cais-soas.com.[4]
- More on Magog from christiananswers.net.[5]
- Wonderful reflection of Josephus' accounts of Genesis to include a table of nations from answersingenesis.org.[6]
- Chapter 10 of *The Islamic Antichrist* by Joel Richardson.

Important things to remember about the makeup of the Antichrist's kingdom:

1. The countries **surround Israel.**
2. The country **due north of Israel is Turkey**, which includes most of the countries listed in the above table.
3. All countries in the list are predominantly **Islamic** in nature.
4. The people of the prince to come (who destroyed Jerusalem and the second temple in 70 CE) were with the Roman Empire but were made up of a vast number of **Middle Eastern reinforcements**.

~ COVENANT OF DEATH ~

In the next section, *Term of Office*, you'll learn that the Antichrist will have authority to persecute and kill God's people for three and a half years and that the period will be the last half of a seven-year timeframe foretold by Daniel. This seven-year period will begin with a covenant between the Antichrist and his *beast* kingdom. Midway through the *week of years*, he'll turn on Israel, dishonoring the agreement and setting himself up in the third temple to be worshipped. He'll exalt himself above God and begin a roughly three-and-a-half-year reign of terror against God's people. Christ's defeat of the "*man of lawlessness*," as Paul called him, and establishment of His 1,000-year kingdom will cancel – or annul – the *covenant of death*. Here's a breakdown of each phase ([ ] inserted by me for clarification):

<u>Establishment of the seven-year covenant</u>:

> *And he will make a **firm covenant with the many for one week** [of years] . . .* —Daniel 9:27.

> *Because you have said, "We have made a **covenant with death**, And with Sheol we have made a pact. The overwhelming scourge will not reach us when it passes by, For we have*

made falsehood our refuge and we have concealed ourselves with deception." —Isaiah 28:15.

Breaking of the covenant and subsequent great tribulation:

> *. . . but in the* ***middle of the week*** *[of years] he will* ***put a stop to sacrifice and grain offering; and on the wing of abominations will come one who makes desolate****, even until a complete destruction . . .* —Daniel 9:27.

> *Therefore when you see the ABOMINATION OF DESOLATION which was spoken of through* ***Daniel*** *the prophet,* ***standing in the holy place*** *(let the reader understand) . . . For then there will be a* ***great tribulation****, such as has not occurred since the beginning of the world until now, nor ever will.* —Matthew 24:15-21.

Canceling of the covenant with Christ's kingdom:

> *Therefore thus says the Lord GOD, "Behold, I am* ***laying in Zion a stone****, a tested stone, A costly cornerstone for the foundation, firmly placed.* ***He who believes in it will not be disturbed****. . . . Your* ***covenant with death will be canceled****, And your pact with Sheol will not stand; When the overwhelming scourge passes through, Then you become its trampling place.*" —Isaiah 28:16-18.

Key points to remember:

1. The covenant will be between the Antichrist's kingdom (currently Islamic nations) and Israel.
2. The covenant will be for seven years.
3. The Antichrist will go against the agreement and persecute God's people (to include all believers in Christ) for nearly three and a half years during the second half of the covenant period.
4. Christ will cancel the covenant upon defeat of the Antichrist and the establishment of His kingdom on earth.

~ TERM OF OFFICE ~

We've introduced the concept that the Antichrist will dishonor the agreement with Israel after three and a half years and then persecute and kill God's people throughout the remaining three-and-a-half-year period. You'll learn more about the latter timeframe in the upcoming topic of *Tribulation & Beheading*. But I think it's important to understand how we arrive at that particular length of time for the Antichrist's authority. The following points demonstrate that there will be a seven-year agreement and that the second half will be a three-and-a-half-year Great Tribulation at the hand of the Antichrist.

Establishing the seven-year period: This will be the final seven years in a 490-year period prophesied by Daniel. The Hebrew word for "week of years" is depicted below by Strong's H7620 (below). This period will conclude the 70 weeks of years as shown to Daniel to do the following (cf. Daniel 9:24):

- Finish the transgression
- Make an end of sin
- Make atonement for iniquity
- Bring in everlasting righteousness
- Seal up vision and prophecy
- Anoint the most holy

All of these goals will be accomplished when Christ gains His kingdom at the seventh trumpet (cf. Revelation 11:15). Sixty-nine weeks of years (483) would pass from the command to rebuild Jerusalem and its walls until Christ's crucifixion (cf. Daniel 9:25-26). Daniel then prophesied about Jerusalem's destruction by forces under Roman control in 70 CE (cf. Daniel 9:26). The last – the 70th – "week of years" (years 484-490) will start with a covenant between the Antichrist (spiritual principality that drove the Roman Empire) and Israel (Daniel 9:27). Let's look at Strong's definition for the word used in the Old Testament to represent this "week of years":

H7620 shâbûaʻ shâbûaʻ shebûʻâh (shaw-boo'-ah, shaw-boo'-ah, sheb-oo-aw') literally sevened, that is, **a week (specifically of years)**: - seven, week.

First 3.5-year period: As previously discussed, the seven-year period will begin with a peace agreement between the Antichrist and Israel. We know almost nothing about the first half of the "week of years" although it's likely that the authorities associated with the Antichrist will be reduced from ten to seven during this time (see study section *Rise to Power*) and the relationship between the Antichrist's kingdom and Israel will begin to deteriorate (see study section *Babylon: Past, Present, & Future*).

Second 3.5-year period: This timeframe will see catastrophe, persecution, rescue, and wrath.

- War in heaven – Satan thrown to the earth and protection of the woman (remnant of Israel) by God
- Persecution of the saints
- Dishonored agreement
- Antichrist in the temple
- Blaspheme against God
- Preaching by the two witnesses
- Ends with gathering of believers and God's wrath just before Christ's kingdom

Keep these points in mind as you read the supporting Scripture below:

- *42 months and 1,260 days = 3.5 years*. The Jewish year is made up of 12 30-day months for a total of 360 days. So 42 months equals 3.5 years or 1,260 days.
- *Time, times, and half a time = 3.5 years*. The Hebrew word for *time* as in Daniel 7:24-25 is *Iddan* (Strong's H5732 below) which suggests a year-long period. The Hebrew word for *time* in Daniel 12:7 is represented by Strong's H4150 and also indicates a year.

H5732 ʽiddân (id-dawn') a set time; **technically a year**: - time.

H4150 môʽêd môʽêd môʽâdâh (mo-ade', mo-ade', mo-aw-daw') properly an appointment, that is, a fixed time or season; specifically a festival; **conventionally a year.**

Key supporting Scripture ([ ] inserted by me for consideration):

<u>Great tribulation (distress) for time, times, and half a time</u>:

*Now at that time Michael, the great prince who stands guard over the sons of your people, will arise [probably because of the war in heaven revealed in Revelation 12]. **And there will be a time of distress such as never occurred since there was a nation until that time**; . . . "**How long will it be until the end of these wonders**?" I heard the man dressed in linen, who was above the waters of the river, as he raised his right hand and his left toward heaven, and swore by Him who lives forever that it would be for a **time, times, and half a time**; and as soon as they finish shattering the power of the holy people, all these events will be completed.* —Daniel 12:1-7.

<u>Antichrist given a three-and-a-half-year authority</u>:

*. . . and they will be given into his hand for a **time, times, and half a time**.* —Daniel 7:25.

*Leave out the court which is outside the temple and do not measure it, for it has been **given to the nations**; and they will tread underfoot the holy city for **forty-two months**.* —Revelation 11:2.

<u>Antichrist's three-and-a-half-year reign will begin with an appearance in the temple and changing of the Law</u>:

And he will make a firm covenant with the many for one week, but in the middle of the week ***he will put a stop to sacrifice*** **and grain offering** and on the wing of **abominations** will come one who makes desolate . . . —Daniel 9:27.

Therefore when you see the ***ABOMINATION OF DESOLATION*** *which was spoken of through Daniel the prophet,* ***standing in the holy place*** . . . —Matthew 24:15.

From the time that the regular sacrifice is abolished and the abomination of desolation is set up, there will be 1,290 days. —Daniel 12:11.

He'll speak out against God during his three-and-a-half-year reign:

He will ***speak out against the Most High and wear down the saints of the Highest One****, and he will intend to make alterations in times and in law; and they will be given into his hand for a* **time, times, and half a time**. —Daniel 7:25.

There was given to him a mouth speaking arrogant words and blasphemies, and authority to act for forty-two months was given to him. —Revelation 13:5.

A remnant of Israel will be protected during the Antichrist's reign:

Then the ***woman*** *fled into the wilderness where she had a place prepared by God, so that there she would be* ***nourished for one thousand two hundred and sixty days****.* —Revelation 12:6.

But the two wings of the great eagle were given to the ***woman****, so that she could fly into the wilderness to her place, where she was* ***nourished for a time and times and half a time****, from the presence of the serpent.* —Revelation 12:14.

Ending of the seven-year period with Christ's kingdom/ annulment of the covenant of death:

> *Then I kept looking because of the sound of the boastful words which the horn was speaking; I kept looking until the beast was slain, and its body was destroyed and given to the burning fire [also see Revelation 19:20].* —Daniel 7:11.
>
> *Then the sovereignty, the dominion and the greatness of all the kingdoms under the whole heaven will be given to the people of the saints of the Highest One; His kingdom will be an everlasting kingdom, and all the dominions will serve and obey Him.* —Daniel 7:27.

Key points to remember:

1. An agreement between the Antichrist and Israel will kick off a final seven-year period (see *Covenant of Death*).
2. Scripture doesn't shed light on what will happen during the first half of the seven-year period.
3. The Antichrist will be given authority to persecute and kill God's people for three and a half years during the second half of the seven-year period. This latter half is known as Jacob's Trouble and the Great Tribulation. NOTE: Hal Lindsey and others incorrectly call the entire seven-year period "seven years of tribulation."
4. The beginning of the second half will be earmarked by a dishonoring of the "*covenant of death*" and the Antichrist's presence in the temple (see *Covenant of Death*).
5. The Antichrist will speak out against God and persecute His people (see *Tribulation & Beheading*).
6. A remnant of Israel (the woman) will be protected during the reign of the Antichrist.
7. The Antichrist's reign will end with Christ's appearing and his defeat.

~ SEALING FOLLOWERS – THE MARK ~

The "mark of the beast" has been speculated about and sensationalized throughout the ages and by such movies as *The Omen* and over the Internet. Although Scripture tells us that understanding the number of the beast will take wisdom, we've seen it in the form of a 666 tattooed into the head of a small boy on TV (as in *The Omen*), believed it to be the Social Security number, and also reasoned it will take the form of an embedded microchip. Sigh. But what will it be *really*? What does Scripture tell us about this mark associated with the Antichrist? What will be its purpose?

Just as God will seal the 144,000 for protection before His wrath, the Antichrist will have sealed his followers for their protection, both physically and fiscally, as he unleashes his terror. That will be the purpose of the mark of the beast – to identify those who've made a choice to follow the Antichrist for the sake of their lives, forsaking the one true God.

> *And he causes all, the small and the great, and the rich and the poor, and the free men and the slaves, to be given a mark on their right hand or on their forehead, and he provides that no one will be able to buy or to sell, except the one who has the mark, either the name of the beast or the number of his name.* —Revelation 13:16-17.

What will the mark be or look like? No one knows for sure, but there are several intriguing clues to consider:

1. It will be a way of identifying someone aligned with the Antichrist or his kingdom.
2. The mark may somehow be physically placed on the right hand or forehead. Or it may instead indicate something you *know* rather than something tattooed into your skin (cf. Exodus 13:9 & 16, and Deuteronomy 6:8 & 11:18). Regardless, it will be a unique identification.
3. The mark will be associated with either the name or the

> number of the Antichrist's name – 666: "*Here is wisdom. Let him who has understanding calculate the number of the beast, for the* ***number is that of a man****; and his number is* ***six hundred and sixty-six****.*" —Revelation 13:18.

Instinctively, many will be looking for a requirement to have 666 tattooed into their skin. Or they may expect to see RFID (Radio Frequency Identification Device) chips inserted just below the surface of the skin. These can be used to store personal information or track individuals or property. And people continue to try to number the names of world leaders to discover the Antichrist's true identity (Hitler and George W. Bush have been strong candidates). But the Bible tells us that understanding the mark will take wisdom. While it may be a physical marking, the marking may instead be more symbolic – acceptance of the Antichrist's ways or moral code – just like God's mark on the Hebrews exiting Egypt was.

God gave the Israelites certain commandments after the exodus from Egypt (cf. Exodus 13:9 & 16 and Deuteronomy 6:8 & 11:18). He told the Israelites to remember how He'd saved them, and to remember His commandments – part of the covenant with Israel – and teach them to subsequent generations. God used the tangible and familiar "forehead" to represent the receiving and committing of His commandments to memory. Likewise, He used the "hand" as an identifier for action related to that knowledge. The learning, retaining, and acting upon God's commandments would prove allegiance to Him while also completing the covenant.

> *And it shall serve as a* ***sign to you on your hand, and as a reminder on your forehead****, that the law of the LORD may be in your mouth; for with a powerful hand the LORD brought you out of Egypt. Therefore, you shall keep this ordinance at its appointed time from year to year.* —Exodus 13:9-10.

> *You shall love the LORD your God with all your heart and with all your soul and with all your might.* ***These words, which I am commanding you today, shall be on your heart****. You shall teach*

> *them diligently to your sons and shall talk of them when you sit in your house and when you walk by the way and when you lie down and when you rise up.* ***You shall bind them as a sign on your hand and they shall be as frontals on your forehead****. You shall write them on the doorposts of your house and on your gates.* —Deuteronomy 6:5-9.

So, the significance of forehead and hand may be that of pledging allegiance through learning of, agreeing to, and acting upon a certain set of commandments initiated by the Antichrist's empire. But what is the significance of the number – 666?

Remember that the number is that of a man, and that this man will be one part of an unholy trinity: Satan, Antichrist, and False Prophet. The number used historically to represent man is **6**, whereas God is represented by the number **7** to indicate perfection. Because of this and the unholy trinity mentioned above, I suggest the number 666 was used in Scripture as a way to represent *some kind* of identification or sign of allegiance that will come from the Antichrist (empowered by Satan) through the False Prophet.

An alliance with the unholy trinity may result in the ability to buy and sell during the time of the Great Tribulation, but it will bring personal destruction at the hand of God. Therefore, we need to increase our faith by learning of God's ways to avoid deception during the Antichrist's reign and should therefore watch for anything that may require you to profess allegiance to him or his kingdom. Anyone not following this advice may be deceived into taking this mark. Here's what anyone doing so will get for their lack of faith:

> *Then another angel, a third one, followed them, saying with a loud voice, "If anyone worships the beast and his image, and receives a mark on his forehead or on his hand, he also will drink of the wine of the wrath of God, which is mixed in full strength in the cup of His anger; and he will be tormented with fire and brimstone in the presence of the holy angels and in the presence of the Lamb. And the smoke of their torment goes up*

> *forever and ever; they have no rest day and night, those who worship the beast and his image, and whoever receives the mark of his name*." —Revelation 14:9-11.

> *So the first angel went and poured out his bowl on the earth; and it became a loathsome and malignant sore on the people who had the mark of the beast and who worshiped his image.* —Revelation 16:2.

Remember the "beheaded" we talked about in the last chapter? They'll be faithful believers who won't take the mark – whatever form it takes. Even though the consequence will be physical death, they'll earn spiritual life and will reign with Christ during His 1,000-year reign on earth.

> *Then I saw thrones, and they sat on them, and judgment was given to them. And I saw the souls of those who had been* ***beheaded*** *because of their testimony of Jesus and because of the word of God, and those who* ***had not worshiped the beast or his image, and had not received the mark*** *on their forehead and on their hand; and they came to life and reigned with Christ for a thousand years*. —Revelation 20:4.

Key points to remember:

1. The Antichrist will require everyone faithful to him to be marked with a number or name. This mark may be physical, but it may also be an understanding and carrying out of the Antichrist's "law" in the same way the Israelites learned God's commandments and acted upon them. Regardless, it will indicate an allegiance to the Antichrist and his kingdom.
2. This allegiance and marking will be necessary to buy or sell during the Antichrist's reign.
3. Those not taking the mark will most likely be beheaded, but they'll be resurrected and will reign with Christ if they are His.

4. The mark will most likely *not look exactly like 666*, which indicates the number of man three times.
5. The mark may not be a microchip since it isn't an identifying mark per-se and would require insertion *into* the skin (the mark will be *on* the right hand or forehead or symbolic as described above).
6. Don't waste your time trying to convert the names of world leaders into numbers for the sake of *counting the number of a name*.
7. Spend your time becoming more knowledgeable of God's Word to ensure you won't be deceived when the Antichrist appears and requires this mark.

~ TRIBULATION & BEHEADING ~

Make no mistake – God's people will suffer incredible tribulation during the Antichrist's reign. Those who persevere and remain faithful will be brought out of that Great Tribulation and saved from God's subsequent wrath. A popular belief these days is that there'll be a secret pre-second-coming gathering of the church before this happens. But the recent concept isn't scriptural. The Bible tells a different version of the end and reminds us that tribulation is often necessary and that believers will go through the Great Tribulation.

Going through trouble grows perseverance, character, and hope:

> *And not only this, but we also exult in our tribulations, knowing that* ***tribulation brings about perseverance; and perseverance, proven character; and proven character, hope****.* —Romans 5:3-4.

Refining comes through testing:

> ***Many will be purged, purified and refined****, but the wicked will act wickedly; and none of the wicked will understand, but*

those who have insight will understand. —Daniel 12:10.

And I will bring the third part ***through the fire, Refine them as silver is refined, And test them as gold is tested*** *. . .* —Zechariah 13:9.

If any man's work is burned up, he will suffer loss; but he himself will be saved, yet so ***as through fire****.* —1 Corinthians 3:15.

I advise you to buy from Me ***gold refined by fire*** *so that you may become rich, and white garments so that you may clothe yourself . . .* —Revelation 3:18.

. . . so that the proof of your ***faith****, being* ***more precious than gold*** *which is perishable, even though tested by fire, may be found to result in praise and glory and honor at the* ***revelation of Jesus Christ*** *. . .* —1 Peter 1:7.

Believers in Christ may suffer tribulation but will escape the wrath of God:

Much more then, having now been justified by His blood, ***we shall be saved from the wrath of God through Him****.* —Romans 5:9.

THE SUN WILL BE TURNED INTO DARKNESS AND THE MOON INTO BLOOD, BEFORE THE GREAT AND GLORIOUS DAY OF THE LORD SHALL COME. AND IT SHALL BE THAT ***EVERYONE WHO CALLS ON THE NAME OF THE LORD WILL BE SAVED****.* —Acts 2:20-21.

You will be hated by all because of My name, but ***the one who endures to the end, he will be saved****.* —Mark 13:13.

The terrible tribulation against God's people (to include Christians) will happen because God will allow the Antichrist to have authority over them for three and a half years. And this period, as we've already discussed, will begin in the middle of the seven-year period foretold by Daniel. The Bible informs us that the Great Tribulation will require *patience* and *perseverance* on the part of the saints. It will result in the *beheading* of many faithful, and will be ended prematurely by the *gathering* of the church and the start of God's wrath. Let's look at some of the supporting Scripture:

Antichrist's authority over the saints:

> *. . . will speak out against the Most High and wear down the saints of the Highest One, and he will intend to make alterations in times and in law; and they* ***will be given into his hand for a time, times, and half a time****.* —Daniel 7:25.

> *. . .* ***Authority was given to them over a fourth of the earth, to kill with sword and with famine and with pestilence and by the wild beasts*** *of the earth. —Revelation 6:8.*

> *There was given to him a mouth speaking arrogant words and blasphemies, and* ***authority to act for forty-two months was given to him****.* —Revelation 13:5.

Terrible time of tribulation:

> *Now at that time Michael, the great prince who stands guard over the sons of your people, will arise.* ***And there will be a time of distress such as never occurred since there was a nation until that time;*** *and at that time your people, everyone who is found written in the book, will be rescued.* —Daniel 12:1.

> *Alas! for that day is great, There is none like it; And it is the time of Jacob's distress, But he will be saved from it.* —Jeremiah 30:7.

> *For then there will be a* ***great tribulation****, such as has not occurred since the beginning of the world until now, nor ever*

will. Unless those days had been cut short, no life would have been saved; but ***for the sake of the elect those days will be cut short.*** —Matthew 24:21-22.

And when the dragon saw that he was thrown down to the earth, he persecuted the woman who gave birth to the male child. . . ***So the dragon was enraged with the woman, and went off to make war with the rest of her children, who keep the commandments of God and hold to the testimony of Jesus.*** —Revelation 12:13-17.

Patience and perseverance required during that time:

Here is the perseverance of the saints who keep the commandments of God and their faith in Jesus. *And I heard a voice from heaven, saying, "Write,* ***'Blessed are the dead who die in the Lord from now on!'"*** *"Yes," says the Spirit, "so that they may rest from their labors, for their deeds follow with them."* —Revelation 14:12-13.

If anyone is destined for captivity, to captivity he goes; if anyone kills with the sword, with the sword he must be killed. ***Here is the perseverance and the faith of the saints.*** —Revelation 13:10.

Saints killed/beheaded for their testimony:

I looked, and behold, an ashen horse; and he who sat on it had the name Death; and Hades was following with him. ***Authority was given to them over a fourth of the earth, to kill with sword and with famine and with pestilence and by the wild beasts*** *of the earth. When the Lamb broke the fifth seal, I saw underneath the altar the* ***souls of those who had been slain because of the word of God, and because of the testimony*** *which they had maintained . . .* —Revelation 6:8-9.

Then I saw thrones, and they sat on them, and judgment was given to them. And I saw the souls of those who had been ***beheaded because of their testimony of Jesus and because of the word of God****, and those who* ***had not worshiped the beast or his image, and had not received the mark*** *on their forehead and on their hand; and they came to life and reigned with Christ for a thousand years.* —Revelation 20:4.

<u>Tribulation ended by the darkening of the sun, moon, and stars and the gathering</u>:

But in those days, ***after that tribulation, THE SUN WILL BE DARKENED AND THE MOON WILL NOT GIVE ITS LIGHT, AND THE STARS WILL BE FALLING from heaven****, and the powers that are in the heavens will be shaken. Then they will see THE SON OF MAN COMING IN CLOUDS with great power and glory. And then He will send forth the angels, and will* ***gather together His elect from the four winds, from the farthest end of the earth to the farthest end of heaven****.* —Mark 13:24-27. (Note: Also see Matthew 24:29-31.)

. . . and behold, a ***great multitude which no one could count, from every nation and all tribes and peoples and tongues****, standing before the throne and before the Lamb, clothed in white robes, and palm branches were in their hands . . . And he said to me, "These are* ***the ones who come out of the great tribulation****, and they have washed their robes and made them white in the blood of the Lamb."* —Revelation 7:9-14.

Key points to remember:

1. The Antichrist will have a three-and-a-half-year authority over God's people.
2. The three-and-a-half-year period will be a terrible time of tribulation never seen before or ever again.
3. Those who refuse the mark of the beast may be killed by beheading.

4. God will cut the three-and-a-half-year time of the Antichrist's authority short.
5. The sign of the termination of the Antichrist's authority and Christ's return will be a complete darkening of the sun, moon, and stars.
6. The gathering of the church will follow the darkening.

~ War to End All Wars ~

Well, this will actually be the *penultimate* war to end all wars since there'll be one more with Satan at the end of Christ's 1,000-year reign. But *War to End All Wars* made a great title for this section, and the topic keeps us on the right track.

Just before the great earthquake produced by the seventh vial of God's wrath, He'll dry up the Euphrates River to pave the way for a showdown between Christ and His heavenly armies and the Antichrist and his forces. The place of this battle will be at Har-Magedon (often seen as Armageddon).

> ***The sixth angel poured out his bowl on the great river, the Euphrates; and its water was dried up, so that the way would be prepared for the kings from the east*** *. . . for they are spirits of demons, performing signs, which go out to the kings of the whole world, to gather them together for the war of the great day of God, the Almighty. . . . And they gathered them together to the place which in Hebrew is called* ***Har-Magedon****.* —Revelation 16:12-16.

In the Revelation given to him by Jesus, John saw the phenomenal bloodshed produced by the destruction of the Antichrist's armies. The first glimpse came during a vision of the second of two *harvests* at the end – the gathering of the wicked for destruction. A second came during a vision of the battle at Armageddon.

> *So the angel swung his sickle to the earth and gathered the clusters from the vine of the earth, and threw them into the great*

wine press of the wrath of God. ***And the wine press was trodden outside the city, and blood came out from the wine press, up to the horses' bridles, for a distance of two hundred miles.*** —Revelation 14:19-20.

Then I saw an angel standing in the sun, and he cried out with a loud voice, saying to all the birds which fly in midheaven, "Come, assemble for the great supper of God, so that you may eat the flesh of kings and the flesh of commanders and the flesh of mighty men and the flesh of horses and of those who sit on them and the flesh of all men, both free men and slaves, and small and great." And ***I saw the beast and the kings of the earth and their armies assembled to make war against Him who sat on the horse and against His army****. And the beast was seized, and with him the false prophet who performed the signs in his presence, by which he deceived those who had received the mark of the beast and those who worshiped his image; these two were thrown alive into the lake of fire which burns with brimstone.* ***And the rest were killed with the sword which came from the mouth of Him who sat on the horse, and all the birds were filled with their flesh****.* —Revelation 19:17-21.

Key points to remember:

1. The battle of Har-Magedon will happen after the sixth vial of God's judgment, which will dry up the Euphrates River.
2. Christ and His armies will defeat the Antichrist at that battle. The amount of bloodshed will be extraordinary.
3. Satan will be bound and then released after 1,000 years to do battle one last time. God will then throw him into the lake of fire.

~ SUMMARY ~

We've learned that the Antichrist will exalt himself above God after entering the temple in Jerusalem. This will kick off a three-and-a-half-year time of great tribulation for God's people (Jews and all Christian believers). God will cut that period short with a darkening of the sun, moon, and stars. Christ will appear at that time with His angels, who'll gather the church for the wedding supper in heaven. God's wrath against those who remain on earth will begin shortly thereafter.

Ezekiel taught us that the Antichrist's kingdom will be made up of eight Middle Eastern countries, one of which will be the ancient area of Magog – southern Russia, northern Iran, eastern Turkey, etc. This will be the origin of the Antichrist. All of these areas composing the Antichrist's kingdom surround Israel and are predominantly Islamic (today). They were also part of the previous kingdoms of Babylon, Mede/Persia, Greece, and Rome as Daniel prophesied they would be.

Daniel revealed to us that the Antichrist's people would destroy the temple first. This happened in 70 CE by armies under Roman command. The "people" would most likely have been Middle Eastern (e.g. Arab and Syrian) and Greek. The Antichrist's kingdom, as discussed above, will be made up of indigenous people from these regions.

The Antichrist will require a mark of allegiance in order to buy or sell during his time of authority. Regardless of the form this mark takes, accepting it will mean certain death at the hands of God during His wrath. Those who stay faithful and don't take the mark will most likely be beheaded. However, they'll be victorious in the end and will reign with Christ (if they're His).

A battle between Christ and the Antichrist will occur at Har-Magedon at the end of God's wrath. After a complete slaughter of the armies gathered there, the Antichrist will be thrown into the lake of fire, and Satan will be bound for 1,000 years. Afterward, he'll be released for a short time only to be defeated again and then thrown into the lake of fire.

In the next chapter, *Babylon: Past, Present, & Future*, we'll take a detailed look at what John describes as "*Babylon the great – the mother of whores*."

CHAPTER NINE

BABYLON: PAST, PRESENT, & FUTURE

Nearly two chapters in the book of Revelation have been devoted to *Babylon*, which will represent at least two things during Daniel's 70th week: the "*mother of whores*" and the location of the Antichrist's rule during the three-and-a-half-year reign of the Antichrist – the Great Tribulation. Old Testament prophets and Jesus had a lot to say about the "whore," God's original and unfaithful bride. They also gave us insight into Babylon as a city – headquarters of the Antichrist. You'll learn that the harlot has been, and will be, *Israel* and the city *Jerusalem*. We'll explore each aspect of end-times Babylon beginning with the whore, or harlot.

✓ **Quick reference:** Ezekiel 16; Revelation 16-18

BABYLON – THE HARLOT

Jesus showed John a vision containing what the Bible calls a *harlot*, *whore*, *prostitute*, and *adulterer*. These terms all describe the same thing in Scripture: an unfaithful bride. When John sees her in the Revelation, she's wearing a banner that displays "*BABYLON – MOTHER OF HARLOTS and ABOMINATIONS.*" After studying this section, you'll learn that the Israelites, the original bride of God, were the only people to have earned the label of "harlot" from Him. Why the additional name of *Babylon* in the Revelation? God had much to say to His people about their idolatry (to include human sacrifice) and indulging in the sorceries of ancient Babylon. And this "great city" under Nimrod's rule provided the first known single worldwide government.

Ancient Israel's adoption of Babylon's evil ways represents a religious adultery through a departure from God's Law and a rebellion against His covenant with Israel. End-times Israel will continue to forsake God and His ways by entering into a covenant with the Antichrist. This is why you'll see Old Testament prophecies concerning ancient Babylon and Israel mirrored in apocalyptic literature contained in the Revelation. In a sense, these are examples of the near-far prophecies, oracles, and apocalyptic literature we discussed in Chapter Four under the *Format* section.

Three key things to remember as you continue your study of this topic:

1. God's bride engaged in adulterous acts (e.g. idol worship, human sacrifice, sorcery, etc.) while under Babylonian rule. Many ancient prophecies were directly related to this.
2. The adulterous acts earned Israel the title of *harlot*.
3. Ancient prophecies regarding Israel's harlotry were concerned with the near-term (problems and consequences of that day) and far-term (the adultery and consequences that will occur during the reign of the Antichrist).

I think the best approach is to start by analyzing what Revelation has to say about the coming Babylon-Harlot and then comparing her characteristics to other Scripture containing the ancient prophecies. Let's set the stage by introducing you to the context in which the future *harlot* appears in Revelation:

> **Revelation 16**: The last of God's wrath is being poured out (six vial judgments). The third vial turns the waters into blood (verse 4). Verses 5-6 tell us that they (the wicked experiencing God's wrath) deserve it since **they've poured out the blood of saints and prophets**. The seventh and final vial causes the greatest earthquake ever known to man. **The great city** (Jerusalem) is split into three parts. God remembers **Babylon the great** as He pours out His wrath on her.
>
> **Revelation 17**: The vision of chapter 16 is continued as the angel executing the seven vials of God's wrath explains that Babylon is the harlot and gives more detail about her demise. What you'll

learn is that God will give Israel to the Antichrist's kingdom to experience destruction in addition to their suffering of God's wrath. This chapter also shows that there'll be a temporary relationship between the harlot and the Antichrist's kingdom, although she'll eventually be made "desolate and naked" by the Antichrist and his people. The last half of the chapter is devoted to highlighting Babylon, the great city.

Revelation 18: The vision started in chapter 16 moves forward with a continued focus on *Babylon* as the great city. The fact that she's responsible for the blood of the saints and prophets is reiterated here.

Our analysis will start with Revelation 17 since it contains much information about the future Babylon-Harlot. Although you'll go through it again in Chapter Sixteen of this study, let's pick it apart now to find Babylon's key features starting with verses 1-6:

> *Then one of the seven angels who had the seven bowls came and spoke with me, saying, "Come here, I will show you the judgment of the great **harlot who sits on many waters**, with whom the **kings of the earth committed acts of immorality, and those who dwell on the earth were made drunk with the wine of her immorality**." And he carried me away in the Spirit into a wilderness; and I saw a woman **sitting on a scarlet beast, full of blasphemous names, having seven heads and ten horns**. The woman was **clothed in purple and scarlet, and adorned with gold and precious stones and pearls**, having in her hand a gold cup full of **abominations and of the unclean things of her immorality**, and on her forehead a name was written, a mystery, "BABYLON THE GREAT, THE MOTHER OF HARLOTS AND OF THE ABOMINATIONS OF THE EARTH." And I saw the woman **drunk with the blood of the saints, and with the blood of the witnesses of Jesus**. When I saw her, I wondered greatly.*
> —Revelation 17:1-6.

From the above passage, we learn that:

- **The harlot sits on many waters**. The use of the phrase "*many waters*" signifies a multitude of different nations and peoples. John corroborates this in Revelation 17:18: "*The woman whom you saw is the* ***great city,*** *which reigns over the kings of the earth.*"
- **The kings of the earth acted immorally with her**. This reminds us of the immoral relationships the harlot has had with world rulers throughout the years, culminating with the relationship to come with the Antichrist and his kingdom.
- **The harlot is riding a scarlet beast with seven heads and ten horns that utters blasphemous words**. Again, this emphasizes the relationship the harlot will have with the Antichrist's kingdom (beast with seven heads and ten horns as we learned from Daniel).
- **The harlot is clothed in purple and scarlet, and adorned with jewels and pearls**. This is echoed in Old Testament prophecy and may just represent physical adornment typical of a harlot. However, the description matches the makeup of the biblical Jewish priest's ephod and breastplate (see FOOD FOR THOUGHT below).
- **The harlot is unclean and full of abominations and immorality, and is called, "BABYLON THE GREAT, THE MOTHER OF HARLOTS AND OF THE ABOMINATIONS OF THE EARTH."** This is a reiteration of how immoral the harlot has been and will be. I believe Old Testament prophets clearly show this is a reference to Israel then and in the future.
- **The harlot is "drunk" with the blood of the saints and witnesses of Jesus**. You'll learn this is probably a reference to Israel as shown through prophecy and by the bloodshed produced by the "covenant of death" she'll enter into with the Antichrist.

The rest of the chapter, Revelation 7:7-18, pertains to Babylon as a city/location. We'll save that for the next topic in this section, *Babylon – the Great City*.

I've stated that Israel is *Babylon, the Harlot*. Why? She's been the unfaithful bride and will commit the most heinous act of adultery at the end by entering into the *covenant of death* with the Antichrist as spoken of by Daniel and Isaiah (see study section *Covenant of Death*). This final act of unfaithfulness to God will end in abuse by her new "lover" and in experiencing the wrath of God. But don't take my word for it – let's look at a sampling of Old and New Testament Scripture that corroborates the claim that Israel will indeed be the harlot of Revelation (the samples follow the analysis of Revelation 17 above):

> **<u>The harlot acts immorally with the kings of the earth</u>**: (Additional Scripture related to Israel and her unfaithfulness/ adultery: Isaiah 57; Jeremiah 3-4, 13, 23, & 30; Ezekiel 23-24; Amos 7.)
>
>> *You also* ***played the harlot with the Egyptians****, your lustful neighbors, and multiplied your* ***harlotry*** *to make Me angry. Behold now, I have stretched out My hand against you and diminished your rations. And I delivered you up to the desire of those who hate you, the daughters of the Philistines, who are ashamed of your lewd conduct. Moreover, you* ***played the harlot with the Assyrians*** *because you were not satisfied; you played the harlot with them and still were not satisfied. You also multiplied your harlotry with the land of merchants, Chaldea, yet even with this you were not satisfied. How languishing is your heart," declares the Lord GOD, "while you do all these things, the actions of a* ***bold-faced harlot****. When you built your shrine at the beginning of every street and made your high place in every square, in disdaining money, you were not like a harlot.* ***You adulteress wife****, who takes strangers instead of her husband!"* —Ezekiel 16:26-32.
>>
>> *. . . with whom the kings of the earth committed* ***acts of immorality****, and those who dwell on the earth were made drunk with the wine of her immorality.* —Revelation 17:2.

> *And he cried out with a mighty voice, saying, "Fallen, fallen is Babylon the great! She has become a dwelling place of demons and a prison of every unclean spirit, and a prison of every unclean and hateful bird. For* ***all the nations have drunk of the wine of the passion of her immorality, and the kings of the earth have committed acts of immorality with her****, and the merchants of the earth have become rich by the wealth of her sensuality."* —Revelation 18:2-3.

The harlot clothed in purple, bejeweled, and decked in gold: (Additional information can be found in Exodus 28 and 39.)

> *He made the* ***breastpiece****, the work of a skillful workman, like the workmanship of the* ***ephod****: of* ***gold and of blue and purple and scarlet*** *material and fine twisted linen. It was square; they made the breastpiece folded double, a span long and a span wide when folded double. And they mounted* ***four rows of stones*** *on it. The first row was a row of ruby, topaz, and emerald; and the second row, a turquoise, a sapphire and a diamond; and the third row, a jacinth, an agate, and an amethyst; and the fourth row, a beryl, an onyx, and a jasper. They were* ***set in gold filigree*** *settings when they were mounted.* —Exodus 39:8-13.

> *And you, O desolate one, what will you do? Although you* ***dress in scarlet****, Although you decorate yourself with* ***ornaments of gold****, Although you enlarge your eyes with paint, In vain you make yourself beautiful. Your lovers despise you; They seek your life.* —Jeremiah 4:30.

> *The woman was clothed in* ***purple and scarlet, and adorned with gold and precious stones and pearls****, having in her hand a gold cup full of abominations and of the unclean things of her immorality . . .* —Revelation 17:4.

> *Woe, woe, the great city, she who was* ***clothed in fine linen and purple and scarlet, and adorned with gold and precious***

***stones** and pearls;* —Revelation 18:16.

<u>The harlot has been (and will be) responsible for the blood of saints and believers in Christ</u>: (Also see Ezekiel 22:2-4 & 23:45.)

*Thus says the Lord GOD, "Because your lewdness was poured out and your nakedness uncovered through your harlotries with your lovers and with all your detestable idols, and because of the **blood of your sons which you gave to idols**,"* —Ezekiel 16:36.

*Indeed **Babylon is to fall for the slain of Israel, As also for Babylon the slain of all the earth** have fallen.* —Jeremiah 51:49. (Compare with Revelation 18:24.)

***Jerusalem**, Jerusalem, **who kills the prophets and stones those who are sent to her**! How often I wanted to gather your children together, the way a hen gathers her chicks under her wings, and you were unwilling. Behold, your house is being left to you desolate!* —Matthew 23:37-38.

*They **killed those who had previously announced the coming of the Righteous One**, whose betrayers and **murderers you have now become** . . .* —Acts 7:52.

*For you, brethren, became imitators of the churches of God in Christ Jesus that are in **Judea**, for you also endured the same sufferings at the hands of your own countrymen, even as they did from the **Jews**, **who both killed the Lord Jesus and the prophets**, and drove us out. They are not pleasing to . . .* —1 Thessalonians 2:14-15.

*And I saw the **woman drunk with the blood of the saints, and with the blood of the witnesses of Jesus**.* —Revelation 17:6.

*And **in her was found the blood of prophets and of saints***

> ***and of all who have been slain on the earth***. —Revelation 18:24. (Compare with Jeremiah 51:49.)

FOOD FOR THOUGHT: The mention of purple, gold, and jewels on the harlot by Old Testament prophets may be very significant – even beyond just confirming that the whore will most likely be Israel. God instructed her to make their priests' ephods and breastplates of these materials and stones (see above). In pages 28-29 of his book *The Islamic Antichrist*, Richardson quotes Islamic writings that tell of an end-times **peace agreement between the Muslim nations and Israel that will be mediated through a Jewish priest (a descendant of Aaron) and will last for seven years.**

Israel, as *Babylon the harlot*, will suffer at the hands of the Antichrist with whom she'll commit her final act of adultery. Ezekiel and Isaiah saw this coming and revealed the outcome in near-far prophecies. John was also shown the same thing by Jesus in the Revelation. As mentioned earlier, Israel will enter into a seven-year *covenant of death* with the Antichrist (see study section *Covenant of Death*). He and his cohorts will turn on her and dishonor the agreement after three and a half years, spawning a three-and-a-half-year period of great tribulation and death for God's people (see study section *Tribulation & Beheading*).

Here are samples of the near-far prophecies and apocalyptic literature revealing how the Antichrist and his kingdom will turn on Israel in the last days, leaving her "*desolate and naked*" (see also Hosea 2:2-5 and Isaiah 47:3) ([ ] added for clarity) :

> *I will also give you into the hands of your lovers, and they will tear down your shrines, demolish your high places,* ***strip you of your clothing, take away your jewels, and will leave you naked and bare***. —Ezekiel 16:39.

> *For thus says the Lord GOD, 'Behold,* ***I will give you into the hand of those whom you hate****, into the hand of those from whom you were alienated. They will deal with you in hatred, take all*

> *your property, and* ***leave you naked and bare****. And the nakedness of your harlotries will be uncovered, both your lewdness and your harlotries. These things will be done to you because you have played the harlot with the nations, because you have defiled yourself with their idols.* —Ezekiel 23:28-30.

> *And the ten horns which you saw, and the beast [Antichrist and his kingdom], these will* ***hate the harlot and will make her desolate and naked****, and will eat her flesh and will burn her up with fire.* ***For God has put it in their hearts to execute His purpose by having a common purpose, and by giving their kingdom to the beast, until the words of God will be fulfilled.*** —Revelation 17:16-17.

Key points to remember:

1. Israel was (and will be) the unfaithful bride of God and the only nation to be labeled as a harlot by Him.
2. The term *Babylon* is used in Revelation to represent Israel and the adulteries she has, and will, commit.
3. Israel has been responsible for the deaths of the prophets and others throughout history. Her final act of adultery (the covenant with the Antichrist/beast kingdom) will cause the death of many saints, including those who believe in Christ and walk in His ways.
4. God instructed His priests' garments to be made of purple, scarlet, gold, and jewels. This is the adornment of the harlot.
5. God will allow the Antichrist and his kingdom to make Israel "desolate and naked" during the three-and-a-half-year Great Tribulation period.

In the next topic, *Babylon – the Great City*, we'll attempt to unravel the other role of the harlot and location of the Antichrist's rule.

BABYLON – THE GREAT CITY

And the mystery of *Babylon* continues. We understand now that one of "*Mystery Babylon's*" roles is that of a whore and that Israel is the most likely candidate for the end-times Babylon-Harlot. End-times Babylon will also be a location. In fact, you'll learn that it's the place or location where the Antichrist will rule over the kings of the earth during his three-and-a-half-year time of authority and great tribulation. Will it be a symbolic authority? A physical city? If a city, then *which* city? I think you'll find it to be both an authority *and* a location—but not the ancient city of Babylon.

Some like Rev. Finis Jennings Dake (author of *God's Plan for Man*) interpret the reference to Babylon in Revelation literally and believe the city of Babylon in Iraq must be rebuilt and become "*that great city, which rules over the kings of the earth*" (cf. Revelation 17:18). We should definitely take Scripture literally whenever possible unless there's good reason based on context and similar passages to do otherwise (as discussed in Chapter Four of this guide). But this is an "otherwise" situation based on context and prophecy.

Here's what we already know about Babylon as an authority/location: the ancient city of Babylon (and much of Iraq for that matter) has been crippled or destroyed. God made it clear through Isaiah's prophecies that physical Babylon would be destroyed and never inhabited again (cf. Isaiah 13 & 14). Israel as a nation will most likely be the *whore of Babylon*. The following is a list of the things we have yet to learn about futuristic Babylon. We'll further define the list and add Scripture references later.

1. Although the "seven mountains" mentioned in Revelation 17:9 also refer to principalities making up the Antichrist's kingdom (past and future), Israel is a city built on seven mountains.
2. By definition, the word *Babylon* in the New Testament figuratively identifies a place of tyranny. Zephaniah called Jerusalem the "*tyrannical city*" (cf. Zephaniah 3:1).

3. Jerusalem is referred to as the "*great city*" in the New Testament (cf. Revelation 11:8) – a title also hung onto the end-times Babylon.
4. Jerusalem will be the "*great city, which reigns over the kings of the earth*" (cf. Revelation 17:18). Don't forget that, according to Daniel, Paul, and Christ, the Antichrist will establish himself in the temple there (cf. Daniel 9:27, 2 Thessalonians 2:4, and Matthew 24:15).
5. Babylon and Jerusalem are both listed in the context of God's end-times wrath (cf. Isaiah 51:17; Jeremiah 4:1-27; Matthew 23:37-38; Luke 13:34-35; Revelation 14:7-8, 16:19, & 18:19).
6. Isaiah prophesied about a future "*fallen, fallen*" Jerusalem (cf. Isaiah 21:9). Jeremiah revealed the same destiny (cf. Jeremiah 51:8). Jesus showed John a "*fallen, fallen*" Babylon at the end of God's wrath (cf. Revelation 18:2). I believe these definitely represent a near-far prophecy. My intent here is to show a relationship between the original Babylon, the first one-world government under Noah's descendant Nimrod, and end-times Babylon, which will be the last one-world-government.

Although the focus here is to determine the physical location of end-times Babylon, you'll learn during our study of Revelation in Chapter Sixteen that it will also represent an ultimate authority. This is where the Antichrist's kingdom will rule the world. And like ancient Babylon, the end-times Babylon will represent an authority over the world's commerce. As you learned in this chapter, the Antichrist and his kingdom, headquartered in Jerusalem, will manage the world's financial system (hence the ability to control buying and selling with a **mark** of allegiance). But let's get back to the location of apocalyptic Babylon and expound upon the items above.

Seven Mountains: According to Revelation 17:9, the seven heads of the beast the harlot sits on represent seven mountains. Church tradition says this proves the *harlot* will sit in Rome since it historically has been known as the "city on seven hills." This is done to pave the way for a doctrine that also states the pope will be either the Antichrist or the False Prophet in charge of an adulterous religious system – the Catholic Church. As you've hopefully learned by now, the harlot will probably be Israel, not Catholicism. And while Rome is indeed a city on seven hills, Jerusalem is a city situated on seven mountains.

> Strong's definition for the Greek word used for mountain - *Oros*: **G3735 oros (or'-os) a mountain (as lifting itself above the plain): - hill, mount (-ain)**. According to one of many sources[7] that also include the writings of historian Flavius Josephus, the seven mountains of Jerusalem are Mount Goath, Mount Gareb, Mount Acra, Mount Bezetha, Mount Zion, Mount Ophel, and Mount Moriah. NOTE: Revelation 17:10 goes on to describe the seven heads as seven past/future kings. Therefore, it's possible the mention of seven mountains isn't a reference to physical mountains at all but to the empires that have risen, or will rise, to become the Antichrist's kingdom. More on this later during our study of Revelation in Chapter Sixteen.

Jerusalem as a place of tyranny: The word *Babylon* in Revelation is based on Strong's G897, the Greek word *Babulon*: "G897 Babulōn (bab-oo-lone') Babylon, the capital of Chaldaea (literally or **figuratively as a type of tyranny**): - Babylon." Zephaniah refers to Jerusalem as a tyrannical city: "*Woe to her who is rebellious and defiled,* ***The tyrannical city!***" (cf. Zephaniah 3:1).

Jerusalem as the *great city*: (Other references to the "*great city*" in Revelation include 14:8, 16:19, 17:18, 18:10, and 18:16-20.)

> *And their dead bodies will lie in the street of the* ***great city which mystically is called Sodom and Egypt****, where also* ***their Lord was crucified****.* —Revelation 11:8.

Jerusalem will be the "*great city, which reigns over the kings*

of the earth": (cf. Revelation 17:18). The Antichrist will set himself up in the temple, and his end-times kingdom will be positioned in Jerusalem as a result. We know that he'll have authority over the entire world at that time and be in Jerusalem in the end (see Chapter Twelve of this guide, *Daniel*; study Chapters Nine, Eleven, and Twelve in particular for additional information).

Figurative Babylon and Jerusalem will experience the end-times wrath of God: (See also Ezekiel 16:35-40.) Isaiah, Jeremiah, and Jesus foretold of the wrath of God Jerusalem will experience. This wrath is reiterated in the Revelation, strengthening a case for Jerusalem and end-times *Babylon* being one and the same. The following is but a sampling:

> *Rouse yourself! Rouse yourself! Arise, O* ***Jerusalem, You who have drunk from the Lord's hand the cup of His anger*** . . . —Isaiah 51:17.

> *If you will return, O Israel, declares the LORD. . . For thus says the LORD, "****The whole land shall be a desolation****, Yet I will not execute a complete destruction."* —Jeremiah 4:1-27.

> *Jerusalem, Jerusalem, who kills the prophets and stones those who are sent to her! . . . Behold,* ***your house is being left to you desolate!*** —Matthew 23:37-38 & Luke 13:34-35.

> *. . . and he said with a loud voice, "Fear God, and give Him glory,* ***because the hour of His judgment has come****; worship Him who made the heaven and the earth and sea and springs of waters." And another angel, a second one, followed, saying, "****Fallen, fallen is Babylon the great****, she who has made all the nations drink of the wine of the passion of her immorality.* —Revelation 14:7-8.

> *And the* ***great city was split into three parts, and the cities of the nations fell. And Babylon the great was remembered***

> ***before God, to give her the cup of the wine of His fierce wrath***. —Revelation 16:19.

> *And they threw dust on their heads and were crying out, weeping and mourning, saying, 'Woe, woe, the **great city**, in which all who had ships at sea became rich by her wealth, **for in one hour she has been laid waste!**'* —Revelation 18:19.

Babylon – past and future – as "*fallen, fallen*": The following Scripture from Isaiah, Jeremiah, and John compare Old and New Testament prophecy and apocalyptic literature regarding "*fallen Babylon*" and is just for reference. My point in including them is to show a relationship between the original Babylon, the first one-world government under Nimrod, and end-times *Babylon*, which will be the last one-world government.

> *Now behold, here comes a troop of riders, horsemen in pairs. And one said, "**Fallen, fallen is Babylon**; And all the images of her gods are shattered on the ground."* —Isaiah 21:9.

> *Babylon has been a golden cup in the hand of the LORD, Intoxicating all the earth. **The nations have drunk of her wine**; Therefore the nations are going mad. Suddenly **Babylon has fallen** and been broken; Wail over her! Bring balm for her pain; Perhaps she may be healed.* —Jeremiah 51:7-8.

> *And another angel, a second one, followed, saying, "**Fallen, fallen is Babylon the great**, she who has made all the nations drink of the wine of the passion of her immorality."* —Revelation 14:8.

> *And he cried out with a mighty voice, saying, "**Fallen, fallen is Babylon the great**! She has become a dwelling place of demons and a prison of every unclean spirit, and a prison of every unclean and hateful bird."* —Revelation 18:2.

Key points to remember:

1. The ancient city of Babylon (and much of Iraq for that matter) has been crippled or destroyed.
2. Israel, as we've learned, will most likely be the *whore of Babylon*. She lives in the land of Israel with the capital of Jerusalem.
3. Israel is a city built on seven mountains. But remember that Scripture also states that the mountains are seven kingdoms and therefore may not represent physical mountains at all.
4. Babylon in the New Testament figuratively represents tyranny; Zephaniah called Jerusalem the "*tyrannical city*."
5. Jerusalem is referred to as the *great city*, as the figurative *Babylon* of Revelation was by Jesus. The Antichrist and his kingdom will establish themselves in Jerusalem and reign from there in the last days.
6. End-times Babylon and Jerusalem are both listed in the context of God's wrath.

Chapter Ten

Deceivers

Satan, as the *father of lies* (cf. John 8:44), has been deceiving the world since Adam and Eve occupied the Garden of Eden roughly 6,000 years ago. Those who learn from him to deceive others become *children of the evil one* as does anyone who becomes deceived and therefore follows attractive but unscriptural doctrine. Deceivers take the form of spiritual weeds – tares – that come up alongside true believers in Christ and often squeeze the life out of the body of Christ. They also come as false messiahs or false prophets. Many of these have been on earth since the time of Christ, but a special false Christ and false prophet will exist during the time of the end just before our Lord's return and subsequent wrath of God.

Our study of deceivers will be divided into three topics:

- **Tares**: "*False grain*" – people within the body of Christ who look like part of the bride but choke the life out of the church through dissension, division, deception, etc.
- **False Prophets**: A type of tare, they deceive through false teaching and ungodly visions and dreams. Jesus called them "*ravenous wolves in sheep's clothing*." The final and ultimate false prophet will support the Antichrist and do great wonders on his behalf.
- **False Messiahs**: People claiming to be Christ, the promised Messiah. Judaism, Islam, and even Christianity suffer from the same type of deception. Jesus described what may be the final false messiah as one who'll deceive many into believing he actually *is* their savior.

✓ **Quick reference:** Revelation 13

Tares

When I think of tares, I'm reminded of Bill (name changed to protect the individual), who masqueraded as a reverend in our church and uttered prophecy from what he called "God-inspired dreams." The revelations were usually frightening – a far cry from the edification God's revelations typically convey. As it turns out, Bill wasn't really an ordained minister or a vessel for God's revelations. And although he claimed to have lost his wife and baby in childbirth, Bill's family of five or six was alive and well and living in another state. Nine months of havoc ended when he was apprehended under a warrant for his arrest. Unfortunately, the damage was done and the church suffered considerable guilt, confusion, and division until well after the ordeal was over.

The Greek word for tares: G2215 zizanion (dziz-an'-ee-on) darnel or false grain: - tares. Jesus gave us a glimpse of the damage they can do and why the church would have to put up with their wicked influence for a time:

> *But while his men were sleeping, his enemy came* ***and sowed tares among the wheat****, and went away. But when the wheat sprouted and bore grain, then the tares became evident also. The slaves of the landowner came and said to him, 'Sir, did you not sow good seed in your field? How then does it have tares?' And he said to them, 'An enemy has done this!' The slaves said to him, 'Do you want us, then, to go and gather them up?' But he said, '****No; for while you are gathering up the tares, you may uproot the wheat with them. Allow both to grow together until the harvest****; and in the time of the harvest I will say to the reapers, "First gather up the tares and bind them in bundles to burn them up; but gather the wheat into my barn."' . . . And He said, "The one who sows the good seed is the Son of Man, and the field is the world; and as for the good seed, these are the sons of the kingdom; and the* ***tares are the sons of the evil one; and the enemy who sowed them is the devil, and the harvest is the end of the age****; and the reapers are angels. So just as the tares*

are gathered up and burned with fire, so shall it be at the end of the age. The Son of Man will send forth His angels, and they will gather out of His kingdom all stumbling blocks, and those who commit lawlessness, and will throw them into the furnace of fire; in that place there will be weeping and gnashing of teeth." —Matthew 13:25-42.

How can we tell the tares apart from true believers? It seems that tares are made evident at the "fruit-bearing stage" when, at the same time, "*the wheat sprouted and bore grain*" (cf. Matthew 13:26). This is verified by Jesus' emphasis upon the good works that a true believer will produce in his/her life: "*By their fruit you will know them*" (cf. Matthew 7:15-20). Thus, tares, as false wheat, look like wheat (even sound like wheat) but the fruit of their character will identify their true spiritual nature and parentage.

The appearance of tares within the body of Christ varies, and a list of the devastating consequences would be endless. Several are related to our study; we'll reveal some of them in Chapter Seventeen. Paul wrote about a very significant deception: the Gentile church in Thessalonica was deceived into thinking the end had already come and that they'd "missed the boat." Paul put them at ease by reminding the believers that at least a couple of things must happen before Christ's return and His gathering of the church: a great falling away from the faith and a revealing of the Antichrist after he displays himself as God in the temple.

Now we request you, brethren, with regard to the ***coming of our Lord Jesus Christ and our gathering together to Him****, that you not be quickly shaken from your composure or be disturbed either by a* ***spirit or a message or a letter as if from us****, to the effect that the day of the Lord has come. Let no one in any way deceive you, for* ***it will not come unless the apostasy comes first, and the man of lawlessness is revealed, the son of destruction, who opposes and exalts himself above every so-called god or object of worship, so that he takes his seat in the temple of God, displaying himself as being God****.* —2 Thessalonians 2:1-4.

The lesson to be learned here: test what you hear or see in the church against the standard of God's Word to avoid deception. Studies like this one will help you learn the standard and strengthen your faith.

Key points to remember:

1. People influenced by Satan infiltrate the church regularly – knowingly or unknowingly. They can take the form of false teachers, false prophets, or people who cause dissension and confusion from within the body of Christ.
2. Test what you hear or see to ensure it's from God and not a deception. The parable of the tares would also teach us to look for the character fruit of a true child of God as evidenced in the fruit of the Spirit.

FALSE PROPHETS

G5578 pseudoprophētēs (psyoo-dop-rof-ay'-tace) a spurious prophet, that is, **pretended foreteller** or **religious impostor**: - false prophet.

Many "religious imposters" or "pretended foretellers" have come and gone throughout the church's history. They cause incredible damage in the church! Jesus, Peter, and John warned us about them in advance – Jesus first, and then Peter and John in letters addressed to the church.

Jesus:

> *Beware of the* ***false prophets****, who come to you in* ***sheep's clothing, but inwardly are ravenous wolves****.* —Matthew 7:15.

> *At that time many will fall away and will betray one another and hate one another. Many* ***false prophets will arise and***

> ***will mislead*** *many.* —Matthew 24:10-11.

Peter:

> *But* ***false prophets*** *also arose among the people, just as there will also be* ***false teachers*** *among you, who will secretly introduce* ***destructive heresies****, even denying the Master who bought them, bringing swift destruction upon themselves.* ***Many will follow their sensuality, and because of them the way of the truth will be maligned*** . . . —2 Peter 2:1-2.

John:

> *Beloved, do not believe every spirit, but test the spirits to see whether they are from God, because many* ***false prophets have gone out into the world****. By this you know the Spirit of God: every spirit that confesses that Jesus Christ has come in the flesh is from God; and* ***every spirit that does not confess Jesus is not from God; this is the spirit of the antichrist****, of which you have heard that it is coming, and now it is already in the world.* —1 John 4:1-3.

Now that we know the definition of false prophet, we should move forward to learning about the *ultimate* false prophet – the great religious imposter who'll be tied to the Antichrist the way Christ is tied to God.

This is probably a good time to expound upon the concept that each part of the holy trinity can be loosely compared to an unholy character. Here's my loose comparison of what we normally think of as the holy trinity – God our heavenly Father, His Son the Christ, and His Holy Spirit – and the unholy trinity: the Antichrist, the False Prophet, and Satan.

10.1 Comparison of the Godly and Ungodly Trinities

Godly Trinity	Ungodly Trinity
God, the father	**The beast** (The Antichrist) 1. Sets himself up as God in the temple 2. Demands worship as God
Jesus, God's Christ 1. Glorifies God 2. Works miracles 3. Promised Messiah	**The False Prophet** 1. Glorifies the Antichrist 2. Works miracles 3. Religious imposter
Holy Spirit, breath of God 1. Spirit that empowers believers 2. Teaches and influences believers in Christ	**Satan** 1. Spirit that empowers the Antichrist 2. Influences the ungodly to trick and deceive

Traditionally, some people compare Christ to the Antichrist and God to Satan when looking at good versus bad. I didn't do that because I focus more on the characteristics of each entity. Christ is to God what the False Prophet will be to the Antichrist. The Holy Spirit is a spiritual principality that convicts and empowers just as Satan does, and will do through the Antichrist. Finally, the Antichrist (while empowered by Satan) will claim to be God and demand worship as such. But remember that the table above reflects my opinion and is meant only to show a loose relationship between a holy and unholy trinity.

Jesus said that false messiahs and false prophets would come *before* the end. He also told His disciples there would be false messiahs and false prophets at the time of the Great Tribulation. In the next subtopic – *False Messiahs* – you'll see why those before the end and those during the time of the end will be different.

So what will be the relationship between the Antichrist and false prophet during the Great Tribulation? The Antichrist won't act alone – he'll have an accomplice. His champion will be the second beast in the Revelation. Unlike the Antichrist *beast* that will come out of the water (symbolic of many peoples and nations), the False Prophet *beast* will come up from the *earth* (Strong's G1093). This implies he'll originate from a particular region of the world (based on the definition below).

> **G1093** gē (ghay) **by extension a region, or the solid part or the whole of the terrene globe** (including the occupants in each application): - country, earth (-ly), ground, land, world.

The Bible classifies this beast as the False Prophet in several places within Revelation. For instance, Scripture confirms he'll be the one who works miracles on behalf of the first beast (Antichrist) and deceives those who take the mark of that first beast (see the Scripture reference below). Both beasts will be destroyed in the same way – by being cast into the lake of fire as outlined below:

> *And the beast was taken, and with him the* ***false prophet that wrought miracles before him****, with which he* ***deceived them that had received the mark of the beast****, and them that worshipped his image. These both were cast alive into a lake of fire burning with brimstone*. — Revelation 19:20.

But Revelation 13 contains the bulk of what we know about the end-times False Prophet.

> *Then I saw* ***another beast coming up out of the earth****; and he* ***had two horns like a lamb and he spoke as a dragon****. He exercises all the authority of the first beast in his presence. And he* ***makes the earth and those who dwell in it to worship the first beast****, whose fatal wound was healed. He* ***performs great signs, so that he even makes fire come down*** *out of heaven to the earth in the presence of men. And he* ***deceives those who dwell on the earth*** *because of the signs which it was given him to perform in the presence of the beast, telling those who dwell on the earth to make an image to the beast who had the wound of the sword and has come to life. And it was given to him to give breath to the image of the beast, so that the* ***image of the***

> ***beast would even speak and cause as many as do not worship the image of the beast to be killed****. And he causes all, the small and the great, and the rich and the poor, and the free men and the slaves,* ***to be given a mark*** *on their right hand or on their forehead . . .* —Revelation 13:11-16.

The False Prophet will do many things on behalf of the Antichrist:

- Cause the world's inhabitants to worship the Antichrist (cf. Revelation 13:12 & 15).
- Do great wonders such as *bringing fire down from heaven* (cf. Revelation 13:13).
- Deceive the world's inhabitants (cf. Revelation 13:14-15).
- Put to death those who refuse to worship the Antichrist or his image (cf. Revelation 13:15).
- Cause all who will accept it to receive a mark on the right hand or forehead in order to buy or sell in those days (cf. Revelation 13:16-18).

Key points to remember:

1. False prophets have, and will, deceive the church. Be on the lookout for false teaching, inaccurate prophecies, a lack of spiritual fruit, sources of division in the church, etc.
2. *The* False Prophet will arise from what will most likely be a particular region or nation.
3. He'll work miracles and deceive many – even the *chosen* if possible.
4. The False Prophet will demand worship of the Antichrist as God.
5. He and the Antichrist will be destroyed when God throws them into the lake of fire at the battle of Armageddon.

In the next topic, *False Messiahs*, we'll take a look at the warning Jesus gave regarding those who've claimed to be Christ and the one at the end who will trick people into believing he really *is* the Messiah. We'll also look at examples of past or present false messiahs in Judaism, Christianity, and Islam.

FALSE MESSIAHS

But as for Me, I have installed ***My King Upon Zion****, My holy mountain. I will surely tell of the decree of the LORD: He said to Me, '****You are My Son****, Today I have begotten You.' Ask of Me, and I will surely* ***give the nations as Your inheritance****, And the very ends of the earth as Your possession.'* ***You shall break them with a rod of iron****, You shall shatter them like earthenware.' Now therefore, O kings, show discernment; Take warning, O judges of the earth. Worship the LORD with reverence And rejoice with trembling. Do homage to the Son, that He not become angry, and you perish in the way, For His wrath may soon be kindled. How blessed are all who take refuge in Him!* —Psalm 2:6-12.

And she gave birth to a son, a male child, who is to ***rule all the nations with a rod of iron****; and her child was caught up to God and to His throne.* —Revelation 12:5.

*Then the seventh angel sounded; and there were loud voices in heaven, saying, "****The kingdom of the world has become the kingdom of our Lord and of His Christ****; and He will reign forever and ever."* —Revelation 11:15.

King David wrote the above psalm after a vision of the coming Messiah, or anointed one who'll save Israel in the last days. During times of unfaithfulness to God and resulting wrath (e.g. Babylonian captivity) Daniel and others like Ezekiel and Isaiah foretold of Israel's end-times salvation. And John reminded the church of the same thing in the Revelation given to him by Christ (e.g. Revelation 12:5 and 11:15 above). The Muslim prophet Mohammed also foretold of a coming Messiah *and* of the return of Jesus. Whether Jewish, Christian, or Muslim, all are waiting for someone, but for whom?

Believers in Christ understand Him to be the promised Messiah and anxiously await His second coming. Jews are still waiting for the Messiah to be born and fulfill hundreds of scriptural prophecies pertaining to his birth, death, resurrection, and judgment of the world. Muslims are awaiting *their* end-times savior, the Mahdi, and Eesa al Maseeh – Jesus the Messiah (but not *the* Messiah). This is the person Muslims consider to be the *prophet* Jesus born to Mary. But to them, He's in no way to be considered God's Son. Islam finds the concept that God had a Son repulsive despite the fact that the Qur'an and supporting Suras explain that Jesus was born of the Virgin Mary, who conceived through God's Holy Spirit. A particular warning from John comes to mind at this time: "*Who is the liar but the one who denies that Jesus is the Christ?* ***This is the antichrist, the one who denies the Father and the Son***." —1 John 2:22.

God will redeem His original chosen, the Jews, through Christ in the last days. This becomes very clear when comparing prophecy, David's revelation through the Psalms, Christ's testimony, and the Revelation given to John. So Christians and Jews are awaiting the same individual albeit for different reasons. But identifying the messiah may be difficult for some since Jesus told us that many would come in His name claiming to be the Christ before the very end. Let's look at the definition of the Greek word Jesus used for *Christ* when prophesying that many would claim to be the savior before the end, along with supporting Scripture:

> **G5547** Christos (khris-tos') anointed, that is, the Messiah, an epithet of Jesus: - Christ.
>
> *And Jesus answered and said to them, "See to it that no one misleads you.* ***For many will come in My name, saying, 'I am the Christ,' and will mislead many****. You will be hearing of wars and rumors of wars. See that you are not frightened, for those things must take place, but that is not yet the end.*" —Matthew 24:4-6.
>
> **Many will come in My name, saying, 'I am He!' and will mislead many** —Mark 13:6.
>
> *And He said, "See to it that you are not misled; for* ***many will come in My name, saying, 'I am He,' and, 'The time is near.'***

Do not go after them." —Luke 21:8.

Jews, Christians, and Muslims have apparently witnessed the arrival of the Messiah—or several Messiahs over the years (if you believe the claims). Here are a few examples (courtesy of Wikipedia and YouTube):

An early Jewish Messiah:

Shimon bar Kokhba was the Jewish leader who led what is known as the Bar Kokhba revolt against the Roman Empire in 132 CE, establishing an independent Jewish state of Israel which he ruled for three years as Nasi ("Ruler"). His state was conquered by the Romans in 135 following a two-year war. Documents discovered in the modern era give us his original name, Simon ben Kosiba, he was given the surname Bar Kokhba, (Aramaic for "Son of a Star", referring to the Star Prophecy of Numbers 24:17, "A star has shot off Jacob") by his contemporary, the Jewish sage Rabbi Akiva. After the failure of the revolt, the rabbinical writers referred to bar Kokhba as "Simon bar Kozeba" ("Son of lies" or "Son of deception").

A complete Roman legion with auxiliaries was annihilated. The new state knew only one year of peace. The Romans committed no fewer than twelve legions, amounting to one third to one half of the entire Roman army, to reconquer this now independent state. Being outnumbered and taking heavy casualties, the Romans refused to engage in an open battle and instead adopted a scorched earth policy which reduced and demoralized the Judean populace, slowly grinding away at the will of the Judeans to sustain the war.

Bar Kokhba took up refuge in the fortress of Betar. The Romans eventually captured it and killed all the defenders. According to Cassius Dio, 580,000 Jews were killed, 50 fortified towns and 985 villages razed. Yet so costly was the

Roman victory that the Emperor Hadrian, when reporting to the Roman Senate, did not see fit to begin with the customary greeting "If you and your children are well, all is well. For I and the army are all in good health." He was the only Roman general known to have refused to celebrate his victory with a triumphal entrance into his capital. In the aftermath of the war, Hadrian consolidated the older political units of Judaea, Galilee and Samaria into the new province of Syria Palaestina, named to complete the disassociation with Judaea . . . . (Courtesy of Wikipedia.)

An example of a self-proclaimed Christian messiah:

David Koresh (August 17, 1959 – April 19, 1993), born Vernon Wayne Howell, was the leader of a Branch Davidian religious sect, believing himself to be its final prophet. Vernon Howell had his name legally changed to David Koresh on May 15, 1990. A 1993 raid by the U.S. Bureau of Alcohol, Tobacco, Firearms and Explosives, and the subsequent siege by the FBI ended with the burning of the Branch Davidian ranch outside of Waco, Texas in McLennan County. Koresh, 54 adults and 21 children were found dead after the fire. Raid began on February 28, 1993 – lasted 51 days.

At the Palestine, Texas camp, Koresh worked it so that everyone was forced to rely on him, and him alone. All previous bonds and attachments, family or otherwise, meant nothing. His rationale was if they had no one to depend on, they had to depend on him, and that made them vulnerable. By this time, he had already begun to give the message of his own "Christhood", proclaiming that he was "the Son of God, the Lamb who could open the Seven Seals." (Courtesy of Wikipedia.)

Another example of a self-proclaimed Christian messiah:

James Warren "Jim" Jones (May 13, 1931 – November 18, 1978) was the founder and leader of the Peoples Temple, which is best known for the November 18, 1978 death of 405 Temple members in Jonestown, Guyana along with the deaths of nine other people at a nearby airstrip and in Georgetown, Guyana. (Courtesy of Wikipedia.)

Example of a Muslim messiah:

"I am real Messiah Mahdi who is called as Zeus Gawd. Watch all my videos to know everything about me & Maseeh Dajjaal." (Courtesy of YouTube.)

Another example of a Muslim messiah also as the prophet Jesus:

"I am Jesus Chrst 2nd Mohd. Maodood ahmed Khan arrived in Hyderabad, India in 2007 A.D. Mirza's entire jamat ahmadiyya is certified Maseeh Dajjaal the anti-christ 666 . . . My slogan is 'Hatred for satan. Love for all' . . ." (Courtesy of YouTube, posted 10-17-2007.) NOTE: Oddly enough, Maodood ahmed Khan (above) also accuses the 19th-century supposed-Mahdi Mirza Ghulam Ahmad of actually being the Antichrist.

On the Mount of Olives, Jesus continued to tell His disciples of the sequence of the end and of the terrible tribulation of the coming Antichrist. It was in that context that Jesus again mentioned a false messiah, but He used a different word this time – *psudochristos* – which translates directly to a *spurious Messiah* or *false Christ*. In the first scenario (as in Matthew 24:4-6) Jesus let us know that people would *claim* to be the true Christ as one of the "birth pangs." The latter part of the end-times sequence given on the Mount of Olives (that reflects the word *psudochristos*) reveals *the* False Prophet or false Christ that will arise during the Great Tribulation resulting from the reign of the Antichrist. The following is the definition for *pseudochristos* (Strong's G5580) and Scripture using that word in the latter part of Jesus' discourse on the Mount of Olives.

G5580 pseudochristos (psyoo-dokh'-ris-tos) a spurious Messiah: - false Christ. (Matthew 24:24 and Mark 13:22)

> *For* ***then there will be a great tribulation****, such as has not occurred since the beginning of the world until now, nor ever will. Unless those days had been cut short, no life would have been saved; but for the sake of the elect those days will be cut short.* ***Then if anyone says to you, 'Behold, here is the Christ,' or 'There He is,' do not believe him. For false Christs*** *and false prophets* ***will arise and will show great signs and wonders, so as to mislead, if possible, even the elect****. Behold, I have told you in advance.* —Matthew 24:21-25.

FOOD FOR THOUGHT: According to the Qur'an (cf. Sura 9:29), pages 65-67 of *The Islamic Antichrist*, and wikiislam, the Muslim prophet Jesus Eesa al Maseeh):

1. Will judge the world.
2. Will defeat the Jewish Antichrist (Dajjal).
3. Will lead the Muslims, soldiers of Jesus, in battle against the Jews and Christians.
4. Will abolish the Jizyah tax thereby giving non-Muslims no choice but to convert to what will be the one-world religion of Islam or die.
5. Will demand worship of the Mahdi by everyone on earth.
6. Will support the Muslim Messiah (Mahdi), who will reign in Jerusalem as a subordinate.

What is the *Jizyah* tax? According to multiple sources including Islam Wiki[8] and page 65 of *The Islamic Antichrist*, it's the extra tax imposed on non-Muslims who live under Muslim rule according to the Qur'an and hadith: "***Fight*** *those who believe not in Allah nor the Last Day, nor hold forbidden that which hath been forbidden by Allah and His Messenger, nor acknowledge the religion of Truth, (even if they are) of* ***the People of the Book [Christians and Jews], until they pay the Jizyah*** *with willing submission, and feel themselves subdued.*" (Qur'an 9:29) ([ ] inserted by me for clarification.)

You'll find that the apocalyptic Muslim Jesus and the False Prophet of Revelation are very similar in nature. We already know from Scripture that the Antichrist will come from what is currently one of several Islamic regions surrounding Israel. We also know that, according to Islam, the Muslim Messiah (Mahdi) will make a seven-year peace agreement with Israel through a priest. So the similarities between the Muslim Jesus and False Prophet of Scripture should come as no surprise.

The following table highlights similarities between the Antichrist and Mahdi, and the false prophet and Muslim prophet Jesus. It's not meant to drive home a point that the Antichrist will be Muslim. However, the prospect based on a comparison of apocalyptic literature is intriguing.

10.2 Comparison of Christian and Muslim Apocalyptic Players

Christian Prophecy	Muslim Prophecy
Antichrist 1. Temporary ruler of the world 2. Will rule from Jerusalem 3. Supported by the False Prophet 4. Will make a seven-year agreement with Israel	**Mahdi** 1. Ruler of the world 2. Will rule from Jerusalem 3. Supported by the prophet Jesus 4. Will make a seven-year agreement with Israel
False Prophet 1. Demands worship of the Antichrist 2. Supports the Antichrist through miracles and signs 3. Kills all who won't worship the Antichrist (primary method: beheading)	**Prophet Jesus** 1. Demands worship of the Mahdi 2. Supports the Mahdi 3. Does away with the Jizyah tax and has anyone who doesn't convert to Islam killed (primary method: beheading)

Sources for learning more about the similarities between Islamic and Christian eschatology (study of end times):

- *The Islamic Antichrist* by Joel Richardson
- Islam Wiki[9]

- The Qur'an online[10]
- A website that addresses questions about Islam[11]
- Islamic prophecies about the Mahdi (to include the seven-year agreement)[12]

CHECKUP

CHAPTERS EIGHT, NINE, & TEN

The following questions are meant to check your understanding of what we've covered so far and provoke additional thoughts and questions to elevate your learning to a higher level. You don't have to answer *Private Challenge/Discussion* questions (or share the answers publicly if you do). They're just for your own consideration or group discussion.

Possible answers to all questions can be found in Appendix D.

1. According to John 8:44, who is the father of lies?

2. When will Satan be permanently removed from heaven and banished to the earth?

3. List three different names for the Antichrist based on 2 Thessalonians 2:1-8.

4. Ezekiel 38:2-6 reveals the names of the country of the Antichrist's origin and the seven other countries not subdued by him. What are these eight countries/regions?

5. The *people* of what will be the region or kingdom of the Antichrist's origin destroyed Jerusalem and the temple in 70

CE as prophesied by Daniel (Daniel 9:26). Based on accounts by Flavius Josephus and in consideration of the part of the world this happened in, what would've been the most likely ethnic background of those people?

6. Scripture such as Daniel 7:25 and Revelation 11:12 and 13:5 indicate the length of time the Antichrist will have authority to persecute and kill God's people. What will be this length of time in days, months, or years?

7. The authority of the Antichrist will be a time of great tribulation. Will believers in Christ have to endure this? Helpful Scripture references include Matthew 24:21-22, Revelation 12:13-17, Revelation 14:12-13, and Revelation 13:10.

8. What sign in the heavens will mark the end of the Great Tribulation and precede the gathering of Christian believers? Helpful Scripture references include Matthew 24:29-31 and Mark 13:24-27.

9. Scripture like Ezekiel 16:37-39, Ezekiel 23:28-30, Matthew 23:37-38, and Revelation 17:16-17 hints at who – or what – the harlot of Babylon *could* be. Who or what do you believe the harlot will be? Why?

10. Isaiah 1:9-10, Revelation 11:8, and Revelation 16:19 offer clues as to the figurative end-times city Babylon. What city or location do you believe this *Babylon* will represent?

11. Private Challenge / Discussion: Several theories exist regarding the Antichrist's identity and the makeup of his end-times kingdom. Views also differ as to whether Christians will go through the Great Tribulation. What do you believe about the Antichrist, his kingdom, and whether Christians will go through the Great Tribulation? How has this study affected your beliefs or views of these topics?

PART FOUR

Revelation & Insight

Chapter Eleven

Introduction to the Apocalypse

For then there will be a great tribulation, such as has not occurred since the beginning of the world until now, nor ever will. . . . ***Behold, I have told you in advance.*** —Matthew 24:21-25.

You may have been taught that Jesus can return at any moment and that His return and our gathering will be a silent surprise. I believe you'll discover that this won't be the case as we go through this section of our study: *Revelation & Insight*. The primary goal of this chapter, the first in the section, is to introduce you to the concept that we've been warned of the end of the age and given many details and signs to watch for. Old Testament prophets Ezekiel, Daniel, Amos, Isaiah, and others left us prophetic and apocalyptic clues, as did Jesus, Peter, and Paul.

The unveiling of future events by these prophets and by our Savior Jesus gives us insight into:

- Kingdoms that would come and go before the final kingdom of the Antichrist.
- The Antichrist and his kingdom.
- The sequence and timing of end-times events.

Some of the many warnings and admonishments you'll read about in greater detail in this section:

> *The Revelation of Jesus Christ, which God gave Him to show to His bond-servants, the things which must soon take place . . . Blessed is he who reads and those who hear the words of the prophecy, and heed the things which are written in it; for the time is near.* —Revelation 1:1-3.

> *For nation will rise against nation, and kingdom against kingdom,*

and in various places there will be famines and earthquakes. But all these things are merely the beginning of birth pangs. —Matthew 24:7-8.

Now at that time Michael, the great prince who stands guard over the sons of your people, will arise. And there will be a time of distress such as never occurred since there was a nation until that time . . . . —Daniel 12:1.

It was also given to him to make war with the saints and to overcome them, and authority over every tribe and people and tongue and nation was given to him. —Revelation 13:7.

The sun will be turned into darkness And the moon into blood Before the great and awesome day of the LORD comes. And it will come about that whoever calls on the name of the LORD Will be delivered . . . —Joel 2:31-32.

But of that day and hour no one knows, not even the angels of heaven, nor the Son, but the Father alone. . . . Therefore be on the alert, for you do not know which day your Lord is coming. —Matthew 24:36-42.

Now we request you, brethren, with regard to the coming of our Lord Jesus Christ and our gathering together to Him . . . for it will not come unless the apostasy comes first, and the man of lawlessness is revealed, the son of destruction, who opposes and exalts himself above every so-called god or object of worship, so that he takes his seat in the temple of God, displaying himself as being God. —2 Thessalonians 2:1-4.

Therefore repent; or else I am coming to you quickly, and I will make war against them with the sword of My mouth. He who has an ear, let him hear what the Spirit says to the churches. To him who overcomes, to him I will give some of the hidden manna, and I will give him a white stone, and a new name written on the stone which no one knows but he who receives it. —Revelation 2:16-17.

Although Joel, Amos, Isaiah, Micah, and Jeremiah gave prophecies (some near-far) before Daniel began revealing future events, Daniel gave us the best sense of timing and more characteristics of the Antichrist and his coming kingdom than any other prophet. He warned us of kingdoms that would come and go before the final authority and gave us prophecies that have since become a matter of historical fact. The fulfillment of prophecy is an example of the assurance that strengthens our faith as discussed in Chapter Three. Daniel also wrote apocalyptic literature that helps us understand what to expect in the last days. We'll cover his dream interpretations, visions, prophecies, and apocalyptic literature in the next chapter: *Daniel's Visions & Interpretations*.

Chapter Twelve

Daniel's Visions & Interpretations

Like Joseph during his time in Egypt, Daniel gained incredible favor and wealth while exiled to Babylon. He was wise and faithful. Through him, God interpreted dreams for King Nebuchadnezzar and gave apocalyptic views of the future. The other prophets before and after Daniel wrote many near-far prophecies that passed on God's admonishments and often ended in an apocalyptic tone, but didn't include as much detail or historical context.

What set apart Daniel's interpretations of the dreams and his apocalyptic visions from the prophecies of his counterparts is the historical context and precise timing of events. The rebuilding of Jerusalem and Christ's death and resurrection are but two examples. Daniel's revelations also give us insight into the timing of the Antichrist's authority and the Lord Jesus Christ's kingdom that will come after his defeat.

Our approach to learning Daniel's writings will be different from how we've tackled the other subjects thus far. Instead of presenting a concept and quoting Scripture references, I'll suggest you read certain passages we'll then summarize in these sections:

- Part I: Chapters 2 & 4 (Nebuchadnezzar's dreams and God's granting of authority).
- Part II: Chapters 7 & 8 (The Antichrist and a type/shadow of the coming Antichrist).
- Part III: Chapters 9, 11, & 12 (Timing and historical context from Greece until the end).

Each part will begin with a RECOMMENDED READING and then proceed with verse and chapter summaries. You'll notice that I haven't listed every chapter in the book of Daniel, leaving out 1, 3, 5, 6, and 10. Why? To allow us to focus on those that apply specifically to our study of the future. This doesn't mean you shouldn't read the others. In fact, I encourage you to look them over as you have time. But don't worry – I'll quote from the non-included chapters or summarize points from them as necessary.

Finally, I found the following resource to be invaluable during the creation of this chapter: *The New American Commentary, Volume 18: Daniel* by Stephen R. Miller. Anyone wishing to do additional reading on this subject should consider it along with *The New Complete Works of Josephus* – especially for the historical value.

PART I: CHAPTERS 2 & 4

RECOMMENDED READING:

1. Daniel 2 and 4
2. Review *Babylon Rule* under Chapter Five of this guide

Chapters 2 and 4 contain two of King Nebuchadnezzar's dreams and interpretations by Daniel, a young exile from Jerusalem. The first was of a statue symbolic of the next four major kingdoms (to include his own), and the dream in chapter 4 regarded the kingdom and a warning to the king to change his ways or suffer the consequences.

~ DANIEL CHAPTER 2 ~

This is where we first see four major kingdoms that would come before the end: Babylonian, Mede/Persian, Greek, and Roman. From an interpretation Daniel gave of the king's dream in this chapter, we learn that the final (Antichrist's) kingdom will be related to the Roman Empire.

2:1-30. Nebuchadnezzar had a dream that bothered him, and he wanted an interpretation. The king threatened the wise men, magicians, and Chaldeans with death if they didn't tell him the dream and then interpret it. When confronted by Arioch (the captain of the king's guard) in an attempt to carry out the king's order to kill all the wise men, Daniel interpreted the dream after God also showed him the dream itself. One very significant thing to point out: Daniel had so much faith that God would show him the dream and interpretation that he agreed to tell them to the king and *then* sought after God to receive the information.

2:31-43. The dream was of a great statue with a head of gold, arms and breastplate of silver, belly and thighs of bronze, legs of iron, and feet/toes of iron mixed with clay. This statue is significant, as the head, arms/breastplate, belly/thighs, and legs represented what would become the next four major *beast* kingdoms—those empires involved with conquest and persecution of the Israelites. We'll study them later, but here are the kingdoms revealed in the interpretation of the dream:

- Head of **gold**: Nebuchadnezzar's Babylonian Empire
- Arms and breastplate of **silver**: Mede/Persian Empire
- Belly and thighs of **bronze**: Greek Empire
- Legs of **iron**: Roman Empire
- Feet of **iron and clay**: Latter-days divided empire (Antichrist's kingdom)

2:44-45. The "*stone cut out of the mountain without hands*" (verse 45) represents Christ. This passage reminds us of His coming kingdom that will last forever.

2:46-49: King Nebuchadnezzar paid homage to Daniel and to God. You'll discover this was the first of several times the king did this until he finally realized the greatness of God and that He grants all authority and can therefore take it away (chapter 4). Shadrach, Meshach, and Abed-nego were placed over the administration of the province of Babylon. Chapter 1 introduced Daniel and these three fellow exiles, and chapter 3 tells of how Daniel's friends were rescued from a fiery furnace without being burned. The account ends with King Nebuchadnezzar again acknowledging the greatness of God.

~ DANIEL CHAPTER 4 ~

In this chapter, you'll learn that King Nebuchadnezzar *finally* realized that God grants all authority and can therefore remove it. Here, the king tells the world of how God showed him through a dream that his authority would be taken away unless he humbled himself. This indeed happened a year later until Nebuchadnezzar came to his senses after seven years and acknowledged that he was in authority only because God allowed it.

4:1-9. King Nebuchadnezzar's introduction explaining how he had a dream he believed could only be revealed and interpreted by Daniel (just like we read in chapter 2).

4:10-18. King Nebuchadnezzar's dream: A great tree grew toward heaven, and it sheltered and fed the animals and all inhabitants of the king's world. An angel ordered it to be cut down, leaving the stump with a band of iron and bronze. He also revealed this about Nebuchadnezzar's future: ". . . *And let him be drenched with the dew of heaven, And let him share with the beasts in the grass of the earth. Let his mind be changed from that of a man And let a beast's mind be given to him, And let seven periods of time pass over him*" —Daniel 4:15-16. The dream ended with the angel exclaiming that the outcome revealed by the dream would show the living that God rules over mankind and gives authority to whomever He wishes.

4:19-27. Interpretation of the king's dream: The tree represented the Babylonian Empire, which would be "cut down" by future kingdoms to include those of Greece and Rome. I believe these are represented by the band of iron and bronze – metals used in the statue the king dreamed about earlier (chapter 2). We'll learn later why these metals represent Greece and Rome. The protection of the band and act of leaving the roots intact and in the ground most likely depicted the return of Nebuchadnezzar's kingdom to him after a time (seven years).

The interpretation continued with Daniel warning the king that, if he didn't change his ways, God would drive him from men and make him like a wild animal for seven years.

4:28-37. How quickly we tend to forget! After 12 months (while Nebuchadnezzar was admiring *his* handiwork) God fulfilled the prophecy by driving him into the wild until the seven years were done and his senses returned. The king then acknowledged and praised the one true God. How do we know the seven periods referenced in verses 16 and 32 are representative of seven years? The Chaldean word *iddan* (Strong's H5732), defined as "technically a year," is used for "period." Therefore, seven of these *periods* equal seven years.

Part II: Chapters 7 & 8

RECOMMENDED READING:

1. Daniel 7
2. Revelation 13:1-10

As with Nebuchadnezzar's dreams in chapters 2 and 4, Daniel's visions of chapters 7 and 8 were received during the reign of the Babylonian Empire. The first one, in chapter 7, unveils the Antichrist, his rise to power, his three-and-a-half-year authority, and his defeat. Of particular note is the end-times beast/kingdom made up of the geographical areas each of the first four kingdoms of Nebuchadnezzar's statue comprises. Daniel's vision of chapter 8 foretells of a *type* of Antichrist that would come first – Antiochus Epiphanes.

~ Daniel Chapter 7 ~

This chapter is devoted to a vision Daniel had of the Antichrist and his kingdom. The main things to understand and remember from your reading:

1. The Antichrist's kingdom will comprise the regions conquered

by the first four beasts/ kingdoms in succession from Daniel's time: Babylonian, Mede-Persian, Greek, and Roman.

2. The Antichrist's kingdom of the future will be related to the ancient Roman Empire (see *The Antichrist: Rise to Power* in Chapter Eight of this guide).
3. The Antichrist will subdue three rulers before heading the eight-leader end-times kingdom (see *The Antichrist: Rise to Power* in Chapter Eight of this guide).
4. Christ and the saints will triumph over the Antichrist at the end of his three-and-a-half -year authority.

7:1-3. Daniel envisioned four beasts coming out of the *sea*. Scripture references like Isaiah 17:12-13 help us understand that *sea* depicts *many peoples* or *nations*. This is confirmed later by Daniel in verse 17 when he refers to the earth as the source of this kingdom.

7:4. The beast like a lion with eagle's wings signified Nebuchadnezzar's kingdom. Winged lion carvings and statues, pervasive throughout the kingdom, represented the Babylonian god Bel/Marduk.

7:5: This beast represented the shared Mede-Persian Empire. Showing the bear on one side most likely indicates the stronger of the two joint forces, the Persian Empire. This empire absorbed the three kingdoms of Babylon, Egypt, and Lydia, possibly represented by the eating of three ribs. It's also possible the ribs represent the three Persian kings between Cyrus II and Xerxes as previously discussed in Chapter Four of this guide. The devouring of flesh may refer to the killing necessary to overcome and absorb the empires.

7:6. The third beast represented the Greek Empire, which would conquer Persia and most Middle Eastern countries around 332 BCE. The *four heads* to which dominion was given depicted the four kingdoms the Greek Empire would be split into upon Alexander the Great's death: Seleucid, Macedonia/Greece, Ptolemy, and Pergamum.

7:7-8. The fourth beast symbolized a near-far prophecy, identifying the Roman Empire that would defeat the Greeks and then rule during Christ's time (the iron legs of Nebuchadnezzar's statue) and the related empire (ten toes of the statue) that Christ will crush in the end (verses 9-12). The latter will be headed initially by ten leaders, but from them another ruler will rise and violently overthrow three of the ten. This is the only major event that must still take place before a peace agreement starting the 70th week of Daniel is reached. This beast that will comprise all geography conquered by the Babylonian, Mede-Persian, Greek, and Roman Empires also appeared in the Revelation Christ gave to John (cf. Revelation 13:1-10).

7:9-12. These passages reflect the future defeat of the Antichrist and his armies by Christ. This can only be the battle of Armageddon and subsequent throwing of the Antichrist into the *lake of fire*. Of interesting note is the reiteration of the Antichrist's "*boasting*" (review 2 Thessalonians 2:3-4; also see Revelation 19:17-21 for John's view of the Antichrist's defeat).

7:13-18. Daniel is told that the four beasts will be four kingdoms that come from the earth before the end. We see an unveiling of Christ's kingdom, which will rule over all nations and people.

7:19-22. Again, this fourth kingdom is a near-far prophecy concerning the Roman Empire and future related kingdom of the Antichrist. Stressed here is the rise of the Antichrist to power through the overthrow of three rulers of a ten-member association. This passage also reminds us that the Antichrist will persecute and kill the saints until Christ defeats him and his kingdom. Revelation 13:6-7 corroborates this.

7:23-26. This is yet another view of the Antichrist's rise to power and kingdom (similar to verses 19-22 above). Revelation 13:5 corroborates a three-and-a-half-year authority over God's people. That Scripture and Daniel 7:25 help us understand that *times, time, and half time* and *42 months* are the same length of time and the same period.

7:27-28: Christ's kingdom will be the last and will rule over all people. The dream troubled Daniel, who kept the vision to himself.

~ DANIEL CHAPTER 8 ~

RECOMMENDED READING:

1. Daniel 8
2. Review *Mede-Persian* rule under Chapter Five of this guide
3. Review *Greek Rule* under Chapter Five of this guide

Through a vision described here, Daniel saw the overthrow of the Persians by the Greeks and the destruction of Jerusalem by Antiochus Epiphanes – a *type* of Antichrist to come. Daniel revealed that there would be a cleansing period of 1,150 days (2,300 evenings and mornings) from the time Antiochus would end daily sacrifice until the practice was restored. That came to pass from 167 - 164 BCE as confirmed by the writings of Judah Maccabeus.

Some people believe this chapter is a continuation of information about the Antichrist prophesied in chapter 7. Others believe the opposite – that the dream in chapter 7 portrayed Antiochus Epiphanes, not the Antichrist. However, neither scenario is possible. Let's contrast the Antichrist *type*, Antiochus, and the future Antichrist to highlight their differences:

12.1 Comparison of Antiochus Epiphanes and the Antichrist

Event or Characteristic	Antichrist (Chapter 7)	Antiochus (Chapter 8)
Origin/Rise to Power	Will arise as a "little horn" (7:8) from a ten-member association and overthrow three of them.	Came up as a "little horn" (8:9) from within the ranks of one of four divisions of the Greek Empire.
Geographical Location	Will be attacked *by* a king of the north (11:40).	*Was* a king of the north.
Changes Laws or Times	Will enter the temple and stop daily sacrifice until defeated by Christ.	Stopped daily sacrifice, which was reinstituted after a 1,150-day cleansing period.
Both Conclude End-time Periods	The end of God's wrath at the end of the establishment of Christ's kingdom.	The end of a period of indignation/wrath starting with the exile to Babylon[13]
Deceive Through Peace	Will deceive through a peace agreement (9:27).	Through peace and deceit (8:25).
Method of Destruction	Will be thrown into the lake of fire.	Died of bowel disease/ ulcers.
Disposition of Kingdom	Will be completely annihilated and replaced by Christ's kingdom.	Continued after Antiochus' death until being absorbed into the Roman Empire.

Although it should be apparent that Antiochus and the Antichrist identify two separate individuals, Satan will have influenced both. Exploring the similarities between all three will help understand this.

12.2 Comparison of Satan, Antiochus, and the Antichrist

Satan	Antichrist	Antiochus Epiphanes
Great boasts like, "*I will ascend above the heights of the clouds; I will make myself like the Most High.*" —Isaiah 14:14.	Great boasts (Daniel 7:8, 11, 20, & 25).	
Said, "*I will raise my throne above the stars of God, and I will sit on the mount of assembly in the recesses of the* ***north***." —Isaiah 14:13. Remember that the Antichrist will be a "king of the north."	Will display himself as God (2 Thessalonians 2:4).	Magnified himself to the level of God. (Daniel 8:8 & 11).
	Empowered by Satan (Revelation 13:2 & 2 Thessalonians 2:9).	Influenced by Satan (Daniel 8:24).
Will persecute (or influence the persecution of) a remnant of Israel and Christian believers during the 3.5-year authority of the Antichrist. —Revelation 12:13 & 17.	Will have authority to persecute and kill God's people (including Christian believers) for 3.5 years.	Killed tens-of-thousands of Jews during his nearly 7-year time of authority.

Now, on to a summary of the verses in chapter 8:

8:1-2. This vision occurred in the third year of the reign of the Regent of Babylon, Belshazzar, in 550 BCE. Daniel envisioned himself at the Ulai Canal in Susa, Elam. The country in his vision, Elam, was just east of Mesopotamia and covered southwestern Iran and a small part of southern Iraq.

8:3-4. The ram with two horns, the one greater which came up last, depicted the consolidated kingdom of the Medes and Persians (cf. Daniel 8:20). The Persian kingdom was the greater of the two powers, thus the greater horn which came up last. Together the two joint powers conquered to the west, north, and south from their initial location in the east (i.e. Persia).

8:5-8. Greece, headed by Alexander the Great and symbolized here by a goat, crushed Persia in 332 BCE during a swift campaign toward the east (compare with verse 21). Upon Alexander's death, the Greek Empire was divided into four parts: Seleucid, Macedonia/Greece, Ptolemy, and Pergamum.

8:9-10. The prophetic utterance "*a rather small horn which grew exceedingly great toward the south, toward the east, and toward the Beautiful Land*" refers to Antiochus Epiphanes, who destroyed Jerusalem after also trying to conquer Egypt beginning in 169 BC (also see verse 23). Verse 10 is most likely referring to the severe persecution of God's people at the hands of Antiochus Epiphanes starting in 169 BCE.[14]

8:11-12. Antiochus magnified himself as God and took away the daily sacrifice. He also desecrated the temple ("*the place of His sanctuary was thrown down*" in verse 11). Just as He'll do with the Antichrist, God gave authority over the Jews to Antiochus because of their sins (transgressions). Please compare this passage with Daniel 8:23-25.

8:13-14. When asked how long the daily sacrifice would be abolished, the messenger replied, "*For 2,300 evenings and mornings; then the holy place will be properly restored.*" This period stretched from 167 until December 164 BCE. This is assuming that 2,300 evenings and mornings equal 1,150 days since each Jewish day started with an evening and included the next morning (daytime). Some believe that the reference actually indicates 2,300 days and that the nearly seven-year period started in 170 BCE with the assassination of the Jewish priest Onias III and ended with the rededication of the temple in December 164 BCE.[15] Regardless, Daniel's prophecy materialized with the horror-filled reign of the ruler Antiochus Epiphanes and concluded with the rededication of the temple and return of daily sacrifice in December 164 BCE.

8:15-19. Daniel's heavenly messenger (Gabriel) is told to reveal the meaning of the vision.

8:20-22. This is where we learn that the ram spoken of in verses 3-4 represents the Mede-Persian Empire. We see here that the *shaggy goat* from verses 5-8 depicts Greece, under the command of Alexander, which would crush the Mede-Persian Empire. Verse 22 tells of Alexander's death and the dividing of his kingdom into quarters.

8:23-25. This passage describes Antiochus Epiphanes, his empowerment by Satan, and his persecution of God's people. Verse 25 hints at his deceit and shrewdness and pride. Apparently, Antiochus' coins were inscribed with *theos epiphanes*, which means "God manifest." His title, Epiphanes, even translates to "the illustrious one."[16] Finally, Antiochus' assault on God's people, His laws, and His holy temple fulfilled the portion of this prophecy in verse 25 which reads, "*He will even oppose the Prince of princes, but he will be broken without human agency*." The latter part of the verse tells us that Antiochus would die, but not at the hands of man in battle. He did in fact die in 163 BCE of "grief/ulcers" (bowel trouble) according to 1 Maccabeus 6:1-16.

8:26-27. Daniel is told to keep the vision a secret. He explains here that the revelation has left him exhausted and weak.

Part III: Chapters 9, 11, & 12

RECOMMENDED READING:

1. Daniel 9
2. Review *Term of Office* in Chapter Eight
3. Review *Covenant of Death* in Chapter Eight

~ DANIEL CHAPTER 9 ~

There's no other place in Scripture where you'll find as much detail about prophetic and apocalyptic timing as you will in this chapter. Daniel's vision here gives specific timing with regard to Christ's first visitation and the time of the end and all that will be accomplished by then.

Important things to take away from this chapter:

1. A total of 490 years (70 weeks of years) were declared to bring an end to sin for the Jewish people and bring in everlasting righteousness, possible only after Christ's return and the establishment of His kingdom.
2. 483 of those years (69 weeks of years) passed from the decree to rebuild Jerusalem until Christ (most likely His baptism by John).
3. Afterward, the people the Antichrist will eventually come from destroyed the city of Jerusalem and the temple in 70 CE.
4. The last seven-year period (the 70th week of years) will start with an agreement between the Antichrist and at least Israel.
5. The antichrist will enter the temple after three and a half years, ending daily sacrifice and creating an abomination until destroyed by Christ.

9:1-2. In 539 BCE (the first year of the reign of Darius, son of Ahasuerus), Daniel realized that the 70-year captivity of Judah beginning in 605 BCE should end soon as prophesied by Jeremiah (cf. Jeremiah 25:11-12 & 29:10). He would've been about 80 years old by this time.

9:3-23. Daniel prayed for his people, repenting for the ways of the Israelites and asking God to have mercy on them and end His wrath. During one of Daniel's prayers, the angel Gabriel visited him and said he'd give insight and understanding in answer to his prayers.

9:24. Seventy weeks (of years) – or 490 years total – (see Strong's H7620 below) had been established for Daniel's people (and for Jerusalem) to do several things:

- Finish the transgression.
- Make an end of sin.
- Make atonement for iniquity.
- Bring in everlasting righteousness.
- Seal up vision and prophecy.
- Anoint the Most Holy. (Note: The word "place" was added later by an interpreter (Most Holy *Place*), but doing so changes the meaning significantly; the word "place" should probably be left out).

  H7620 shâbûaʻ shâbûaʻ shebûʻâh (shaw-boo'-ah, shaw-boo'-ah, sheb-oo-aw') Literally sevened, that is, **a week (specifically of years)**: - seven, week.

There's been much debate over the meaning of verse 24. Therefore, two major questions should be answered at this point:

1. Are the "sevens" days or years?
2. When will the "70 sevens" end?

In response to the first question, most scholars accept that a "seven" here depicts a "week of years." The definition seems to support this interpretation. Hebrews of the time would've been very familiar with the concept of either seven years (as in the Sabbatical year) or days. However, using a day instead of year in this context wouldn't work (i.e. 490 days would get us to no significant point in time and wouldn't allow the fulfilling of prophecy). Like most others in this case, I accept the definition of a "week of years."

When will the 490-year period (70 weeks of years) end? Most of the six requirements above (e.g. finish the transgression, bring in everlasting righteousness, and anoint the Most Holy) will only be possible once Christ appears for the second time and gains His kingdom (cf. Revelation 10:7 & 11:15). One could argue that the third goal, *make atonement for iniquity*, was fulfilled when Christ was crucified and became the ultimate sacrifice for mankind. That would be fine – these six very important things necessary for Israel's redemption have been, or will be, done within the 490-year period.

One issue that has spawned differences in opinion about the timing of Christ's return is this: how to consider the 490-year timeframe. Should it be taken sequentially, or did the clock stop at year 483 BCE not to restart again until the peace agreement at the end?

This couldn't be a contiguous 490-year timeframe if it started in 458 BCE and won't end until Christ gains His kingdom, which hasn't happened yet. If so, 490 years from 458 BCE would earmark 33 CE, which is just past the time of Christ's crucifixion. Verse 25 reveals that the peace agreement will start the last *week*, which couldn't happen until well after the "*people of the prince to come*" would destroy Jerusalem in 70 CE. The first 69 weeks of years ended before that with the crucifixion of Christ as you'll see in the next verse.

9:25. Seven of the seven-year periods (49 years) and then another 62 weeks of years (434 years) –483 years total – would pass from the time the decree to rebuild Jerusalem was issued until *Messiah the Prince* would come and then be killed. Consequently, 483 years passed from when the decree to rebuild the city was issued in 458 BCE until Jesus was baptized and began His ministry. The first "7 sevens," or 49-year period, extended from the decree until the work was done in roughly 409 BCE. The second period of "62 sevens," or 434 years, stretched from that time until Christ.

A slightly different but popular school of thought is that the 483-year timeframe started instead with the decree to Nehemiah in

445 BCE and not with the one to Ezra in 458 BCE. While the decree in 445 fits the requirement, the end-date would be after the crucifixion of Christ and therefore doesn't fit the prophecy.[17]

Regardless, *a* decree was issued 483 years before the latter part of Christ's life as Daniel prophesied, and the city was rebuilt during troublesome times as shown in Nehemiah 4. The following is an excerpt from that passage:

> *So we carried on the work with half of them holding spears from dawn until the stars appeared. At that time I also said to the people, "Let each man with his servant spend the night within Jerusalem so that they may be a guard for us by night and a laborer by day." So neither I, my brothers, my servants, nor the men of the guard who followed me, none of us removed our clothes, each took his weapon even to the water.* —Nehemiah 4:21-23.

9:26a. "*Then after the sixty-two weeks the Messiah will be cut off and have nothing . . .*" Once the first period of 49 years (*7 weeks*) and then the second period of 434 years (*62 weeks*) have passed, the Messiah would be "*cut off and have nothing.*" The original Hebrew word for "*cut off*" is kârath, Strong's H3772. It suggests destruction or death as in Jeremiah 9:21 and 11:19. The rest of the passage "*. . . and have nothing*" is represented by the Hebrew word *'ayin* (Stong's H369). Basically, the word means to "be non-existent." Several theories about what this means include the possibility that Daniel was referring to the fact that the Jews despised and rejected Jesus. The simplest explanation is that Daniel was revealing that the Messiah would be killed (cut off) and then wouldn't exist on the earth after the resurrection and ascension into heaven. This is the view I hold.

9:26b. "*. . . and the **people** of the prince who is to come will destroy the city and the sanctuary.*" As discussed in the topic of *Rise to Power* in Chapter Eight of this guide, people of the Roman Empire destroyed the city of Jerusalem and the temple in 70 CE. The reference to *prince* – or *principality* – in verse 26 may be a depiction of the spirit influencing the kingdom leader. This is certainly the case where, in the next chapter, the angel speaking to Daniel mentions being detained by the "*prince of Persia*" (cf. Daniel 10:14). In Daniel 10:20, the angel continues by telling him about having to fight the "*prince of Persia*" and of the next *prince*, the authority of the Greek kingdom.

9:26c. "*And its end will come with a flood; even to the end there will be war; desolations are determined.*" Roman forces under control of Titus Flavius Vespasianus indeed swept through Jerusalem like a flood and destroyed the city and temple. Jewish rebellions against the eastern forces of Rome continued until the middle of the second century CE.

9:27a. "*And* ***he*** *will make a firm covenant with the many for one week [of years], but in the middle of the week [of years]* ***he*** *will put a stop to sacrifice and grain offering . . .*" Our earlier training on antecedents will come in handy here as we decide who *he* above is referring to. The last noun before the "*he*" is the "*prince*" from the previous verse, who'll come from the people who destroyed Jerusalem and the temple in 70 CE. We know that forces under Roman control destroyed the temple, and that many if not most were of Middle Eastern descent. Remember too that Ezekiel showed us that the end-times kingdom will be made up of Middle Eastern countries that surround Israel. Bottom-line: This verse most likely tells us that someone from the Middle East will establish a seven-year agreement with Israel and then dishonor it after three and a half years, abolishing daily sacrifice at that time.

9:27b. "*. . . and on the* ***wing of abominations*** *will come one who makes* ***desolate*** *. . .*" This difficult passage uses the Hebrew words *kânâ* (Strong's H3671) for "*wing*" and *shiqqûts* (Strong's H8251) for "*abominations*." Together they symbolize the overspreading of filthy *idolatry*, most likely representing Israel's deception by the Antichrist and its entering into the *covenant of death*. Jesus and Paul tell us that this *abomination of desolation* will also set himself up in the temple, and Jesus lets us know this will happen at the start of the Great Tribulation (cf. Matthew 24:15-28 & 2 Thessalonians 2:4). The Hebrew word for "*desolate*" is *shâmêm*, which has several definitions that include "to stun," "make amazed," and "devastate." We know the passage is referring to the coming Antichrist, so this Scripture comes to mind: "*. . . and they worshiped the beast, saying, 'Who is like the beast, and who is able to wage war with him?'*" —Revelation 13:4.

9:27c. "*. . . even until a complete* ***destruction****, one that is* ***decreed****, is poured out on the one who makes* ***desolate***." The rest of 9:27 shows us that the one who comes on the "*wing of abominations*" (i.e. the Antichrist) will be destroyed as decreed (cf. Daniel 7:25-26).

12.3 Israel's 490-year Redemption Plan

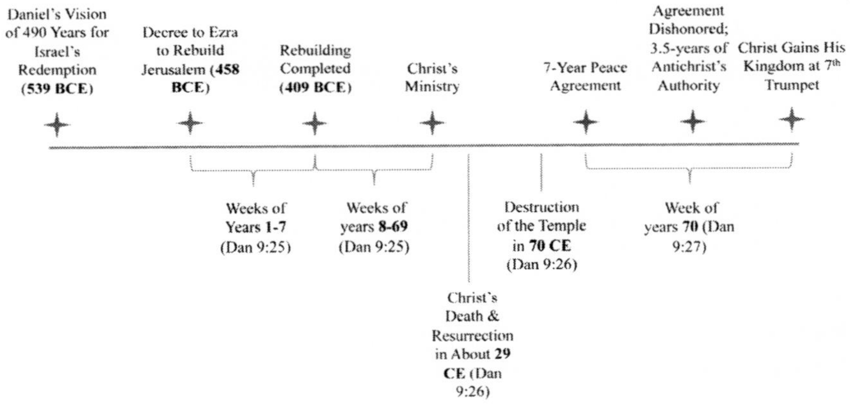

~ DANIEL CHAPTERS 11 & 12 ~

RECOMMENDED READING: Daniel 11 and 12

Although we won't cover Daniel 10 in detail, chapters 10 – 12 really go together and the vision contained in them supports a single theme: a panoramic view of the rise of the Antichrist *type*, Antiochus Epiphanes, to the rise of the actual Antichrist and his time of authority. The setting is Palestine, the geographical focal point for Antiochus *and* the Antichrist.

Chapter 10 is a recollection of the visitation by Gabriel to deliver the end-times message. The vision outlined in chapters 11 and 12 chronicles the major events leading to the rise and defeat of Antiochus, and the time of the end to include the Antichrist's great time of tribulation. As with chapter 9, I found *The New American Commentary – Volume 18* (Daniel) by Stephen R. Miller to be invaluable to writing about the historical fulfillment of the prophecies given in chapter 11. Many of these historical facts can be confirmed by sources like the writings of Judah Maccabeus and historian Flavius Josephus. I highly recommend Miller's book, Maccabeus' writings, and the *Complete Writings of Flavius Josephus* (at least *The Jewish Wars*) to anyone wishing to do a more in-depth study of the book of Daniel. Nearly all historical information in our summary of Daniel chapter 11 has come from Miller's book.

For ease of understanding, we'll divide chapters 11 and 12 into the following digestible portions:

1. Introduction and prophecies leading *up to* Antiochus Epiphanes (cf. **11:1-20**).
2. Prophecies concerning Antiochus IV Epiphanes (cf. **11:21-35**).
3. Prophecies concerning the end times to include the Antichrist and great time of tribulation (cf. **11:36** through **12:3**).
4. The remainder of the message as depicted by **12:4** through **12:13**.

1. Introduction and prophecies leading up to Antiochus Epiphanes (11:1-20).

11:1. Gabriel tells Daniel that he had come two years earlier to comfort and protect the king of Persia in the first year of his reign. Gabriel makes it clear in verses 10:13 and 10:20 that evil principalities (demons) influence rulers and that spiritual battles do take place.

> *But the prince of the kingdom of Persia was withstanding me for twenty-one days; then behold,* ***Michael, one of the chief princes****, came to help me, for I had been left there with the kings of Persia.* —Daniel 10:13.

> *Then he said, "Do you understand why I came to you? But I shall now return to fight against the* ***prince of Persia****; so I am going forth, and behold, the* ***prince of Greece*** *is about to come."* —Daniel 10:20.

11:2. Four more kings would arise in Persia after Cyrus II; the fourth would wage war against Greece. The three kings to rule after Cyrus, but before the fourth, were (refer to figure 5.13) Cambyses, Smerdis, and Darius I Hystapses. Xerxes was the fourth – known for his wealth and expedition against the king of Greece as prophesied by Daniel.

11:3-4. The "*mighty king*" of verse 3 was Alexander, who came to power in 336 BCE. As unveiled in verse 4, his kingdom was divided into four parts after his death in 323 BCE (see also Daniel 7:6 & 8:5-8).

11:5. Highlights Ptolemy I Soter – ruler of Egypt. The commander who would "*gain ascendancy*" over Ptolemy I was Seleucus I Nicator, who ended up controlling the largest portion of the Greek kingdom. It included Babylonia, Syria, and Media. Thus the Seleucid era, out of which Antiochus Epiphanes came, began.

11:6. Foretells of clashes between the Ptolemies (Egypt) and Seleucids (Syria) until a peace agreement was established through the marriage of Berenice, the daughter of Ptolemy (king of the south), to Antiochus II Theos (king of the north).

11:7-9. In retaliation for his sister's murder, the king of the south (Ptolemy III) attacked and plundered Syria. A peace agreement between Egypt and Syria in 240 BCE allowed the fighting to stop and Ptolemy to pursue other interests.

11:10-12. The sons of Seleucus II (Selecus III and Antiochus III the Great) carried on the wars with Egypt. Antiochus III eventually launched a great campaign countered by Ptolemy IV Philopator. Both armies consisted of tens of thousands of troops. At the end of the battle in 217 BCE, Ptolemy (Egypt – king of the south) had won a great victory, but his supremacy would be short-lived.

11:13-14. Antiochus III regained superiority over Egypt. Jews aiding Antiochus ("*violent ones from among your people . . .*") eventually "*fell down*" (cf. verse 14) when the leaders of Jerusalem and Judah who had rebelled were punished by Egyptian leader General Scopas.

11:15-17. Antiochus "the invader" defeated General Scopas at Sidon in 198 BCE. This gave Syria complete control over Phoenicia and Palestine, the *Beautiful Land*. To seal a peace agreement, Antiochus gave Cleopatra to Ptolemy V to become his wife. Cleopatra's love for her husband kept Antiochus from realizing a plan to completely control Egypt.

11:18-19. Antiochus and his Syrian army were eventually overcome by Romans led by Lucius Scipio and Greek allies at Thermopylae and then defeated at the battle of Magnesia (Turkey) in 190 BCE. An angry mob killed Antiochus upon his return home after he attempted to pillage the temple of Zeus at Elymais in search of funds.

11:20. Antiochus' successor was Selucus IV Philopator, who died after a short reign by poisoning at the hands of his tax collector and prime minister. Apparently, his attempts to raise funds included an attempt to raid the temple in Jerusalem.

2. **Prophecies concerning Antiochus IV Epiphanes (11:21-35).**

11:21. Upon Selucus' death, the throne was seized by Antiochus IV Epiphanes – "*a despicable person.*" He earned this title because of the severe persecution and slaughter of the Jewish people, and the desecration of God's temple.

11:22-24. The Syrians, under control of Antiochus IV, squashed an attempt by Ptolemy VI Philometor to regain territories in 169 BCE as Antiochus came to power. Ptolemy is the "*prince of the covenant*" because of the agreement he made with Antiochus in order to collaborate in the regaining of his throne. Ptolemy broke the agreement. Antiochus retaliated without warning during a "*time of tranquility*" and plundered the Egyptian treasures. Apparently, Antiochus dispersed his spoils amongst his followers.

11:25-26. This passage refers to Antiochus' campaign against Egypt in 169 BCE (cf. 11:22-24).

11:27. Ptolemy VI, who lost his throne while imprisoned, and Antiochus tried unsuccessfully to regain the Egyptian throne from Ptolemy VII despite the collaboration between the two. The two Ptolemies ended up sharing the throne.

11:28. Antiochus IV put down a rebellion in Palestine on his way home after plundering Egypt (cf. 11:22-26). He massacred as many as 80,000 Jewish men, women, and children in the process and looted the temple with the help of Menelaus, the high priest.

11:29. Antiochus again returned to Egypt in 168 BCE. However, he was unsuccessful in his invasion attempt.

11:30a. "*For ships of Kittim will come against him; therefore he will be disheartened and will return . . .*" The Roman fleet from Cyprus (ancient Kittim) came to Alexandria and stopped Antiochus with the threat of war. Humiliated, he retreated.

11:30b. "*. . . and become enraged at the holy covenant and take action; so he will come back and show regard for those* *who forsake the holy covenant.*" This passage through verse 35 foretells of what would be another fierce encounter with the Jews. Here, Antiochus is taking his anger out on God's people and showing favor to those who forsook God and His covenant. This sets the stage for a changing of the law and times.

11:31. Antiochus forbade the Jews to honor the Law of the covenant and partake in related practices (i.e. daily sacrifice, circumcision, feasts, etc.) under penalty of death if they disobeyed. The setting up of the *abomination of desolation* in the temple probably foretold of the erection of an altar dedicated to Zeus in December 167 BCE. Antiochus also offered sacrifices of swine on the temple altar in December of that year as indicated in the writings of Judah Maccabeus.

11:32-33. Many of the Jews would be fooled and deceived by flattery, forsaking their God and His ways. Others would stand their ground and fight back. The priest Mattathias and three of his sons were in this group and would later become known as the Maccabees (the name Maccabeus means "*hammer*" and was originally given to Judah, one of the three sons). Those with insight may include teachers of the Law, but the point here is that those not deceived suffered significantly during the revolt against Antiochus and the Syrian forces.

11:34-35. Many would have been helped by the forces initially fighting back against the Syrians. Some joined the forces, but out of necessity to avoid punishment that awaited Antiochus' collaborators. This time, as rough as it was, would've purified the Jews by ridding Israel of sinful practices and strengthening the faith of God's people. This passage concludes with a statement that suggests this era, while coming to a close, wouldn't be the end of *the* age.

3. **Prophecies concerning the end times to include the Antichrist and time of great tribulation (11:36 through 12:3).**

11:36. This verse picks up where Antiochus IV Epiphanes left off and marks the beginning of the end. Here we're reminded that *the* Antichrist will exalt himself above God and speak blasphemies against Him until destroyed (cf. 7:8, 11, & 20. 25; 2 Thessalonians 2:4; Revelation 13:5-6).

11:37-39. The Antichrist won't honor any God (an atheistic position) but will instead demand worship *as* God (see the references above). "*But instead he will honor a god of fortresses*" most likely refers to his military might and trust in weapons of war. We know he won't acknowledge a deity and will be a great military power: "*. . . and they worshiped the beast, saying, 'Who is like the beast, and who is able to wage war with him?'*" —Revelation 13:4. Those who'll give allegiance to the Antichrist will be greatly rewarded (i.e. with the ability to buy and sell).

11:40. The "king of the north" is either the Antichrist, which is unlikely, or ruler of a kingdom to the north of Palestine that will come against the Antichrist near the end of time. There's not enough information to determine which countries north and south of Israel are being referenced here, but it might be worthwhile to consider the countries listed in figure 8.1. The Antichrist will apparently overcome them and many other countries at this time.

11:41. He'll enter Palestine and continue his rampage. Edom, Moab, and Ammon (modern-day Jordan) will remain untouched. It's hard to say why, but most likely because this area will be an ally.

11:42-43. Egypt will be one of many countries that won't escape him. He'll plunder Egypt with Libya and Ethiopia (ancient Cush) as his companions. "*. . . at his heels*" (cf. 11:43) is represented by the Hebrew word *mits'âd* (Strong's H4703), which translates to "companionship; in step." The fact that Libya and Ethiopia will be associated with the Antichrist should come as no surprise based on what Ezekiel wrote (cf. 38:2-6).

11:44. Rulers in the east and in the north will most likely oppose the Antichrist's kingdom. His response will be to destroy with great wrath.

11:45. The Antichrist will set up his headquarters in Jerusalem at Mount Zion (the *Holy Mountain*), probably in the temple (cf. Matthew 24:15 & 2 Thessalonians 2:4). *"Between the seas"* probably depicts Jerusalem, which is between the Mediterranean and Dead Sea – the location of Mount Zion. Daniel revealed in 9:27 that the Antichrist will dishonor a seven-year agreement by entering the temple, stopping daily sacrifice, etc., as also confirmed by Jesus (cf. Daniel 9:27 & Matthew 24:15). So the timing of this verse is probably midway through the seven-year agreement. This is important because it sets the stage for the next verse, 12:1a, where we'll see the start of the Great Tribulation. This time of distress – or the Antichrist's authority – will last for three and a half years (the second half of the seven-year agreement period).

12:1a. "*Now at that time Michael, the great prince who stands guard over the sons of your people, will arise.*" We know from 10:13 that Michael is one of the *chief princes* (archangels). Here we learn that he is the chief principality who has been given the special job of watching over Israel. Why must he leave his post at this point, which is probably midway through Daniel's 70th week of years (in the middle of the "peace agreement")?

> Revelation 12 reveals the answer: Michael must leave to fight against Satan and his forces in heaven at the start of the three-and-a-half-year protection of a remnant of Israel (the woman), which also earmarks the beginning of the Great Tribulation as you'll learn in verse 12:1b.
>
> > *Then the woman fled into the wilderness where she had a place prepared by God, so that there she would be nourished for* ***one thousand two hundred and sixty days****.* ***And there was war in heaven, Michael and***

> ***his angels waging war with the dragon****. The dragon and his angels waged war, and they were not strong enough, and there was no longer a place found for them in heaven. And the great dragon was thrown down, the serpent of old who is called the devil and Satan, who deceives the whole world; he was thrown down to the earth, and his angels were thrown down with him.* —Revelation 12:6-9.

12:1b. "*And there will be a time of distress such as never occurred since there was a nation until that time;*" The war between Michael and Satan will end with the devil and his forces being thrown to the earth. Angered, Satan through the Antichrist will execute great wrath upon Israel and believers in Christ. As stated in Zechariah 13:8, two-thirds of the people of Israel will be wiped out during this time.

> *So* ***the dragon was enraged with the woman, and went off to make war with the rest of her children, who keep the commandments of God and hold to the testimony of Jesus****.* —Revelation 12:17.

> *Therefore when you see the* ***ABOMINATION OF DESOLATION*** *which was spoken of through Daniel the prophet,* ***standing in the holy place*** *(let the reader understand) . . . For then there will be a* ***great tribulation, such as has not occurred since the beginning of the world until now, nor ever will****.* —Matthew 24:15-21.

12:1b-2. "*. . . and at that time your people, everyone who is found* ***written in the book****, will be* ***rescued****. Many of those who sleep in the dust of the ground will* ***awake, these to everlasting life****, but the others to disgrace and everlasting contempt.*" This passage is probably referring to the gathering of everyone who is a part of the bride of Christ at Christ's appearing following the Great Tribulation (cf. Matthew 24:29-31). Those not "awakened" at that time will be present at the great judgment of God after

Christ's 1,000-year reign (cf. Revelation 20:11-15). References to the Book of Life can be found in Psalm 69:28, Malachi 3:16, Luke 10:20, and Revelation 3:5 & 20:12.

12:2-3. Verse 3 honors the righteous and those who lead others to righteousness. My belief is that these are those *rescued* in verses 12:1b-2. Compare with Matthew 13:43.

4. **The remainder of the message including timeframe of the end.**

12:4. Daniel is told to seal up (preserve, as in Jeremiah 32:9-12) this prophecy. The meaning will become clear when the end draws near and knowledge (of the end) increases as people go about seeking it ("*. . . until the end of time; many will go back and forth, and knowledge will increase*").

12:5-6. Daniel sees two heavenly beings standing on each of the river's banks, and one asks Gabriel how long it will be until the ***end** of these wonders*. What *wonders*? He's referring to what we just read about: Michael arising, the Great Tribulation, and the rescuing of those whose names are in the Book of Life.

12:7. The "*man dressed in linen*" (Christ?) answered Daniel's question: "*. . . **time, times, and half a time**; and as soon as they finish shattering the power of the holy people, all these events will be completed.*" Daniel used the same terminology (*time, times, and half a time*) to refer to the authority of the Antichrist and persecution of the saints (cf. 7:25). Jesus referred to this period as a 42-month time of the nations (cf. Revelation 11:2). Both timeframes equal 1,260 days, also referenced in verse 11 below.

12:8-10. Daniel didn't understand the prophecy, which he's told to preserve *until the time of the end*. He is told many will be tried and purified; some will be wicked and won't understand the prophecy. He's also told that the wise will understand though. Gabriel continues by going into more detail about the timeframe in verse 11.

12:11a. "*From the time that the regular* ***sacrifice is abolished and the abomination of desolation is set up*** *. . .*" Earlier in the vision, Daniel was shown that the last seven-year period will begin with a covenant, and that the Antichrist will dishonor the agreement halfway into the period. One of his acts of defiance will be to stop daily sacrifice (cf. Daniel 9:27). So we can tell from this passage that whatever timeframe the speaker is about to reveal will start at this point – midway through the seven-year period of Daniel.

12:11b. "*. . . there will be 1,290 days.*" We already know that the tribulation period at the hands of the Antichrist will last for three and a half years. So why add an extra 30 days? Nothing in Scripture tells us definitively, but there are clues that suggest the time will be needed to execute the remainder of God's wrath (seven vial judgments).

> Remember that the 70th week of years will conclude the 490-year time for Israel to put an end to sin, anoint the Most Holy, bring in everlasting righteousness, etc. This conclusion will only be possible at Christ's return and the establishment of His kingdom. As a result, it's likely that the reign of the Antichrist and therefore the seven-year period will end there. Christ will gain His kingdom at the seventh trumpet judgment (cf. Revelation 11:15). But God's wrath won't be finished yet according to the Revelation (e.g. chapters 16-19). The seven vial judgments, which will come after the trumpet judgments (and therefore after the 1,260-day authority of the Antichrist), will include the battle of Armageddon and the destruction of both *Babylon* and the Antichrist. These are the events that will most likely take place during the 30-day period after the end of the 1,260-day authority of the Antichrist.

12:12. "*How blessed is he who keeps waiting and attains to the* ***1,335 days****!*" This verse reveals an additional 45-day period after the 1,290 days have passed. There's no indication in Scripture as to the purpose of this timeframe, but I suspect it will be needed for cleaning and purification following the aftermath of Armageddon. Perhaps it will be needed to prepare for the start of Christ's 1,000-year kingdom. Regardless of its purpose, it *will* occur as Daniel prophesied.

12:13. Daniel is told to go about his business, and that he'll rise again at the end of the age after *entering into rest*. This passage reminds us that the final resurrection and great judgment will conclude this age and usher in a new heaven and earth (cf. Revelation 20:11-15 & 21:1).

12.4 Timeline of Daniel Chapters 11-12

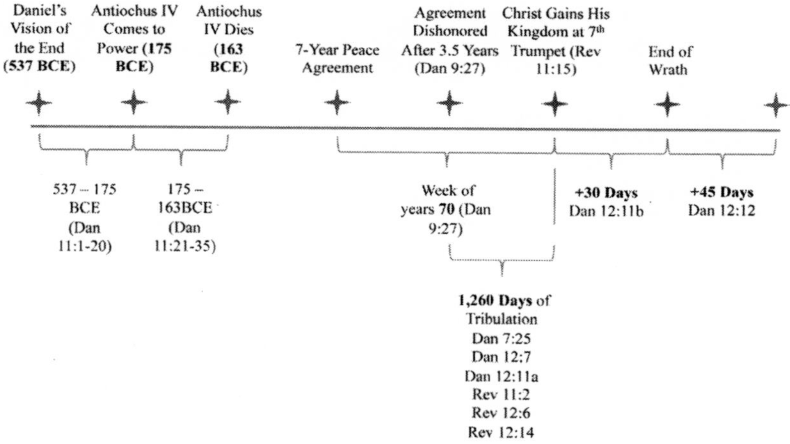

CHECKUP
CHAPTER TWELVE

The following questions are meant to check your understanding of what we've covered so far and provoke additional thoughts and questions to elevate your learning to a higher level. Answers to all questions can be found in Appendix D.

1. According to Daniel 2, what were the five parts of Nebuchadnezzar's statue? What empire does each part represent?

2. What is the "*stone cut out of the mountain without hand*" of Daniel 2:34 and 45?

3. List the three kingdoms depicted in Daniel 7:1-6.

4. Daniel 7:7-8 reveals a fourth beast that will come after the Greek Empire. Which empire does it represent in the near-term? In the far-term?

5. What is the theme of Daniel 7:23-26?

6. List at least three similarities between the Antichrist in chapter 7 and Antiochus Epiphanes in chapter 8.

7. When will the "70 sevens" of years foretold in Daniel 9:25 begin?

8. What two major events happened during the first 69 of Daniel's 70 weeks of years?

9. According to Daniel 9:27, what will kick off Daniel's 70th week of years? What will happen in the middle of it after three and a half years?

10. What will happen in last half of Daniel's 70th week (based on 11:45-12:2)?

11. Daniel 12:11 tells us of an event or action that will start the 1,260 days (3.5 years) + 30 days for a total of a 1,290-day period. What will it be?

12. Those who attain a certain number of days from the removing of the daily sacrifice will be blessed according to Daniel 12:12. What is that total number of days? Do we know what the last 45-day period during that time will be used for?

Chapter Thirteen

Other Old Testament Prophets

It's hard to believe, but God was showing prophets the final disposition of Israel (and of this world) before the nation was even 900 years old. That was nearly 3,000 years ago! What God revealed must've seemed strange to them. These prophets lived in troublesome times, and the oracles they received from God contained warnings of judgment against the Israel of their day while sometimes ending with a far-term prophecy or apocalyptic tone. This was certainly the case with Isaiah's messages.

I've gathered significant Old Testament prophecies and apocalyptic literature as revealed by the prophets in the following tables. A few others may have uttered prophecies related to the coming apocalypse, but we'll focus on those that have done so significantly with one exception: we've already covered Daniel's writings extensively, so we'll include him in the following table for reference only. You'll find a list of the prophets we'll highlight below along with the approximate timeframe of their prophecies and the empire in power during these times.

My recommendation is to preview the tables and choose a handful of chapters sporting topics that grab your interest, reading those in particular. Chapter numbers in **boldface** reflect likely near-far prophecies. All years are BCE.

13.1 Old Testament Prophets

Prophet	Approximate Timeframe as a Prophet	Kingdom Era
Joel	850	Assyrian
Amos	760	Assyrian
Isaiah	740-700	Assyrian
Micah	736-690	Assyrian
Zephaniah	640-621	Assyrian
Jeremiah	627-580	Assyrian / Babylonian
Daniel	605-530	Babylonian / Persian
Ezekiel	593-570	Babylonian
Obadiah	580	Babylonian
Zechariah	520-518	Babylonian / Persian

Joel (850 BCE): Prophecies of the son of Pethuel were few, but they revealed a lot about the end times – the Day of Lord wrath and subsequent dwelling of God in Jerusalem in particular. His words were echoed in the apocalyptic writings of Daniel (e.g. the Great Tribulation and the stopping of daily sacrifice) and in the Revelation given to John (e.g. the Day of the Lord destruction, darkening of the sun, moon, and stars, and the *winepress of the wrath of God*). Joel's prophecies came to light during the time of the Assyrian Empire – well before the Babylonians took many Hebrews captive in 605 BCE.

13.2 Joel's Apocalyptic Literature References

Chapter	Topics or Key Words Related to End-times Prophecy or the Apocalypse
1	The Great Tribulation Sacrifice/offering stopped Day of the Lord destruction

Chapter	Topics or Key Words Related to End-times Prophecy or the Apocalypse
2	Day of the Lord Darkness before the Day of the Lord Escape to Mount Zion and Jerusalem / kingdom of God
3	Gather nations to valley of Jehoshaphat for the battle of Armageddon Sickle / winepress of the wrath of God God dwelling in Zion

Amos (760 BCE): The context of Amos' prophecies was the reign of the Assyrian Empire. This sheepherder from Tekoa prophesied about the coming wrath of God, the fate of the tribe of Dan, and Christ's end-times kingdom. The information regarding the tribe of Dan is helpful because it sheds light on why that name was replaced by the name of Manasseh, one of Joseph's sons, in the list of those protected from God's wrath in Revelation 7.

13.3 Amos' Apocalyptic Literature References

Chapter	Topics or Key Words Related to End-times Prophecy or the Apocalypse
5	Day of the Lord – a day of darkness Exile beyond Damascus
8	Earthquake, famine, and mourning Darkness in the Day of the Lord Fate of the tribe of Dan
9	End-times destruction of Jerusalem, but not the annihilation of the people of Israel Christ's kingdom

Isaiah (740-700): As with Amos and Joel, Isaiah's prophecies came during the time of the Assyrian Empire. The son of Amoz wrote a lot about the end of the age. He referred to the Antichrist as "*the King of Assyria,*" "*the destroyer,*" and "*a cruel master.*" This isn't surprising considering the incredible hardships God's people faced at the hands of the Assyrians. There was probably no better icon to use in that day for the future Antichrist than the current king of Assyria. Isaiah penned many passages related to the Day of the Lord (wrath of God) and of Christ's kingdom; some of them were most likely near-far oracles.

13.4 Isaiah's Apocalyptic Literature References

Chapter	Topics or Key Words Related to End-times Prophecy or the Apocalypse
1	God's end-times wrath against Israel Israel's redemption at the end
2	Day of the Lord wrath Hiding in the rocks (compare 2:10, 2:19, and 2:21 with Revelation 6:16-17) Day of reckoning End-times kingdom on Mount Zion
3-4	Christ's kingdom after the wrath
10-12	Antichrist labeled as the *King of Assyria* Remnant of Israel in the last days God's work in Mount Zion and Jerusalem in the last days Christ's kingdom Destruction of the wicked by Christ
13	Day of the Lord wrath Darkening of sun, moon , and stars at the Day of the Lord Destruction of Babylon, never to be inhabited again
14	Antichrist labeled as the *King of Babylon* Lucifer; ascension to heaven/God (compare with Antichrist's description) Prophecy of Zion
15-16	Oracle for Moab (associated with the Antichrist) Christ from Sela to Zion (route of the 144,000 and woman?) Christ's kingdom Moab *degraded* within *three years*

Chapter	Topics or Key Words Related to End-times Prophecy or the Apocalypse
17-18	Oracle for Damascus Will look to Christ at the end Whirring wings from beyond *Cush* Feeding of flesh by birds (compare with Revelation 19:17-21)
19	Oracle for Egypt Egypt handed over to a *cruel master* (Antichrist) at the end Five cities with allegiance to God and Israel City of Destruction; Savior and champion Egypt and Assyria worship God
24	Day of the Lord Darkening before the Day of the Lord wrath Splitting of the earth at the end Reign of Christ
25-27	Kingdom of God and Christ Moab (Antichrist's kingdom) trodden down Great judgment (compare 26:19 to Daniel 12:1-2) Hide until indignation is done
28	Covenant with death (compare 28:15 and 28:18 to Daniel 9:27) Cornerstone in Zion (Christ and His kingdom)
29	War against Zion (Armageddon) Wrath of God Kingdom of Christ
30	Wrath of God Christ's kingdom
31	God's wrath *Assyrian* (Antichrist) will fall but not by the sword of man
33	Destroyer destroyed Kingdom of God/Christ
34	Sky rolled up like a scroll (compare Isaiah 34:4 to Revelation 6:14) Day of the Lord vengeance
35	Day of the Lord vengeance Ransomed of the Lord (Israel) return God's kingdom on Mount Zion
43	Return to Israel Babylon's fate
49	Israel's salvation

Chapter	Topics or Key Words Related to End-times Prophecy or the Apocalypse
51	Ransomed of the Lord (Israel) Everlasting joy in Zion
54	Israel's salvation
56	Return of the dispersed in the last days
59-62	Christ the redeemer at Mount Zion Salvation Judgment and wrath at the end
63	Winepress of wrath at the end (compare 63:3 with Revelation 14:19-20)
65	New heaven and earth
66	Christ Wrath of God Witness to **Tarshish**, **Put**, **Lud**, **Meshech**, **Tubal**, and **Javan** (Noah's grandsons, mostly of his son Japheth); part of the Antichrist's end-times kingdom Everlasting judgment against the wicked

Micah (736-690): The Moresheth, whose name translates to "*who is like Yahweh,*" also received his revelations from God during the time of the Assyrians. Most of Micah's writings contain warnings to *repent or else*.

13.5 Micah's Apocalyptic Literature References

Chapter	Topics or Key Words Related to End-times Prophecy or the Apocalypse
2	Remnant returning Lord as King
4-5	Israel's redemption The Antichrist labeled as *the Assyrian* Armageddon

Zephaniah (640-621): This son of Cushi painted a fairly complete picture of the return of the Jews and the wrath of God that will be realized in the last days. Like Isaiah and Micah, Zephaniah compared the Antichrist (or at least his kingdom) to Assyria. His reference to Jerusalem as the "*tyrannical city*" – one label for the New Testament figurative Babylon – should sound familiar based on our earlier study of the Antichrist in Chapter Eight of this guide.

13.6 Zephaniah's Apocalyptic Literature References

Chapter	Topics or Key Words Related to End-times Prophecy or the Apocalypse
1-3	Day of the Lord wrath / complete destruction / darkness Destruction of Assyria Jerusalem the *tyrannical city* Return of the dispersed to Israel at the end

Jeremiah (627-580): Priest and son of Hilkiah, this prophet was most likely also the author of the book of Lamentations in the Old Testament. His writings reflect a very common theme: Israel had committed spiritual adultery, and the harlot would suffer God's wrath through the Babylonian Empire and at His hand at the end of time.

13.7 Jeremiah's Apocalyptic Literature References

Chapter	Topics or Key Words Related to End-times Prophecy or the Apocalypse
3	God's people, the harlot, will return to Israel at the end
7	Dead bodies – food for birds (compare with Isaiah 18:6 and Revelation 19:17-21) Valley of Hinnom called the *Valley of Slaughter*
9	Coming wrath of the Lord

Chapter	Topics or Key Words Related to End-times Prophecy or the Apocalypse
23	The remnant will return at the end Christ's kingdom Spiritual adultery God's wrath
25	Israel's wickedness God's wrath (near-far)
30-31	Time of the Great Tribulation (Jacob's Trouble) Christ as king and the return of the remnant of Israel in the last days Israel's adultery God's end-times wrath
32-33	Christ's kingdom at the end God's mercy and the restoration of Israel

Ezekiel (593-570): We owe a lot to this prophet whose name means "*God will strengthen.*" Ezekiel was a priest and the son of Jeremiah "Buzi," who shouldn't be confused with the prophet Jeremiah. Ezekiel's visions and resulting revelations came during his exile to Babylon and give us a good view of God's end-times wrath and Israel's fate. Most significantly, they help us to understand the makeup of the Antichrist's kingdom as we've already discussed in Chapter Eight of this guide.

13.8 Ezekiel's Apocalyptic Literature References

Chapter	Topics or Key Words Related to End-times Prophecy or the Apocalypse
1-2	Four living creatures in heaven (compare to Revelation 4)
26-27	Destruction of Tyre; "I will bring you down to the pit" Fine merchandise (just as in the description of the great city in Revelation 17-18) Persia, Lud, and Put as part of the military power Javan, Meshech, Tarshish, Tubal, and Beth-Togarmah as traders and customers

Chapter	Topics or Key Words Related to End-times Prophecy or the Apocalypse
28	Arrogant king of Tyre; "I am a God" King of Tyre as Satan Reference to Satan in the Garden of Eden Wrath of God in the end times
30-31	Day of the Lord Destruction for Egypt, Ethiopia, Put, Lud, Arabia, and Libya Return of the remnant of Israel Salvation on Mount Zion
34	Christ's kingdom
37	Return of those dispersed at the end Christ's kingdom Covenant
38	Gog – Antichrist Antichrist's kingdom made up of Magog, Meshech, Tubal, Persia, Ethiopia, and Put Gomer and Beth-Togarmah Great earthquake at the end before the Antichrist's destruction God's wrath to include pestilence, blood, hail, fire, and brimstone

Obadiah: His name means "*servant of Yahweh*" and he wrote the shortest prophetic book in the Bible at just one chapter containing 21 verses. The fact that this is the shortest introduction is a mere coincidence.

13.9 Obadiah's Apocalyptic Literature References

Chapter	Topics or Key Words Related to End-times Prophecy or the Apocalypse
1	Day of the Lord wrath Escape to Mount Zion at the end

Zechariah: This prophet's name means "*the Lord has remembered.*" Zechariah prophesied during the time of Mede-Persian rule, and most of his writings were apocalyptic, revealing details about the return of the dispersed of Israel, the Antichrist, and the battle of Armageddon.

13.10 Zechariah's Apocalyptic Literature References

Chapter	Topics or Key Words Related to End-times Prophecy or the Apocalypse
1-3	Red and white horse Four horns Four craftsmen Zion as a place of escape at the end Kingdom of Christ and God Stone with seven eyes
8	Return of the remnant of Israel Kingdom of God
9	Christ as king riding on a donkey (first coming) Christ's kingdom (second coming)
10	Dispersion and return to Israel at the end Destruction of Assyria in the last days
12-13	Armageddon Two-thirds of the Jews will perish; one-third refined by fire (similar to Ezekiel 5:12) Christ's kingdom
14	Nations gathered against Israel by God at the end God will come with all His holy ones Standing on the Mount of Olives; the mount is split Horrible consequences for those who come against Israel Kingdom of God established

After considering the information contained in the tables above, you should've seen some common elements in the apocalyptic writings:

- Return of the remnant of Israel after being scattered by God.
- Different names for the Antichrist or his kingdom (cruel master, king of Assyria, Moab, etc.).

- The Antichrist's association with Satan.
- Darkening of the sun, moon, and stars at the Day of the Lord.
- Day of the Lord wrath of God at the end of time.
- Armageddon – the armies gathered against Israel and their destruction.
- Christ's kingdom.
- Salvation on Mount Zion.

In the next chapter, we'll move into the New Testament era and consider what Christ had to say about the end-times events surrounding His second coming.

Chapter Fourteen

Mounting Suspense

. . . They will see the SON OF MAN COMING ON THE CLOUDS OF THE SKY with power and great glory. And He will send forth His angels with A GREAT TRUMPET and THEY WILL GATHER TOGETHER His elect from the four winds, from one end of the sky to the other. —Matthew 24:30-31.

Without Christ and the promise of His appearing and our gathering, there'd be no hope and therefore no point in this study. So it stands to reason that we should pay very close attention to everything Jesus said – especially with regard to His return and the end of the age.

We can categorize what He said about the end and His return like this:

1. Statements Jesus made to His disciples while on earth. Our focus will be primarily on those made on the Mount of Olives.
2. Things He shared with Paul during and after his spectacular conversion on the road to Damascus.
3. Events revealed in the Revelation given to John.

We'll present a detailed breakdown of category #1 in Part One of this chapter. Part Two of this chapter will provide an introduction to the Revelation (category #3 above). In the next chapter, *Chapter Fifteen – Peter & Paul Weigh In*, we'll take a look at end-times Scripture written by Peter and Paul (category #2 above).

I've chosen this particular order of presentation because I believe it will be helpful to discuss the disclosures in the order in which they occurred. And even though we won't cover the Revelation until Chapter Seventeen, I've included an introduction to it here because Old Testament prophecies and Jesus' input while on earth are echoed in His later Revelation to John. My hope is that providing an introduction to Revelation in this chapter will show a clear relationship between those elements and whet your appetite for the coming overview in Chapter Sixteen.

Let's begin our New Testament journey with *Part I: Mount of Olives Discourse*.

PART I: MOUNT OF OLIVES DISCOURSE

RECOMMENDED READING:

- Matthew 24 and 25
- Mark 13
- Luke 21

One day, while walking through the temple structures, Jesus' disciples marveled at the buildings and pointed out their magnificence. In response, Jesus explained that a time would come when they'd be utterly destroyed and dismantled (cf. Matthew 24:1-2; Mark 13:1-2; Luke 21:5-6).They wondered when this would happen, but other questions were on their minds too.

Jesus' disciples knew He'd return one day and that His arrival would herald the end of the current world/age. They just didn't know when. Probably a bit concerned about the future, Peter, James, John, and Andrew privately asked Jesus three questions (cf. Matthew 24:3; Mark 13:3-4; Luke 21:7):

1. When will the destruction of the temple happen?
2. What will be the sign of Christ's return?
3. What will be the sign of the end of the age (world)?

What makes Jesus' answer difficult to interpret is the fact that He had to respond to questions about multiple events spanning thousands of years. So we have to try to pull out basic facts and match them to eras as best we can under the circumstances.

Our job is made more difficult by the near-far makeup of the discourse. For example, Jesus talks about false messiahs, war, famine, earthquakes, and persecution. These were things that happened during His day with a climax between 70 – 135 CE under Roman oppression and will happen again under the Antichrist's time of great tribulation. Unfortunately, the near-far nature of this discourse on the Mount of Olives, which contains both prophetic and apocalyptic writing, has caused dissension among Christians. Some, such as those taking a preterist view, believe all events contained therein have already taken place and climaxed with the destruction of Jerusalem in 70 CE. Others holding to a pre-tribulation rapture position are adamant that everything in the writing pertains to Jews and not Christian believers. We'll compare and contrast these and other end-times positions in Chapter Seventeen of this guide.

Not to add insult to injury, but we'll have one more challenge: the books of Matthew, Mark, and Luke contain accounts from different perspectives and with a different audience in mind. We'll do our best though to line up related verses and match them to the appropriate responses by Christ to His disciples' questions. Most will line up nicely while a few could fit into timeframes 1 and 2 (defined below). I'll identify those as "gray area" verses that most likely fit into near-far apocalyptic writing covering the time from Christ until the end.

You'll discover that the Mount of Olives response by Jesus can be broken down into these broad timeframes:

1. Events or conditions that will come *before* the end, but not *be* the end:
    a. Destruction of Jerusalem and the temple in 70 CE.
    b. Things that will continue with greater intensity and frequency:
        i. Claims of being Christ by some
        ii. War
        iii. Famine
        iv. Earthquakes
    c. Persecution and death

2. Events surrounding Christ's return:
    a. Persecution and death.
    b. Antichrist in the temple.
    c. Gospel preached just before the end.
    d. Christ's appearing and our gathering.
    e. Mourning by the rest of the earth
3. A description of the kingdom of heaven (only in Matthew's account).

The table below presents a side-by-side comparison of all three Mount of Olives accounts. The writings cover timeframes 1 and 2 (above). Cells filled with gray contain Scripture that could be considered near-far prophecies. Early church members and apostles were definitely persecuted and martyred for their faith (e.g. Stephen, Paul, and James). This still happens occasionally and will happen with greater magnitude as the end draws near. However, the "*abomination*" spoken of by Daniel hasn't appeared in the temple yet. Nor has Christ appeared with His angels to gather the elect. So we can safely say those events are apocalyptic and not near-far (hence the lack of gray in those Scripture cells).

My recommendation is to read and compare the verses one row at a time. Then read the comment and look up Scripture references if they exist for a particular row before moving to the next one.

14.1 Comparison of Mount of Olives Scripture

Matthew	Mark	Luke	Comments
TIMEFRAME #1 – *Before* the end			
24:4 And Jesus answered and said to them, See to it that no one misleads you.	**13:5** And Jesus began to say to them, See to it that no one misleads you.	**21:8a** And He said, See to it that you are not misled;	

Matthew	Mark	Luke	Comments
24:5 For many will come in My name, saying, 'I am the Christ,' and will mislead many.	**13:6** Many will come in My name, saying, 'I am He!' and will mislead many.	**21:8b** for many will come in My name, saying, 'I am He,' and, 'The time is near.' Do not go after them.	The "*He*" was inserted by the translator and is not part of the text. The resulting "*I am*" therefore shows the imposters will claim to be God (as will the Antichrist). See Revelation 6:2 (Seal #1).
24:6 You will be hearing of wars and rumors of wars. See that you are not frightened, for those things must take place, but that is not yet the end.	**13:7** When you hear of wars and rumors of wars, do not be frightened; those things must take place; but that is not yet the end.	**21:9** When you hear of wars and disturbances, do not be terrified; for these things must take place first, but the end does not follow immediately.	See Revelation 6:3-4 (Seal #2).
24:7a For nation will rise against nation, and kingdom against kingdom,	**13:8a** For nation will rise up against nation, and kingdom against kingdom;	**21:10** Then He continued by saying to them, Nation will rise against nation and kingdom against kingdom,	
24:7b and in various places there will be famines and earthquakes.	**13:8b** there will be earthquakes in various places; there will also be famines.	**21:11a** and there will be great earthquakes, and in various places plagues and famines;	See Revelation 6:5-6 (Seal #3).

Matthew	Mark	Luke	Comments
		21:11b and there will be terrors and great signs from heaven.	This is an introduction to 21:25-26. Other things must happen first.
24:8 But all these things are merely the beginning of **birth pangs**.	**13:8c** These things are merely the beginning of **birth pangs**.		The events of false Christs, war, famine, and earthquakes will happen with greater intensity and frequency as the end draws near.
24:9 Then they will deliver you to tribulation, and will kill you, and you will be hated by all nations because of My name.	**13:9a** But be on your guard; for they will deliver you to the courts, and you will be flogged in the synagogues, and you will stand before governors and kings for My sake,	**21:12** But ***before*** all these things, they will lay their hands on you and will persecute you, delivering you to the synagogues and prisons, bringing you before kings and governors for My name's sake.	
	13:9b as a testimony to them.	**21:13** It will lead to an opportunity for your testimony.	See Matthew 10:18.

Matthew	Mark	Luke	Comments
	13:10 The gospel must first be preached to all the nations.		This seems a bit out of place since it doesn't fit into the context. The passage is most likely related to Matthew 24:14. Don't be fooled into believing that Christ can't come back until we've preached to every human on the planet (as some do). The preaching referred to here, in Matthew 24:14, and in Revelation 14:6-7 will be a distinct milestone in end-times events: (1) birth pangs; (2) **the preaching**; (3) the end. See my comment on Matthew 24:14.
	13:11a When they arrest you and hand you over, do not worry beforehand about what you are to say,	**21:14** So make up your minds not to prepare beforehand to defend yourselves;	See Matthew 10:19.

Matthew	Mark	Luke	Comments
	13:11b but say whatever is given you in that hour; for it is not you who speak, but it is the Holy Spirit.	**21:15** for I will give you utterance and wisdom which none of your opponents will be able to resist or refute.	See Matthew 10:20.
TIMEFRAME #2 – The Time of the End			
24:10 At that time many will fall away and will betray one another and hate one another.	**13:12** Brother will betray brother to death, and a father his child; and children will rise up against parents and have them put to death.	**21:16** But you will be betrayed even by parents and brothers and relatives and friends, and they will put some of you to death,	See Matthew 10:21. See Revelation 6:7-12 (Seals #4 & #5).
	13:13a You will be hated by all because of My name,	**21:17** and you will be hated by all because of My name.	See Matthew 10:22.
24:11 Many false prophets will arise and will mislead many.			These can probably be put into the "tares" category and most likely contribute to the "falling away" in 24:10.
24:12 Because lawlessness is increased, most people's love will grow cold.			

Matthew	Mark	Luke	Comments
		21:18 Yet not a hair of your head will perish.	
24:13 But the one who endures to the end, he will be saved.	**13:13b** but the one who endures to the end, he will be saved.	**21:19** By your endurance you will gain your lives.	See Matthew 10:22. See Revelation 6:7-12 (Seals #4 & #5).
24:14 This gospel of the kingdom shall be preached in the whole world as a testimony to all the nations, and then the end will come.			See Revelation 14:6-7. This may possibly be done by the two witnesses of Revelation 11.
24:15 Therefore when you see the ABOMINATION OF DESOLATION which was spoken of through Daniel the prophet, standing in the holy place (let the reader understand),	**13:14a** But when you see the ABOMINATION OF DESOLATION standing where it should not be (let the reader understand),	**21:20** But when you see Jerusalem surrounded by armies, then recognize that her desolation is near.	See Daniel 9:27, 11:45, & 12:7-11. Also see 2 Thessalonians 2:3-4.

Matthew	Mark	Luke	Comments
24:16 then those who are in Judea must flee to the mountains.	**13:14b** then those who are in Judea must flee to the mountains.	**21:21** Then those who are in Judea must flee to the mountains, and those who are in the midst of the city must leave, and those who are in the country must not enter the city;	
24:17 Whoever is on the housetop must not go down to get the things out that are in his house.	**13:15** The one who is on the housetop must not go down, or go in to get anything out of his house;		
24:18 Whoever is in the field must not turn back to get his cloak.	**13:16** and the one who is in the field must not turn back to get his coat.		
		21:22 because these are days of vengeance, so that all things which are written will be fulfilled.	God's end-times wrath (cf. Isaiah 34:8, 61:2, 63:4, Jeremiah 46:10).
24:19 But woe to those who are pregnant and to those who are nursing babies in those days!	**13:17** But woe to those who are pregnant and to those who are nursing babies in those days!	**21:23a** Woe to those who are pregnant and to those who are nursing babies in those days;	
24:20 But pray that your flight will not be in the winter, or on a Sabbath.	**13:18** But pray that it may not happen in the winter.		Jewish law restricts movement on the Sabbath.

Matthew	Mark	Luke	Comments
24:21 For then there will be a great tribulation, such as has not occurred since the beginning of the world until now, nor ever will.	**13:19** For those days will be a time of tribulation such as has not occurred since the beginning of the creation which God created until now, and never will.	**21:23b** for there will be great distress upon the land and wrath to this people;	The time of the Antichrist's authority/wrath (e.g. Daniel 7:21 & 25; 12:1; Revelation 7:9-15).
		21:24a and they will fall by the edge of the sword, and will be led captive into all the nations;	This has been happening from 66 CE with the beginning of the dispersion from Israel. It will also happen again during the tribulation of the Antichrist (cf. Revelation 13:10) and is therefore a near-far prophecy.
		21:24b and Jerusalem under foot by the gentiles until the times of the gentiles are fulfilled.	Gentile control of Jerusalem for 42 months (3.5 years) at the end. See Romans 11:25 and Revelation 11:2.

Matthew	Mark	Luke	Comments
		21:25 There will be signs in sun and moon and stars, and on the earth dismay among nations, in perplexity at the roaring of the sea and the waves,	See Revelation 6:12-13 (Seal #6).
		21:26a men fainting from fear and the expectation of the things which are coming upon the world;	See Revelation 6:15-17 (Seal #6).
24:22 Unless those days had been cut short, no life would have been saved; but for the sake of the elect those days will be cut short.	**13:20** Unless the Lord had shortened those days, no life would have been saved; but for the sake of the elect, whom He chose, He shortened the days.		These passages indicate that God will cut the time of the Antichrist's authority short – not that the days will be shorter (e.g. only 22 hours instead of 24) as I've heard some claim.
24:23 Then if anyone says to you, 'Behold, here is the Christ,' or 'There He is,' do not believe him.	**13:21** And then if anyone says to you, 'Behold, here is the Christ'; or, 'Behold, He is there'; do not believe him;		

Matthew	Mark	Luke	Comments
24:24 For false Christs and false prophets will arise and will show great signs and wonders, so as to mislead, if possible, even the elect.	**13:22** for false Christs and false prophets will arise, and will show signs and wonders, in order to lead astray, if possible, the elect.		Because of the context of the Great Tribulation and the word used for "Christs" here, the passage is probably referring to the Antichrist and False Prophet of the end (see False Messiahs in Chapter Ten of this guide).
24:25 Behold, I have told you in advance.	**13:23** But take heed; behold, I have told you everything in advance.		
24:26 So if they say to you, 'Behold, He is in the wilderness,' do not go out, or, 'Behold, He is in the inner rooms,' do not believe them.			
24:27 For just as the lightning comes from the east and flashes even to the west, so will the coming of the Son of Man be.			

Matthew	Mark	Luke	Comments
24:28 Wherever the corpse is, there the vultures will gather.			This is the first "*when you see this, then you'll see that*" moment. Compare with Job 39:27-30. Vulture or eagle is used here depending on the translation. The King James Version uses "*eagle*." Preterists have used this verse in an attempt to prove Christ's second coming happened in 70 CE since the Roman military staffs sported eagles.

Matthew	Mark	Luke	Comments
24:29a But immediately after the tribulation of those days THE SUN WILL BE DARKENED, AND THE MOON WILL NOT GIVE ITS LIGHT,	**13:24** But in those days, after that tribulation, THE SUN WILL BE DARKENED AND THE MOON WILL NOT GIVE ITS LIGHT,		See Revelation 6:15-17 (Seal #6).
24:29b AND THE STARS WILL FALL from the sky, and the powers of the heavens will be shaken.	**13:25** AND THE STARS WILL BE FALLING from heaven, and the powers that are in the heavens will be shaken.	**21:26b** for the powers of the heavens will be shaken.	
24:30a And then the sign of the Son of Man will appear in the sky,			
24:30b and then all the tribes of the earth will mourn,			
24:30c and they will see the SON OF MAN COMING ON THE CLOUDS OF THE SKY with power and great glory.	**13:26** Then they will see THE SON OF MAN COMING IN CLOUDS with great power and glory.	**21:27** Then they will see THE SON OF MAN COMING IN A CLOUD with power and great glory.	

Matthew	Mark	Luke	Comments
24:31 And He will send forth His angels with A GREAT TRUMPET[18] and THEY WILL GATHER TOGETHER His elect from the four winds, from one end of the sky to the other.	**13:27** And then He will send forth the angels, and will gather together His elect from the four winds, from the farthest end of the earth to the farthest end of heaven.		See 2 Thessalonians 2:1. "from the four winds" and "from the farthest end of the earth to the farthest end of heaven" depict the gathering of the *elect* from every part of the earth.
When You See *This*, Then You'll See *That*			

Matthew	Mark	Luke	Comments
		21:28 But when these things begin to take place, straighten up and lift up your heads, because your redemption is drawing near.	Jesus is only stating again that, "When you see *this*, then you'll see *that*" in a similar fashion to the verse about the eagle and carcass in Matthew 24:28. Unfortunately, some allegorize the budding fig tree parable to symbolize Israel and its becoming a nation in 1948.
24:32a Now learn the parable from the fig tree:	**13:28a** Now learn the parable from the fig tree:	**21:29** Then He told them a parable: Behold the fig tree and all the trees;	
24:32b when its branch has already become tender and puts forth its leaves, you know that summer is near;	**13:28b** when its branch has already become tender and puts forth its leaves, you know that summer is near.	**21:30** as soon as they put forth leaves, you see it and know for yourselves that summer is now near.	
24:33 so, you too, when you see all these things, recognize that He is near, right at the door.	**13:29** Even so, you too, when you see these things happening, recognize that He is near, right at the door.	**21:31** So you also, when you see these things happening, recognize that the kingdom of God is near.	

Matthew	Mark	Luke	Comments
24:34 Truly I say to you, this generation will not pass away until all these things take place.	**13:30** Truly I say to you, this generation will not pass away until all these things take place.	**21:32** Truly I say to you, this generation will not pass away until all things take place.	Be careful here! "*This generation*" is tied to the audience addressed in the previous passages – not to the disciples' generation. To support a belief that Christ returned in 70 CE, some have claimed that "*this generation*" depicts the generation of the disciples Christ was talking to. The generation that will see "*these things*" (e.g. the Antichrist, signs in the heavens, etc.) will also witness Christ's return.
24:35 Heaven and earth will pass away, but My words will not pass away.	**13:31** Heaven and earth will pass away, but My words will not pass away.	**21:33** Heaven and earth will pass away, but My words will not pass away.	

Matthew	Mark	Luke	Comments
24:36 But of that day and hour no one knows, not even the angels of heaven, nor the Son, but the Father alone.	**13:32** But of that day or hour no one knows, not even the angels in heaven, nor the Son, but the Father alone.		Remember this from the marriage ceremony in Chapter Seven?

Several concepts I hope you'll walk away with after a review of the Scriptures contained in the above table:

1. The "birth pangs" in Timeframe #1 of those claiming to be "I Am," and wars, famine, and earthquakes increasing with greater frequency and intensity as the end draws near. They're repeated by Christ to John with the unveiling of the events protected by seals 1, 2, and 3 in the book of Revelation.
2. As stated by Paul, two things must precede our gathering:
    a. A falling away from the faith.
    b. The abomination (Antichrist) in the temple (which hasn't been rebuilt yet).
3. Martyrdom of the saints during the reign of the Antichrist (the beheaded as we learned earlier in Chapter Six) is represented by events protected by seals 4 and 5 in the Revelation.
4. Our gathering and the Day of the Lord wrath found in Timeframe #2 will be preceded by a complete darkening of the sun, moon, and stars – also reflected by the sixth seal events in the book of Revelation.

As clear as these points seem to be, some people claim that the Mount of Olives discourse between Jesus and His disciples was directed at the Jews and not Christian believers. This is done to remove complications inherent in a pre-tribulation rapture belief. The sequence of events as described by Jesus strongly suggests that true believers in Christ – *elect* believers – will be on earth during the Great Tribulation of the Antichrist's reign. This is in direct conflict with a pre-tribulation rapture position. We'll discuss the conflict and differences further in Chapter Seventeen. We're not done with the discourse though.

The remainder of Matthew 24, Mark 13, and Luke 21 admonish the reader to be alert to ensure this terrible time of tribulation and God's subsequent wrath don't surprise and overtake His chosen. Let's summarize the rest of the verses in each book beginning with Matthew 24:37-39.

> *For the coming of the Son of Man will be just like the days of Noah. For as in those days before the flood they were eating and drinking, marrying and giving in marriage, until the day that Noah entered the ark, and they did not understand until the flood came and took them all away; so will the coming of the Son of Man be.* —Matthew 24:37-39.

Matthew 24:37-39: Christ's appearing, our gathering, and subsequent wrath will come as a surprise to the non-elect just as God's wrath through the great flood did.

> *Then there will be two men in the field; one will be taken and one will be left. Two women will be grinding at the mill; one will be taken and one will be left. Therefore be on the alert, for you do not know which day your Lord is coming. But be sure of this, that if the head of the house had known at what time of the night the thief was coming, he would have been on the alert and would not have allowed his house to be broken into. For this reason you also must be ready; for the Son of Man is coming at an hour when you do not think He will.* —Matthew 24:40-44.

Matthew 24:40-44: When Christ returns some will be taken to the marriage supper—and some won't. We must remain alert and watchful since we won't know the exact time of Christ's appearing and the gathering. This passage is similar to what's recorded in Mark 13:33-37.

> *Who then is the faithful and sensible slave whom his master put in charge of his household to give them their food at the proper time? Blessed is that slave whom his master finds so doing when he comes. Truly I say to you that he will put him in charge of all his possessions. But if that evil slave says in his heart, 'My master is not coming for a long time,' and begins to beat his fellow slaves and eat and drink with drunkards; the master of that slave will come on a day when he does not expect him and at an hour which he does not know, and will cut him in pieces and assign him a place with the hypocrites; in that place there will be weeping and gnashing of teeth.* —Matthew 24:45-51.

Matthew 24:45-51: Those who follow Christ and His commandments, and therefore aren't practicing sinful behavior, will partake of the marriage with Christ and God's everlasting kingdom. The alternative will be judgment and the consequence of hell for everyone else. See Matthew 8:11-12, 13:42, 13:50, 22:13, 25:30, and Luke 13:28 for related references.

> *Take heed, keep on the alert; for you do not know when the appointed time will come. It is like a man away on a journey, who upon leaving his house and putting his slaves in charge, assigning to each one his task, also commanded the doorkeeper to stay on the alert. Therefore, be on the alert--for you do not know when the master of the house is coming, whether in the evening, at midnight, or when the rooster crows, or in the morning – in case he should come suddenly and find you asleep. What I say to you I say to all, 'Be on the alert!'* —Mark 13:33-37.

Mark 13:33-37: Jesus' warning is pretty self-explanatory: be alert! We won't know the exact time of His appearing, our gathering, and the subsequent wrath of God on the rest of the earth. But we're admonished to keep watch.

> *Be on guard, so that your hearts will not be weighted down with dissipation and drunkenness and the worries of life, and that day will not come on you suddenly like a trap; for it will come upon*

> *all those who dwell on the face of all the earth. But keep on the alert at all times, praying that you may have* ***strength to escape all these things that are about to take place****, and to stand before the Son of Man.* —Luke 21:34-36.

Luke 21:34-36: Jesus is warning the elect to be alert and stay pure. The Greek word for "strength" is *katischuō* (Strong's G2729) and it means "to prevail against." In context, we're to pray that we can prevail against the wickedness of the world and therefore escape the wrath of God that will come in "*that day.*" Those who do prevail will escape God's wrath and stand before Christ.

Paul echoed this sentiment in one of his letters to the church in Thessalonica:

> *Now as to the times and the epochs, brethren, you have no need of anything to be written to you. For you yourselves know full well that* ***the day of the Lord will come just like a thief in the night****. While they are saying, "Peace and safety!" then* ***destruction will come upon them suddenly*** *like labor pains upon a woman with child, and* ***they will not escape****. But you, brethren, are not in darkness, that the day would overtake you like a thief; for you are all sons of light and sons of day. We are not of night nor of darkness; so then let us not sleep as others do,* ***but let us be alert and sober****. For those who sleep do their sleeping at night, and those who get drunk get drunk at night. But since we are of the day, let us be sober, having put on the breastplate of faith and love, and as a helmet, the hope of salvation. For* ***God has not destined us for wrath****, but for obtaining salvation through our Lord Jesus Christ, who died for us, so that whether we are awake or asleep, we will live together with Him.* —1 Thessalonians 5:1-10.

In addition to instructing us to be watchful, Jesus gave His disciples several scenarios as examples of the gathering and God's kingdom in Matthew 25. There are three divisions, or parables, within the chapter: a parable of ten virgins, a parable of the talents, and a view of the great judgment of God at the end of the age.

> **Verses 1-13**: The parable of the ten virgins waiting for the bridegroom. Five were wise, prepared, and watchful. The others weren't and missed the bridegroom's arrival and opportunity for marriage. Being alert and prepared is a repetitive theme in what Jesus told His disciples on the Mount of Olives.
>
> **Verses 14-30**: This passage, a repeat of Matthew 24:45-51, reminds us that we need to be faithful and obedient to Christ's commandments and with the resources He's given us as we await His return.
>
> **Verses 31-40 & 41-45**: Moving on, Christ gave His disciples a glimpse of the great judgment that will conclude the current age. This approach is similar to that taken in the Revelation. There, Jesus took John through a sequence spanning from the early church through the Great Tribulation and God's wrath, and then to the great judgment at the very end.

Each major division is as follows:

> *Then the kingdom of heaven will be comparable to ten virgins, who took their lamps and went out to meet the bridegroom. Five of them were foolish, and five were prudent. For when the foolish took their lamps, they took no oil with them, but the prudent took oil in flasks along with their lamps. Now while the bridegroom was delaying, they all got drowsy and began to sleep. But at midnight there was a shout, 'Behold, the bridegroom! Come out to meet him.' Then all those virgins rose and trimmed their lamps. The foolish said to the prudent, 'Give us some of your oil, for our lamps are going out.' But the prudent answered, 'No, there will not be enough for us and you too; go instead to the dealers and buy some for yourselves.' And while they were going away to make the purchase, the bridegroom came, and those who were ready went in with him to the wedding feast; and the door was shut. Later the other virgins also came, saying, 'Lord,*

lord, open up for us.' But he answered, 'Truly I say to you, I do not know you.' Be on the alert then, for you do not know the day nor the hour. —Matthew 25:1-13.

For it is just like a man about to go on a journey, who called his own slaves and entrusted his possessions to them. To one he gave five talents, to another, two, and to another, one, each according to his own ability; and he went on his journey. Immediately the one who had received the five talents went and traded with them, and gained five more talents. In the same manner the one who had received the two talents gained two more. But he who received the one talent went away, and dug a hole in the ground and hid his master's money. Now after a long time the master of those slaves came and settled accounts with them. The one who had received the five talents came up and brought five more talents, saying, 'Master, you entrusted five talents to me. See, I have gained five more talents.' His master said to him, 'Well done, good and faithful slave. You were faithful with a few things, I will put you in charge of many things; enter into the joy of your master.' Also the one who had received the two talents came up and said, 'Master, you entrusted two talents to me. See, I have gained two more talents.' His master said to him, 'Well done, good and faithful slave. You were faithful with a few things, I will put you in charge of many things; enter into the joy of your master.' And the one also who had received the one talent came up and said, 'Master, I knew you to be a hard man, reaping where you did not sow and gathering where you scattered no seed. And I was afraid, and went away and hid your talent in the ground. See, you have what is yours.' But his master answered and said to him, 'You wicked, lazy slave, you knew that I reap where I did not sow and gather where I scattered no seed. Then you ought to have put my money in the bank, and on my arrival I would have received my money back with interest. Therefore take away the talent from him, and give it to the one who has the ten talents.' For to everyone who has, more shall be given, and he will have an abundance; but from the one who does not have, even what he does have shall be taken away. Throw out the worthless slave into the outer darkness; in that place there will be weeping and gnashing of teeth. —Matthew 25:14-30.

But when the Son of Man comes in His glory, and all the angels with Him, then He will sit on His glorious throne. All the nations will be gathered before Him; and He will separate them from one another, as the shepherd separates the sheep from the goats; and He will put the sheep on His right, and the goats on the left. Then the King will say to those on His right, 'Come, you who are blessed of My Father, inherit the kingdom prepared for you from the foundation of the world. For I was hungry, and you gave Me something to eat; I was thirsty, and you gave Me something to drink; I was a stranger, and you invited Me in; naked, and you clothed Me; I was sick, and you visited Me; I was in prison, and you came to Me.' Then the righteous will answer Him, 'Lord, when did we see You hungry, and feed You, or thirsty, and give You something to drink? And when did we see You a stranger, and invite You in, or naked, and clothe You? When did we see You sick, or in prison, and come to You?' The King will answer and say to them, 'Truly I say to you, to the extent that you did it to one of these brothers of Mine, even the least of them, you did it to Me.' —Matthew 25:31-40.

Then He will also say to those on His left, 'Depart from Me, accursed ones, into the eternal fire which has been prepared for the devil and his angels; for I was hungry, and you gave Me nothing to eat; I was thirsty, and you gave Me nothing to drink; I was a stranger, and you did not invite Me in; naked, and you did not clothe Me; sick, and in prison, and you did not visit Me.' Then they themselves also will answer, 'Lord, when did we see You hungry, or thirsty, or a stranger, or naked, or sick, or in prison, and did not take care of You?' Then He will answer them, 'Truly I say to you, to the extent that you did not do it to one of the least of these, you did not do it to Me.' These will go away into eternal punishment, but the righteous into eternal life. —Matthew 25:41-45.

In summary, Jesus told His disciples there'll be false messiahs, wars, famine, and earthquakes leading up to the end. He also said that these things will increase in intensity and frequency as the end draws near. Jesus revealed the death and persecution they'd go through on account of Him from that time until the end. And He unveiled end-times events to come much later, including the tribulation of the Antichrist and gathering of believers. In Matthew's account, we also read the parables and additional warnings to stay watchful and faithful. Finally, we saw in Matthew's account a description of the great judgment of God at the very end of the age. Guess what? You'll see all this again and in greater detail as we study the Revelation Christ gave to John roughly 60 years later. Although that particular part of our study won't happen until Chapter Sixteen, the next part of this chapter will introduce the Revelation.

Part II: Introduction to the Revelation

The Revelation of Jesus Christ, which God gave Him to show to His bond-servants, the things which must soon take place; and He sent and communicated it by His angel to His bond-servant John, who testified to the word of God and to the testimony of Jesus Christ, even to all that he saw. Blessed is he who reads and those who hear the words of the prophecy, and heed the things which are written in it; for the time is near. —Revelation 1:1-3.

God revealed what would happen at the end of time to Christ, who showed John, who then wrote most of what he saw down for the churches in Asia Minor. Christ had already given the concepts to His disciples on the Mount of Olives, but the Revelation unveils much more detail about the time of the end and corroborates what Jesus said about events *not yet* the end (e.g. false messiahs, wars, famine, and earthquakes).

Knowing the basic structure of the apocalyptic Revelation will help immensely in our study. Let's start our overview of this structure by making a few very clear and adamant claims:

1. The book is divided into distinct sections, and most of it is **sequential** from beginning to end. Christ's Revelation takes us sequentially from about 90 CE through the gathering and wrath to the great judgment. Please see the breakdown below for more information.
2. While the Revelation does make use of some symbols, they're **easy to understand** and already explained for us with just a few exceptions (e.g. the *whore of Babylon*).
3. The visions contained within the book are **for the church** – saints and servants of the Lord Jesus Christ. Everything within it pertains to the bride of Christ – then, now, and in the future until the very end. A popular rapture belief perpetuated by the media, such as the "Left Behind" series, is that the apocalyptic writing is instead meant for a "tribulation force" made up of believers who'll be left behind after the gathering of the church. This is unscriptural and part of a deceptive and potentially dangerous doctrine.
4. The book of Revelation is ***not* symbolic** as a whole, and while it does contain some symbols, it should be taken as literally as possible! Many people have emphatically claimed that the opposite is true – that the *entire* Revelation is symbolic. Why? To support a particular end-times view that contrasts the message given in a literal interpretation of Revelation.

Now is as good a time as any to introduce different methods used to interpret Revelation. Although we'll compare and contrast different end-times positions in Chapter Seventeen, discussing the basic approaches others take to studying the apocalyptic writing may be beneficial to you as you prepare to go through it.

Four significant approaches have been taken in trying to understand the Revelation: Preterist, Historic, Futurist, and Spiritual (Idealist/Symbolic). All have been spawned from attempts to make Revelation (and the Mount of Olives discourse) fit historical events or hidden meaning (as with the *spiritual* approach). The latter is without boundaries, perpetuated by the likes of Augustine and Origen,[19] and won't be discussed here.

Classical preterism sees the fulfillment of Revelation's prophecies as having already occurred in the past, particularly in 70 CE with the destruction of Jerusalem. Proponents believe that the Revelation would have had more relevance to the original readers.[20] While it's true that much of what Jesus told His disciples in response to their question regarding the destruction of the temple (in 70 CE) has already occurred, much hasn't. For instance, you'd be hard-pressed to find evidence that the incredible destruction of God's *Day of the Lord* wrath and Christ's second coming have already happened. For this reason, some preterists claim to be only *partial* preterists. Expositors of this view believe that while many of the events of the Mount of Olives discourse and of the Revelation have occurred (e.g. with the destruction of Jerusalem), others won't be realized until sometime in the future (e.g. the return of Christ, new heaven and earth, etc.).

Historicism (historic Protestant interpretation of the Revelation) is an all but extinct view held by the likes of John Wycliffe, John Calvin, and Sir Isaac Newton.[21] This position teaches that God revealed the entire church age in advance through the symbolic visions of the Apocalypse.[22] Examples include:

- The breaking of the seven seals were said to have been fulfilled by barbaric invasions of the Roman Empire.
- Arab hordes that attacked the Roman Empire were represented by scorpions from the bottomless pit in chapter 9.
- The beast of chapter 13 represents the Roman papacy (an assertion that the pope is the Antichrist is also made here).

The biggest challenge with this approach is that it requires much conjecture since multiple historical events may fit a single prophecy. You should definitely avoid taking this approach for the same reasons you should avoid pursuing a Spiritual/Idealist/Symbolic approach!

Most popular among evangelical writers and Bible teachers of today is a *futurist* approach to an interpretation of the Revelation. This method dictates that everything past chapter 3 awaits future fulfillment. Whereas historicism attempts to match past events to Scripture as an explanation of prior fulfillment, futurists look forward to eventual fulfillment. Many who subscribe to this approach also hold to a dispensationalist view. It insists that church history has been divided into seven segments (i.e. dispensations) that closely correspond to the different churches in Asia Minor as recorded by John (more on this in Chapter Seventeen of this guide).

Although I'm not a proponent of dispensationalism, I do appreciate the *futurist* method of analyzing the Revelation because it allows the reader to take a literal approach to interpretation whereas other methods must often take passages non-literally. Anyone assuming God meant something other than what He revealed literally must also take responsibility for their interpretation. Therefore, my recommendation (as already discussed) is to take Scripture at face value wherever possible unless context strongly suggests you do otherwise, and doing so results in no contradictions.

The following is a very high-level summary of what we'll study by chapter:

- Chapters 1-5 (90 CE): Introduction by John, letters from Christ to the churches of Asia Minor, and an invitation to heaven to watch the end-times events.
- Chapter 6: Seals 1-6 depicting birth pangs and Great Tribulation.
- Chapter 7: Protection of the 144,000 Jews; bride of Christ seen in heaven.
- Chapters 8-9: Seal 7; trumpet judgments 1-6.
- Chapter 10: Seventh trumpet judgment.
- Chapters 11-13: Three-and-one-half-year period of Great Tribulation detailed.
- Chapter 14: A glimpse of *Babylon's* destruction, preaching of the gospel before God's wrath, gathering of believers, and God's wrath – all things that will happen near the end of the three-and-a-half-year Great Tribulation or shortly thereafter by the end of the trumpet judgments.

- Chapters 15-16: Seven vial judgments that will complete God's wrath.
- Chapters 17-18: Description (and destruction) of *Babylon* near the end of God's wrath; Antichrist kingdom details.
- Chapter 19: Armageddon at the end of God's wrath; marriage supper of Christ.
- Chapter 20: Thousand-year reign of Christ; great judgment following Christ's kingdom.
- Chapter 21: New heaven and earth after the judgment.
- Chapter 22: Final admonishments and closure.

Chapters 1-5 provide an introduction by John and letters to the seven churches in Asia Minor. Why only seven? The early church was segmented by geographical boundaries. You would've found one church in each city or town instead of hundreds of thousands of fairly autonomous and relatively small church organizations worldwide (as you'll find today). Christ's letters to these churches contain admonishments and warnings based on their behavior at the time. These chapters also reveal John's invitation to heaven to view the end-times events and prepare for the breaking of the seven seals – only possible by Christ, who had earned the right.

Chapter 6 shows seals 1-3 broken to reveal events that have happened, and will continue to with greater intensity and frequency. Seals 4 and 5 are broken to reveal the persecution and death (beheading) that will happen at the hands of the Antichrist and his kingdom during his three-and-a-half-year authority. Broken seal 6 of chapter 6 reveals the darkening of the sun, moon, and stars preceding Christ's return. It concludes with the realization by the rest of the world that God's wrath is coming.

Chapter 7 details the protection of the 144,000 Jews in anticipation of God's impending wrath, and the bride of Christ gathered at the darkening of the sun, moon, and stars can be seen here.

Chapters 8-10 outline the first six of seven trumpet judgments (the beginning of God's wrath). The seventh trumpet will herald the kingdom of Christ – the anointing of the Most Holy – ending the 70th week of Daniel.

Chapters 11-13 give great detail about the kingdom and three-and-a-half-year authority of the Antichrist – the last half of Daniel's 70th week. Each of these three chapters offers a different view of this timeframe. Why stick this information into the middle of the sequence of God's wrath? The seventh trumpet judgment marks the end of the three-and-a-half-year Great Tribulation at the hands of the Antichrist, so it's probably as good a place as any to present a summary of that time.

Chapter 14 tells of events concluding the three-and-a-half-year authority of the Antichrist (preaching of the gospel, gathering, and wrath). The vision also updates the disposition of the 144,000.

Chapters 15-19 contain information pertaining to the rest of God's wrath including the battle of Armageddon. You'll also find much detail regarding *Babylon.*

Chapters 20-22 will take us through Christ's 1,000-year kingdom, reveal details about the new heaven and earth, and offer closure to the Revelation.

As you'll discover, the entire unveiling is sequential and closely related to what Christ already told His disciples on the Mount of Olives. The diagram below closely resembles the first one we looked at back in Chapter Two. The primary difference is the insertion of references from the book of Revelation. We'll break it down into multiple detailed timelines later in Chapter Sixteen. Each detailed view will depict a specific timeframe and will contain appropriate references.

14.2 Timeline of the Book of Revelation

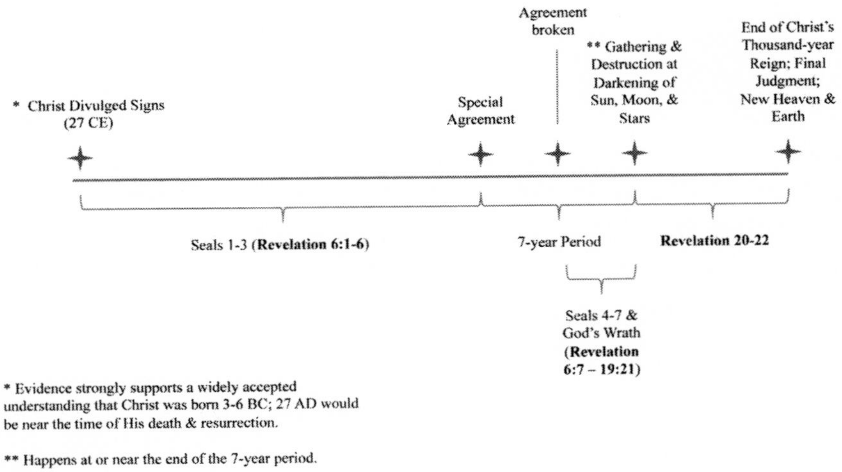

SUPPLEMENTAL READING (Either the KJV or NASB version of the Bible is recommended; read at least three verses before and after scriptural references to understand the context better):

1. Introduction by John: Revelation 1:1-9
2. Saints on earth and in Great Tribulation during the Antichrist's reign:
    a. Revelation 13:7 & 10 (Antichrist at war with the saints, who must persevere)
    b. Revelation 14:12 (further perseverance of the saints)
3. Closure: Revelation 22:7-21

CHECKUP

CHAPTER FOURTEEN

The following questions are meant to check your understanding of what we've covered so far and provoke additional thoughts and questions to elevate your learning to a higher level. Answers to all questions can be found in Appendix D.

1. What three basic questions did several of Jesus' disciples ask Him on the Mount of Olives?

2. Which events mentioned in Matthew 24 will, according to Christ, lead to, but not be, the end?

3. Christ described the events in question #3 as "*birth pangs*." Why did He call them that?

4. Who was Christ quoting when He mentioned the "*Abomination that causes desolation*" in Matthew 24:15? What will be the "*holy place*" mentioned in the same verse? (NOTE: Scripture we studied from Daniel 9 and 12, and 2 Thessalonians 2:4 may be helpful here.)

5. What event or timeframe will the appearing of the abomination in the temple usher in?

6. Why will God cut short the time referenced in question #5 (Matthew 24:22 and Mark 13:20)?

7. Matthew 24:29, Mark 13:24-25, Luke 21:25-26, and Revelation 6:12-14 describe signs that will appear in the sky when God cuts short the Antichrist's time of authority. Their presence will be seen at the time Christ appears with His angels to gather the elect. What will these signs be?

8. The signs from question #7 and the subsequent gathering will be good news to some (as in Luke 21:28), but not to others. Why do you think the Bible tells us that some will mourn at that time (cf. Matthew 24:30 and Revelation 6:15-17)?

9. What do you think Christ's intention was behind what He said in Matthew 24:28 & 32, Mark 13:28, and Luke 21:29-30?

10. What are the three major themes portrayed in the parables of Matthew 25?

CHAPTER FIFTEEN

PETER & PAUL WEIGH IN

John, Peter, and Paul had more to say about the time of the Antichrist, our gathering, God's wrath, and final judgment than anyone else since the time of Christ. You'll see most of John's input in the Revelation given to him by Christ in approximately 90 CE. In the interest of exposing you to all end-of-the-age Scripture, we'll address Peter and Paul's apocalyptic writings here before moving on to a comprehensive overview of the Revelation.

Peter, like the other apostles and disciples, preached a message of Jesus' resurrection from the dead. This single act of love by God and by Christ provided the greatest sacrifice and gift known to mankind. A belief in that resurrection strengthens our faith and hope in Christ's return, also preached by Peter and others. We understand from their message that what we hope for will bring salvation and save us from the wrath of God (to include possible lake-of-fire consequences after the great judgment).

Let's take a look at several of Peter's messages that presented end-times themes of salvation and judgment.

> *Blessed be the God and Father of our Lord Jesus Christ, who according to His great mercy has caused us to be born again to a living hope through the resurrection of Jesus Christ from the dead, to obtain an* ***inheritance*** *which is imperishable and undefiled and will not fade away, reserved in heaven for you, who are protected by the power of God through faith for a* ***salvation ready to be revealed in the last time****.* —1 Peter 1:3-5.

> *. . . then the Lord knows how to rescue the godly from temptation, and to keep the* ***unrighteous*** *under* ***punishment for the day of judgment*** *. . .* —2 Peter 2:9.

Peter also warned us of end-times mockers who'll follow their own lusts:

> *Know this first of all, that in the last days mockers will come with their mocking, following after their own lusts, and saying, "Where is the promise of His coming? For ever since the fathers fell asleep, all continues just as it was from the beginning of creation."* —2 Peter 3:3-4.

He continues in what was most likely his last letter to the church by describing the coming destruction that awaits the wicked: the Day of the Lord / Day of God. Peter goes on to tell us that we should look forward not to that time, but to the new heavens and earth where righteousness will dwell in the age to come after this one.

> *But the* ***day of the Lord*** *will come like a thief, in which the heavens will pass away with a roar and the elements will be destroyed with intense heat, and the earth and its works will be burned up. Since all these things are to be destroyed in this way, what sort of people ought you to be in holy conduct and godliness, looking for and hastening the coming of the* ***day of God****, because of which the heavens will be destroyed by burning, and the elements will melt with intense heat! But according to His promise we are looking for* ***new heavens and a new earth****, in which righteousness dwells.* —2 Peter 3:10-13.

Paul's messages echoed the same sentiment and instructions but often included more detail about the end times. He was also a prolific writer – more so than anyone else in the New Testament – and gave the early church much-needed guidelines through several letters. Let's take a look at some of the most significant of his end-times writings.

Christ was resurrected as the first-fruits. Those who are Christ's will be made alive again at His coming and kingdom. Christ will then hand His kingdom over to God at some point, who'll introduce an everlasting kingdom. We'll see this again during our study of Revelation.

But now Christ has been raised from the dead, the first fruits of those who are asleep. For since by a man came death, by a man also came the resurrection of the dead. For as in Adam all die, so also in Christ all will be made alive. But each in his own order: Christ the first fruits, after that those who are Christ's at His coming, then comes the end, when He hands over the kingdom to the God and Father, when He has abolished all rule and all authority and power. –1 Corinthians 15:20-24.

We'll be changed and given imperishable bodies at Christ's appearing. The "*last trump*" mentioned in 15:52 is most likely associated with the Feast of Trumpets, which Christ will fulfill upon His return. Some (e.g. those who hold to a post-tribulation position) believe the "*last trumpet*" is indicative of the seventh trumpet judgment in Revelation 10:7 and 11:15.

Just as we have borne the image of the earthy, we will also bear the image of the heavenly. Now I say this, brethren, that flesh and blood cannot inherit the kingdom of God; nor does the perishable inherit the imperishable. Behold, I tell you a mystery; we will not all sleep, but we will all be changed, in a moment, in the twinkling of an eye, at the last trumpet[23]*; for the trumpet will sound, and the dead will be raised imperishable, and we will be changed. For this perishable must put on the imperishable, and this mortal must put on immortality. But when this perishable will have put on the imperishable, and this mortal will have put on immortality, then will come about the saying that is written, "DEATH IS SWALLOWED UP in victory."* —1 Corinthians 15:49-54.

For our citizenship is in heaven, from which also we eagerly wait for a Savior, the Lord Jesus Christ; who will transform the body of our humble state into conformity with the body of His glory, by the exertion of the power that He has even to subject all things to Himself. —Philippians 3:20-21.

There have been, are, and will be tares in the church until Christ returns. In the following passage, you'll see that some of them convinced members of the first-century church that the resurrection of the end had already taken place in Paul's time and that they'd missed it. This is similar to what he addressed in 2 Thessalonians 2 and not unlike much of the nonsense we hear today. The only defense against false teaching is a good offense built by learning the gospel and thereby strengthening our faith to withstand errant and dangerous doctrine.

> *But avoid worldly and empty chatter, for it will lead to further ungodliness, and their talk will spread like gangrene. Among them are Hymenaeus and Philetus, men who have gone astray from the truth saying that the resurrection has already taken place, and they upset the faith of some. Nevertheless, the firm foundation of God stands, having this seal, "The Lord knows those who are His," and, "Everyone who names the name of the Lord is to abstain from wickedness."* —2 Timothy 2:16-19.

Rewards await the faithful.

> *. . . in the future there is laid up for me the crown of righteousness, which the Lord, the righteous Judge, will award to me on that day; and not only to me, but also to all who have loved His appearing.* —2 Timothy 4:8.

True believers are looking forward to the blessed hope and appearing of Christ as our redemption.

> *For the grace of God has appeared, bringing salvation to all men, instructing us to deny ungodliness and worldly desires and to live sensibly, righteously and godly in the present age, looking for the blessed hope and the appearing of the glory of our great God and Savior, Christ Jesus, who gave Himself for us to redeem us from every lawless deed, and to purify for Himself a people for His own possession, zealous for good deeds.*—Titus 2:11-14.

We must establish ourselves blameless and holy when Jesus comes for us with all His angels (also see Matthew 24:31 and Jude 1:14).

> *. . . so that He may establish your hearts without blame in holiness before our God and Father at the coming of our Lord Jesus with all His saints.* —1 Thessalonians 3:13.

> *Now may the God of peace Himself sanctify you entirely; and may your spirit and soul and body be preserved complete, without blame at the coming of our Lord Jesus Christ.* —1 Thessalonians 5:23.

The dead in Christ will be raised first, and then those alive in Christ will be resurrected when He appears to gather the elect. Redemption will be heralded by a trumpet blast and shout[24] (see also Matthew 24:31).

> *But we do not want you to be uninformed, brethren, about those who are asleep, so that you will not grieve as do the rest who have no hope. For if we believe that Jesus died and rose again, even so God will bring with Him those who have fallen asleep in Jesus. For this we say to you by the word of the Lord, that we who are alive and remain until the coming of the Lord, will not precede those who have fallen asleep. For the Lord Himself will descend from heaven with a shout, with the voice of the archangel and with the trumpet of God, and the dead in Christ will rise first. Then we who are alive and remain will be caught up together with them in the clouds to meet the Lord in the air, and so we shall always be with the Lord.*—1 Thessalonians 4:13-17.

Certain events will precede the gathering of the elect (contrary to a belief of an imminent and pre-tribulation return of Christ). According to Paul, a falling away from the faith and the establishment of the Antichrist in the temple must happen first. The temple must still be built, and the covenant of death spoken of by Isaiah and Daniel must still come three and a half years before the Antichrist's time of authority begins. We could be waiting for quite a while but are warned by Peter, Paul, and Christ to persevere and remain blameless.

> *Now we request you, brethren, with regard to the* ***coming of our Lord Jesus Christ and our gathering together to Him****, that you not be quickly shaken from your composure or be disturbed either by a spirit or a message or a letter as if from us, to the effect that the day of the Lord has come. Let no one in any way deceive you, for* ***it will not come unless the apostasy comes first, and the man of lawlessness is revealed, the son of destruction, who opposes and exalts himself above every so-called god or object of worship, so that he takes his seat in the temple of God, displaying himself as being God****. Do you not remember that while I was still with you, I was telling you these things? And you know what restrains him now, so that in his time he will be revealed. For the mystery of lawlessness is already at work; only he who now restrains will do so until he is taken out of the way. Then that lawless one will be revealed whom the Lord will slay with the breath of His mouth and bring to an end by the appearance of His coming; that is, the one whose coming is in accord with the activity of Satan, with all power and signs and false wonders, and with all the deception of wickedness for those who perish, because they did not receive the love of the truth so as to be saved.* —2 Thessalonians 2:1-10.

In the next chapter, we'll undertake a comprehensive overview of the Revelation given to John by Jesus Christ.

CHAPTER SIXTEEN
THE UNVEILING

You've probably read half or more of the book of Revelation by now while going through this self-study. My intent was to introduce many of the verses and concepts early on and to provide repetition to make your study of Revelation more meaningful. I hope that's been the case.

In this chapter, we'll undertake a comprehensive overview of the book of Revelation similar to what we did with the book of Daniel. This will be broken down into seven parts as follows:

16.1 Division of the Study of the Revelation by Part and Theme

Part	Theme
Part I: Revelation 1 – 4	Introduction by John and letters to the churches in Asia Minor.
Part II: Revelation 5 – 8:1	Breaking of seals 1-7, the gathering, and protection of the 144,000.
Part III: Revelation 8:2 – 10	Trumpet judgments 1-6 (the beginning of God's wrath).
Part IV: Revelation 11 – 13	Several perspectives of the Antichrist's 3.5-year period of authority that will end with trumpet #7.
Part V: Revelation 14 – 16	Events just before and just after the end of the 3.5-year period of authority; vial judgments 1-6 (almost the end of God's wrath).
Part VI: Revelation 17 – 19	Babylon and the battle of Armageddon (end of God's wrath).
Part VII: Revelation 20 – 22	Christ's 1,000-year kingdom; new heaven and earth; closure

As discussed in Chapter Fourteen, the Revelation is sequential, relatively easy to read, written for the church, and not symbolic as a whole. Take your time when reading Scripture references. My recommendation is to read the Revelation one chapter at a time and then compare what you've read to the appropriate overview given here.

Let's begin our study of the ultimate in apocalyptic unveiling with *Part I: Revelation 1-4*.

PART I: REVELATION 1 – 4

RECOMMENDED READING:

1. Review the appropriate portion of Chapter Fourteen of this guide – *Part II: Introduction to the Revelation*
2. Revelation 1-4

The first four chapters of the Revelation offer an introduction by John and instructions in the form of letters from Christ to the seven churches of Asia Minor (at the time of John's vision in 90 CE). John also reported what he saw after being invited to heaven to view the visions of the end.

Translation of the Greek word used for *angel* in these passages (*aggelos*) depicts a *messenger*. This may mean that each letter is addressed to a messenger or leadership of the appropriate church instead of an actual angel. This interpretation would make more sense than a scenario where Christ is telling John to write to angels – especially when Christ has regular access to them Himself. Regardless of your position on this topic, the message and the intended audience aren't affected. The translation of "*messenger*" therefore is a secondary issue and not worth fretting over.

~ REVELATION CHAPTER 1 ~

In this opening dialog, you'll receive an introduction from John and learn that the audience of this apocalyptic writing is seven churches of Asia Minor. The prophecy contained within it was, and is, applicable to:

- These seven churches and their behavior at the time of the writing in approximately 90 CE.
- Any church since then exhibiting similar qualities and behavior. They can learn from the warnings or admonishments given to the seven churches by Christ, who labeled each church with particular positive and negative attributes.
- The future Middle East and the regions comprised by ancient Asia Minor from the time the "*covenant of death*" is entered into with the coming Antichrist.

Some modern-day church denominations hold to a belief that each church and its letter in the Revelation are symbolic and correspond to a different "church age." For instance, they believe the church of Sardis is the church during the Reformation (1500-1700 CE) and that the church of Philadelphia represents the current church from 1700 CE to the present. The rationale is that behavior and circumstances of the churches in the letters parallel that of various eras in the history of the church.[25] The assumption therefore is that Christ will return soon since we are in the "final church age."

This is man's wisdom at work, and you should avoid this way of thinking at all cost. While we can learn from the behavior and potential consequences of the churches in Asia Minor, we should take the letters at face value and be careful not to make something out of nothing. Good hermeneutics dictates we seek the historical meaning. Thus, there's no reason to employ allegory or symbolism (such as dispensationalism does to this part of the book) where originally none was intended (though each letter employs some symbolism which would have been understood by the readers).

Key Points or Considerations:

1. The Revelation was meant for the seven churches of Asia Minor in the "near" part of a near-far prophecy that spans current behavior and consequences as of 90 CE to the end of this age.
2. Seven lampstands are the seven churches of Asia Minor.

3. Seven stars are messengers from the seven churches of Asia Minor.
4. Christ's weapon in apocalyptic writing is the sword.

1:1-6. God gave this Revelation of end-time events to Christ to give to the servants of the church through John, who then wrote them down for the seven churches in Asia Minor. His greeting included God, Christ, and the spirits of each of the seven churches he was writing to. Why address these seven churches in particular? John was most likely their apostle and responsible for their spiritual well-being and growth. Also, they were located for the most part in what is western Turkey today in the middle of what will be regions making up the Antichrist's kingdom.

> Although many may have been taught that Revelation won't apply to them because the church will be gone before these events unfold, the book teaches a different ending and offers encouragement right off the bat.
>
> > *Blessed is he who reads and those who hear the words of the prophecy, and heed the things which are written in it; for the time is near*. —Revelation 1:3.

1:7-8. "*BEHOLD, HE IS COMING WITH THE CLOUDS, and every eye will see Him, even those who pierced Him; and all the tribes of the earth will mourn . . .*" is a quote from Zechariah echoed by others. Christ even referred to this Scripture on the Mount of Olives (cf. Daniel 7:13; Matthew 24:30 & 26:64; Mark 13:26 & 14:62; Zechariah 12:10; John 19:37).

1:9-11. Persecution of the first-century church was in full swing, and many had suffered tribulation and death as a result. In fact, John had been exiled to the Island of Patmos just off the coast of Greece. The year would've been approximately 90 CE.

1:12-16. This passage describes Christ, and you'll learn shortly that the seven lampstands represent the seven churches of Asia Minor, to whom this Revelation is addressed. The description of Christ in

Daniel 7:9-10 also reveals a white head and hair like snow or wool.

> *I kept looking Until thrones were set up, And the Ancient of Days took His seat;* ***His vesture was like white snow And the hair of His head like pure wool****. His throne was ablaze with flames, Its wheels were a burning fire. A river of fire was flowing And coming out from before Him . . .* —Daniel 7:9-10.

After reading verse 16, it would be good to remember that the weapon of Christ is a sword. Paul informs us in Ephesians 6:17 that the *sword* of the Spirit is the Word of God, also equated with Christ in Revelation 19:13. Revelation 9:15 & 21 reveal the sword Christ uses to strike down the nations at the battle of Armageddon.

1:17-19. Christ explains to John that He is the first and the last – the resurrected one who holds the power of death and hell. He instructs John to write down the things that *are* (current affairs contained in the letters to the seven churches of Asia Minor) and the things that *will be* (end-times events to follow).

1:20. The seven stars Christ is holding in His hand represent messengers from the seven churches of Asia Minor. Again, the Greek word for "messenger" is *aggelos*, which is often translated as "angel" even though it wouldn't make much sense for Christ to tell John to write a message to angels who are always in the presence of God and Christ. Therefore, the messengers John is told to write to are probably people who represent each church – perhaps elders or pastors. The golden lampstands represent the churches.

16.2 Map of the Seven Churches of Asia Minor

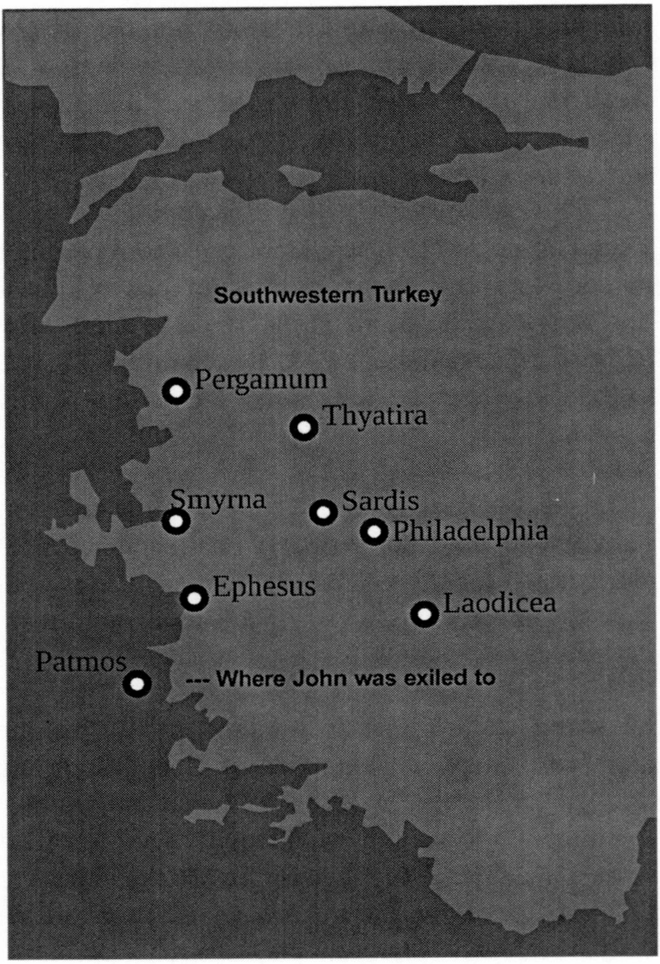

(Courtesy of Wikipedia)

~ REVELATION CHAPTER 2 ~

In this chapter, you'll read the letters given to these four churches of Asia Minor: Ephesus, Smyrna, Pergamum, and Thyatira. The church at Smyrna, like that at Philadelphia, is praised and Christ has nothing against them.

2:1-3. This passage is specifically for the church at Ephesus, which was 60 miles northeast of Patmos and 35 miles south of Izmir, Turkey. The city was the largest and most important in the Roman province of Asia. Christ begins by encouraging and praising the church for their patience and perseverance in the face of evil and in the midst of false apostles.

2:4-7. But they had forgotten Christ and His ways. They must repent or suffer the consequences, which include the removal of the church. True to His word, there is no church there today, and Islam is the pervasive religion in the region. Conversely, those who overcome evil and persevere will be present in God's everlasting kingdom (cf. Revelation 22:2). Christ commends them for hating the evil ways of the Nicolaitans, who were followers of a heretic named Nicolas.

2:8-11. The text here is for the church at Smyrna (modern-day Izmir, Turkey), which is where Polycarp[26] was martyred. He was one of John's disciples. The city was 13 miles south and 35 miles north of Ephesus and the second-largest in Asia. Christ acknowledges their tribulation and poverty and the fact that some falsely claim to be Jews. He encourages them to remain faithful despite the tribulation and imprisonment that will befall them soon in order to receive everlasting life. If they do, they'll avoid the lake of fire judgment of God – the *second death* (cf. Revelation 20:14 & 21:8). I'm unsure of the significance of the "*ten days of tribulation*" and can find no significant information related to the statement. Perhaps it corresponds to trouble witnessed during the Roman occupation.

2:12-13. Christ addresses the church at Pergamum in this passage. Its location was 15 miles from the Aegean coast, and 70 miles north of

Smyrna. The city was the oldest in Asia. Christ begins by commending the believers at Pergamum for their undeterred faith – even in the face of the murder of one of their fellow believers, Antipas.

2:14-15. Some in this church held to the teaching of Balaam, causing Jews to eat food sacrificed to idols and commit immoral acts. Others held to the teachings of the Nicolaitans as did the church at Ephesus.

2:16-17. Christ warned the church to repent or suffer the same fate that the Antichrist and his followers will experience in the last days, which will include defeat at the battle of Armageddon (cf. Revelation 19:15). He also offered encouragement by reminding the reader that great rewards await the faithful. The "*white stone with a new name*" may be symbolic of a "ticket" or "pass" (to heaven) as was the practice of the day. Here's what the New Commentary says on the subject:

> In ancient times, white stones were given to people (with their names written on them) as invitations to special banquets. (This is similar to the practice in modern times of sending engraved invitations.) If this is what Jesus was alluding to, the white stone with the new name could very well signify an open invitation to his wedding feast (Rev_19:9).

2:18-19. Thyatira, halfway between Pergamum and Sardis, is the focus of these verses although the city was the least significant in Asia. John's description of Christ as having "*eyes like a flame of fire, and his feet are like burnished bronze*" probably portrays a Christ about to judge – especially considering their evil ways and the consequences they'll suffer if they don't repent. But He starts this letter with encouragement and commends the church's deeds, love, faith, and perseverance.

2:20-21. The reference to Jezebel here probably depicts the same spirit of rebellion and sin that we see today in the church. Originally, Jezebel was the queen of King Ahab hundreds of years before John's time. She incited her husband to act wickedly and was responsible for the death of many of God's prophets. She also led Israel to worship the goddess Ashteroth, the "*Queen of Heaven*" (cf. Jeremiah 44:17, 18, & 25). Jezebel came to a bitter end, but the spirit of rebellion and destruction of authority exist today. *She* hasn't repented, though Christ has given her the opportunity.

2:22-23. Anyone acting under the influence of that *Jezebel* spirit will suffer God's wrath unless they repent. Christ reminds us that everyone will reap what they sow.

2:24-29. Christ encourages those in the church who aren't practicing sin to continue their good works until He comes. At that time, they'll receive authority over the nations and receive the "*morning star*." Just as Christ was the "*hidden manna*" to the church of Pergamum, He was also the morning star (cf. Revelation 22:16) to the church of Thyatira. Of course, He's still these things to those who believe in Him.

> The "*Spirit*" in verse 29 may be a reference to the *Holy Spirit* based on Scripture such as 1 Corinthians 3:16.

~ REVELATION CHAPTER 3 ~

Contained in this section are the letters to the last three churches: Sardis, Philadelphia, and Laodicea.

3:1-2. Sardis was 50 miles east of Smyrna and 30 miles southeast of Thyatira. Christ called the church "dead" and warned it to "*wake up, and strengthen the things that remain, which were about to die*."

> No repentance; Jesus will come like a thief and they won't know the hour; a few haven't defiled their garments. He that overcomes won't be blotted out of the Book of Life.

3:3. The church is warned to repent or suffer God's wrath in the Day of the Lord. A key point to remember: it will be the *Day of the Lord* destruction that comes suddenly and without warning on the unfaithful world – not the appearing of Christ and the gathering of the church. This is in sharp contrast to what those who hold to a pre-tribulation rapture are taught.

> *Therefore if you do not wake up, I will* ***come like a thief****, and you will not know at what hour I will come to you.* —Revelation 3:3.

> *For you yourselves know full well that* ***the day of the Lord will come just like a thief*** *in the night. While they are saying, "Peace and safety!" then destruction will come upon them suddenly like labor pains upon a woman with child, and they will not escape.* —1 Thessalonians 5:2-3.

> *But the* ***day of the Lord will come like a thief****, in which the heavens will pass away with a roar and the elements will be destroyed with intense heat, and the earth and its works will be burned up.* —2 Peter 3:10.

Also in sharp contrast to man's wisdom is the biblical concept that we can give up our salvation and fall from grace. Those in the church at Thyatira faced this possible outcome as did members of the church at Sardis as you'll see in verse 5 (below).

3:4-6. A few in the church are righteous. They and the others who overcome sin and remain that way will be dressed in white and walk with Christ. We'll see the manifestation of this in Revelation 7:

> *Then one of the elders answered, saying to me, "These who are* ***clothed in the white robes****, who are they, and where have they come from?" I said to him, "My lord, you know." And he said to me, "****These are the ones who come out of the great tribulation****, and they have washed their robes and made them white in the blood of the Lamb."* —Revelation 7:13-14.

In verse 5, Christ makes it very clear that our names can be removed from His Book of Life. Included in this group of people who can lose their salvation will be anyone taking the mark of the beast during the Antichrist's reign.

3:7-8. The city of Philadelphia was 28 miles southeast of Sardis. From Christ's message, the church there was faithful and obedient and will therefore reap great reward for keeping His Word and not denying Him. Interestingly, there's no complaint against this group. Only two of the churches in Asia Minor could boast this – Smyrna and Philadelphia.

3:9. As with Smyrna, some at this church claim to be Jews.

3:10-11. Because of their faithfulness, Christ will *keep* them from the "*hour of testing*" that will come upon the whole world to *test* everyone. He admonishes them to remain faithful and persevere so they can keep their heavenly rewards (crowns).

This difficult passage is used by many as proof of a pre-tribulation rapture. They interpret "*will keep you*" as meaning "completely remove you out of," yet a closer look at the Scripture presented in these 2 verses and the original Greek wording reveal something else entirely. Let's look at the definitions of the original Greek words used for *keep*, *hour*, *testing*, and *test*:

- "*I also will **keep** you*": tēreō (Strong's G5083). Defined: To guard by keeping an eye on.
- "*from the **hour***": hōra (Strong's G5610). Defined: Figurative day, hour, season; time.
- "*of **testing***": peirasmos (Strong's G3986). Defined: Putting to proof by adversity or temptation.
- "*upon the whole world to **test***": peirazō (Strong's G3985). Defined: Scrutinize; Examine; Try.

Ability to use this very small piece of Scripture to support an end-times theology also relies on two more things:

1. An assumption that the "*hour of testing*" is referring to the future Great Tribulation of the Antichrist. While this

may be possible, remember that the letters were written for real, honest-to-goodness institutions of John's time. We know too from the testimonies of martyrs like Polycarp that the persecution of the church in the first and second centuries got much worse and probably felt like the "*hour of testing*" foretold by Christ.

2. Modern doctrine that insists the church of Philadelphia represents a faithful church that will be raptured out of the Great Tribulation. One major problem with this is that a dispensation theology associated with church ages, also popular with pre-tribulation rapture believers, mandates that the ancient church of *Laodicea* – not Philadelphia – represents this current church age.

Because of the context, definitions of the Greek words used, and the understanding gleaned from other Scripture that the saints won't escape the Great Tribulation of the Antichrist, verses 10 and 11 could be paraphrased to read: "*I will watch over you during a time that I will allow for testing of the world, but I will come quickly. Persevere through the testing to keep your reward.*"

3:12-13. We'll see the reference to the bride of Christ and the temple of God in His everlasting kingdom again in Revelation 21.

> *And I saw the holy city, new Jerusalem, coming down out of heaven from God, made ready as a bride adorned for her husband. And I heard a loud voice from the throne, saying, "Behold, the tabernacle of God is among men, and He will dwell among them, and they shall be His people, and God Himself will be among them . . .* —Revelation 21:2-3.

> *He who overcomes will inherit these things, and I will be his God and he will be My son.* —Revelation 21:7.

> *There will no longer be any curse; and the throne of God and of the Lamb will be in it, and His bond-servants will serve Him; they will see His face, and His name will be on their foreheads.* —Revelation 22:3-4.

3:14-16. The final audience was in Laodicea, 40 miles southeast of Philadelphia and 100 miles east of Ephesus. If you follow the churches on the map in figure 16.2 (clockwise starting with the Isle of Patmos) you'll see that it forms something of a route that could've been a Roman mail route as some have suggested.

> Neither hot nor cold in their faith, this church was "*lukewarm*." Therefore, Christ said He will *spit them out of His mouth*. This can't be a good outcome . . .

3:17-19. Laodicea was known for its wealthy and finely dressed citizens, and for the manufacturing of eye salve. Christ warns the church members to repent and obtain from Christ:

1. Valuable refining and disciplining as if by fire. (See the section *Tribulation & Beheading* in Chapter Eight of this guide.) Proverbs 3:12 reminds us that "*whom the Lord loves He reproves, even as a father corrects the son in whom he delights.*"
2. White garments of the righteous (e.g. Revelation 7:13).
3. The ability to see the truth and no longer be blinded (e.g. 2 Thessalonians 2:10-11).

3:20-22. We need to overcome sin and remain righteous in order to be with Christ in God's kingdom. Essential to this is giving ourselves to Christ in the new covenant and maintaining a relationship with Him.

~ REVELATION CHAPTER 4 ~

Here we see the invitation of John to preview end-times events. He receives a magnificent view of heaven that reveals the throne of God and part of His entourage: 24 elders and the "*four living creatures*," all giving glory to God.

Key Points or Considerations:

1. John is invited to heaven to view the end-times sequence of

events. This is *not* symbolic of a pre-tribulation rapture of the church.

2. The 24 elders mentioned here are part of God's hierarchy and not representative of a special few in a church raptured before the time of great tribulation of the Antichrist.

4:1. John is invited to heaven for a preview of end-times events. Those who hold to a pre-tribulation rapture position see this as a symbolic representation of the gathering of the church. Since John's invitation comes before the scrolls are opened, some believe the rapture will therefore happen before any of the end-of-the-world events take place. My recommendation is to take this passage at face value and accept it as it is – an invitation to heaven for the unveiling John must later pass on to the church.

4:2-3. John sees the throne of God. Emerald and jasper were precious stones used in the making of the Jewish priest's breastplate (cf. Exodus 28:17 & 20; 39:10 & 13). God's radiance as a rainbow can be seen in Ezekiel's account (cf. 1:28).

4:4. The 24 elders (seen next in verse 10) are just that – elders in God's hierarchy, not raptured saints.

4:5-6a. John further describes the throne of God.

4:6b-9. You'll find a description of the "*four living creatures*" of heaven here. Isaiah saw the same thing in his vision of the temple of God in heaven (cf. Isaiah 6:1-3).

4:10-11. John sees the 24 elders worshipping God and casting their crowns before Him. One pre-tribulation rapture belief I've heard: "The elders are casting crowns. Since the 24 elders are raptured believers and we won't get crowns until Christ rewards the gathered church, this must mean John is in heaven after the rapture. This proves we'll be in heaven before the tribulation . . ."

Please be careful not to buy into this. The 24 elders are part of

God's hierarchy, and their crowns – just as with Christ's crown – are heavenly crowns not isolated to a reward given at the end to the gathered bride of Christ. John has just been invited to heaven to view the end-times events and is simply describing activities happening at the throne of God as he's about to receive his apocalyptic visions.

PART II: REVELATION 5 – 8:1

RECOMMENDED READING:

1. Review the appropriate portion of Chapter Fourteen of this guide – *Part II: Introduction to the Revelation*
2. Revelation 5-7
3. Revelation 8:1

The main focus of this section is the unveiling of events by breaking the seven seals of the scroll containing the visions. Having earned the right through the purchase of mankind by His sacrifice, Christ is the only one who can break the seals. Included in this section is a glimpse of the church gathered after the darkening of seal 6. We'll also see 144,000 of God's elect sealed for protection against His impending wrath.

~ REVELATION CHAPTER 5 ~

The Lamb of God is about to break the scroll's seals to unveil last-days scenarios.

5:1-4. God is holding a book protected by seven seals. As was the custom, a portion of the scroll would be written on, sealed, and then the process repeated as often as necessary to write a multi-sectioned document and preserve each section. A strong angel asked, "*Who is worthy to open the book and to break its seals?*" No one in heaven, on the earth, or under the earth was worthy. John was deeply grieved because of this.

5:5. One of the elders comforted John by telling him, "*behold, the Lion that is from the tribe of Judah, the Root of David, has overcome so as to open the book and its seven seals*." Because Christ *overcame*, He was worthy to open the book and unseal its sections.

He overcame by purchasing us from the world through His death and resurrection as you'll read in verses 9-10.

5:6-8. John sees a lamb "*as if slain*" with seven horns and seven eyes, which represent the seven spirits of God sent out into all the earth. The lamb was Christ, who indeed was slain for our sinful nature at His crucifixion. Compare this passage with that of Zechariah 3:9, which most likely refers to the coming kingdom of Christ that will remove the iniquity of that land as also prophesied by Daniel (cf. 9:24).

'For behold, the stone that I have set before Joshua; on one stone are seven eyes. Behold, I will engrave an inscription on it,' declares the LORD of hosts, 'and I will remove the iniquity of that land in one day.' —Zechariah 3:9.

Seven is often used to depict perfection. So the seven horns may be symbolic of Christ's perfect and everlasting authority. He *has* been given the keys to hell and death, after all. The 24 elders are worshipping Christ at this point in John's vision.

5:9-10. The 24 elders confirm that Christ alone is worthy to open the book and seals because He has purchased the right to do so. "*Worthy are You to take the book and to break its seals; for You were slain, and purchased for God with Your blood men from every tribe and tongue and people and nation. You have made them to be a kingdom and priests to our God; and they will reign upon the earth.*"

5:11-14. Thousands upon thousands of angels, elders, and other creatures praise God and Christ and give them glory.

~ REVELATION CHAPTER 6 ~

Major events or eras Jesus told His disciples about on the Mount of Olives can also be seen here from the birth pangs to the darkening of the sun, moon, and stars that will precede the gathering of Christ's bride and the wrath of God.

Key Points or Considerations:

1. Each of the six seals broken in this chapter reveals scenarios that parallel those given by Christ on the Mount of Olives (e.g. Matthew 24:5-30).
2. The first seal represents the false messiahs Jesus mentioned in Matthew 24:4-5, not *the* Christ or *the* Antichrist. It and the next two seal events are *birth pangs* that will happen with greater intensity and frequency as the end draws near (e.g. Matthew 24:5-8).
3. Christ's weapon in apocalyptic writing is the sword (not bow).
4. The fourth and fifth seals depict the persecution and death that the Antichrist will be granted authority to execute (e.g. Matthew 24:10-26).
5. Seal 6 depicts the darkening of the earth and the mourning of those about to experience God's wrath (e.g. Matthew 24:29-30).

6:1-2. Christ breaks the first seal and reveals the contents. John sees a white horse whose rider is wearing a crown and bent on conquering. The rider's weapon is a bow. Being clothed in white signifies righteousness and the crown depicts authority. While this sounds a lot like Christ, the rider is carrying a bow – not a sword, which is the weapon of Christ. You may remember this discussion from our overview of Revelation 1:12-16.

> The scene unveiled by the breaking of seal 1 is identical to the first birth-pang Jesus told His disciples about on the Mount of Olives: "*For many will come in My name, saying, 'I am the Christ,' and will mislead many.*" —Matthew 24:5.

Some make the claim that this rider in white represents the Antichrist that will come in the end, but that's not possible. According to Jesus, this is one of several birth pangs that will increase with intensity and frequency as the end draws near. It comes before the Antichrist and other end-times events as foretold by Jesus. Finally, seals 4 and 5 preserve Scripture related to the time of the Antichrist – the Great Tribulation. These are after the rider in white seen in seal 1.

6:3-4. Christ breaks the second seal and reveals a red horse whose rider has been given authority to take peace from the world. Compare this to the second birth-pang Jesus told His disciples about on the Mount of Olives:

You will be hearing of wars and rumors of wars. See that you are not frightened, for those things must take place, but that is not yet the end. For nation will rise against nation, and kingdom against kingdom . . . —Matthew 24:6.

6:5-6. The third seal is broken and John sees a black horse whose rider is holding a pair of scales. He hears, "*A quart of wheat for a denarius, and three quarts of barley for a denarius; and do not damage the oil and the wine.*"

This scene depicts the famine Jesus told His disciples about in advance: "*. . . and in various places there will be famines and earthquakes.*" —Matthew 24:7.

6:7-8. With the breaking of the fourth seal, John sees a pale horse whose rider is death; hell followed. Authority over one-fourth of the earth was given to them to kill with sword, famine, pestilence, and by the wild beasts of the earth.

This is the time of the Antichrist's authority – the Great Tribulation – and most likely the time of testing Christ talked about in Revelation 3:10.

There are four significant things to know and remember about this passage:

1. Just as death and persecution by the "*abomination that causes desolation*" (cf. Matthew 24:15) follow the third birth-pang of famine in Jesus' Mount of Olives discourse, this event unveiled by the breaking of seal 4 follows the famine hidden by seal 3.
2. In seal 5, John sees those who'll be martyred for their faith during the Great Tribulation of the Antichrist (*abomination that causes desolation*) as depicted in seal 4.
3. The Greek word for "*beasts*" in verse 8 (wild *beasts* of the earth) is *therion* (Strong's G2342), which represents a particularly venomous creature and is the only word used to describe the Antichrist in the Revelation (e.g. Revelation 13, 14, 15:2, 16:2, etc.).
4. God will grant the Antichrist and his kingdom authority over all the earth to kill and persecute for three and a half years (cf. Daniel 7:25; Revelation 13:7-8).

6:9-11. Christ breaks the fifth seal and John sees the souls of those martyred for their faith during the timeframe of seal 4. Those killed during that time ask, "*How long, O Lord, holy and true, will You refrain from judging and avenging our blood on those who dwell on the earth?*" They're given a white robe and told to "*wait until the number of their fellow servants and their brethren who were to be killed even as they had been would be completed also.*"

The martyrs mentioned here are in the context of the Antichrist's time of great tribulation. Christ tells us in Revelation 20:4 that they'll be resurrected and will reign with Him during His 1,000-year kingdom (see also the section *Beheaded* in Chapter Six of this study guide).

6:12-14. Breaking the sixth seal unveiled a great earthquake and complete darkening of the sun, moon, and stars. This is the darkening Jesus told His disciples about that will precede the gathering of the bride of Christ and the wrath of God (cf. Matthew 24:29; Mark

13:24-25; Luke 21:25-26; Joel 2:2 & 3:14-15).

6:15-17. Everyone on the earth at this time will hide themselves in caves and among the rocks of the mountains, saying to the rocks, "*Fall on us and hide us from the presence of Him who sits on the throne, and from the wrath of the Lamb; for the great day of their wrath has come, and who is able to stand?*"

> Isaiah saw this coming as well: "*Men will go into caves of the rocks and into holes of the ground before the terror of the LORD and the splendor of His majesty, when He arises to make the earth tremble*." —Isaiah 2:19.

~ Revelation Chapter 7 ~

Two very important components in the end-times sequence of events are described in this chapter:

1. God seals a remnant of Israel (144,000) for protection against His impending wrath which will be addressed beginning with the next chapter.
2. John sees the bride of Christ in heaven after her gathering just after the darkening of the sun, moon, and stars of Matthew 24:30 and the sixth seal depiction.

7:1-3. After John views the darkening of the sun, moon, and stars and mourning of the sixth seal, he's shown a scene where four angels have stopped the wind from blowing on the earth. Another angel coming from the east has the seal of God and tells the four angels to wait to harm the earth until they've "*sealed the bond-servants of our God on their foreheads*."

> I've often wondered about the significance of holding back the wind and have come to realize that we'd be in great distress without it. Planes would have difficulty taking off and landing. Wind generators would stop. There'd be no natural cooling or

evaporation. Pollination would be nearly impossible. Smog and pollution would be stationary, producing toxic breathing environments. And I'm sure this is just the "tip of the iceberg."

7:4-8. The angel seals 144,000 of God's people with His seal. This list contains 12,000 from each of the 12 tribes of Israel. You may remember from the section *144,000 From the 12 Tribes of Israel* in Chapter Six of this guide that the original tribe of Dan was replaced by the tribe of Manasseh (most likely due to the sinful behavior of its members and idol worship).

7:9. John then saw "*a great multitude which no one could count, from every nation and all tribes and peoples and tongues, standing before the throne and before the Lamb, clothed in white robes . . .*"

Several key things to keep in mind about this passage:

1. John sees this great multitude just *after* the sixth seal is broken and *before* the seventh seal.
2. The sixth seal revealed the darkening of the sun, moon, and stars that precedes the gathering of the bride of Christ.
3. There are so many people that their number can't be counted.
4. The multitude is made up of people from every nation and language on earth.

Popular among pre-tribulation rapture proponents is the belief that this multitude is a "tribulation force" made up of people who've been *left behind* after the rapture but who've since repented and accepted Christ. This isn't scriptural or possible. One compelling reason is the fact that those left behind won't repent of their sinful behavior and will blaspheme God during the time of His wrath (cf. Revelation 9:20-21; 16:9 & 11). It would be pretty hard to get a tribulation force "*which no one could count*" under those circumstances.

I've also heard a theory that this multitude will be made up of tribulation Jews on their way to Petra. Please remember that this group is made up of a very large number of people "*from every nation and all tribes and peoples and tongues.*"

So who are the members of the multitude? They make up the bride of Christ that will be gathered at the darkening following the Great Tribulation as unveiled in Matthew 24:29 and seal 6.

7:10-12. This great multitude along with all those seen by John in 5:11-14 are praising God.

7:13. One of the elders asks John if he knows who these people making up this uncountable multitude dressed in white robes are and where they came from.

7:14. John doesn't know the answer, so the elder tells him, "***These are the ones who come out of the great tribulation**, and they have washed their robes and made them white in the blood of the Lamb.*"

Again, this vision came to John after the darkening revealed in the sixth seal. We learned from Christ in Matthew 24, Mark 13, and Luke 21 that the darkening will follow the Great Tribulation of the Antichrist. That darkening will precede the gathering of the church. John is seeing the church that had been gathered (raptured) from out of the Great Tribulation of the Antichrist when he sees the multitude.

7:15-17. "*They will hunger no longer, nor thirst anymore; nor will the sun beat down on them, nor any heat; for the Lamb in the center of the throne will be their shepherd, and will guide them to springs of the water of life; and God will wipe every tear from their eyes.*"

This multitude, the gathered bride of Christ, will serve God and He will protect them. Compare the Scripture in this passage to that found in Revelation 21:4.

Behold, the tabernacle of God is among men, and He will dwell among them, and they shall be His people, and God Himself will be among them, and He will wipe away every tear from their eyes; and there will no longer be any death; there will no longer be any mourning, or crying, or pain; the first things have passed away. —Revelation 21:3-4.

~ Revelation 8:1 ~

I've broken this single verse out of chapter 8 and used it to conclude this section because it's the last of the seven seal revelations. This event sets the stage for God's wrath against the rest of the world *not* gathered by Christ and His angels at His appearing.

8:1. Christ breaks the seventh and final seal, revealing a silence in heaven for *about* half an hour. As you'll learn from the rest of chapter 8, the silence is used for prayer and preparation for God's impending wrath that will begin with seven "trumpet" judgments.

16.3 Timeline of the Seven Seals
Revelation 6 – 8:1

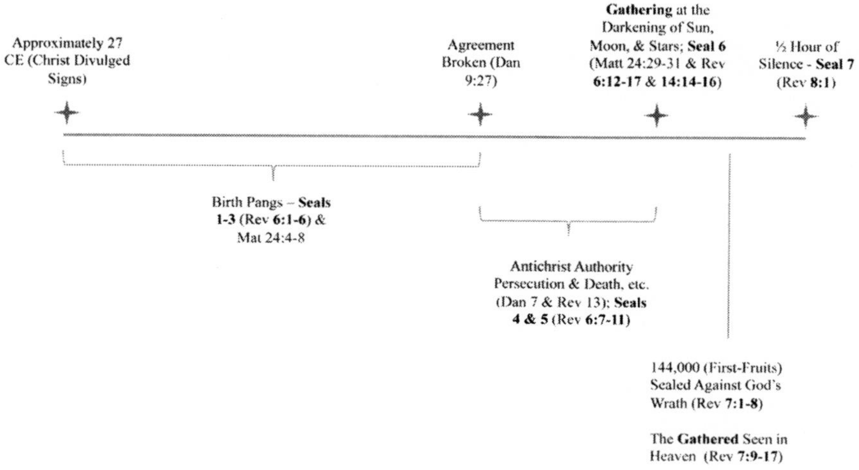

PART III: REVELATION 8: 2 – 10

RECOMMENDED READING:

1. Review the appropriate portion of Chapter Fourteen of this guide – *Part II: Introduction to the Revelation*
2. Revelation 8:2-13
3. Revelation 9 & 10

These chapters detail the first half of God's wrath: the seven trumpet judgments. Chapter 10 introduces the seventh trumpet judgment that will usher in Christ's kingdom, ending the three-and-a-half-year authority of the Antichrist.

~ REVELATION 8:2 – 8:13 ~

John sees the first four of seven trumpet judgments being executed.

8:2. John sees seven angels with seven trumpets. As you'll learn, these are trumpets of God's judgments – not to be confused with the trumpet blast that will be heard at the gathering of the bride of Christ (cf. Matthew 24:31; 1 Corinthians 15:52; 1 Thessalonians 4:16).

8:3-6. Another angel (not one of the seven) gathered the prayers of the saints and added them to an incense censer; the smoke went before God. It seems at this point that all heavenly hosts to include the multitude John had just seen were praying in preparation for God's impending wrath. The angel threw the censer to the earth, causing an earthquake as the other seven angels prepared to administer God's wrath.

8:7. The first angel sounded its trumpet, producing hail and blood, which were then thrown to the earth. One-third of the earth (including vegetation) was burned up.

8:8-9. The second angel sounded its trumpet. "*Something like a great mountain burning with fire was thrown into the sea; and a third of* *the sea became blood, and a third of the creatures which were in the sea and had life, died; and a third of the ships were destroyed.*"

8:10-11. Angel number three sounded, destroying one-third of the rivers and streams and poisoning the water. Many people will die because of this.

> The waters are poisoned by a *star* that is called *wormwood*. The Greek word for *star* is *astēr* (Strong's G792), which figuratively or literally means to be "*strewn across the sky*." Wormwood is used only once in the New Testament, but its Old Testament origin is the Hebrew word *la'ănâh* (Strong's H3939). It basically just means "bitter." (NOTE: Jeremiah also referred to this event as recorded in Jeremiah 23:15.)
>
> The wormwoods are members of the family of *Compositae* and belong to the genus Artemisia, a group consisting of 180 species. It's likely the reference to wormwood in Revelation 8 here was made just to show how bad the waters would become after the sounding of the third angel's trumpet.

8:12. One-third of the natural lights will go out with the sounding of the fourth angel.

8:13. As bad as things have been to this point with the first four trumpet blasts, things are about to get worse.

~ Revelation Chapter 9 ~

Trumpet judgments five and six can be seen here: demons or demonic forces in the form of scorpions that can hurt (but not kill) those who've accepted the mark of the Antichrist and of 200 million "*horsemen*." These two judgments represent woes one and two.

Key Points or Considerations:

1. God's wrath will be just that – His judgment. This is

regardless of whether we recognize elements that fit within our own frames of reference. It's best to continue to look at the execution of God's wrath in that light.

2. To follow point #1, the fact that China is the only country capable of having an army of 200 million soldiers doesn't make it the vehicle of destruction of trumpet judgment 6 as some believe.
3. God's wrath will be divided into three "*woes*." Trumpet judgment 5 will comprise the first one.

9:1-2. At the sounding of the fifth trumpet, the bottomless pit (i.e. hell, Hades, etc.) is opened to make way for the plague of special locusts you'll learn more about in verses 3-11.

9:3-4. Locusts with power as scorpions are allowed to hurt only the "*men who do not have the seal of God on their foreheads*."

9:5-6. They can't kill but can torment for five months with a sting (as with a scorpion). Those stung will wish they were dead. Many during the cold war era believed the scorpions are symbolic of modern military weapons such as the Apache helicopter.

All I can say to that is this: John is witnessing God's wrath, not man's. It would be better for us to take the prophecy at face value and believe the plague will come from God as stated instead of trying to put the judgment into our own frame of reference, which changes regularly and is very limited.

9:7-10. The *locusts* described here have these features:

- Their heads appeared to sport crowns.
- Their faces will be like those of men.
- Hair like the hair of women.
- Teeth like the teeth of lions.
- Breastplates of iron.

- The "*sound of their wings will be like the sound of chariots, of many horses rushing to battle.*"
- Their tails will be like those of scorpions, the sting of which will hurt for five months.

9:11. Their king is Satan – angel of the abyss – called *Abaddon* (Hebrew) and *Apollyon* (Greek). You may wish to review the section of Chapter Eight titled *The Dragon – Satan*. As with the Assyrians and their defeat by the Babylonians, God will permit the use of this satanic force to accomplish His purposes.

9:12. The **first woe** consisting of **trumpet judgment 5** is past – two more to go.

9:13-15. The sixth angel sounds its trumpet. In response, four angels bound at the great river Euphrates are released for the single purpose of killing one-third of mankind.

9:16-19. The number of armies of the horsemen controlled by the four angels is 200 million. The riders have red breastplates. The horses' heads are like those of lions, and they breathe fire, smoke, and brimstone. The horses, which have power to do harm in their mouths and tails, kill one-third of mankind.

> Again, a popular approach is to label these as man's weapons of war. While God has indeed used man's forces to accomplish His purposes in the past (as with the ancient Babylonians), He hasn't said so in this case. There's no hint that these resources belong to anyone other than God. It would be better to take the apocalyptic writing at face value as a result.

9:20-21. Those not killed still won't repent and stop their sinful behavior. Not only does this highlight the sinful and rebellious nature of man, but it serves as a reminder that not many if any will repent and be saved during the time of God's wrath.

~ REVELATION CHAPTER 10 ~

John is shown things he isn't allowed to disclose. We also learn from this chapter that the "*mystery of God*" will be completed at the seventh trumpet, bringing to a close the time of the gentiles as foretold by the prophets and apostles.

Key Points or Considerations:

1. The *mystery of God* is the inheritance of what was offered to Israel – the salvation of Christ – but has now been given to the rest of the nations (the gentiles).
2. The seventh trumpet will usher in Christ's kingdom, end the three-and-a-half-year authority of the Antichrist, and conclude the 490-year timeframe of Daniel's vision (cf. Daniel 9).
3. Some believe the seventh trumpet and the trumpet heralding Christ's appearance at the gathering of the bride will be the same thing. This doctrine therefore holds that the trumpet judgments will not be part of God's wrath and that all believers in Christ will experience those woeful judgments. We'll discuss this further in Chapter Seventeen of this guide, *Exploring End-times Positions*. Although a "trumpet" is common to both scenarios, my recommendation at this point is that you consider the seventh and final trumpet judgment and the trumpet blast at the gathering of the church as separate and unrelated events.

10:1-2. A "*strong angel*" (probably a description of Christ) shows an open book to John. The word *angel* is used here to depict a messenger, which could indeed be Christ – especially considering that the Revelation is being given to John by Him. His feet are on the sea and on the land, most likely symbolizing the nations of the earth. The scenario would be appropriate considering that the time of the gentiles is about to come to an end with the sounding of the seventh trumpet.

10:3-4. The *angel* cries out "*as when a lion roars,*" and the seven peals of thunder bellow. The mention of a lion's roar is intriguing and supports a belief that this is Christ, "*the **lion** of the tribe of Judah*" (cf. Revelation 5:5). John is instructed to seal up and refrain from writing down what he heard from the "*seven thunders*." We never discover in the Revelation what John had to keep secret. Perhaps it's best. Considering the horrific things we *will* read about, I can't imagine how much worse the things we *won't* read about could be!

10:5-7. The messenger declares that there will be no more delay in **finishing** the mystery of God. This *mystery* is the inheritance of the kingdom of God by the gentiles. Christ is showing John that the time of the gentiles will end at the seventh trumpet blast, which we'll explore further when we cover the next chapter of Revelation.

> Here are several verses explaining the *mystery* of God and Christ, revealing that it's the gift of Christ to the gentiles – the nations of the world:
>
> > *For I do not want you, brethren, to be uninformed of this **mystery**--so that you will not be wise in your own estimation – that a partial hardening has happened to Israel **until the fullness of the Gentiles has come in*** . . . —Romans 11:25.
> >
> > *Now to Him who is able to establish you according to my gospel and the preaching of Jesus Christ, according to the revelation of the **mystery** which has been kept secret for long ages past, but now is manifested, and by the Scriptures of the prophets, according to the commandment of the eternal God, **has been made known to all the nations, leading to obedience of faith*** . . . —Romans 16:25-26.
> >
> > . . . *that by revelation there was made known to me the **mystery**, as I wrote before in brief. By referring to this, when you read you can understand my insight into the **mystery of Christ**, which in other generations was not made known to the sons of men, as it has now been **revealed to His holy***

> ***apostles and prophets*** *in the Spirit; to be specific,* ***that the Gentiles are fellow heirs and fellow members of the body, and fellow partakers of the promise in Christ Jesus through the gospel*** . . . —Ephesians 3:3-6.

> *. . . that is, the* **mystery** *which has been hidden from the past ages and generations, but has now been manifested to His saints, to whom God willed to* ***make known what is the riches of the glory of this mystery among the Gentiles, which is Christ in you, the hope of glory***. —Colossians 1:26-27.

Scripture contained in verses 5-6 is reminiscent of what Daniel saw and recorded in Daniel 12:7 as follows:

> *I heard the man dressed in linen, who was above the waters of the river, as he raised his right hand and his left toward heaven, and swore by Him who lives forever that it would be for a time, times, and half a time; and as soon as they finish shattering the power of the holy people, all these events will be completed.*—Daniel 12:7.

Interestingly, the end of the "*time, times, and half a time*" as stated in 12:7 above will be at the seventh trumpet judgment (cf. Revelation 11:15). So it's appropriate that the messenger in Daniel and Revelation (again, most likely Christ) is using similar verbiage.

10:8-11. John is told to eat the book the messenger was holding. The contents are bittersweet as he still had more horrors to write about, yet an end to this age will come, ushering in a new heaven and earth along with God's everlasting kingdom.

Part IV: Revelation 11 – 13

RECOMMENDED READING:

1. Review the appropriate portion of Chapter Fourteen of this guide – *Part II: Introduction to the Revelation.*

2. Review section *Two Witnesses* in Chapter Six of this guide.
3. Review section *False Prophets* in Chapter Ten of this guide.
4. Revelation 11-13.

The seventh trumpet judgment introduced by chapter 10 will usher in Christ's kingdom, ending the three-and-a-half-year authority of the Antichrist. Appropriately, chapters 11-13 detail that timeframe and describe the Antichrist's kingdom, the False Prophet, God's two witnesses, and the pursuit of the elect by Satan (through influence of the Antichrist).

~ REVELATION CHAPTER 11 ~

John is shown a temple where the outer courts will be given to the nations (gentiles) for three and a half years. He also sees a vision of God's two witnesses who will prophesy during that timeframe. Verses 13-15 outline the seventh and final trumpet judgment that will herald Christ's kingdom and signal the end of the Antichrist's three-and-a-half-year reign. This will also mark the end of the 490 years given to Israel to accomplish certain goals (such as end sin and bring in everlasting righteousness).

Verses 16-19 offer a quick summary by the 24 elders of heaven of everything the rest of the Revelation will detail from Christ's kingdom until God's kingdom in the new age.

Key Points or Considerations:

1. This is the only place in Scripture where we read about the two witnesses.
2. The temple John sees is on earth, not in heaven, nor is it a *spiritual* temple.
3. The seventh trumpet judgment will herald the end of the Antichrist's reign and the beginning of the 1,000-year kingdom of Christ.

11:1-2. John is told to measure the temple. He's told to avoid measuring the outer court because it has been given to the gentiles. John is also told that the nations (gentiles) will control Jerusalem for 42 months (three and a half years). Keep in mind that the temple was destroyed 20 years before this vision in 70 CE. But it will be rebuilt before the end based on what we learned from Daniel, Jesus, and Paul.

11:3. Two witnesses of God will prophesy for 1,260 days (three and a half years). This is the same length of time the messenger in Daniel 12:7 said would exist from the time daily sacrifice is stopped until the shattering of God's people is finished. We know from Daniel 7:25 that it will also be the time of authority of the Antichrist.

> As a result, we can conclude that the two witnesses will present their testimony during the time of the Antichrist's authority – the Great Tribulation.

11:4-6. These two heavenly beings who normally stand before God will have the power to consume and destroy anyone who wishes to harm them. They'll also be able to stop the rain, turn water into blood, and strike the earth with plagues as desired. This is reminiscent of Moses' delivery of God's message to the Pharaoh and the consequences of his refusal to listen (cf. Exodus 3:10 – 12:33).

> As we discussed in the section of Chapter Six titled *Two Witnesses*, various opinions exist as to the identity of the witnesses. There's no way to know for sure. Regardless of whether they'll be Moses, Elijah, Enoch, or angels, their message will be the same: "Repent, for the time of God's judgment is at hand."

11:7-10. At the end of their three-and-a-half-year ministry, Satan will kill the two witnesses. Their bodies will be allowed to lie out in the open in Jerusalem for three days. The nations will rejoice over the death of these heavenly messengers.

11:11-12. God will resurrect the two witnesses after three days and bring them back to heaven.

11:13-14. Several key points are made in this passage, which reflects the timeframe of an hour after their resurrection:

1. A **great earthquake** will take place.
2. One-tenth of the city will fall during the earthquake.
3. Seven thousand people will die in the earthquake.
4. Those not killed will give glory to God.
5. This, the **second woe, has passed**.

Let's pause for a moment to discuss the timing of the *second woe*. You may remember from our earlier overview of Revelation 9 that the *first woe* will consist of trumpet judgment 5. The second woe will comprise trumpet judgment 6. What will follow the judgment of the second woe is trumpet 7, which will herald the beginning of Christ's reign on earth.

11:15. "*The kingdom of the world has become the kingdom of our Lord and of His Christ; and He will reign forever and ever.*"

We can glean several things from this passage to include that the 1,000-year kingdom of Christ will begin just after the second *woe* is over and, as reported in Revelation 10:7, the mystery of God (time of the gentiles) will be complete at this time.

Just as the complete darkening of the sun, moon, and stars will be a pivotal point marking the gathering of the bride of Christ (e.g. Matthew 24:29-31) and preparation for God's impending wrath (e.g. Revelation 6:12-17), the seventh trumpet blast will mark several things:

1. The end of the last three-and-a-half-year section of the overall 490-year period of Daniel (cf. Daniel 9:27 & 12:6-7).
2. The end of the three-and-a-half-year testimony of God's two witnesses (cf. Revelation 11:3-12).
3. The end of the time of the gentiles to include the 42 months (three and a half years) Jerusalem will be controlled by the nations (Revelation 10:7 & 11:2).

4. The end of the second woe (Revelation 11:14).
5. A great earthquake during the second woe (Revelation 11:13).
6. The start of Christ's 1,000-year kingdom (Revelation 11:15). Goals that Christ's kingdom will accomplish for God's people and Jerusalem according to Daniel 9:24:
    a. Finish the transgression.
    b. Make an end of sin.
    c. Bring in everlasting righteousness (Christ's kingdom and then God's everlasting kingdom).
    d. Seal up vision and prophecy.
    e. Anoint the Most Holy (Christ as King).

11:16-19. The 24 elders in heaven praise God and worship Him, exclaiming that the time of His future and everlasting reign has begun. The elders recount the events *leading up to* the new-age reign of God to include His wrath, the great judgment, the rewarding of God's elect, and the destruction of the wicked.

Verse 19 gives a glimpse of the temple of God in heaven, which will come to earth at the beginning of the new age after the great judgment. Also represented here in advance is the completion of God's wrath with the seventh bowl judgment (the great earthquake and hail seen in Revelation **16:18-21**).

Therefore, verses 16-19 represent in a couple of paragraphs what we know as chapters 8:2 – 22:5 of this Revelation: the wrath of God, 1,000-year reign of Christ, great judgment, and new heaven and earth.

~ Revelation Chapter 12 ~

While Chapter Eleven gave us a glimpse of the three-and-a-half-year authority of the Antichrist as it will relate to the two witnesses of God, this chapter offers a view of Satan's influence in the Antichrist's pursuit and persecution of God's *elect* during that time.

Key Points or Considerations:

1. God put stars and resulting constellations in the heavens to signal events and seasons. Several constellations will align themselves just before the war in heaven.
2. Satan and "*the dragon*" represent the same being. He has had, and will continue to have, access to heaven until he's cast down after the war in heaven (12:7-9).
3. The "*woman*" is a remnant of God that will be kept safe by Him during the three-and-a-half-year reign of the Antichrist. This may very well be the 144,000 also sealed by God for protection against His judgments (cf. Revelation 7:1-8).
4. This passage confirms that believers in Christ will suffer the wrath of Satan (through the Antichrist), sharply contrasting an opposing theory that all Christians will be gathered before this time in a pre-tribulation rapture.

12:1-2. John sees a sign in the heavens: "*A great sign appeared in heaven: a woman clothed with the sun, and the moon under her feet, and on her head a crown of twelve stars . . .*"

And why shouldn't there be signs in the heavens? God Himself said He put them there for signs and seasons: "*Let there be lights in the expanse of the heavens to separate the day from the night, and let them be for signs and for seasons and for days and years . . .*" —Genesis 1:14.

John witnesses the constellations of Virgo (the woman), Coma Bernice (the twelve stars), and Hydra and Corax (the dragon with seven heads and ten horns) in a particular alignment before the war in heaven. I believe the purpose in showing John this vision of the constellations and their specific position (verses 1-5) is twofold:

1. To help us understand who the *woman* and the *dragon* are to set the stage for the rest of this passage (verses 6-17).
2. To show us the position the constellations will be in just

> before the three-and-a-half-year authority of the Antichrist, which will begin with Satan losing his access to heaven and the persecution of God's people that will follow.

In verse 1, the sign John sees is the constellation Bethulah (Virgo) – the *virgin*. She represents Israel (hence the 12 stars) who "*gave birth*" to a Son – Christ (cf. 12:4).

Interestingly, this constellation is seen every couple of years or so in Jerusalem in late September to early October at the time of Rosh Hashanah, the Feast of Trumpets. Why might this be significant? John's report of the position of these stars at a particular point in time is more real and credible if we believe Christ will fulfill the fall feasts at His return just as He did with the spring feasts during His first coming.[27]

If you're interested in learning more about the signs God has placed in the heavens, you may want to check out sites like biblicalastronomy.com or watchmanbiblestudy.com.[28]

12:3-4. Appearing in the sky is another sign: a great red dragon with seven heads, ten horns, and seven crowns (these should be constellations Hydra and Corax). The dragon represents Satan (cf. Revelation12:9). A sweeping away of "*a third of the stars of heaven*" most likely represents the angels Satan has corrupted and taken with him (see 12:9 for possible confirmation).

John's dragon has seven heads, ten horns, and seven crowns. As previously discussed in our study, Satan will influence and guide the Antichrist and his end-times kingdom; this passage just serves as a reminder. Additional references to this "*beast*" that will be controlled by Satan:

- The Antichrist's kingdom that "*comes out of the sea*" (cf. Revelation 13:1).
- The Antichrist's kingdom and a temporary relationship with the *Babylon harlot* (cf. Revelation 17:3, 7, 12, & 16).

- The Antichrist's kingdom as foretold by Daniel (cf. Daniel 7:7-8, 20, & 24).

Also in this passage is the statement that "*the dragon stood before the woman who was about to give birth, so that when she gave birth he might devour her child.*" This shows the position Hydra and Corax will be in with regard to Virgo at the time of the war in heaven.

Satan has influenced many kings and nations over the years, driving them to nearly annihilate the Jews and diminishing the salvation offered through Christ. In fact, what is most likely represented here is the fact that he caused King Herod Agrippa to order the murder of all children two years of age and younger in an attempt to kill Christ (cf. Matthew 2:16-18).

12:5. The son of the "*woman*," Christ, is shown being caught up to God's throne (His resurrection). There should be no doubt that the subject here is Christ. But just in case you need something else to chew on, please consider the following Scripture: Psalm 2:9, Revelation 2:27, and Revelation 19:15.

This ends the vision of the constellations and their alignment at the time Satan and Michael (and their angelic forces) will war in heaven.

12:6. The *woman* (a remnant of Israel) flees into the wilderness (also see 12:14). Perhaps this group will be the 144,000 God also seals for their protection before His wrath.

At least a portion of Israel will be kept safe in an isolated location for 1,260 days (three and a half years). Scripture here mentions that the place is prepared for her by God, so we should accept the destination as a literal location – not a *spiritual* wilderness, or dispersal to all the gentile nations. Also, Isaiah foretold of the movement of Christ from Sela (Petra) to Mount Zion at the end of the Antichrist's reign and the beginning of His own kingdom (cf. Isaiah 16:1-5).

> Wikipedia defines *Sela* as ". . . meaning rock; Arabic: as-Sala‘; Greek: πέτρα; Latin: **petra** was the **capital of Edom**, situated in the great valley extending from the Dead Sea to the Red Sea (2 Kings 14:7)."

12:7-9. Israel flees into the desert at the same time there'll be war in heaven. Satan and his angels will ultimately lose and be thrown down to the earth. Why will this be a problem? Because of the incredible wrath and destruction Satan will execute through the Antichrist after losing the war.

> Let's take a moment to address a popular belief that the war in heaven has already happened before Adam and Eve were created, and that Satan was thrown to earth at that time. This position isn't scriptural and is based on taking Isaiah 14:12-14 out of context. Isaiah 14 is an apocalyptic writing that contains an unveiling of the last days. In it, Isaiah is witnessing the Antichrist (labeled as the "*Assyrian*" here), Satan's influence on him, and his eventual destruction.

> We must also consider the context and timing of verses 6-17 of this chapter in Revelation, which will occur three and a half years before the end (as noted by *1,260 days* in verse 6 and "*time, times, and half a time*" in verse 14). Also, as discussed in the section *The Dragon – Satan* in Chapter Eight of this guide, Satan has had access to God and heaven since well after the time of Adam and Eve as shown by the writings of Job (cf. Job 1:6-11). This "*accuser of our brethren . . . who accuses them before our God day and night*" (cf. 12:10) won't lose that access until he's cast to earth after the war in heaven, which will occur at the beginning of the Antichrist's time of great tribulation three and a half years before the end.

12:10-13. This Scripture unveils the terrible time of great tribulation. Many of God's people will lose their lives at the hands of the Antichrist, who'll be influenced by Satan.

12:14. We again see that a portion of Israel (probably the 144,000) will be protected by God for three and a half years. Compare this verse to 12:6 for further confirmation and support for understanding that 1,260 days and "*time, times, and half a time*" are the same length of time and will represent the same timeframe (the three-and-a-half-year authority of the Antichrist).

> The message behind "*two wings of the great eagle*" is most likely the same as that in Exodus 19:4 where God is reminding Israel how He gathered them up and protected them during the exodus from Egypt. Be careful not to read anything more into this, believing as some have that the Scripture represents a symbol of America or that Jews will be "airlifted" out by cargo planes in the last days.[29]

12:15-16. Satan's attempt to destroy this *woman* by water will be thwarted.

12:17. Enraged and filled with wrath (since he knows his time is short), Satan will go after those who "*keep the commandments of God and hold to the testimony of Jesus.*"

~ Revelation Chapter 13 ~

You'll get a lot of good information here about the Antichrist and his associate, the False Prophet. This chapter corroborates what Daniel prophesied (cf. chapter 7) and reminds us that God will give him authority over His elect for three and a half years (cf. 13:5). Also outlined here is the worship that the False Prophet will demand for the Antichrist and the mark he'll force mankind to take in order to buy or sell during the Antichrist's reign.

13:1-2. The beast John witnesses represents the Antichrist's end-times kingdom and is the fourth beast in Daniel 7:7. Notable features of this kingdom that comprises the four beasts Daniel first foretold of in Daniel 7:3-6:

- There were ten horns and seven heads with blasphemous names.
- It was like a leopard (Greece in Daniel's visions).
- Its feet were like those of a bear (Persia in Daniel's visions).
- It had a mouth like that of a lion (Babylon in Daniel's visions).
- Satan will give the Antichrist, who'll lead the beast, his power and throne and great authority.

The features are significant because they show that the Antichrist's kingdom will comprise all regions conquered by the previous Babylonian, Greek, and Persian Empires. The geography will be what is currently the Middle East made up of predominantly Muslim nations (you may wish to refresh your memory by reviewing the section of Chapter Eight titled *The Antichrist*).

Although we'll cover the topic again in greater detail in our overview of Revelation 17, this might be the best time to introduce information found there about this beast – the Antichrist's kingdom. What we'll discuss will help you to make sense of the "heads" and of the next couple of verses. Let's start by looking at the Scripture contained in Revelation 17:9-11:

> *Here is the mind which has wisdom. The* ***seven heads*** *are . . .* ***seven kings; five have fallen, one is, the other has not yet come****; and when he comes, he must remain a little while. The beast which was and is not [the Antichrist], is himself also an* ***eighth and is one of the seven****, and he goes to destruction.* —Revelation 17:9-11.

The seven heads represent seven kings/kingdoms that will have controlled the Middle Eastern regions throughout history from the inception of the 12 tribes of Israel until the destruction of the Antichrist and his empire. They're broken down as follows:

- Five that have *fallen* by 90 CE: Egypt, Assyria, Babylon, Persia, and Greece.
- One that *is* (at the time of the Revelation to John): Roman Empire.

- The other that *hasn't come* (by John's time) but would be in power for a short time in the future: most likely the Ottoman Empire (Turks) since they assimilated the lands previously ruled by the eastern half of the Roman Empire.
- A final, eighth kingdom: the Antichrist's empire.

13:3-4. One of the beast's seven heads looks as if it had been slain, but the fatal wound is then healed. Knowing this, the whole world is amazed and follows this kingdom. A popular belief exploited by the *Left Behind* series and other similar sources is that the Antichrist himself will receive a fatal head wound and then be resurrected miraculously.

While this may be entertaining and one possible interpretation, a more likely scenario will be where one of the previous heads (kingdoms) will be revived and become very powerful. My opinion is that this revived kingdom will be that of the Antichrist since we now know from our discussion of Chapter Seventeen (above) that the principality of the Antichrist will have also been from one of the previous seven kingdoms (Revelation 17:9-11).

You'll learn in verse 14 that the fatal wound was caused by a weapon of war (represented by the word *sword*). This supports a position that the Antichrist's kingdom will be a revived kingdom previously defeated through war (as all the previous *beast* empires had been).

13:5-6. The Antichrist will speak out against God and have authority over His people for 42 months just as Daniel prophesied (cf. 7:25). Again, this shows that 42 months and *time, times, and half a time* equal the same timeframe (three and a half years) just like 12:6 & 14 showed us that 1,260 days *and time, times, and half a time* are the same. So, to review: 42 months = 1,260 days = *time, times, and half a time*. All three refer to a three-and-a-half-year period of 42 30-day Jewish months.

13:7. Satan, through the Antichrist, will have the authority (given by God) to "*make war with the saints and overcome them.*" Daniel foretold of this time hundreds of years before the Revelation was given to John (cf. 7:21 & 25).

13:8. Everyone whose names are *not* in the Book of Life will worship the beast. This is confirmed by Revelation 14:11. It's critical to understand that our names *can* be removed from the Lamb's Book of Life. For instance, those who worship the beast and/or take his mark will have their name blotted out.

13:9-10. People will go into captivity and be killed by weapons of war during the Antichrist's authority. Perseverance and the faith of the saints will be tested from this time on. Luke foretold of the captivity and death in his account of Jesus' response on the Mount of Olives (cf. 21:24). Paul refers to this type of activity in his letter to the Romans (8:35). Finally, these verses just offer another view of the Great Tribulation of the Antichrist as also seen in the unveiling by the broken fourth seal (cf. Revelation 6:8).

13:11-12. Verses 11-18 pertain to the false prophet of the Antichrist. This beast will come from "*the earth,*" suggesting his origin will be a particular region. This entity will be very deceitful, appearing as a lamb while speaking as a *dragon*. The False Prophet will take action on behalf of the Antichrist, having all his authority while in the Antichrist's presence. All inhabitants of the earth will be made to worship the Antichrist by this false prophet.

13:13-14. The False Prophet will perform great signs and wonders to include bringing down fire from heaven. Mankind is deceived by these signs and wonders and told to make an image to the Antichrist (or his kingdom). Again, the significance of the statement "*the wound of the sword and has come to life*" is that the Antichrist or his kingdom will have come from one of the previous empires that had suffered what appeared to be a complete military defeat.

13:15. This associate of the Antichrist will bring the image of the beast to life and kill anyone who doesn't worship it. We don't know what this image will be like or of what form the worship of it will take, although many have wondered whether it will somehow be connected to the world via the Internet.

13:16-18. Everyone wishing to buy or sell will be forced to accept a mark on the right hand or forehead. It will either be the name of the Antichrist or the number of his name (somehow related to 666). Subtopic *Sealing Followers – the Mark* in section *The Antichrist* (Chapter Eight) addresses this Scripture in greater detail.

16.4 Timeline of the Antichrist's Reign and Trumpet Judgments
Revelation 8:2 – 13

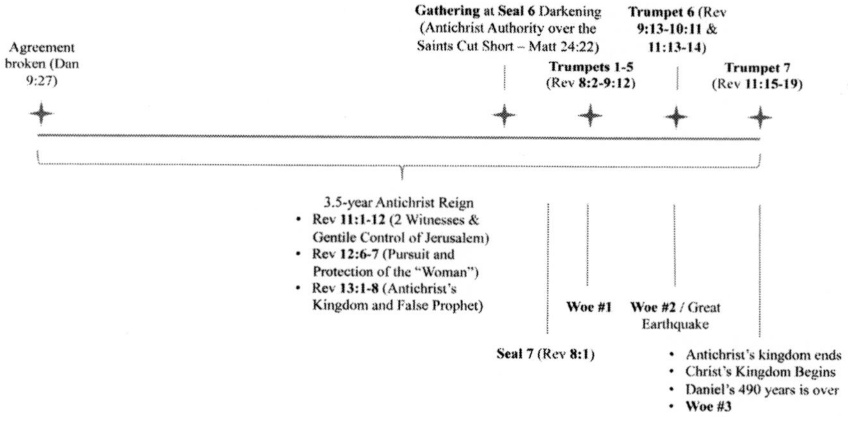

PART V: REVELATION 14 – 16

RECOMMENDED READING:

1. Review the appropriate portion of Chapter Fourteen of this guide – *Part II: Introduction to the Revelation*
2. Revelation 14-16

This section highlights the 144,000 who'll be with Christ at the beginning of Christ's reign on earth and during the last of God's wrath: the seven bowl judgments. In chapter 14, John also sees several angels who will preach the gospel to all nations before the end, gather the bride of Christ, and administer God's wrath.

~ Revelation Chapter 14 ~

Interestingly, this chapter through verse 5 continues the vision from chapter 13. It then offers additional information related to the preaching of the gospel to all nations before the end, the gathering of the elect, and the execution of God's wrath against everyone else.

Key Points or Considerations:

1. Verses 1-5 continue the vision of chapter 13 and describe the 144,000 as seen with Christ at the beginning of His kingdom and just before the execution of the seven bowls of God's wrath.
2. Verses 6-7 depict the preaching of the gospel to all nations. This is most likely the end-times event Christ spoke of on the Mount of Olives (e.g. Matthew 24:14).
3. Verse 8 signals the destruction of figurative *Babylon*, which will be described further in Revelation 16, 17, and 18.
4. The two harvests in this chapter reflect the gathering of the elect (e.g. Matthew 24:30) and the destruction of the wicked (those not gathered by Christ) by the wrath of God. Both are represented as harvests of grapes.

14:1-5. Christ appears on Mount Zion with the 144,000. The voices, making up the sound John hears coming from heaven, sing a new song to God, the four living creatures, and the 24 elders. The only ones on earth who'll be able to learn this new song being sung in heaven will be the 144,000 Jews protected by God's seal.

> Revelation 15:2-4 will reveal that the voices singing in heaven are those of the souls beheaded for their faith during the reign of the Antichrist, and that the time of this vision is just before the seven vial judgments (the last seven plagues) of God will be administered.

This group is most likely the "*woman*" from Revelation 12, who God will keep safe for the duration of the Antichrist's wrath in a place prepared by Him for this very purpose (cf. 12:6). Why do I suggest the 144,000 and the *woman* are the same?

1. Petra (ancient Sela) will be the starting point of an end-times trip to Mount Zion to obtain His kingdom and will therefore most likely be the location where God will keep the group safe for the three-and-a-half-year authority of the Antichrist (Isaiah 16:1-5).
2. The 144,000 follow Christ "*wherever He goes.*"

Scripture divulges qualities of the 144,000 such as:

- They've not had sexual relations with women.
- They don't lie.
- They're blameless.

See *144,000 from the 12 Tribes of Israel* from Chapter Six of this study for more about this group.

14:6-7. An angel gives a final warning to the earth: "*Fear God, and give Him glory, because the hour of His judgment has come; worship Him who made the heaven and the earth and sea and springs of waters.*" It's possible that the angel's gospel represents the three-and-a-half-year testimony of the two witnesses, but there's no definitive proof. Regardless, this instance of preaching the gospel is most likely that part of the end-times progression as noted by Christ on the Mount of Olives (cf. Matthew 24:14 and Mark 13:10).

14:8. Scripture here depicts the destruction of "*Babylon*" (see *Babylon – the Great City* in Chapter Nine of this guide for additional information).

14:9-11. Another angel warns that anyone receiving the mark of the beast will suffer God's wrath. This would be appropriate because anyone accepting the mark will have made a choice not to follow

Christ and will not be gathered with the bride of Christ at His appearing. Also contained in this reference is a reminder that their name will be blotted from the Lamb's Book of Life and that they'll suffer an eternity in hell as a result (cf. Revelation 13:8).

14:12-13. The saints who persevere during this time of the Antichrist and remain faithful will receive their rest and reward during the "*harvest*" coming in 14:15-16.

14:14. Christ is about to reap these two harvests at the end of the Antichrist's time:

1. The bride of Christ (e.g. Matthew 29-31) in verses 15 & 16.
2. Everyone else not gathered in the first harvest. These humans will suffer God's incredible wrath (cf. verses 18-20).

14:15-16. Christ is told to put in His "*sickle and reap, for the hour to reap has come, because the harvest of the earth is ripe*." This harvest follows the blessing given to the righteous in 14:13.

14:17-20. God's wrath, which will follow the "*rapture*," is shown here as the second harvest. It will conclude with the battle of Armageddon and the resulting incredible bloodshed (cf. 19:15-21).

> *I will gather all the nations And bring them down to the valley of Jehoshaphat. Then I will enter into judgment with them there . . . Let the nations be aroused And come up to the valley of Jehoshaphat, For there I will sit to judge All the surrounding nations.* ***Put in the sickle, for the harvest is ripe. Come, tread, for the wine press is full****; The vats overflow, for their wickedness is great. Multitudes, multitudes in the valley of decision! For the day of the LORD is near in the valley of decision.* —Joel 3:2-14.

~ Revelation Chapter 15 ~

Primarily, this chapter reflects the preparation of the remainder of God's wrath.

15:1. John sees seven angels holding seven plagues that will finish the wrath of God. NOTE: Some believe the plagues administered by these angels *are* the complete wrath of God to then be able to say that the previous trumpets *are not* part of His judgments of wrath. But as you can see here, they will complete God's wrath, made up of the seven trumpet judgments (cf. 8:2-11:15) *and* the seven plagues.

15:2. The vision continues with a view in heaven of those who had remained faithful during the time of the Antichrist. Because they won't worship the Antichrist or his image or accept his mark, they'll be killed by beheading (cf. 20:4). John is probably seeing the souls of those who were martyred for their faith (cf. 6:9-11 – the fifth seal).

15:3-4. These souls in heaven sing the song that no other on earth but the 144,000 can learn. Therefore, these must be the voices John hears singing the song in 14:2-3:

> *And I heard a voice from heaven, like the sound of many waters and like the sound of loud thunder, and the voice which I heard was like the sound of harpists playing on their harps.* ***And they sang a new song before the throne and before the four living creatures and the elders*** . . . —Revelation 14:2-3.
>
> Christ is on Mount Zion at this point with the 144,000; the rest of God's wrath is about to begin.

15:5-8. The angels prepare to administer the seven vials (bowls) full of the remainder of God's wrath. John sees them in God's temple in heaven and notes that no one will be able to re-enter the heavenly temple until the angels have finished releasing the seven plagues.

~ REVELATION CHAPTER 16 ~

The remainder of God's wrath is administered here. Also reflected in this Scripture is the destruction of figurative *Babylon*, which I believe will be Jerusalem based on what we've learned so far in this guide (e.g. Chapter Eight).

16:1. The angels are told to administer the seven bowls filled with wrath.

16:2. Angel #1's plague: Everyone who accepts the mark of the Antichrist and worships his image will receive a "*loathsome and malignant sore.*"

16:3. Angel #2's plague: Everything left alive in the oceans after the second trumpet judgment will die after the water turns to blood.

16:4-7. Angel #3's plague: All fresh water of the earth is turned to blood as the salt waters had been. Although Scripture doesn't say so, everything left alive after the third trumpet judgment will probably die at this point.

16:8-9. Angel #4's plague: Inhabitants of the earth are "*scorched with fierce heat.*" Despite this, survivors curse God and won't repent.

16:10-11. Angel #5's plague: The Antichrist's kingdom and its inhabitants are made to suffer great pain. They still won't repent of their behavior.

16:12-16. Angel #6's plague: The Euphrates River is dried up to make way for forces coming from the east. Spiritual principalities from, or associated with, the Antichrist, Satan, and the False Prophet gather the armies of the world for the battle of Armageddon.

16:17-21. Angel #7's plague: Hailstones weighing about 100 pounds will come down upon the inhabitants of the earth, yet they still won't repent.

At that time, the greatest earthquake known to man will split Jerusalem into three parts. This is when *Babylon* will be destroyed. Chapters Seventeen and Eighteen will reveal additional information about the quake and its destruction.

16.5 Timeline of the Seven Bowl Judgments
Revelation 14 – 16

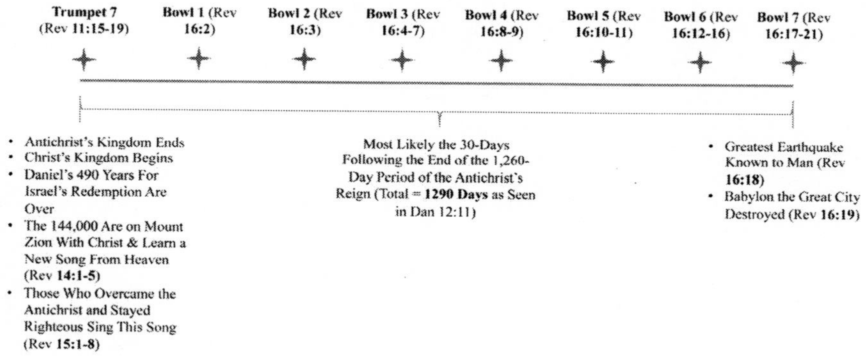
Trumpet 7 (Rev 11:15-19)
Bowl 1 (Rev 16:2)
Bowl 2 (Rev 16:3)
Bowl 3 (Rev 16:4-7)
Bowl 4 (Rev 16:8-9)
Bowl 5 (Rev 16:10-11)
Bowl 6 (Rev 16:12-16)
Bowl 7 (Rev 16:17-21)
• Antichrist's Kingdom Ends
• Christ's Kingdom Begins
• Daniel's 490 Years For Israel's Redemption Are Over
• The 144,000 Are on Mount Zion With Christ & Learn a New Song From Heaven (Rev 14:1-5)
• Those Who Overcame the Antichrist and Stayed Righteous Sing This Song (Rev 15:1-8)
Most Likely the 30-Days Following the End of the 1,260-Day Period of the Antichrist's Reign (Total = 1290 Days as Seen in Dan 12:11)
• Greatest Earthquake Known to Man (Rev 16:18)
• Babylon the Great City Destroyed (Rev 16:19)

PART VI: REVELATION 17 – 19

RECOMMENDED READING:

1. Review the appropriate portion of Chapter Fourteen of this guide – *Part II: Introduction to the Revelation*
2. Review *Babylon – the Harlot* in Chapter Nine
3. Review *Babylon – the Great City* in Chapter Nine
4. Revelation 17-19

Scripture contained in this section focuses on end-times Babylon (the *harlot* and *great city*), the marriage celebration in heaven, and the battle of Armageddon.

~ REVELATION CHAPTER 17 ~

Half of this chapter describes "*Babylon the Great, the Mother of Harlots*," an unfaithful bride that will enter into a temporary alliance with the Antichrist and his kingdom. The second half goes into great detail about that kingdom foretold by Daniel (cf. chapter 7).

Key Points or Considerations:

1. Israel's role throughout history as God's unfaithful bride and the description of her clothing and adornment make her an ideal candidate for the harlot.
2. The spiritual principality that will drive/influence the Antichrist's kingdom was also associated with one of the first five kingdoms to rule that region of the world: Egypt, Assyria, Babylon, Persia, or Greece.
3. *Babylon*, the *great city* highlighted in verse 18, will most likely *not* be New York City or the World Bank as some suggest, but Jerusalem instead. The most compelling reason of several is that the Antichrist and his kingdom will rule the world during this time from that location.

17:1-2. One of the angels administering God's wrath in chapter 16 is about to show John the judgment and destruction of "*the great harlot who sits on many waters . . . .*" This unfaithful bride, whom I believe to be Israel (see *Babylon – the Harlot* in Chapter Nine of this guide), has engaged in immoral acts with the nations of the earth. My opinion is that this is a reference to her and her unfaithful act of entering into the *covenant of death* with the Antichrist (thus *cheating* on God in a sense).

17:3. The *harlot* will have a relationship with the Antichrist's kingdom.

17:4-6. The woman's clothing and adornment are interesting and mirror that worn by Israel's priests (e.g. Exodus 39:8-13). If the harlot is indeed Israel, then it's possible the *covenant of death* will be orchestrated by one of her priests.

Scripture here has labeled the woman as "*Babylon the Great, the Mother of Harlots and of the Abominations of the Earth.*" This is indeed a mystery as declared by the passage. As you've discovered though, multiple descriptions of *Babylon* in the Revelation closely resemble those given to ancient Babylon by prophets at the height of that empire and during the exile of Judah. Hebrews in Babylon adopted sinful practices of astrology, divination, idol worship, and child sacrifice. The influence on God's people was devastating, and the sinful behavior earned her the title of *harlot* by her *husband*, God.

We also see here that the *harlot* will be responsible for the blood of the saints. This has been true of Israel throughout history and mirrors what Jesus and Paul said during their ministries on earth (cf. Matthew 23:37; Acts 7:52; 1 Thessalonians 2:14-15). But the ultimate bloodshed of God's people will come at the hands of the Antichrist, made possible by the *covenant of death* entered into by Israel through deception. This is most likely the focus of 17:6 even though, as we've seen in Scripture, Israel has always had a hand in the bloodshed of her saints.

17:7. The angel is about to demystify the *harlot* and the *beast* she'll have a relationship with (Antichrist's kingdom).

17:8. As discussed in our overview of Revelation 13, the *beast* the harlot is riding will be empowered by Satan, and its spiritual principality also influenced the kingdom before John's time (before the Roman Empire). Those of the earth not in Christ's Book of Life, which has existed since the beginning of the world, will be unwise as to the Antichrist and his kingdom.

17:9-11. So Christ in His mercy offers wisdom to help us discern good from evil and avoid the end-times deception. The following explores these verses and matches the kingdoms to specific timeframes based on what we know of historical fulfillment:

Here is the mind which has wisdom. The ***seven heads*** *are . .*

. ***seven kings; five have fallen, one is, the other has not yet come;*** *and when he comes, he must remain a little while. The beast which was and is not [the Antichrist], is himself also an* ***eighth and is one of the seven****, and he goes to destruction.* —Revelation 17:9-11.

The seven heads represent seven kings/kingdoms. Some have already come and gone by John's time, but not all. History and Scripture help us to understand which kingdoms the seven heads represent:

- Five that have *fallen* by 90 CE:
  1. **Egypt** (722 BCE)
  2. **Assyria** (605 BCE)
  3. **Babylon** (539 BCE)
  4. **Persia** (331 BCE)
  5. **Greece (**63 BCE)
- One that *is* (at the time of the Revelation to John): **Roman Empire**.
- The other that *hasn't come* (by John's time) but would be in power for a short time in the future: This can only be the **Ottoman Empire** (Turkish) which captured Constantinople in 1453 and lasted until 1918. Each of the empires above conquered the next, assimilating the people and geographical regions in the process. In keeping with this progression, the Turks conquered the Roman Empire and acquired all its territory in the Middle East.
- A final, eighth kingdom: Interestingly, Christ tells John these things about the principality of the Antichrist:
  - "*Was, but is not*": This informs us that the principality will be from one of the "*five that have fallen.*"
  - "*Also an eighth*": He'll be the principality of the eighth kingdom (Antichrist's kingdom).
  - "*One of the seven*": The Antichrist's spiritual principality will be from one of the previous seven kingdoms. Of course, we already know this because he "*was, but is not.*"

- "*Goes to destruction*": We know that the Antichrist will be thrown into the lake of fire along with his false prophet after being defeated by Christ at the battle of Armageddon (cf. Revelation 19:20).

17:12-14. The ten horns of the Antichrist's beast represent ten kings/ authorities that will initially reign with the Antichrist, giving him all power and authority that is theirs to give. We see here a reference to the battle of Armageddon.

Insight given here mimics Scripture penned by Daniel regarding the makeup of the Antichrist's kingdom, tribulation of God's people, and the ultimate defeat of the Antichrist by Jesus:

> *I kept looking, and that horn was waging war with the saints and overpowering them until the Ancient of Days came and* ***judgment was passed in favor of the saints of the Highest One, and the time arrived when the saints took possession of the kingdom.***—Daniel 7:21-22.

> *As for the* **ten horns***, out of this kingdom ten kings will arise; and another will arise after them, and he will be different from the previous ones and will subdue three kings. He will speak out against the Most High and wear down the saints of the Highest One, and he will intend to make alterations in times and in law; and they will be given into his hand for a time, times, and half a time.* ***But the court will sit for judgment, and his dominion will be taken away, annihilated and destroyed forever.*** —Daniel 7:24-26.

17:15. *Water* in Scripture represents multitudes of people, from separate languages and nations in this case. The reference suggests there'll be something of an international element to the Antichrist's kingdom.

17:16-17. The ten rulers associated with the Antichrist will make the harlot "*desolate and naked.*" Just as Israel's label as a *harlot* and her responsibility in the *bloodshed of the saints* makes her a good candidate for the Babylon harlot, so does this outcome, which Christ said Israel was destined for:

> ***I will also give you into the hands of your lovers, and they will tear down your shrines, demolish your high places, strip you of your clothing, take away your jewels, and will leave you naked and bare.*** —Ezekiel 16:39.

> *For thus says the Lord GOD, 'Behold,* ***I will give you into the hand of those whom you hate****, into the hand of those from whom you were alienated. They will deal with you in hatred, take all your property, and* ***leave you naked and bare****.'*—Ezekiel 23:28-29.

> ***Jerusalem****, Jerusalem, who kills the prophets and stones those who are sent to her! How often I wanted to gather your children together, the way a hen gathers her chicks under her wings, and you were unwilling.* ***Behold, your house is being left to you desolate!*** —Matthew 23:37-38.

17:18. "*The woman whom you saw is the great city, which reigns over the kings of the earth.*" This passage has led some to believe the harlot is New York City because of the United Nation's presence there. But in context it's referring to the *great city* from which the Antichrist will rule at the time of his destruction. This will be Jerusalem, an integral part of the *harlot* Israel, based on Old Testament prophecy, the Antichrist's presence in the temple as foretold by Daniel, Jesus, and Paul, etc.

~ REVELATION CHAPTER 18 ~

The saga of future, figurative Babylon continues with this section of Scripture related to her destruction as the harlot and as the location of the Antichrist and his associates – "*the great city, which reigns over the kings of the earth*" (cf. 17:18).

Several themes discussed here had already been foretold in what were likely near-far prophecies aimed at *ancient* Babylon by Jeremiah and Isaiah as you'll see below.

18:1-6. "*Fallen, fallen is Babylon the great!*" The entire world will be involved in immoral acts with her as it had been during the time of *ancient* Babylon. We've already seen this mentioned in 14:8 & 17:2, but you can read about it in Isaiah's oracle concerning the "*Wilderness of the Sea*" (cf. 21:1-10).

> Jeremiah uttered the same basic message, which may very well be a near-far prophecy for ancient Babylon and future, figurative Babylon considering the recurrence of it in the vision to John well after original Babylon had been destroyed.
>
> > *Flee from the midst of Babylon, And each of you save his life! Do not be destroyed in her punishment, For this is the LORD'S time of vengeance; He is going to render recompense to her.* ***Babylon has been a golden cup in the hand of the LORD, Intoxicating all the earth. The nations have drunk of her wine****; Therefore the nations are going mad. Suddenly* ***Babylon has fallen*** *and been broken . . .*—Jeremiah 51:6-8.

18:7-19. The arrogance of this figurative Babylon is seen by Scripture references such as "*I SIT as A QUEEN AND I AM NOT A WIDOW, and will never see mourning*" and "*For this reason in one day her plagues will come . . .*"

> Isaiah's prophecy about ancient Babylon mimics the description given to John about the *future Babylon*:
>
> > *Yet you said, 'I will be a queen forever.' These things you did not consider Nor remember the outcome of them. Now, then, hear this, you sensual one, Who dwells securely, Who says in your heart, 'I am, and there is no one besides me. I will not sit as a widow, Nor know loss of children.' But these two things will come on you suddenly in one day: Loss*

> *of children and widowhood. They will come on you in full measure in spite of your many sorceries, in spite of the great power of your spells.* —Isaiah 47:7-9.

Verse 16 reflects the same message contained in 17:4: "*. . . saying, Woe, woe, the great city, she who was clothed in fine linen and purple and scarlet, and adorned with gold and precious stones and pearls . . .*"

18:20-23. These verses contain more information regarding the destruction of future, figurative Babylon.

18:24. Just like Scripture contained in 17:6, this verse addresses the fact that the *harlot* will be responsible for the blood of the prophets, saints, and all who'll be slain during the reign in "*Babylon.*"

Jeremiah foretold of this too in his prophecy about ancient Babylon and its impending destruction by the Assyrians: "*Indeed Babylon is to fall for the slain of Israel, as also for Babylon the slain of all the earth have fallen.*" —Jeremiah 51:49.

I find it very interesting and significant that Christ quoted ancient prophecies to John in these visions about the future *Babylon.* What this reminds us of is that the harlot's behavior and immorality will rival that of ancient Babylon, warranting the same destruction orchestrated by God.

~ REVELATION CHAPTER 19 ~

We'll get to learn John's vision about the marriage to Christ by His betrothed (the church) and of the destruction of the Antichrist and his armies in this passage.

Key Points or Considerations:

1. Verse 15 serves as yet another reminder that the weapon of

Christ is the sword (not the bow as is the weapon of false messiahs in seal 1 of chapter 6).

2. The bride of Christ and the group of warriors seen with Christ in verse 14 will *not* be the same, but rather distinct groups in heaven.

19:1-5. The hosts of heaven are glorifying God and praising Him for the destruction He will bestow upon "*Babylon.*" This is the judgment of Babylon we read about in Revelation 18.

19:6-10. A mighty voice in heaven praises God and declares that it's time for the marriage of the bride of Christ to the groom. Note that this occurs just after the judgment/destruction of *Babylon*.

19:11-16. Christ is seen here riding a white horse and is called "*Faithful and True,*" "*The Word of God,*" and "*King of Kings, and Lord of Lords.*" John sees Christ and the armies of heaven following Him, also on white horses. The white clothing and white horses reflect the purity and righteousness of those in heaven including Christ, His bride, and the warriors.

We're reminded here that the weapon of Christ is the sword. So although the white horse and rider in the first seal of Revelation 6 may suggest righteousness, the rider carries a bow and isn't Christ – the rider represents false righteousness of *false messiahs* as previously discussed in this study (e.g. Chapter Fourteen).

Before moving on, we must address a minor sticking point. Because the gathered church and heaven's warriors are dressed in white, some believe that the bride attending the marriage supper of Christ and the warriors in this passage will be one and the same. This is unlikely since heaven has a hierarchy separate from the bride of Christ that includes warriors, and the bride is seen later coming down from heaven in the Revelation given to John. Please see *The Bride: Marriage* in Chapter Seven of this guide for additional information.

19:17-18. The birds of the sky are being called together for the "*great supper of God.*" This gives us a rough idea of the amount of carnage that will be produced by Christ's destruction of the Antichrist and his armies. Ezekiel, Isaiah, and Jeremiah also prophesied about this feast:

> *You will fall on the mountains of Israel, you and all your troops and the peoples who are with you; I will give you as food to every kind of predatory bird and beast of the field.* —Ezekiel 39:4.

> *They will be left together for mountain birds of prey, And for the beasts of the earth; And the birds of prey will spend the summer feeding on them, And all the beasts of the earth will spend harvest time on them.*—Isaiah 18:6.

> *The dead bodies of this people will be food for the birds of the sky and for the beasts of the earth; and no one will frighten them away.*—Jeremiah 7:33.

19:19-21. Christ defeats the Antichrist and his armies, throwing him and the False Prophet into the lake of fire and killing the rest.

Part VII: Revelation 20 – 22

RECOMMENDED READING:

1. Review the appropriate portion of Chapter Fourteen of this guide – *Part II: Introduction to the Revelation*
2. Revelation 20-22

A lot will take place in the timeframe reflected by the remaining three chapters of Revelation. Once the Antichrist and his false prophet are thrown into the lake of fire, and his armies destroyed, Satan will be bound and held captive in hell (the abyss) for 1,000 years. At the end of that time, he'll be released for one more confrontation. The next few passages also unveil the great judgment of God, His kingdom, and a warning to leave the Revelation as is.

~ REVELATION CHAPTER 20 ~

In this chapter, John reports on Satan's 1,000-year captivity in hell and Christ's reign during that time. With Him will be those beheaded for their faith (seen first after the breaking of the fifth seal in chapter 6 of this Revelation). At the conclusion of the 1,000 years, Satan will be released for one final confrontation before being destroyed by the lake of fire. John witnesses the great judgment and destruction of those not found in Christ's Book of Life.

Key Points or Considerations:

1. Yes, there *is* a lake of fire. As I said at the beginning of this study, we'll be in one group or the other in the end and will either join the rest of the bride of Christ in heaven or suffer the lake-of-fire judgment seen here.
2. Although *everyone* found in the Book of Life will be present in the New Jerusalem (cf. Revelation 21:27), there's no indication that anyone other than the 144,000 and those beheaded during the Antichrist's time will be with Christ on earth during His reign.

20:1-3. Satan is thrown into hell, which is sealed to hold him there for 1,000 years. He'll be released for a short time at the end of 1,000 years to gather the nations together against God for a final battle just as he did at the battle of Armageddon (cf. 20:8-9). It will be interesting to see what a world without Satan's influence for 1,000 years will be like.

NOTE: Some believe there will be no 1,000-year (millennial) reign of Christ, or that it's symbolic of the Christian era we're currently in. We'll discuss this further in the next chapter of our study. Significant points to keep in mind:

1. While some spiritualize or allegorize the binding of Satan to mean that Christians have power over him, his evil influence has been at work and will be until he truly is *bound.*

2. The nations are still deceived and corrupted by Satan and his spiritual principalities. This will not be the case during the millennial reign of Christ while Satan is *bound*.
3. This millennial reign of Christ is sandwiched in between the end of God's wrath when Satan is restrained in hell and the great judgment preceding the new age.

20:4-6. John sees the souls of those beheaded for their faith and for not following the Antichrist (he previously saw them after the breaking of the fourth seal in Revelation 6). They'll come to life and reign with Christ for 1,000 years in what is called the "*first resurrection.*" After being raised to life, they'll become priests of God and Christ and won't suffer the lake of fire death that those not in the Book of Life will suffer at the great judgment (cf. 20:11-15).

20:7-9. Satan will again gather the nations for battle against God as he'll also influence *Gog of Magog* to do at the battle of Armageddon. Fire from heaven will devour this great army as it surrounds Jerusalem containing Christ's kingdom and its holy inhabitants. Where will the nations come from? Remember that one-third of Israel will still be left alive when Christ's kingdom begins (Ezekiel 5 and Zechariah 13). And although most of mankind will have been killed by the plagues of God's wrath, some will be alive afterward to help repopulate the earth.

20:10. Satan will be thrown into the lake of fire upon the crushing defeat described in verse 9. As previously discussed in Chapter Eight of this guide, hell and the lake of fire are generally different locations. *Hell* (generally), *Hades*, and the *abyss* are different labels for the same place – a temporary repository for souls (and for Satan during his 1,000-year incarceration) located deep within the earth. The lake of fire will be a place filled with fire and brimstone where Satan, his angels, and any human not found in Christ's Book of Life will be tormented *forever and ever*.

Let's pause for a moment to discuss the concept of "*forever and ever*." From a very young age, I'd heard that the consequences of sin without Christ would be death. But I'd also heard that anyone not "saved" would be thrown into *hell* where they'd burn *forever*. Fear of cooking without dying for eternity did the trick—for a while. Two things for you to consider on this issue:

1. The Greek word used for "*forever*" in verse 10 is *aiōn* (Strong's G165) – the same word used for "*age*" as in "*end of the age*" from Matthew 24:3. This introduces a strong possibility that the torment from the lake of fire will end at the conclusion of *this* age after the great judgment and as the new age begins when God's kingdom is established.
2. Christ called the lake of fire the second death (cf. 20:14), again suggesting a completion and final disposition of those raised for judgment and then thrown into the fire and brimstone.

Regardless, you'll definitely want to be a part of the bride of Christ. Otherwise, your final destination will most likely be separation from God, torment for a time, and then—nothing.

20:11-15. Here John witnesses the great judgment of God. Everyone not transformed at Christ's appearing and the gathering of the bride will be raised at this time. Included in this group will be those who lived and died before the gift of salvation from Christ was possible; they'll be judged by their works. The other half of this group will be anyone who had the opportunity to accept Christ and receive this great gift of salvation but didn't.

~ Revelation Chapter 21 ~

Here John sees the passing of this age and the dawning of a new one where God will dwell with mankind on earth. Of special note is the list of sinful behavior, the practice of which will keep us out of the Lamb's Book of Life and therefore out of God's kingdom. There will only be two choices, so it stands to reason that anyone who *practices* sinful behavior will end up in the lake of fire after God's end-of-the-age judgment.

21:1-2. John has witnessed the passing of the previous age (the one we're in now) and the dawn of the new age and a New Jerusalem coming out of heaven from God.

21:3-5. God declares that the tabernacle of God is now among men. He will dwell with them and protect them. There will be no more sadness, death, or pain. This is what Isaiah wrote about when he penned:

> *He will swallow up death for all time, And the Lord GOD will wipe tears away from all faces, And He will remove the reproach of His people from all the earth; For the LORD has spoken.* —Isaiah 25:8.

21:6-8. Christ tells John that He is the "*beginning and the end*" – the one who'll give freely from the "*springs of the water of life.*" This passage also serves as a reminder that people who *practice* sinful behaviors such as these will *not* inherit the kingdom of God. Here's a list of the sinful practices and what Scripture says about them:

- Cowardice
- Unbelief (in Christ as the Son of God)
- Acts **abominable** to God. Several of many based on Scripture such as Leviticus 18, Deuteronomy 7, 22, 23, and Proverbs 15 are:
  - Sexual immorality:
    - Gay and lesbian sexual acts (these contradict God's intended relationships)
    - Bestiality
    - Pursuit of nudity (in context, this may be abominable because of the sexual acts, adultery, or incest the pursuit of sensuality can lead to)
    - Adultery

    - Graying the lines between the roles and dress of men and women (e.g. Deuteronomy 22:5)
    - Idolatry (also listed below)
    - Mistreatment of the weak or of the property of others
- Murder
- Immorality
- Sorcery
- Idolatry
- Lying

21:9. One of the angels who'd taken part in dispensing the seven vial (bowl) judgments invites John to see the bride of Christ.

21:10-21. John then sees the holy city – New Jerusalem – coming from heaven. He notes the following features:

- 12 gates (three in each direction) made up of a single pearl with 12 angels at each gate.
- The names of the 12 tribes, one on each gate.
- 12 foundation stones representing each of Christ's12 apostles.
- Footprint: 1,500 miles long by 1,500 miles wide (2,250,000 square miles).
- Walls that are 72 yards thick.
- Walls made up of various precious stones.
- Streets of pure gold.

21:22-27. There'll be no physical temple because God and Christ will be the temple, and no additional light will be needed because they'll illuminate the city. It will always be open to those whose names were in the Lamb's Book of Life at the great judgment preceding the new heaven and earth. No one inside will practice the sinful behavior we listed earlier in our discussion of verses 6-8 because those who do have been tossed into the lake of fire at that judgment.

~ REVELATION CHAPTER 22 ~

The unveiling of the new heaven and earth, and of God's kingdom, continues with verses 1-5. Jesus finishes the Revelation by issuing a warning to change nothing about it or suffer lake-of-fire consequences. I've encountered a significant number of people who do modify this Revelation, declare it symbolic, or disregard it altogether to fit a particular eschatological standpoint. If you fall into one of these categories, I beg you to reconsider your position based on Christ's warning in this last chapter of His Revelation.

22:1-2. John sees the water of life and the tree of life.

22:3-5. The kingdom of God and Christ will last until the end of *that* age – however long that may be. We're reminded of the amazing illumination of God's glory as we also saw in 21:23-25. This ends the apocalyptic visions and descriptions spanning from the time of the letters to the churches in chapters 2-3, through the time of the birth pangs and Antichrist, and until the new heaven and earth.

22:6-7. The angel tells John that what he has seen is true and meant for the servants of the church. Christ then tells John that He'll come quickly. Those who listen and heed the prophecy contained in the Revelation will be blessed.

22:8-9. The angel also tells John that he's a servant of God just like John is, just like the prophets were, and just as those who heed the words of the Revelation will be.

22:10-11. John is instructed to make the prophecy known, "*for the time is near.*" Those who are righteous and holy must keep themselves that way.

22:12-13. Christ reiterates that He'll come quickly and that judgment will follow. Some people mistake this for a separate pre-great-judgment judgment meant only for the gathered church. There'll be just one judgment where Christ will "*render to every man according* *to what he has done.*" Remember that Christ's appearing (second coming), His 1,000-year reign, and the final judgment (mentioned in this passage) will all be part of this current age.

22:14-15. We're reminded that the righteous will inherit the kingdom while everyone else who practiced the kind of sin we discussed in our overview of 21:6-8 won't.

22:16. Jesus again states that the Revelation given to John is for the churches.

22:17. Those who wish to be partakers of God's kingdom are encouraged to do so.

22:18-21. Anyone modifying the Revelation given to John will lose their inheritance and suffer the lake of fire judgment. This passage reminds us that we can give up our salvation under certain circumstances.

16.6 Timeline of the Rest of the Revelation
Revelation 17 – 21

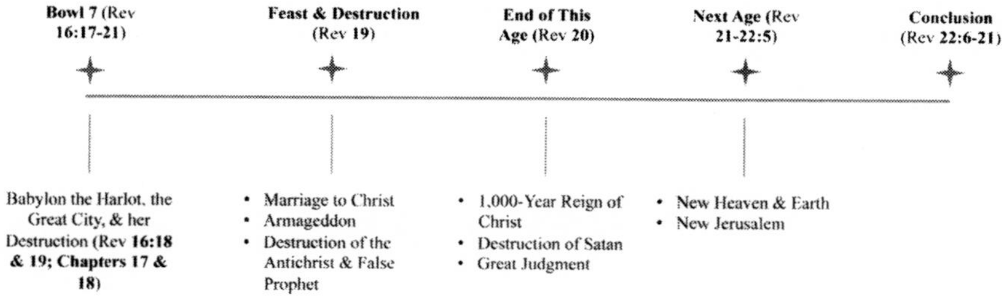

CHECKUP
CHAPTER SIXTEEN

The following questions are meant to check your understanding of what we've covered so far and provoke additional thoughts and questions to elevate your learning to a higher level. You don't have to answer *Private Challenge/Discussion* questions (or share the answers publicly if you do). They're just for your own consideration or group discussion.

Answers to all questions can be found in Appendix D.

1. Who is the author of the Revelation? Who gave it to that author?

2. What do the seven lampstands of Revelation 1 represent?

3. What do the seven stars of Revelation 1 represent?

4. In His letters to the churches, Christ has nothing against two of them. Which are they?

5. Why is Christ the only one who can break the seals and reveal the end-times events in chapter 5?

6. Which timeframe is unveiled by broken seals 4 and 5 in Revelation 6:7-11?

7. Revelation 6:12-17 covers the breaking of the sixth seal, which outlines the darkening of the sun, moon, and stars that will precede ________________ and ____________ (also check out Matthew 24:29-31).

8. What is the background or nationality of the multitude reflected in Revelation 7:9-17 (seen by John immediately after the darkening of the sixth seal)?

9. From what did the multitude in question #8 come out of?

10. Which trumpet judgment comprised woe #1 of Revelation 9:12?

11. Which trumpet judgment or other events comprise woe #2 of Revelation 11:14?

12. The seventh trumpet blast (Revelation 11:15) will pinpoint certain apocalyptic events. What will they be?

13. Which two three-and-a-half-year-long scenarios are unveiled in Revelation 11?

14. Which three-and-a-half-year-long scenario is unveiled in Revelation 12?

15. What will be happening during the three-and-a-half-year timeframe unveiled in Revelation 13?

16. Please summarize what's happening in Revelation 14:2-3 and 15:2-4. Things to consider:
    a. Who's singing the song in heaven?
    b. What group contains the only earthly beings that can learn the song?
    c. What's the context of this vision?

17. What's the theme of Revelation 17 and 18?

18. Revelation 17:9-11 gives insight as to the spiritual principality (or principalities) that will be involved with the Antichrist's end-times kingdom. Please describe who the following entities were or will be (when John wrote down the Revelation):
    a. The five that *have fallen*.
    b. The one that *is*.
    c. The one that *will come*.
    d. The *eighth* ruler.

19. What are the primary points or themes of Revelation 19?

20. According to Revelation 20:4-6, who'll be with Christ during His 1,000-year reign?

21. Are hell and the lake of fire the same thing?

22. *Private Challenge / Discussion*: Do you believe the judgment reflected in Revelation 20:11-15 and the "sheep and goat" judgment of Matthew 24 describe the same event? Why? Why not?

23. *Private Challenge / Discussion*: Revelation 21:8 gives a short list of sinful behavior that will keep us out of God's kingdom and put us into the lake of fire at the great judgment. What do you think someone practicing any of those behaviors could do to become one who "*overcomes*" as in 21:6-7?

24. Who is the intended audience of the Revelation?

25. *Private Challenge / Discussion*: The word *church* isn't used in the Revelation after the seven letters of chapters 2 and 3. A popular theory of those who hold to a pre-tribulation rapture: this is proof that the rapture will happen before any of the events of the Great Tribulation (reign of the Antichrist). What are your thoughts now that you've gone through the entire Revelation? Do you agree? Why? Why not?

26. What consequences await those who modify the Revelation given by Christ (22:18-21)?

PART FIVE

Putting It all Together

Chapter Seventeen

Exploring End-times Positions

Most Christians believe *something* about the end of time and the return of Christ. But if it's true that 95% of those professing to be Christians don't read their Bibles on a regular basis (as statistics suggest), then most end-times beliefs come only from church tradition. While tradition can be good for passing along proper beliefs and customs, it can also be destructive when perpetuating faulty doctrine if recipients don't question or prove the information by examining it against Scripture. For that reason, I believe everyone should undergo a thorough self-study of all Scripture before forming a belief system regardless of whatever tradition they've been exposed to.

Traditionally, one of four methods of studying apocalyptic Scripture will dictate what one accepts with regard to the timing of Christ's return to earth and His millennial reign. As you learned in Chapter Fourteen of this guide, readers of biblical prophetic and apocalyptic writings have generally taken one of several approaches to their interpretation. Each has produced different schools of thought regarding Christ's second coming and the likelihood of a literal 1,000-year kingdom on earth. We'll explore these in greater detail after a brief overview of the different positions and their relationships to one another.

Review of the most common approaches to the study of apocalyptic literature: (see Chapter Fourteen of this guide for additional information):

- **Spiritual**: Also called *Idealist* or *Symbolic*; proponents of this method work to discover hidden meaning in the Revelation and tend to take the Scripture symbolically or allegorize what they read (as Augustine and Origen did centuries ago). An inherent danger is missing the writer's real meaning thereby misleading others with faulty interpretations through esoteric interpretations of Scripture that can change with each person's study.

- **<u>Preterist</u>**: Most in this category believe that all events portrayed in the Mount of Olives discourse and the Revelation were fulfilled by 70 CE. The rationale? Roman atrocities committed during the siege of Jerusalem, along with the destruction of the temple, matched Jesus' prophecies listed in His Mount of Olives discourse. Also, language used in Scripture, to include the Revelation, indicated the events would happen "soon." This position states that the wrath of God has already taken place and that Christ's 1,000-year reign (cf. Revelation 20) is a symbolic one currently underway. Under this view, the only unfulfilled event is the final judgment, which will happen after a symbolic reign of Christ. As a result, a *post-millennial* view is generally held by preterists.
- **<u>Historicist</u>**: This approach isn't commonplace these days but is mentioned for your benefit. Supporters, which have included John Wycliffe and John Calvin, believe that God has revealed the entire church age through apocalyptic symbols contained in the Revelation. Seventh-day Adventists have adopted many of the Historicist viewpoints. As previously stated in Chapter Fourteen of this guide, examples of this approach include the association of the seals to barbaric invasions, scorpions to invading Arab hordes, the *beast* to the Roman Catholic Church, and the Antichrist to the pope. As with a Spiritual approach, much conjecture is necessary since there's no way to accurately pinpoint specific historic events to apocalyptic literature. As such, there's also no accountability since there's no way to prove or disprove that events resembling elements of prophecy or apocalyptic literature are truly fulfillments of those writings. Many proponents of this approach hold to a *pre-millennial* reign of Christ and *post-tribulation* rapture of the church.
- **<u>Futurist</u>**: Popular with most evangelical writers and

Bible teachers of today, this approach holds that none of the events in Revelation (with the exception of the letters to the churches in Asia Minor) have come to pass yet. This is certainly the most literal approach to interpreting the Revelation.

Attitudes toward the millennial reign of Christ:

- **A-millennial**: This view (as well as the post-millennial position), which came out of a "pro-Catholic" and "Christendom" mentality, disregards a literal 1,000-year reign of Christ as specified in Revelation 20. The timeframe outlined in that chapter is considered to be a "very long time" representing the current church age.
- **Post-millennial**: As with a-millennialism, expositors of this position disregard a literal 1,000-year kingdom but teach an earthly symbolic kingdom versus an ongoing heavenly reign. Because a-millennialism and post-millennialism teach that Christ's kingdom has come – either through a heavenly kingdom proxied by the pope or through an earthly reign of the church – both are labeled as "kingdom now" theologies.
- **Pre-millennial**: Supporters tend to take the Revelation literally, believing that Christ will return and gather the church *prior* to a 1,000-year kingdom on earth.

The timing of Christ's second coming as related to the millennial reign of Christ:

- **A-millennial**: This position is generally associated with a belief that Christ will return for the church at some undetermined point in the future.
- **Post-millennial**: Supporters tend to believe that Christ's second coming and the great judgment will occur at the *end* of a symbolic earthly reign by the church and that this won't (or can't) happen until nearly the entire world has been converted to Christianity.

- **Pre-millennial**: This view, which takes a more literal and sequential approach to the Revelation, teaches that Christ will return for the church before a literal 1,000-year reign of Christ on earth. Different positions regarding the exact timing of Christ's appearing and the gathering of the church exist within this view:
  - **Pre-tribulation Rapture**: Christ's return will happen *before* Daniel's seven-year period.
  - **Mid-tribulation Rapture**: Christ's return will happen exactly in the *middle* of Daniel's seven-year period.
  - **Pre-wrath Rapture**: Christ's return and the gathering of the church will occur at some point *during* the last half of the Antichrist's reign just before God's wrath begins.
  - **Post-tribulation Rapture**: Christ will gather the church at the *end* of Daniel's seven-year period. This view doesn't consider the trumpet judgments to be part of God's wrath.

We've already discussed the different approaches to studying the Revelation in Chapter Fourteen (Historicist, Preterist, Spiritual, and Futurist). This chapter of our study will focus on the remaining two significant sticking points: the millennial reign of Christ and the timing of His return. As a result, it's divided into two sections: *The Millennial Reign – Fact or Fiction* and *The Timing of Christ's Second Coming.*

You've most likely already formed an opinion regarding Christ's return and the end of the world. It may have come from a comprehensive study of Scripture (as I've attempted to present with this guide). Or it may have been formed after hearing your church's doctrine. It may even have come from discussions with your peers. Regardless, not everyone will agree with all viewpoints on the subject of Christ's return and related events. I'm going to present major end-times views and offer challenges as I and others see them. My desire is to educate, not offend or change your mind.

But there's a good chance the information will contrast what you believe. Should that happen, please consider everything you've learned here and then decide the best course of action or belief.

As you've already gathered, I take a literal approach to the study of Scripture. I consider historical and scriptural context and compare references in an attempt to build a complete and solid picture of what the Bible presents on a particular topic. As a result, I consider passages as figurative or symbolic *only* when there's no other obvious answer. And even then I look for explanations in Scripture to explain symbols. This practice reduces the risk of interpreting Scripture based on my own reasoning or frames of reference. Approaching end-of-the-age studies in this regard has helped form my own particular stance regarding Christ's return and events surrounding it.

Because others are often curious, I'd describe my understanding of this subject as follows:

- **Approach to the Revelation**: ***Futurist***. However, I believe Scripture shows that some events (such as several listed in Matthew 24) have come to fruition in the past (e.g. 70 CE).
- **Belief of the Millennium**: ***Pre-millennial***. However, I'm not a proponent of some of the typical pre-millennial manmade concepts (e.g. dispensationalism).
- **Timing of Christ's return**: ***Pre-wrath***. This is based on a sequential and literal reading of the Revelation and Matthew 24. Doing so suggests Christ will return and cut short the Great Tribulation, which will affect all *elect*, and gather the church just before God's destructive wrath begins.

In the interest of building faith and maintaining an attitude of love, peace, and joy, I'd like you to consider the following before proceeding to the next section:

1. Make sure you understand *why* you believe what you do about Christ's return and the end of the world. It's important

to have a good reason for your beliefs, and that your belief system is founded on solid study, not tradition or hearsay.

2. Each viewpoint we'll consider is based on some element of biblical and historical truth; none is completely false. Unfortunately, each is also most likely incomplete because they don't consider *all* Scripture or historical evidence.
3. Remember that no matter how hard we try to get things right, we're human and view evidence with different backgrounds, educational levels, and perceptions. We're not all going to agree on everything as a result but can learn from analyzing what each of us thinks about these topics.
4. Consider each point, contrast the support with what you already know (or believe you know), and then re-evaluate your understanding of these matters.

The Millennial Reign – Fact or Fiction

"What's this millennial reign?" "What's it based on?" "Why are there differing views as to what it is or whether it will take place?" Good questions, all. It's hard to believe such a division within the church can occur over a single concept, but this is often a major sticking point among believers in Christ – even well-educated Bible scholars.

First, the "millennial reign" describes a period of Christ's kingdom occurring before the great judgment (as explained in Revelation 21:11-15). Sources introducing it:

- **Old Testament**: Prophets like Amos, Ezekiel, Zechariah, Jeremiah, and Isaiah foresaw Christ's coming kingdom. References include Amos 9:11-15, Ezekiel 37:24-28, Zechariah 14:17-21, Jeremiah 30:18-20 & 37:15-17, and Isaiah 27:9-13. Scripture firmly shows that a reign on earth will be established after the destruction of the Antichrist's kingdom, and that it will be governed by Christ. Old and New Testament Scripture also shows that a new heaven and earth will follow. However, it's not clear from Old Testament apocalyptic writing as to how much time will pass from the establishment of Christ's reign to the new heaven and earth and everlasting kingdom of God.

- **Revelation 20:1-10**: Those taking a-millennial or post-millennial stands interpret this passage non-literally. Pre-millennial advocates understand this to be a literal reign of Christ on earth.
    - A literal interpretation of this passage reveals a physical 1,000-year reign of Christ on earth after the destruction of the Antichrist and his armies. His kingdom will conclude with the great judgment (cf. Revelation 20:11-15) and new heaven and earth (cf. Revelation 21:1). God's everlasting kingdom will follow (in a literal understanding) (cf. Revelation 21 and 22:1-5).
    - A non-literal interpretation of this passage enables a-millennialists to believe this to be a symbolic reign of Christ in heaven with the pope and Catholic Church as Christ's proxies on earth. Post-millennialists also take a non-literal approach, claiming the period is symbolic of the church age which began at Christ's ascension and will continue until His return.

Why do pre-millennialists consider the millennial reign to be a future literal reign while others (e.g. a-millennialists and post-millennialists) don't? The position one takes depends on whether you approach Bible interpretation as literally as possible or whether you believe the events portrayed in Revelation have already occurred. For instance, a literal approach presumes there really will be a physical, earthly reign of Christ, which will follow other yet-to-be filled events (e.g. Great Tribulation, gathering of the church, and God's wrath). A-millennialists tend to follow a Spiritual/Symbolic approach to interpreting the Revelation and therefore don't hold to a physical, earthly reign. Post-millennialists typically believe the events revealed in the Revelation have already occurred. Therefore, there's no room in the interpretation for future, unfulfilled events such as a physical reign of Christ on earth.

Now that we understand the basic differences between these views, let's explore each in greater detail.

~ A-MILLENNIAL ~

Again, this view disregards a literal 1,000-year reign of Christ as specified in Revelation 20, explaining that the timeframe is just a "very long time" representing the church age. Therefore, proponents believe the 1,000-year period symbolizes the time from Christ's resurrection until His return regardless of how long it takes. Also part of this position is an understanding that Christ's current "very long reign" is occurring in heaven and that the Catholic Church is His proxy on earth during this time. A-millennialism, which follows the spiritual or symbolic teachings of Augustine, is the one traditionally held by the Catholic Church. [30]

In supporting this position, a-millennialists have spiritualized or disregarded several major scriptural events or entities:

1. End-times Israel.
2. The binding of Satan as outlined in Revelation 20:1-3.
3. A 1,000-year reign of Christ as described in Revelation 20:4-10.
4. The fact that there will be humans still alive on the earth after God's wrath is complete.

Proponents of this belief follow an Augustinian view that Christ is the true Israel and therefore we, as His followers, are as well.[31] The view also purports that "since Christ is the true temple, we are to look for no other." As a result, the church is seen as a replacement for the Jewish nation.

Following the same approach, this theology also symbolizes the binding of Satan at Christ's appearing (cf. Revelation 20:1-3).[32] Although a literal interpretation would put the "binding" at Christ's second coming, this approach claims that "he's considered to have been bound, but not absolutely, at the cross," which would've happened at Christ's crucifixion. This binding is reportedly in only one respect – to keep Satan from deceiving the gentiles. Also believed is that Satan has already been cast to earth (cf. Revelation 12:7-13) but in a symbolic fashion.

The mention of a 1,000-year period too is taken non-literally and considered to represent a church age that will come to an end at Christ's return. And at least one a-millennialist has explained that a millennial reign won't be possible because he believes there'll be no one left alive on earth after God's wrath. He went on to interpret Revelation 19:21 to mean that "all mankind" (instead of the Antichrist's armies as Scripture reveals) was then killed by Christ at the conclusion of the battle of Armageddon.[33]

Challenges:

1. A spiritual replacement of Israel by the church negates the many prophecies regarding the gathering and protection of a remnant of Israel at the end. Also, there's nothing in Scripture to indicate believers in Christ have replaced Israel as God's chosen. There is, however, plenty that describes Israel's redemption and her place in Christ's kingdom once the "*fullness of the gentiles has come in*" (cf. Romans 11:25-26).
2. The Bible defines a future war in heaven that will precede the casting of Satan to the earth at the start of the Great Tribulation. Revelation 9:11, 11:7, and 17:8 describe the abyss also mentioned in chapter 20. There's no indication that any of these events or the abyss itself should be taken symbolically. Most significantly, anyone claiming that Satan has already been "bound at the cross" to keep him from deceiving the nations should explain how he and his angels are still able to influence mankind and empower the likes of Hitler and his military leaders, mass-murderers, etc.
3. We've learned from Zechariah (chapter 13) that two-thirds of the nation of Israel will perish at the end and that one-third will still remain alive. Also, the context of Revelation 19:21 is the battle of Armageddon. The rest, who are "*killed*

with the sword which came from the mouth of Him who sat on the horse," will be the armies of the Antichrist – not the remainder of mankind in general. Therefore, *some* people of the gentile nations along with a remnant of Israel will still be alive at the onset of Christ's kingdom on earth.

~ Post-Millennial ~

As with a-millennialism, expositors of this position disregard a literal 1,000-year kingdom. The primary difference between the two is that post-millennialism teaches an indefinite earthly kingdom versus an ongoing heavenly reign with earthly proxies (as with a-millennialism). The premise here is that Christ will return after an unknown length of earthly evangelism by the church during which time nearly the entire world will become saved. Kenneth Gentry summed up this millennial view as follows:

> Postmillennialism expects the proclaiming of the Spirit-blessed gospel of Jesus Christ to win the vast majority of human beings to salvation in the present age. Increasing gospel success will gradually produce a time in history prior to Christ's return in which faith, righteousness, peace, and prosperity will prevail in the affairs of people and of nations. After an extensive era of such conditions the Lord will return visibly, bodily, and in great glory, ending history with the general resurrection and the great judgment of all humankind. Hence, our system is postmillennial in that the Lord's glorious return occurs after an era of "millennial" conditions.[34]

Many who subscribe to a post-millennial view also follow a preterist approach to understanding the Revelation, believing that the Great Tribulation occurred in the generation living when Jesus spoke (i.e. around 70 CE). According to Doug Wilson, that timeframe kicked off a "new heaven and earth – a new creation."[35] He has also stated that we're in "an eventual reunification of heaven and earth" and that the Golden Age of worldwide Christianity (which according to the position would also include a converted Israel) could come along as late as 3500 CE.

Another quote by Gentry from *Three Views on the Millennium and Beyond* suggests that post-millennialism, like a-millennialism, supports a "replacement" theory whereby Israel would be more or less replaced or at least assimilated by the church:[36]

> . . . the house of God of Jacob and "Zion" refer to the church. Isaiah says that Christ's church will be "established" in "the top of the mountains," indicating she will be permanently fixed, rendered permanently visible. . . . "All nations will stream" (Isaiah 2:2) into the church to worship the Lord, who saves them. . . . Christianity will become the agent of gracious redemptive influence in the world. . . . With overwhelming numbers converting to Christ and being discipled in God's law, great socio-political transformation naturally follows (Isaiah 2:4).

In parallel with a-millennialism, post-millennialism professes a long-ago spiritual binding of Satan that has permitted the flourishing of the church during the current age. Points made by Gentry related to the millennium and the binding of Satan:[37]

> The thousand years in Revelation 20 seem to function as a symbolic value, not strictly limited to a literal thousand year period. . . . The "thousand years", then serve as John's symbolic portrayal of the long-lasting glory of the kingdom Christ established at his first coming.
>
> In Revelation 20:1-3 John portrays the negative implications of Christ's triumph over Satan, when "the dragon, that ancient serpent, who is the devil or Satan" (v.2) is spiritually bound . . . This binding restricts him from successfully accomplishing his evil design in history.
>
> While Satan is bound, Christ rules and his redeemed people participate with him in that rule (Rev. 20:4). . . .Thus, the saints

reigning "with Christ" on thrones while Satan is bound beautifully pictures his redemptive kingdom already established.

The "millennial" era has already lasted almost two thousand years; it may continue another thousand or ten thousand more, for all we know.

That a-millennialism and post-millennialism share similarities should be expected. A-millennialism was (and still is) the primary millennial theology of the Catholic Church. Post-millennialism became a part of the Reformers' theology (e.g. Calvinism), which was born out of the doctrine of the Catholic Church. Therefore, both support a symbolic 1,000-year period, spiritual binding of Satan, and replacement or assimilation of Israel by the church.

Challenges:

1. As with a-millennialism, professing a spiritual replacement or assimilation of Israel by the church requires spiritualization and conjecture since Scripture doesn't explicitly link future Israel to the church or directly compare Israel to Christ. In fact, Old Testament prophecies and apocalyptic writing suggest otherwise if you take them literally.
2. A post-millennial concept dictates that Satan was "constricted" to allow the church to flourish and become the dominant worldwide religion. However, the Christian population is dwindling and becoming less influential in world politics. A trend toward world domination by the Christian faith, even after nearly 2,000 years, appears elusive and is currently nonexistent. Also, Jesus told us that although many are called "*few are chosen*" (cf. Matthew 22:14). Christianity as a worldwide religion with nearly every inhabitant saved or at least under Christian authority before the birth of a "Golden Age" seems unlikely based on this passage alone.

~ PRE-MILLENNIAL ~

Supporters of this doctrine tend to take the Revelation literally and therefore believe that Christ will return and gather the church *prior* to a 1,000-year kingdom on earth. This view considers the Revelation to be mostly sequential (e.g. the end of God's wrath in chapter 19, then the millennial reign and great judgment in chapter 20, and then the new heaven and earth outlined in chapters 21 and 22). Pre-millennial proponents tend to differ, though, on the timing of Christ's second coming.

Unlike a-millennialism or post-millennialism, pre-millennialism proposes that:

1. Christ's second coming will occur *before* He begins His reign on earth.
2. Christ's reign on earth will be a physical, not a spiritual, kingdom.
3. That kingdom will last for 1,000 years before climaxing with a final conflict with Satan and the great judgment.
4. The binding of Satan in preparation for Christ's millennial reign will be physical and last nearly 1,000 years as stated in Revelation 20.

Although a historicist approach to the Revelation was predominant prior to the 19th century, a futuristic method is now probably most common. As discussed previously, those in favor of this approach see most events identified in the Revelation as unfulfilled. Because this position interprets Revelation 20 literally, and the interpretation doesn't conflict with other Scripture, nothing concrete can be said in opposition to the basic tenets themselves. This view does carry some "religious baggage" with it though.

A popular companion to modern pre-millennialism is dispensationalism, which insists God has "dealt with humanity through a series of distinct periods."[38] The idea, perpetuated by John Darby in the early 19th century, has grown into a concept whereby the church age has been divided into seven periods, each corresponding to a particular church listed in Revelation 2-3.

The idea of multiple church eras has been used to support a pre-tribulation rapture theory and introduce interesting doctrine. Here's what Craig Blaising[39] has written regarding the progression of dispensationalism:

> One of the most distinctive forms of premillennialism is that of classical dispensationalism, which developed in the context of nineteenth-century premillennial prophecy conferences. Its key ideas were first formulated by John Nelson Darby, an early leader in the Brethren movement. . . . Representative expressions of classical dispensationalism can be found in the notes of the Scofield Reference Bible and especially in the Systematic Theology of Lewis Sperry Chafer.
>
> Of course, dispensationalists are also known for their emphasis on a pretribulational Rapture.
>
> Historicist premillennialism refers to a distinctive type of apocalypticism . . . They read church history as having fulfilled many of the visions of Daniel and Revelation . . . They followed a basic formula whereby days in biblical prophecy equaled years in the history of the church. . . . Dispensationalists rejected the year-day formula and took a strictly literal approach to the days and months numbered in Daniel and Revelation . . .
>
> Dispensational apocalypticism became popular during the era of the Cold War and occasioned all kind of speculations about events during that period of history. One example of this, certainly the most well-known, is the writings of Hal Lindsey.

Challenges:

1. Because of the futuristic nature of this position, many have tried to set dates for Christ's return and failed. Past examples include several of Edgar C. Whisenant's claims that Christ

would return as early as 1988.[40] Family Radio, which believes that the church age is likely at an end,[41] touts a date of May 21, 2011 for Christ's second coming.[42]

2. The futuristic nature of this position also presents a temptation among its supporters to engage in "media exegesis" – always looking in the news for current signs of the times. Doing this can keep us from tackling the weightier matters of our faith (e.g. taking care of our fellow man and making disciples). It can cause us to misinterpret Scripture in the same way those who've tried to apply *past* events to fulfillment have.
3. Pre-millennialism has produced at least four viewpoints regarding the actual return of Christ and gathering of the church: pre-tribulation rapture, mid-tribulation rapture, pre-wrath rapture, and post-tribulation rapture. Desperation to "see" current events as signs of the last days and a desire to support individual views (even within the realm of a literal approach to Scripture) have contributed to this pre-millennial rapture division.

THE TIMING OF CHRIST'S SECOND COMING

That Christ will return to judge all – living and dead – seems to be a point all Christian believers agree on regardless of their approach to the Revelation or understanding of the millennium. Unfortunately, several different viewpoints as to the timing of His return exist and tend to muddy the eschatological waters.

In this section, we'll relate each millennial position to its most common viewpoint regarding Christ's return in relation to that particular millennial belief. What you'll discover is that while this characteristic of a-millennialism and post-millennialism is pretty straightforward, several different views exist within the pre-millennialism doctrine. Before delving into the different theories, let's define and discuss the terms related to Christ's *appearing* and His *coming*. This will be important to properly understanding the pre-tribulation and mid-tribulation rapture positions.

~ APPEARING VERSUS COMING ~

Christ came (appeared) once as a sacrifice for mankind and will come (appear) a second time as foretold by Paul:

> *. . . so Christ also, having been offered once to bear the sins of many, will* ***appear a second time*** *for salvation without reference to sin, to those who eagerly await Him.* —Hebrews 9:28.

The New Testament mostly uses several Greek words to describe Christ's second coming and related events.[43] Although advocates of a pre-tribulation or mid-tribulation rapture prescribe them to separate events divided by a significant interval, Scripture uses the words to represent a single second coming/appearing of Christ and events that will be revealed during His time on earth.

- **Parousia** (Strong's G3952): This term is tied to Christ's *coming* and commonly describes the gathering of the church. It represents the relief that will be provided believers when Christ is *revealed* (*apokalupsis*).
- **Epiphaneia** (Strong's G2015): This term is tied to Christ's *appearing*, which will happen at His *coming* (*parousia*).
- **Apokalupsis** (Strong's G602): This term is tied to events (such as relief for believers) that will be *revealed* at His *coming*.

Other Scripture references utilize different Greek words than the three above but are still related to Christ's coming/appearing.[44] Let's now move on to an analysis of each major rapture position.

~ A-MILLENNIAL ~

Under this end-times position, Christ will return to earth, raise the dead, and execute final judgment after an indefinite period during which good and evil will coexist (although Satan is said to be "spiritually bound" during this time). According to the doctrine, we're currently in that period which will conclude with Christ's second advent. This is the predominant view of the Catholic Church.

Challenges:

1. See those listed under *The Millennial Reign – Fact or Fiction.*
2. A spiritualized approach to the events leading up to Christ's return, the millennial reign, or God's wrath could make it difficult to understand the "*blessed hope*" we have of Christ's appearing or the wrath "*we're not destined for*" with any clarity (cf. 1 Thessalonians 5:9 & Titus 2:13).

~ POST-MILLENNIAL ~

Expositors of this theology generally hold to a preterist doctrine, which "places the prophecies of intense evil and foreboding gloom in the first century, focusing on the events surrounding the forty-two-month long Neronic persecution (A.D. 64-68), cf. Rev. 13:5), the forty-two-month long Jewish war with Rome (A.D. 67-70, cf. Rev. 11:1-2), and the destruction of the temple (A.D. 70, cf. Matt. 23:36-24:34)."[45]

Gentry, arguing for the post-millennial preterist position (above), goes on to describe the Mount of Olives discussion and Revelation through preterist eyes:[46]

> Another feature of theonomic postmillennialism (though not essential to it) is its preterist approach to a number of the great judgment passages of the New Testament. The preterist (Latin: "gone by") approach to certain prophecies holds that the Great Tribulation (Matt. 24:21) occurred in the generation living when Christ spoke (Matt. 24:34); the book of Revelation expects its events to transpire "soon" (Rev. 1:1, 22:7, 12), because in John's day "the time is near" (Rev. 1:3, 22:10); and the Antichrist was a first-century phenomenon (1 John 2:18, 22; 4:3; 2 John 7).

Preterists generally believe that Christ's millennial reign is symbolic and began with His crucifixion and resurrection. This current age will end with Christ's second advent, which will follow a Golden Age. During that time, nearly everyone on earth including Israel will be serving Him (according to the preterist position).

Challenges:

1. See those listed under *The Millennial Reign – Fact or Fiction.*
2. The preterist approach insists John wrote the Revelation prior to 70 CE, that Nero was the Antichrist, and that the Great Tribulation has already occurred. Although many of the events Jesus spoke of in His discourse on the Mount of Olives *did* occur with the 67-70 CE Jewish war, Nero doesn't fit into the biblical Antichrist model (e.g. from input given by Daniel, Jesus, and Paul). Also, evidence supports a much later writing of the Revelation (around 90 CE – well after the destruction of Jerusalem and Nero's rule).
3. This position disregards a literal interpretation of Revelation 20 permitting a doctrine that includes a "spiritual binding" of Satan and an indefinite and symbolic reign of Christ. In fact, many proponents see Revelation 20 as a complete symbolic representation of the entire church age.
4. Although there's no historical evidence that anything like the description of the Day of the Lord wrath to come or return of Christ have happened, supporters of this position claim there have been many "Day of the Lord" occurrences ending with the destruction of Jerusalem. This precludes a literal requirement to anticipate a single day of reckoning that will follow Christ's appearing and precede the great judgment.
5. According to Daniel and Christ, the Great Tribulation will be a time like no other – past, present, or future. Preterism teaches that this terrible time occurred in 70 CE. However, other historical events since then have certainly proven to be worse than the siege of Jerusalem (e.g. the killing of roughly 100 million by the bubonic plague during the Middle Ages, Hitler's reign of terror against the Jews, etc.).

~ Pre-millennial ~

If you take a literal approach to understanding Scripture, then it's easy to see why many believe in a physical 1,000-year reign of Christ. But if it's supposed to be so *easy*, then why are there several dissenting viewpoints within that doctrine regarding the timing of Christ's return in relation to the millennial reign? The answer may be found in an examination of what the proponents of each viewpoint believe about these related topics: the Great Tribulation, God's wrath, and Christ's return.

On a positive note, each pre-millennial position seems to affirm a gathering of the church before the start of God's wrath. This is in keeping with Paul's statement to believers in Thessalonica:

> *But since we are of the day, let us be sober, having put on the breastplate of faith and love, and as a helmet, the hope of salvation.* ***For God has not destined us for wrath, but for obtaining salvation*** *through our Lord Jesus Christ . . .* — 1 Thessalonians 5:8-9.

In context, Paul had just explained that the Day of the Lord (God's wrath) will come as a surprise to those in darkness. But what will God's wrath comprise? When will it come? We'll explore each viewpoint's position on these things along with the common understanding of each regarding the Great Tribulation. Let's start by looking at the pre-tribulation rapture position.

Pre-tribulation Rapture: This perspective exposits that Christ's return will happen *before* Daniel's seven-year period, the entire time of which will be filled with God's wrath. It's the predominant viewpoint held by evangelical churches and has been since the late 19th century. I say *churches* instead of *Christians* because most church members tend to adopt the doctrine of their denomination without question. In my opinion and experience, this particular end-times theology makes use of conjecture and spiritualism in interpretation of this topic more than the other pre-millennial views.

It hurts me to say this, as it's the view I held for most of my life until I began studying the Bible and became responsible for my own faith and understanding of Scripture.

Pre-tribulation rapture doctrine, unlike the longer-standing rapture beliefs of a-millennialism and post-millennialism, is a recent phenomenon with a clear beginning. According to Richard R. Reiter, "The most influential promulgator of pretribulational dispensationalism was Irish Bible teacher John N. Darby." The Niagara Bible Conference of 1878 popularized pre-millennial doctrine in North America. Initially, the conference's doctrinal statement wasn't specifically dispensational and "left room for all premillennialists." Although the original intent was to unite pre-millennialists and resolve minor conflicting views, pre-tribulationalism and its pre-70th-week rapture doctrine gained widespread support (until the mid-20th century) and emerged as the dominant view following the conference and subsequent meetings. The Sea Cliff Bible Conference of 1901, bolstered by wealthy Plymouth Brethren, followed the pre-tribulation dispensationalism mantra fathered by John Darby. The final outcome of the Niagara cooperation, which spanned the initial conference to subsequent meetings like the Sea Cliff Conference, was the Scofield Reference Bible and staunch support for a pre-tribulation rapture doctrine and dispensationalism.

Also unique to this position is a very distinct separation of Christ's *appearing* and His *second coming* into different events. This is done to substantiate a belief that Christ will *appear* in the clouds to gather the church in an imminent and silent rapture before Daniel's 70th week and then *come again* at the end of that period to defeat the Antichrist. As discussed at the beginning of this section, *The Timing of Christ's Second Coming*, His coming (*parousia*), appearing (*ephipaneia*), and revelation (*apokalupsis*) all refer to the same period encompassing the gathering, reward, judgment, and kingdom.[47]

Understanding of Daniel's 70th week of years and the Great Tribulation: Pre-tribulation rapture supporters see this entire time as a period of man's wrath at the hands of the Antichrist[48] *and* of God's wrath. Believing this makes it necessary to see the gathering of the church *before* the seven-year period begins since, as Paul said, we're not destined for wrath.

Understanding of God's wrath: This position exposits that God's wrath is called the *Great Tribulation* and that it will last for the entire seven-year period (Daniel's 70th week). As such, it's represented by the seven seals (called judgments under this view) which supposedly also correspond to the seven trumpet and seven bowl judgments.[49]

Understanding of Christ's return: Pre-tribulation rapture proponents believe that Christ's appearing and His coming represent two different events.[50] According to Hal Lindsey, "One passage of Scripture speaks of Christ's **coming in the air and in secret**, like a thief coming in the night. Another part of the Scripture describes Christ's **coming in power and majesty** to the earth . . ."

Challenges: This stance produces several significant challenges, most related to a strong push to substantiate a secret pre-second-coming "any moment (imminent)" gathering. Some of the most common examples are as follows:

1. "*Jesus can come back at any moment!*" Dr. John Walvoord, a prominent evangelical leader, argued that the doctrine of *imminency*, defined as "a Rapture that is possible at any moment," was "the central feature of pretribulationalism."[51] This is a belief that disregards the signs Christ said would precede His appearing and the gathering of the church (e.g. the seven-year agreement, Antichrist, Great Tribulation, darkening of the skies, etc.). It also doesn't take into account the landmark events related to a falling away from the faith and the entrance of the Antichrist as portrayed in 2 Thessalonians 2. Parallel with this component of pre-tribulationalism is

a "thief in the night" concept whereby proponents insist that Jesus will "come back like a thief in the night!"[52] In context, the "*thief in the night*" – taken from passages like 1 Thessalonians 5:2 – is actually referring to the Day of the Lord wrath that will fall on end-times unbelievers and doesn't represent the gathering of the church.

2. "*The word* apostasy *in 2 Thessalonians is symbolic of the pretribulation rapture*." Some, in an effort to strengthen the pre-tribulation rapture position, have restated the *apostasy* of 2 Thessalonians 2:3 to mean *departure* or *withdrawal* (rapture) instead of the more common translations of *falling away* (of the faith) or *rebellion*.[53]
3. A common viewpoint among pre-tribulation rapture champions is that the church of Philadelphia mentioned in Revelation 3:10 directly represents believers – the church that will be "kept out of the tribulation altogether."[54] Much time and effort has been spent by advocates in trying to prove that the statement by Christ of "*keep you from the hour of testing*" actually means to be taken "*out from within*" – completely removed (raptured) before the Great Tribulation.[55] This is a liberal and questionable translation. Also, placing such emphasis on the church of Philadelphia is in direct conflict with the pre-tribulation companion of dispensationalism, which dictates that the church of Laodicea is the one that represents the current church age.
4. Common to a pre-tribulation rapture theory is the belief that John's invitation to heaven to view end-times events (cf. Revelation 4:1) is proof of a pre-tribulation rapture. Hal Lindsey's statement, "John has been called up into heaven to be shown the things which must happen after the Rapture . . ."[56] exemplifies this perspective and emphasizes a belief that the gathering (rapture) will happen before the events portrayed in the Revelation. **Food for thought**: What would be the point of Christ revealing end-times events to a church that wouldn't be present during that era?

5. The view of most dispensationalists is that the signs Jesus gave His disciples on the Mount of Olives were for Jews, not Christians.[57] Dismissing these signs permits a secret pre-tribulation rapture theory. However, it's important to remember that Jesus revealed these signs to His disciples, who would be responsible for founding and growing His church. Also remember that Paul reiterated some of these signs (such as a falling away from the faith and of the Antichrist in the temple that would take place *before* the gathering [cf. 2 Thessalonians]) to Christian believers. Finally, as previously learned in this study, Christ revealed the end-times events to John for the benefit of His bride, the church.
6. "*The word* ***church*** *isn't mentioned after Revelation 3, which proves the rapture will happen and that the* church *will be removed before the tribulation events outlined in the rest of the book.*" The Greek word *ekklesia* is used in the Revelation to directly address the seven churches in Asia Minor. Therefore, it isn't used until a conclusion in chapter 21 because the dictation of the letters is finished with chapter 3. Christians present during the time of Great Tribulation are referred to as "saints" in the remainder of the book.
7. Essential to a pre-tribulation perspective is the belief that God's Holy Spirit is the *restrainer* that must be removed to allow Satan to implement great tribulation through the Antichrist (cf. 2 Thessalonians 2:6). Included in the idea: "*This is proof of a pre-tribulation rapture since the church can't exist without the Holy Spirit, and it will be removed before the tribulation . . .*" God's Word actually presents His Spirit in ways contrary to that of a *restrainer*. Additionally, Daniel helps us understand that the *restrainer* is most likely the archangel Michael (cf. Daniel 12:1), which is credible considering his position of military authority in heaven. A few significant verses related to the Holy Spirit's actual character or purpose:[58]
   a. Comforts (cf. Acts 9:31)

b. Provides spiritual gifts (cf. 1 Corinthians 12)
c. Helps and teaches (cf. John 14:26)

Mid-tribulation Rapture: Proponents insist that Christ's return will happen exactly in the *middle* of Daniel's seven-year period. According to Gleason Archer, the Antichrist will shatter the power of the saints and succeed in attaining absolute dictatorship over the world before a mid-70th-week rapture that will occur at the seventh trumpet of Revelation 11:15-19.[59]

Unlike the traditional pre-tribulation rapture position, this doctrine does take Scripture more at face value and therefore precludes the need to dismiss or spiritualize passages that place believers on earth during the Antichrist's time of authority.

Understanding of Daniel's 70th week of years and the Great Tribulation: Mid-tribulation rapture supporters consider a seven-year period as do those who advocate other pre-millennial rapture positions. However, this stance associates the Great Tribulation with the wrath of God, not with the time of the Antichrist's authority.[60] Therefore, they conclude that the Great Tribulation – wrath of God in this case – will occur during the second half of the seven-year period after a mid-70th-week rapture.

Understanding of God's wrath: As with a pre-tribulation rapture position, proponents here consider the rapture and God's "Day of the Lord" wrath as two separate events. Supporters believe that when Jesus said "*and then the end will come*" (cf. Matthew 24:14) He may have been referring only to God's wrath – to the "final horror of the three and a half years during which the wrath of God will be poured out upon the earth."[61] Interestingly, Gleason Archer makes this comment that sums up his belief about the Great Tribulation and its association with the wrath of God:

> If the Great Tribulation is to be identified with the second half of the final seven years prior to Armageddon, during

which the bowls of divine wrath will be poured out upon the earth, then the view we are about to advocate is really a form of pretribulation rapture.[62]

Understanding of Christ's return: Mid-tribulation rapture advocates believe that Christ will return at the seventh trumpet call, and that the call will come exactly midway through the seven-year period defined by Daniel. Again, they see the first three and a half years as the wrath of man at the hands of the Antichrist, and the entire second three-and-a-half-year timeframe as the wrath of God.

Challenges: Many if not most of the issues inherent in the pre-tribulation rapture theory aren't present here since there's no need to dismiss or spiritualize passages that place believers on earth during the Antichrist's time of authority. And, as with other pre-millennial rapture positions, they do claim that the church will be taken before God's wrath. However, there are several points that deserve consideration:

1. While it takes a more literal and sequential approach to the Revelation than the pre-tribulation rapture theory does, this position holds that "John does not follow a neatly segmented chronological sequence in the series of visions revealed to him . . ."[63]
2. An understanding that the Great Tribulation will be the time of God's wrath instead of the Antichrist's reign of terror may disregard Revelation 7:9-14 which states: "*After these things I looked, and behold, a great multitude which no one could count, from every nation and all tribes and peoples and tongues, standing before the throne and before the Lamb, clothed in white robes, and palm branches were in their hands; . . . These are the ones who come out of the great tribulation, and they have washed their robes and made them white in the blood of the Lamb.*"
3. There's no indication in Scripture that the Antichrist's

wrath against God's chosen (Jew or Christian believer) will begin *before* the middle of Daniel's 70th week (cf. Daniel 9:27).

4. There's no indication in Scripture that *God's* wrath will start in the middle of Daniel's 70th week or that it will take up an entire three-and-a-half-year period. Remember, Daniel and Christ said the following about the Antichrist and the time of his authority:
    a. It will be a time of persecution against the saints granted for three and a half years (cf. Daniel 7:25 & Revelation 11:2).
    b. The three-and-a-half-year period of authority will begin in the middle of the seven-year period (cf. Daniel 9:27).
    c. God will cut that time of persecution short with Christ's appearing and the gathering of the church (cf. Matthew 24:21-22).
    d. God's wrath (trumpet and bowl judgments) of an undetermined length of time will follow the gathering as seen in Matthew 24:29-31 and Revelation 7:9-17 (between the sixth and seventh seals).

Pre-wrath Rapture: This stance, advocated by authors Marvin Rosenthal and Robert Van Kampen, takes a very literal approach to Scripture. As such, it exposits that Christ's return and the gathering of the church will occur at some point *during* the last half of the Antichrist's reign just before God's wrath begins. Robert Van Kampen, deceased author of *The Sign*, summed up the view this way:

> The prewrath position is really quite simple: the true and faithful church will be raptured (or rescued) when the Antichrist's great tribulation (persecution) against God's elect is cut short by Christ's coming (Matt. 24:22, 29-31). First he will rescue the faithful who will be undergoing Satan's wrath, and then He will destroy the wicked who remain on earth during the Day of the Lord, God's wrath. The wrath of God is never equated with the persecution of God's elect![64]

Understanding of Daniel's 70th week of years and the Great Tribulation: The pre-wrath rapture view understands that Daniel's 70th week of years is as of yet unfulfilled (as do the other pre-millennial rapture positions). But unlike the pre-tribulation or mid-tribulation rapture positions, this one holds that the Great Tribulation will be a period of the Antichrist's wrath, not God's wrath, which is labeled by Scripture as the *Day of the Lord.* It also states that the Antichrist will dishonor his agreement in the middle of the seven-year period and begin a three-and-a-half-year Great Tribulation against the saints – God's elect (both Jew and Christian).

Understanding of God's wrath: This view keeps a literal label of the Day of the Lord for the end-times wrath of God, called the Great Tribulation by pre-tribulation and mid-tribulation rapture believers. Within the pre-wrath rapture perspective is a very literal approach to Matthew 24 and the Revelation that positions the Day of the Lord *after* the darkening of the sun, moon, and stars at the sixth seal and silence of the seventh seal. This view also takes the judgments of God (trumpets and bowls) at face value.

Understanding of Christ's return: Pre-wrath doctrine declares that Christ will return for His church as God cuts short the Great Tribulation of the Antichrist. This is in keeping with a literal approach to Scripture and reflected by Robert Van Kampen in this statement from *The Sign*:

> Simply stated, the prewrath view contends that the church will go through Antichrist's persecution that begins at the midpoint of Daniel's seventieth week, but will be **raptured before the end of this specific seven-year time period, when Christ cuts short this time of intense persecution** by removing the object of his hatred, the elect of God, and then retaliates with the Day of the Lord's wrath against those who remain.[65]

Challenges: Because this view takes a very literal approach to Scripture, it's difficult to find significant challenges beyond contention over personal opinions of an author expositing this position. For instance, Robert Van Kampen, as a supporting author, has declared these personal and potentially contentious opinions:

1. End-times Babylon will be both Rome and the Catholic Church. This view may disregard Scripture that tends to implicate Jerusalem and Israel instead.[66]
2. In *The Sign*, Van Kampen states that the seventh beast empire was Nazi Germany and that the Antichrist will be Hitler incarnate. Although intriguing, this position may not consider Old Testament prophecy or a trend whereby each subsequent "*beast*" kingdom assimilated the previous empire's regions. Hitler's Germany doesn't follow the mold or fit prophecy.

Post-tribulation Rapture: In this perspective, Christ will gather the church at the *end* of Daniel's seven-year period or shortly thereafter. This view doesn't consider the trumpet judgments to be part of God's wrath, but does consider the last half of the seven-year period to include both the Antichrist's persecution *and* the wrath of God.[67] Two things are central to a placing of the rapture at the end of Daniel's 70th week:

1. A belief that the Day of Christ (cf. Thessalonians 2:2) and the Day of the Lord are the same.
2. An understanding that the seventh trumpet, during what others refer to as God's wrath, will actually herald the gathering of the church.

In pages 5-6 of his book *A Biblical Study of the Return of Christ*, Roy W. Anderberg declares these points in outlining the post-tribulation rapture doctrine:

- That the coming (*parousia*) of Christ is the same event as His appearing and revelation, and it is a single onetime event.

- That the *parousia* occurs at the end of the week or shortly thereafter.
- That the cosmic events associated with the *parousia* in Matthew 24 are the same ones that Isaiah, Joel, Peter, Jesus, John, and Paul prophesied or wrote about.
- That the Day of the Lord is connected directly with the *parousia* and happens immediately after the rapture.
- That the Day of the Lord is at the end of the week and Christians will not be surprised as it approaches.
- That the sixth seal initiates the same cosmic events and introduces the wrath of God upon unbelievers. The believers are not the subjects of God's wrath.
- That the end of the world (age) and the time of harvest occur simultaneously at the end of the week or shortly thereafter.
- That the last day and the last trump also occur simultaneously at the end of the week or shortly thereafter.
- That the two witnesses are killed and resurrected at the end of the 70th week.
- That the Holy Spirit remains with the saints during the entire 70th week.
- That the "restrainer" in 2 Thessalonians 2 is not the Holy Spirit but Michael (one of the chief princes and defender of Israel). He would be a better contender for the position.
- That the rapture is neither silent nor secret, and is the same coming (*parousia*) that Jesus talks about in Matthew 24, transpiring at the end of the week or shortly thereafter.

According to Richard R. Reither, we've "seen the resurgence of posttribulationism through the scholarly growth of that perspective and diverse challenges to the dominance of pretribulationism among American Evangelicals."[68] This may be attributed to the literal approach the position takes to the rapture (as opposed to that of the pre-tribulation rapture theory).

Understanding of Daniel's 70th week of years and the Great Tribulation: In keeping with the other pre-millennial rapture positions, post-tribulation rapture advocates see Daniel's 70th week as something that will be fulfilled in the future. Mr. Anderberg put it this way:

> Post-tribulation doctrine which sees the first half of the 70th week as a pseudo time of peace in Israel, and that the coming of Christ is a single final event occurring at the end of the 7 year period. Advocates view the 2nd half of the week as the tribulation period.[69]

Understanding of God's wrath: Expositors of this position view the seventh trumpet of the Revelation as the gathering of the church (cf. Revelation 10:7 & 11:15) and therefore don't consider any of the trumpets and their outcomes to be judgments of God. As a result, their belief is that God's wrath comprises only the bowl judgments (cf. Revelation 16). As with all other pre-millennial rapture positions, supporters don't believe the church will experience God's wrath. However, this means they put the wrath of God at the extreme end or outside of the 70th week of Daniel.

Understanding of Christ's return: As with mid-tribulation rapture believers, proponents of this view understand that the return of Christ will happen at the seventh trumpet call. They also associate the appearing (*parousia*) of Christ and the resurrection/gathering of the church with the resurrection of Revelation 20:4.[70]

Challenges: This and the pre-wrath rapture positions are based on a very literal approach to Scripture and are therefore almost identical with one exception: this view associates the rapture with the seventh trumpet, placing it at the *very end* of Daniel's seven-year period instead of sometime *near the end.* Several related points to consider:

1. A post-tribulation rapture position sees the *Day of Christ* and *Day of the Lord* as the same event. Yet

Scripture identifies the Day of Christ as the time of the gathering of the church at His appearing (cf. Philippians 1:6 & 10, & 2:16; 1 Corinthians 1:8) and the Day of the Lord as the subsequent wrath of God (cf. 1 Thessalonians 5:2; 2 Thessalonians 2:2; 2 Peter 3:10). None necessarily indicate they'll both occur at the same time.

2. Although this perspective takes a very literal and sequential approach to understanding Scripture such as the Mount of Olives discourse and the Revelation, an insistence upon placing the rapture at the seventh trumpet wrecks that trend. For instance, a literal approach would see the gathering *out of the Great Tribulation* in Revelation 7 as having occurred after the darkening of the sixth seal, but before the silence of the seventh seal. According to the sequence of the Revelation, God's trumpet judgments will follow the silence of seal 7. However, a post-tribulation view that associates the gathering with the last (seventh) of those trumpet judgments would have to either disregard the gathering of chapter 7 or change the sequence of things.
3. This position also equates the "*last trumpet*" that will herald the gathering of the church (cf. 1 Corinthians 15:52; 1 Thessalonians 4:16) with the seventh trumpet of God's trumpet judgments. Scripture isn't clear on this. Although it's conceivable, holding that viewpoint requires taking a nonlinear approach to the Revelation (see the above paragraph). Also, the "*last trumpet*" will be a means of heralding the gathering and may very well be the last trumpet of Rosh Hashanah – one of the fall feasts Christ may fulfill upon His return.

CHAPTER EIGHTEEN

REVIEW & CONCLUSION

Congratulations! You've completed the study (unscathed, hopefully). I know it was exhaustive and very comprehensive. You've most likely forgotten much of what you read by now depending on how long you've been working on this. That's okay – we'll go through a brief review and highlight the most important points to remember. Beyond that, this study guide can always serve as a reference should you wish to dig deeper into a particular topic or look up specific information related to the end of our world.

Chapter One: ***Why Worry About This*****?** I hope you learned here that we should study this (and all Scripture). A lack of biblical knowledge and understanding could open the door for spiritual death, deception, and a falling away from the faith.

Chapter Two: ***A Glimpse of the End.*** We've been in the "last days" since the time of Christ but await the "end of this age" (world). Our current age will end with the great judgment of God, which will usher in a new heaven and earth. Specific events that will conclude this age:

1. Birth pangs of false messiahs, violence (war), earthquakes, and famine. These will increase in intensity and frequency as the end draws near.
2. A seven-year agreement between Israel and the Antichrist's kingdom.
3. Breaking of the agreement and a three-and-a-half-year Great Tribulation at the hands of the Antichrist and his kingdom.
4. Darkening of the sun, moon, and stars that will highlight a "cutting short" of the Great Tribulation and herald Christ's appearance.
5. Gathering of the church by the angels of Christ at His appearing.

6. Wrath of God against the rest of the world.
7. One thousand years of peace.
8. Great judgment.

Chapter Three: *Faith – Truth or Consequences.* Faith is the assurance of things unseen (the things of God and of Christ in our case). How do we gain that assurance? We're assured and build our faith through exposure to the gospel, which in turn teaches us truth through the testimony of the prophets, historical events, Christ's teachings, the apostles' writings, and apocalyptic unveiling. No gospel, no faith or foundation. The Christian faith is also something we belong to as believers in Christ. And the Scripture tells us that many will fall away from it at the end.

Primary points to remember regarding faith:

- Faith is built on hearing the gospel and responding.
- A lack of faith from having no or little exposure to the gospel opens the door for deception.
- A lack of faith and subsequent deception allows wicked doctrine based on man's wisdom to take root and keep some from the faith.
- Being scripturally ignorant can be deadly.

Chapter Four: *How to Study...or Not!* The primary goal of writing is to convey a message. A non-literal approach to interpretation distorts or hides the intended communications. So take Scripture literally wherever possible. This will preclude your being responsible for a personal interpretation, as will be the case if you symbolize or spiritualize Scripture unnecessarily. Consider the context of a passage starting with the verse, then the chapter, then the biblical book, and then the entire Bible itself. Compare similar references for confirmation or further explanation. Take Scripture non-literally only when no other choice is likely. In the case of symbols, look within the Scripture itself for explanations. In addition, take into account the historical setting and background of the writer and intended audiences. And pay particular attention to the use of grammar to make sure you're able to follow the subjects accurately. You'll find the use of tools such as a concordance and computer software very helpful in your studies.

Chapter Five: ***Brief History of Israel & the Temple of God.*** The purpose of this chapter was to provide you with the history of Israel from its inception to the present, dividing it up into eras that match those of ruling kingdoms identified in Daniel's visions and in the Revelation. Here you received a snapshot of the times of the kings and prophets, and of Israel's homecoming as prophesied long ago. This chapter concluded with a history of the temple and the status of its rebuilding.

Chapter Six: ***Key End-times Players.*** At the end of time during the reign of the Antichrist, two categories of people will exist: God's *elect* (both Jew and non-Jew) who remain faithful and resist allegiance with the Antichrist or his kingdom, and everyone else *not* faithful to God and Christ. Key players in the elect group will be remnants of Israel in the form of those God has brought back home to Israel and 144,000 (specifically chosen) who'll be sealed for protection during God's wrath against a wicked earth. Other key participants will include two special witnesses who'll be killed for their testimony and raised again, and those who'll be martyred through beheading during the reign of the Antichrist.

Chapter Seven: ***The Elect Bride.*** Here you read about the bride of Christ – those who've entered into a "marriage" covenant with Him and are awaiting His return. Much emphasis was placed on detailing the Jewish marriage process and equating it to what Christ has done for us and our relationship with Him. The church is currently in a betrothal period that will end when Christ's angels gather the church for the marriage supper of the Lamb in heaven.

Chapter Eight: ***Satan & the Antichrist.*** This chapter offered a brief synopsis of Satan and introduced hell, the abyss, and the lake of fire, explaining the differences between them. We also discussed in great detail the coming Antichrist. Separate topics included the seven-year agreement (covenant of death), length of time of his authority as allowed by God (three and a half years), the "mark" displaying allegiance, and his defeat after the battle of Armageddon. Middle Eastern regions that will make up the final kingdom of the Antichrist can be found in the table below.

18.1 Antichrist's Kingdom Makeup (Review)

Name in Ezekiel 38	Region/Country
Magog (Antichrist's origin)	Scythians; Southern Russia; North of Iran; Eastern Turkey; probably includes Republics of Kazakhstan, Kyrgyzstan, Uzbekistan, Turkmenistan, Tajikistan, and perhaps northern parts of modern Afghanistan.
Meshech	Near Phrygia (biblical region) in central and western Asia Minor (north of Cyprus in central Turkey)
Tubal	Eastern Asia Minor (around Georgia)
Persia	Iran
Ethiopia	Originally Cush, most likely Sudan instead of Ethiopia
Put	Libya (west of Egypt)
Gomer	Central Turkey (Cappadocia of biblical times)
Beth-togarmah	Southeastern Turkey near the Syrian border

Important things to remember about the makeup of the Antichrist's kingdom:

1. The countries surround Israel.
2. The country due north of Israel is Turkey, which includes most of the countries listed in the above table.
3. All countries in the list are predominantly Islamic in nature.
4. The people of the *prince to come* (they destroyed Jerusalem and the second temple in 70 CE) were led by the Roman Empire but made up of a vast number of Middle Eastern reinforcements.

Key points to remember regarding the *covenant of death*:

1. The covenant will be between the Antichrist's kingdom (currently Islamic nations) and Israel.
2. The covenant will be for seven years. FOOD FOR THOUGHT: Islamic prophecy foretells of a seven-year peace agreement with Israel.
3. The Antichrist will go against the agreement and persecute God's people (to include all believers in Christ) for nearly three and a half years during the second half of the covenant period.
4. Christ will cancel the covenant upon defeat of the Antichrist and the establishment of His kingdom on earth.

Key points to remember regarding the *time of the Antichrist's authority*:

1. An agreement between the Antichrist and Israel will kick off a final seven-year period.
2. Scripture doesn't shed light on what will happen during the first half of the seven-year period.
3. The Antichrist will be given authority to persecute and kill God's people for three and a half years during the second half of the seven-year period. This latter half is known as the time of *Jacob's Trouble* and the *Great Tribulation*. NOTE: Hal Lindsey and other pre-tribulation rapture supporters incorrectly call the entire seven-year period "*seven years of tribulation.*"
4. The beginning of the second half will be earmarked by a dishonoring of the *covenant of death* and the Antichrist's presence in the temple.
5. The Antichrist will speak out against God and persecute His people.
6. God will protect a remnant of Israel (the *woman*) during the three-and-a-half-year reign of the Antichrist.
7. The Antichrist's reign will end with Christ's appearing and defeat of the Antichrist.

Key points to remember about the *mark of the beast*:

1. The Antichrist will require everyone faithful to him to be marked with a number or name. This mark may be physical, but it may also be an understanding and carrying out of the Antichrist's "law" in the same way the Israelites learned God's commandments and acted upon them. Regardless, it will indicate an allegiance to the Antichrist and his kingdom.
2. This allegiance and marking will be necessary to buy or sell during the Antichrist's reign.
3. Those not taking the mark will most likely be beheaded, but they'll be resurrected and will reign with Christ if they are His.
4. The mark will most likely *not look exactly like 666*, which indicates the number of man three times.
5. The mark may not be a microchip since it isn't an identifying mark per-se and would require insertion *into* the skin (the mark will be *on* the right hand or forehead or symbolic as described above).
6. Don't waste your time trying to convert the names of world leaders into numbers for the sake of *counting the number of a name*.
7. Spend your time becoming more knowledgeable of God's Word to ensure you won't be deceived when the Antichrist appears and requires this mark.

Key points to remember about the *time of great tribulation and beheading*:

1. The Antichrist will have a three-and-a-half-year authority over God's people.
2. The three-and-a-half-year period will be a terrible time of tribulation never seen before or again.
3. Those who stay faithful to Christ and refuse the mark of the beast may be killed, many by beheading.
4. God will cut the three-and-a-half-year time of the Antichrist's authority short.

5. The sign of the termination of the Antichrist's authority and Christ's return will be a complete darkening of the sun, moon, and stars.
6. The gathering of the church will follow the darkening.

Key points to remember about the *battle of Armageddon*:

1. The battle of Har-Magedon (Armageddon) will happen after the sixth vial of God's judgment, which will dry up the Euphrates River.
2. Christ and His armies will defeat the Antichrist at that battle. The amount of blood shed will be extraordinary.
3. Satan will be bound and then released after 1,000 years to do battle one last time. God will then throw him into the lake of fire.

Chapter Nine: *Babylon: Past, Present, & Future.* God used Babylon to punish Israel long ago. During her exile and assimilation by that kingdom, she engaged in wicked activity that took the form of child sacrifice, sorcery, and idol worship – all abominations to God. Because of her unfaithfulness to Him, God called Israel a "*harlot*" and detailed her wrath-filled future in many prophecies. This trend and other key apocalyptic points suggest Israel will also be the end-times harlot called *Babylon* – most likely because of the ancient association she had with that kingdom and its wicked practices.

We also discussed the possibility that Jerusalem will be the "*great city*" associated with end-times *Babylon* and offered scriptural and historical evidence as support.

Key points to remember about *Babylon – the harlot*:

1. Israel was (and will be) the unfaithful bride of God and the only nation to be labeled as a *harlot* by Him.
2. The term *Babylon* is used in the Revelation to represent Israel and the adulteries she has, and will, commit.
3. Israel has been responsible for the deaths of the prophets

and others throughout history. Her final act of adultery (the covenant with the Antichrist/beast kingdom) will cause the death of many saints including those who believe in Christ and walk in His ways.

4. God instructed His priests' garments to be made of purple, scarlet, gold, and jewels. This is also the adornment of the *harlot*.
5. God will allow the Antichrist and his kingdom to make Israel *desolate and naked* during the three-and-a-half-year Great Tribulation period.

Key points to remember about *Babylon – the great city*:

1. The ancient city of Babylon (and much of Iraq for that matter) has been crippled or destroyed.
2. Israel, as we've learned, will most likely be the *whore of Babylon*. She lives in the land of Israel with the capital of Jerusalem.
3. Israel is a city built on seven mountains. But remember that Scripture also states that the mountains are seven kingdoms and may therefore not represent physical mountains at all.
4. Babylon in the New Testament figuratively represents tyranny; Zephaniah called Jerusalem the "*tyrannical city*."
5. Jerusalem is referred to as the *great city*, as the figurative *Babylon* of the Revelation was by Jesus. The Antichrist and his kingdom will establish themselves in Jerusalem and reign from there in the end times.
6. End-times Babylon and Jerusalem are both listed in the context of God's wrath.

Chapter Ten: *Deceivers.* This final category of people definitely not in God's camp is represented by tares (deceivers from within the body of Christ), false prophets, and false messiahs. These plague Christian, Jewish, and Islamic faiths alike.

Key points to remember about *tares*:

1. People influenced by Satan infiltrate the church regularly –

knowingly or unknowingly. They can take the form of false teachers, false prophets, or people who cause dissension and confusion from within the body of Christ.
2. Test what you hear or see to ensure it's from God and not a deception. The parable of the tares would also teach us to look for the character fruit of a true child of God as evidenced in the fruit of the Spirit.

Key points to remember about *false prophets*:

1. False prophets have, and will, deceive the church. Be on the lookout for false teaching, inaccurate prophecies, a lack of spiritual fruit, sources of division in the church, etc.
2. *The* False Prophet will arise from what will most likely be a particular region or nation.
3. He'll work miracles and deceive many – even the *chosen* if possible.
4. The False Prophet will demand worship of the Antichrist as God.
5. He and the Antichrist will be destroyed when God throws them into the lake of fire at the battle of Armageddon.

Chapter Eleven: *Introduction to the Apocalypse.* The primary goal of this chapter was to introduce you to the concept that we've been warned of the end of the age and given many details and signs over thousands of years. Old Testament prophets Ezekiel, Daniel, Amos, Isaiah, and others left us prophetic and apocalyptic clues as did Jesus, Peter, and Paul.

The unveiling of future events by these prophets and by Jesus gives us insight into:

- Kingdoms that would come and go before the final kingdom of the Antichrist.
- The Antichrist and his kingdom.
- The sequence and timing of end-times events.

Chapter Twelve: *Daniel's Visions & Interpretations.* Through the interpretation of King Nebuchadnezzar's dreams and from his own visions, Daniel received insight into the sequence of kingdoms from the Babylonian Empire to the Antichrist's kingdom to come.

- **Daniel 2** recorded the interpretation of one of King Nebuchadnezzar's dreams. It revealed a statue made of several different metals, each representing a separate authority from the Babylonian Empire until the end-times kingdom of the Antichrist. Most notably, Daniel foretold of the end-times authority made up of regions that had been associated with the ancient Roman Empire and of its defeat by Christ.
- **Daniel 4** was a reflection by King Nebuchadnezzar himself. In it, he detailed a vision of insanity and restoration – both of which came to fruition because he failed to understand that God grants all authority.
- **Daniel 7** introduced the three-and-a-half-year authority of the Antichrist and foretold of his demise. It also offered a brief description of his rise to power.
- **Daniel 8** contained a prophecy fulfilled by Antiochus Epiphanes, a *type* or *shadow* of the coming Antichrist. He inflicted great persecution against Israel in roughly 169 BCE.
- **Daniel 9** outlined the timeframe of 490 total years for Israel's redemption. This is where we learn of the coming seven-year agreement, which is most likely also the *covenant of death* prophesied by Isaiah (cf. 28:15).
- **Daniel 11** chronicled significant historical events from the time of the Persian Empire to that of Greece (cf. 11:2-20). It also provided in verses 21-35 details regarding the reign and terror of Antiochus Epiphanes (*shadow* of the coming Antichrist) introduced in chapter 8. Finally, 11:36-12:3 contain apocalyptic writing concerning the Antichrist to come.
- **Daniel 12** is a continuation of the sequence that began in chapter 11. Verses 4-13 provide more information regarding the time of the Antichrist's authority and Great Tribulation.

Chapter Thirteen: *Other Old Testament Prophets.* Others before Christ wrote apocalyptic literature about the end of the world and events leading up to it – primarily the Antichrist's kingdom, the Great Tribulation, God's "Day of the Lord" wrath, Christ's kingdom, and a new heaven and earth. All of these passages work together with Christ's teachings and the Revelation to provide a clear view of the end times. Some, but not all, of the writings contained near-far prophecies that foretold of near-term destruction (i.e. at the hands of Babylon) while also interjecting apocalyptic literature that gave glimpses of the end.

Chapter Fourteen: *Mounting Suspense.* The main purpose of this chapter was to compare and contrast what Jesus told His disciples on the Mount of Olives in answer to the questions they asked about the destruction of Jerusalem, His return, and the end of the world. All three accounts from the Gospels of Matthew, Mark, and Luke were listed side-by-side and analyzed. Several key points to remember from this chapter:

1. The discourse on the Mount of Olives contains information pertaining to the destruction of Jerusalem, which occurred in 70 CE, *and* related to Christ's future return.
2. Information revealed on the Mount of Olives was repeated in the Revelation (e.g. in the broken seals of Revelation 6).
3. The generation that sees the signs Jesus described will also see His return.

Additionally, this chapter included an introduction to the Revelation that contained a general outline of the book and offered insight into different approaches to interpreting it. Although some take more of a spiritual or symbolic approach to understanding it (as with a-millennialists and post-millennialists), my recommendation is to take each passage literally unless there's a very good reason to do otherwise.

Chapter Fifteen: *Peter & Paul Weigh In.* Peter and Paul (especially Paul) had much to say about Christ's appearing and our gathering. Some of the more significant passages are referenced here.

Chapter Sixteen: *The Unveiling.* Here you underwent an exhaustive overview of the Revelation given to John by Christ, which is sequenced as follows:

- **Chapters 1-5**: Introduction by John, letters from Christ to the churches of Asia Minor, and an invitation to heaven to watch the end-times events.
- **Chapter 6**: Seals 1-6 depicting birth pangs and Great Tribulation.
- **Chapter 7**: Protection of the 144,000 Jews; bride of Christ seen in heaven.
- **Chapters 8-9**: Seal 7; trumpet judgments 1-6.
- **Chapter 10**: Seventh trumpet judgment.
- **Chapters 11-13**: Three-and-one-half-year period of Great Tribulation detailed from several perspectives.
- **Chapter 14**: A glimpse of *Babylon's* destruction, preaching of the gospel before God's wrath, gathering of believers, and God's wrath – all things that will happen near the end of the three-and-a-half-year Great Tribulation or shortly thereafter by the end of the trumpet judgments.
- **Chapters 15-16**: Seven vial judgments that will complete God's wrath.
- **Chapters 17-18**: Description (and destruction) of *Babylon* near the end of God's wrath; details about the Antichrist kingdom.
- **Chapter 19**: Armageddon at the end of God's wrath; marriage supper of Christ.
- **Chapter 20**: Thousand-year reign of Christ; great judgment following Christ's kingdom.
- **Chapter 21**: New heaven and earth after the judgment.
- **Chapter 22**: Final admonishments and closure.

Key points to remember about *the Revelation*:

1. The book is divided into distinct sections and most of it is

sequential from beginning to end. Christ's Revelation takes us sequentially from about 90 CE through the gathering and wrath to the great judgment. Please see the breakdown below for more information.

2. While the Revelation does make use of some symbols, they're **easy to understand** and already explained for us with just a few exceptions (e.g. the *whore of Babylon*).
3. The visions contained within the book are **for the church** – saints and servants of the Lord Jesus Christ. Everything within it pertains to the bride of Christ – then, now, and in the future until the very end. A popular rapture belief perpetuated by media such as the "Left Behind" series is that the apocalyptic writing is instead meant for a "tribulation force" made up of believers who'll be left behind after the gathering of the church. This is unscriptural and part of a deceptive and potentially dangerous doctrine.
4. The book of Revelation is ***not* symbolic** as a whole, and while it contains some symbols, it should be taken as literally as possible! Many people have emphatically claimed that the opposite is true – that the *entire* Revelation is symbolic. Why? To support a particular end-times view that contrasts the message given in a literal Revelation.

Chapter Seventeen: *Exploring End-times Positions.* In this chapter, we compared and contrasted the most popular end-times views with regard to a millennial reign of Christ and His return to earth as follows:

Attitudes toward the millennial reign of Christ:

- **A-millennial**: This view disregards a literal 1,000-year reign of Christ as specified in Revelation 20. The timeframe outlined in that chapter is considered to be a "very long time" representing the current church age.
- **Post-millennial**: As with a-millennialism, expositors of this position disregard a literal 1,000-year kingdom but teach an earthly symbolic kingdom versus an ongoing

heavenly reign.

- **Pre-millennial**: Supporters tend to take the Revelation literally, believing that Christ will return and gather the church *prior* to a 1,000-year kingdom on earth.

The timing of Christ's second coming as related to the millennial reign of Christ:

- **A-millennial**: This position is generally associated with a belief that Christ will return for the church at some undetermined point in the future.
- **Post-millennial**: Supporters tend to believe that Christ's second coming and the great judgment will occur at the *end* of a symbolic earthly reign by the church and that this won't happen until nearly the entire world has been converted to Christianity.
- **Pre-millennial**: This view, which takes a more literal and sequential approach to the Revelation, teaches that Christ will return for the church before a literal 1,000-year reign of Christ on earth. Different positions regarding the exact timing of Christ's appearing and the gathering of the church exist within this view.
  - **Pre-tribulation Rapture**: Christ's return will happen *before* Daniel's seven-year period.
  - **Mid-tribulation Rapture**: Christ's return will happen exactly in the *middle* of Daniel's seven-year period.
  - **Pre-wrath Rapture**: Christ's return and the gathering of the church will occur at some point *during* the last half of the Antichrist's reign just before God's wrath begins.
  - **Post-tribulation Rapture**: Christ will gather the church at the *end* of Daniel's seven-year period. This view doesn't consider the trumpet judgments to be part of God's wrath.

In conclusion, I'd like to thank you for taking the time to study this very difficult subject and for keeping an open mind and heart while doing so. I pray you've found it to be valuable and thought-provoking and that your faith is now stronger as a result. Please continue to build your faith through regular study of Scripture and share that faith with others. This is how you'll be able to respond to Christ's Great Commission.

> *Go therefore and make disciples of all the nations, baptizing them in the name of the Father and the Son and the Holy Spirit, teaching them to observe all that I commanded you; and lo, I am with you always, even to the end of the age.*
> —Matthew 28:19-20.

APPENDIX A

STUDY PLAN

The purpose of this section is to help you develop a plan or routine that will allow you, either in a group or through individual study, to methodically and effectively study this subject. The following table shows at a glance the estimated personal and group time needed to go through this study.

Section Session/ Week	Personal Time	Group Session/ Week
PART ONE:		
Chapter One	45 minutes	2
Chapter Two	45 minutes	2
PART TWO:		
Chapter Three	30 minutes	3
Chapter Four	60 minutes	3
PART THREE:		
Chapter Five	60 minutes	4
Chapter Six	60 minutes	5
Chapter Seven	90 minutes	5
Chapter Eight	60 minutes	6
Chapter Nine	60 minutes	6
Chapter Ten	90 minutes	7
PART FOUR:		
Chapter Eleven	30 minutes	8
Chapter Twelve (Part I)	45 minutes	8
Chapter Twelve (Part II)	60 minutes	9
Chapter Twelve (Part III)	90 minutes	9
Chapter Thirteen	60 minutes	10
Chapter Fourteen (Part I)	60 minutes	11

Chapter Fourteen (Part II)	60 minutes	11
Chapter Fifteen	45 minutes	12
Chapter Sixteen (Part I)	45 minutes	13
Chapter Sixteen (Part II)	45 minutes	13
Chapter Sixteen (Part III)	60 minutes	13
Chapter Sixteen (Part IV)	60 minutes	14
Chapter Sixteen (Part V)	60 minutes	14
Chapter Sixteen (Part VI)	60 minutes	15
Chapter Sixteen (Part VII)	60 minutes	15
PART FIVE:		
Chapter Seventeen	60 minutes	16
Chapter Eighteen	60 minutes	17
TOTAL TIME:	**26 hours**	

Individual Study: Plan to spend roughly 30 hours reading the chapters, doing Scripture reading, and answering questions. All can be done at your leisure; however, I recommend going through the study sequentially. This will ensure you learn fundamental building blocks you'll need later. Appendix A.1 contains a sample template you may wish to use in planning your study sessions. Some key points and tips to keep in mind as you go through this study:

- Stay focused to ensure the course duration doesn't extend longer than desired.
- Back up your beliefs and opinions with Scripture.
- Write down your questions and research answers throughout the week. Become comfortable with admitting you need additional study or research if you don't know or understand a topic. Even after lengthy study, you'll discover that while there are some things we can know with certainty, Scripture doesn't always answer all our questions and often leaves us with more questions than when we started. Feel free to email me for clarification of

any issue or with recommendations for improvement.[71]

Group Study: The beauty of a group study is the interaction and discussion that's sure to develop each week, as this topic is almost never taught or discussed in church. Curiosity needs to be satisfied and people need the opportunity to explain what they believe and why. This will lead to a better understanding of the subject and result in a much more interesting time. Some key points and tips anyone wishing to lead a group study (e.g. 18-week Sunday school session) should keep in mind:

- Consider using the template in Appendix A.2 when preparing a course schedule.
- Encourage discussion but maintain order and focus to ensure the course duration doesn't extend longer than desired.
- Encourage attendees to back up their beliefs and opinions with Scripture.
- Encourage questions. Write them down and research answers throughout the week so you can address questions during the following session. Become comfortable with saying, "Based on our/my study so far, I don't know" if asked a question you can't answer. Even after lengthy study, you'll discover that while there are some things we can know with certainty, Scripture doesn't always answer all our questions and often leaves us with more questions than when we started. Feel free to email me for clarification of any issue or with recommendations for improvement.[72]
- When going through Checkup questions, cover the *Private Challenge / Discussion* questions but don't seek answers unless the group is comfortable with your doing so. These are meant to encourage thought-provoking and personal reflections, and any attempt to prompt or force answers from the individuals could prove to be embarrassing or uncomfortable.

APPENDIX A.1

STUDY PLAN TEMPLATE – INDIVIDUAL

Hour or Session	Date(s)	Chapter/ Topic	Activities
1		Chapter 1	Read chapter 1 and the SUPPLEMENTAL READING.
2		Chapter 2	Read chapter 2, the Quick References, and SUPPLEMENTAL READING. Answer Checkup questions for chapters 1 and 2.
3		Chapter 3	Read chapter 3 and the SUPPLEMENTAL READING.
4		Chapter 4	Read chapter 4 and the Quick References. Answer Checkup questions for chapters 3 and 4.
5		Chapter 5	Read chapter 5.
6		Chapter 6	Read chapter 6.
7		Chapter 7	Begin reading chapter 7 and the Quick References.
8		Chapter 7	Finish reading chapter 7 and the Quick References. Answer Checkup questions for chapters 6 and 7.
9		Chapter 8	Read chapter 8 and the Quick References.
10		Chapter 9	Read chapter 9 and the Quick References.
11		Chapter 10	Read chapter 10 and the Quick References.
12		Chapter 10	Answer Checkup questions for chapters 8, 9, and 10.
13		Chapter 11	Read chapter 11.

Hour or Session	Date(s)	Chapter/ Topic	Activities
14		Chapter 12	Read chapter 12 Parts I and II. Start with the RECOMMENDED READING.
15		Chapter 12	Read chapter 12 Part III. Start with the RECOMMENDED READING.
16		Chapter 12	Answer Checkup questions for chapter 12.
17		Chapter 13	Read chapter 13.
18		Chapter 14	Read chapter 14 Part I. Start with the RECOMMENDED READING.
19		Chapter 14	Read chapter 14 Part II and the SUPPLEMENTAL READING. Answer Checkup questions for chapter 14.
20		Chapter 15	Read chapter 15.
21		Chapter 16	Read chapter 16 Part I. Start with the RECOMMENDED READING.
22		Chapter 16	Read chapter 16 Part II. Start with the RECOMMENDED READING.
23		Chapter 16	Read chapter 16 Part III. Start with the RECOMMENDED READING.
24		Chapter 16	Read chapter 16 Part IV. Start with the RECOMMENDED READING.
25		Chapter 16	Read chapter 16 Part V. Start with the RECOMMENDED READING.
26		Chapter 16	Read chapter 16 Part VI. Start with the RECOMMENDED READING.
27		Chapter 16	Read chapter 16 Part VII. Start with the RECOMMENDED READING. Answer Checkup questions.
28		Chapter 17	Begin reading chapter 17.
29		Chapter 17	Finish reading chapter 17.
30		Chapter 18	Read chapter 18.

APPENDIX A.2

Study Plan Template - Group

Week or Session	Date(s)	Chapter/Topic	Activities
1		Introduction	Read the Foreword and Introduction. Discuss group expectations and review course schedule.
2		Chapters 1 & 2	Read chapters 1 and 2, the Quick References, and SUPPLEMENTAL READING. Answer Checkup questions for chapters 1 and 2. ***Group***: Discuss answers to Checkup questions.
3		Chapters 3 & 4	Read chapter 3 and the SUPPLEMENTAL READING. Read chapter 4 and the Quick References. Answer Checkup questions for chapters 3 and 4. ***Group***: Discuss perceptions of faith, and consequences of not knowing the gospel. Discuss answers to Checkup questions.
4		Chapter 5	Read chapter 5. ***Group***: Discuss the different historical/biblical eras.
5		Chapters 6 & 7	Read chapters 6 and 7 and the Quick References for chapter 7. Answer Checkup questions for chapters 6 and 7. ***Group***: Discuss "God's chosen." Despite Scripture references, there will most likely be differences of opinion. Discuss answers to Checkup questions.

Week or Session	Date(s)	Chapter/Topic	Activities
6		Chapters 8 & 9	Read chapters 8 and 9 and the Quick References. ***Group***: Compare and contrast beliefs and possibilities related to the Antichrist and Babylon (harlot and location).
7		Chapter 10	Read chapter 10 and the Quick References. Answer Checkup questions for chapters 8, 9, and 10. ***Group***: Explore other examples of "deceivers" in the world (generally) and within the church (specifically). Discuss answers to the Checkup questions.
8		Chapters 11 & 12	Read chapter 11, and chapter 12 Part I. Start with the RECOMMENDED READING. ***Group***: Discuss what you've learned from Daniel's writings so far to include the focus on humility, authority, and Nebuchadnezzar's status.
9		Chapter 12	Read chapter 12 Parts II and III. Start with the RECOMMENDED READING. Answer Checkup questions for chapter 12. ***Group***: Discuss the timing from Daniel 9 and the sequence of events from chapter 11 through chapter 12. Discuss answers to Checkup questions.
10		Chapter 13	Read chapter 13. ***Group***: Discuss the common themes and select several chapters and verses related to those the group may be interested in to read and discuss further.

Week or Session	Date(s)	Chapter/Topic	Activities
11		Chapter 14	Read chapter 14 to include RECOMMENDED READING and SUPPLEMENTAL READING assignments. Answer Checkup questions for chapter 14. ***Group***: Compare and contrast the accounts given by Matthew, Mark, and Luke. Discuss the relevance of the Revelation to the church. Discuss answers to Checkup questions.
12		Chapter 15	Read chapter 15. ***Group***: Discuss the different points made by Peter and Paul regarding the end times. Discuss why it would've been possible to believe the end had come.
13		Chapter 16	Read chapter 16 Parts I, II, and III. Start with the RECOMMENDED READING. ***Group***: Discuss the letters to the churches, the seven seals, and the seven trumpet judgments.
14		Chapter 16	Read chapter 16 Parts IV and V. Start with the RECOMMENDED READING. ***Group***: Discuss what chapters 11-13 have to say about the 1,260-day (3.5-year) period of the Antichrist's authority.
15		Chapter 16	Read chapter 16 Parts VI and VII. Start with the RECOMMENDED READING. Answer Checkup questions. ***Group***: Discuss Babylon, the battle of Armageddon, and the new heaven and earth.

Week or Session	Date(s)	Chapter/Topic	Activities
16		Chapter 17	Read chapter 17. ***Group***: Explore different end-times positions. Discuss personal views and supporting Scripture (only if comfortable doing so).
17		Chapter 18	Course review and closure.

NOTE: You should complete all readings by the day before the date listed to the right of the "Week or Session" block.

APPENDIX B

END OF THE AGE DEFINITIONS & REFERENCES

Key Words/ Phrases	Definition	References
Age (World) – End of	Can represent the physical earth (see Strong's G1093 below) as in Revelation 21:1 *(. . . And I saw a new heaven and a new earth . . .)* but also represents an era. Most verses to the right use the Greek word aiōn (Strong's G165 below) to depict the current "age." We're in the "last days" but the end of the current era/world/age won't occur until after the following events have passed: Antichrist, 3.5-year great tribulation, God's wrath, Christ's 1,000-year kingdom, and the great judgment. G165: aiōn (ahee-ohn') properly an age; by extension perpetuity (also past); by implication the world; specifically (Jewish) a messianic period (present or future): - age, course, eternal, (for) ever (-more), [n-]ever, (beginning of the, while the) world (began, without end). G1093: gē (ghay) Contracted from a primary word; soil; by extension a region, or the solid part or the whole of the terrene globe (including the occupants in each application): - country, earth (-ly), ground, land, world.	Ps 19:4 Isa 62:11-12 Matt 12:32 Matt 13:39-40 & 49 Matt 24:3 Matt 28:20 Gal 1:4 Eph 1:21 Eph 2:7 Col 1:26 Titus 2:12 Heb 6:4-5 Heb 9:26

Key Words/ Phrases	Definition	References
Antichrist, The	The wicked principality that will enter into a *covenant of death* with God's people roughly seven years before Christ's second coming/appearing. Midway through the timeframe, he'll dishonor the agreement, set up shop in the third temple, and begin a 3.5-year reign of terror. The coming Antichrist will be empowered by Satan (e.g. see Ezekiel 28) and is called the *mystery of iniquity* by Paul and *abomination of desolation* by Christ. Also see *Beast*. Some characteristics of the *Antichrist*: • 2 Thess 2:3 Gathering won't occur until the Son of Destruction • 2 Thess 2:4 Exalts himself above God and sits in the temple • 2 Thess 2:7 Mystery of lawlessness • 2 Thess 2:8 Lawless One, destroyed at Christ's coming • 2 Thess 2:9 Empowered by Satan • Matt 24:15 & Mark 13:14 Abomination of Desolation (standing in the temple) See Chapter 8 of this guide for additional information.	Isa 14:12-17 Isa 16:4, 6, & 14 Isa 25:10 Ezek 28 Dan 7 Dan 9:26-27 Dan 11:36-45 Hab 3:1-19 Matt 24:15 Mark 13:14 2 Thess 2:3-9 1 John 2:18 1 John 4:3

Key Words/ Phrases	Definition	References
Babylon Harlot	A figurative term used to identify a spiritual "*harlot*" and place of tyrannical authority during the 3.5-year reign of the Antichrist. The *harlot* is most likely Israel based on Old Testament references, and the location of the figurative entity will most likely be Jerusalem: • Jerusalem – that "*great city*" as Sodom and Egypt were in Rev 11:8. • The context of Rev 16:19 suggests Jerusalem and Babylon are synonymous. • Isaiah referred to Jerusalem as a *harlot* (Isa 1:21). Other key points related to the term *Babylon/ Harlot*: • Responsible for persecution/death of the saints (Rev 17:6 & 18:24). • Arrogant: "*I sit a queen, and am no widow, and shall see no sorrow . . .*" • Destroyed by the Antichrist and his kingdom (Rev 17:16). A popular belief that the Babylon Harlot is the Catholic Church and that the Antichrist will be a pope has existed at least since the time of Martin Luther in the 16th century. This is unlikely considering today's lack of authority, military might, and location of the Catholic Church headquartered in Rome. It's also unlikely since Scripture doesn't support this theory. See Chapter 9 of this guide for additional information.	Isa 1:21 Isa 47:1-15 Jer 4:30 Jer 51:49 Ezek 16 Zech 2:4-7 Rev 16:18-19 Rev 17:1-18 Rev 18

Key Words/ Phrases	Definition	References
Beast	The beasts of Revelation 4-6 are living creatures (G2226 below) found at the throne of God, but the term often symbolizes kingdoms or authorities. The only *beast* word used to represent the Antichrist or his kingdom in the New Testament is G2342 (therion) – something dangerous/venomous. This sets the Antichrist or his realm of authority apart from other kingdoms represented by the term *beast* elsewhere in Scripture. A related beast reference is a label used to identify the False Prophet of the Antichrist (Rev 11:13-17). The *beast* kingdom headed by the Antichrist will be composed of eight leaders/authorities (seven plus the Antichrist). G2226: zōon (dzo'-on) A live thing, that is, an animal: - beast. G2342: thērion (thay-ree'-on) A dangerous animal: - (venomous, wild) beast. See *Antichrist* (above) and Chapter 8 of this guide.	Rev 6:8 Rev 11:7-8 Rev 13:1-4 Rev 13:16-18 Rev 14:9 & 11 Rev 15:2 Rev 16:2 Rev 16:13 Rev 17:3 Rev 17:7-8 Rev 17:11-13 Rev 19:20 Rev 20:4 & 10
Bride of Christ	Everyone who's given themselves to Christ since the time of His ministry around 27 CE. This group has entered into a covenant with Him and is referred to as the bride who'll attend the *marriage supper of the Lamb.* This *marriage* will happen in heaven after the bride is raptured (gathered) from the earth just before God's wrath begins against the rest of the world. References to the right are related to both bride and groom. See Chapter 6 of this guide for additional information.	Matt 9:14-15 John 3:28-30 Rev 19:7-9 Rev 21:1-2 & 9 Rev 22:17
Christ's Appearing (*Epiphaneia*)	*Epiphaneia* (G2015) These passages refer to Christ's appearance when He *comes*. The things His return to earth will include: • Defeat of the Antichrist • His kingdom • Judgment of the living and dead • Rewards for the righteous	2 Thess 2:8 1 Tim 6:14 2 Tim 4:1 & 8 Titus 2:13

Key Words/ Phrases	Definition	References
Christ's Coming (*Parousia*)	*Parousia* (G3952) All of these passages refer to Christ's coming at the end and the subsequent gathering of the church. His first visit brought His birth, life, death, resurrection, and ascension to heaven – a fulfilling of the *spring* feasts of the Lord. The purpose of His second coming will be to gather those faithful to Him, destroy the unfaithful, and establish a 1,000-year reign in Jerusalem – a likely fulfilling of the *fall* feasts. The Greek word used to represent Christ's second coming is *parousia* (Strong's G3952 below). In context and when comparing Scripture, we find that it's a presence (not a quick "here and gone") and that several events will happen during His coming/ appearing – *parousia*: gathering of the saints by His angels, accompanying the 144,000, and the 1,000-year reign. The following are several examples of the use of this particular word: • Mat 24:3 As He was sitting on the Mount of Olives, the disciples came to Him privately, saying, "Tell us, when will these things happen, and what will be the sign of Your coming, and of the end of the age?" • 1 Cor 15:23 But each in his own order: Christ the first fruits, after that those who are Christ's at His *coming*. • 2 Thess 2:1 Now we request you, brethren, with regard to the *coming* of our Lord Jesus Christ and our gathering together to Him, • 1 Jn 2:28 Now, little children, abide in Him, so that when He appears, we may have confidence and not shrink away from Him in shame at His *coming*. Common to a pre-tribulation rapture position is the belief that Christ's appearing at the gathering won't be His actual second coming, and that the second coming will happen later when Christ defeats the armies at Armageddon. They separate *appearing* and *coming* into two separate events. Unfortunately, this introduces an unscheduled visit before the second coming (appearing) which the Bible relates directly to the gathering.	Matt 24:3, 27, 37, & 39 1 Cor 15:23 1 Thess 2:19 1 Thess 3:13 1 Thess 4:15 1 Thess 5:23 2 Thess 2:1 & 8 James 5:7-8 2 Pet 3:4 1 John 2:28

Key Words/ Phrases	Definition	References
Christ's Coming (*Parousia*) *continued*	This position isn't scriptural and creates a serious theological problem that requires much allegorizing and symbolizing to rationalize. The Bible records only one second appearing/coming. Heb 9:28 so Christ also, having been offered once to bear the sins of many, **will appear a second time for salvation without reference to sin, to those who eagerly await Him**. G3952: *parousia* (par-oo-see'-ah) a being near, that is, advent (often, return; specifically of Christ to punish Jerusalem, or finally the wicked); (by implication) physical aspect: - coming, presence. Related to Christ's coming are things that will be revealed when He comes. The Greek word for revelation in this case is *apokalupsis* (G602). Passages using the word (as it relates to Christ's return) are affiliated with the gathering of the church that will happen at His coming. They promise relief at the revelation of Christ (2 Thessalonians 1:7) and reflect longing and eagerness in waiting for what will be praise, glory, honor, and grace when we see Him. Related Scripture: • Romans 8:19 • 1 Corinthians 1:7 • 2 Thessalonians 1:7 • 1 Peter 1:7 • 1 Peter 1:13 • 1 Peter 4:13	Matt 24:3, 27, 37, & 39 1 Cor 15:23 1 Thess 2:19 1 Thess 3:13 1 Thess 4:15 1 Thess 5:23 2 Thess 2:1 & 8 James 5:7-8 2 Pet 3:4 1 John 2:28

Key Words/ Phrases	Definition	References
Christ's Kingdom	See *1,000 Year Reign of Christ.* References on the right may also include the kingdom/reign of God that will be eternal and will occur after Christ's 1,000-year kingdom and the great judgment. See Chapter 16 of this guide for additional information.	Isa 11:1-16 Isa 24:23 Isa 25:8-12 Isa 27:13 Isa 28:5-18 Isa 62:1-12 Obad 1:17-21 Zech 9:9-17 2 Tim 4:1-4
Covenant of Death	The agreement the Antichrist will enter into with God's people (Daniel 9:27 & Isaiah 28:15) roughly seven years before Christ returns to earth. He'll go against the covenant after 3.5 years and begin a reign of terror against God's chosen – Jew and Christian alike. The agreement will be cancelled by the destruction of the Antichrist and binding of Satan by God (Isaiah 28:16-18). See Chapter 8 of this guide for additional information.	Isa 28:15-18 Dan 9:27

Key Words/ Phrases	Definition	References
Daniel's 70th Week (of Years)	The 70th week of years – or final seven years – in a 490-year period prophesied by Daniel. The Hebrew word for "week of years" is depicted below by Strong's H7620. This seven-year period will conclude the 70 weeks of years as shown to Daniel to do the following: • Finish the transgression of the people of Israel. • Make an end of sin. • Make atonement for iniquity. • Bring in everlasting righteousness. • Seal up vision and prophecy. • Anoint the Most Holy. All of these goals will be accomplished when Christ gains His kingdom at the seventh trumpet (Revelation 11:15). 69 weeks of years (483 years) would pass from the command to rebuild Jerusalem and its walls until Christ's crucifixion (Dan 9:25-26). Daniel then prophesied about Jerusalem's destruction by Roman forces (Dan 9:26). The last (70th) "week of years" (years 484-490) will start with a covenant between the Antichrist (spiritual principality that drove the Roman Empire) and "many" to include Israel (Dan 9:27). H7620 shâbûaʻ shâbûaʻ shebûʻâh (shaw-boo'-ah, shaw-boo'-ah, sheb-oo-aw') Literally sevened, that is, a week (**specifically of years**): - seven, week. See Chapter 12 of this guide for additional information.	Dan 9:24-27

Key Words/ Phrases	Definition	References
Darkening of the Sun, Moon, & Stars	Extremely important sign that will precede Christ's return and the gathering of Christians and God's wrath. This critical landmark helps us understand that the gathering and wrath of God that follows will occur in close proximity. Scriptural examples: • **Joel 2:10 & 31**: Before the Day of the Lord destruction (God's wrath) • **Matt 24:29**: Before Christ appears and His angels harvest Christians • **Rev 6:12-13**: Before the rest of the earth realizes God's wrath is about to begin. Not to be confused with a partial darkening that will occur *during* the time of God's wrath (Rev 8:12). Also see *Seal 6*.	Isa 13:10 Joel 2:10 & 31 Joel 3:15 Ezek 32:7 Amos 5:18 Zeph 1:15 Matt 24:29 Luke 21:25 Acts 2:20 2 Pet 3:10 Rev 6:12-13
Day of Christ / Jesus / the Lord Jesus / Redemption	Christ's appearing and the gathering of Christians by the Lord's angels. Redemption. Unlike the Day of the Lord that includes God's wrath, this day is a manifestation of the blessed hope of Christian believers – the *rapture*. Scripture shows that the Day of Christ, Day of Jesus, Day of the Lord Jesus, and Day of Redemption all refer to the same event: Christ's appearing and our gathering.	1 Cor 1:7-8 1 Cor 5:4-5 2 Cor 1:14 Eph 4:30 Phil 1:6 & 10-11 Phil 2:15-16 2 Thess 2:1-2
Day of the LORD / Day of God	Great destruction of the earth and its inhabitants by God after the gathering of Christian believers. The great wrath of God will be preceded by a complete darkening of the sun, moon, and stars. This time will also include the battle of Armageddon (Rev 16:14). See *God's Wrath* for additional information and greater detail.	Isa 2:10-19 Isa 13:6 -13 Isa 24 Jer 30:7-8 Joel 1:15 Joel 2:1-32 Amos 5:16-18 Amos 9:11-15 Obad 1:15-21 Zeph 1:14-15 Zech 14 Mal 4 Acts 2:17-21 Rom 2:16 1 Thess 5:1-9 2 Pet 3:10-18 Rev 16:14

Key Words/ Phrases	Definition	References
Day Equals 1,000 Years	An assumption by some that one of God's days equals 1,000 of our years. A byproduct of this assumption is a theory that the 6,000 years *since* creation were represented by the six days *of* creation, and that the seventh day represents the coming 1,000-year reign of Christ. Proponents of this theory believe Christ will return very soon since about 6,000 years have passed from the creation of our world. While there may be something to this, scriptural comparison between day and 1,000 years in context is meant to show that God's timing is His timing and that He'll do what He wants *when* He's ready.	Ps 90:4 2 Pet 3:8-9
Dragon (Satan)	Satan, who'll empower the Antichrist. The reference of Isaiah 14:12-17 describes him directly; the others to the right include the word *dragon*. See Chapter 8 of this guide for additional information.	Isa 14:12-17 Rev 12 Rev 13:2, 4 & 11 Rev 16:13 Rev 20:2

Key Words/ Phrases	Definition	References
Elect/ Chosen	God's chosen – Jew and Christian alike. The Old Testament word used to describe the Jews as God's chosen (e.g. in Isaiah 45:4 and 65:9) is Strong's H972 (see below). The New Testament uses the Greek word *eklektos* (Strong's G1588) to refer to those in Christ as God's chosen. For instance, it's used to label those who'll be gathered (raptured) in Matthew 24. The same word is used for *elect* and *chosen*, and both depict followers of Christ. Examples include: **Elect**: Matt 24:31 And He will send forth His angels with A GREAT TRUMPET and THEY WILL GATHER TOGETHER His *elect* from the four winds, from one end of the sky to the other. Rom 8:33 Who will bring a charge against God's elect? **Chosen**: Matt 22:14 For many are called, but few are *chosen*. Rev 17:14 These will wage war against the Lamb, and the Lamb will overcome them, because He is Lord of lords and King of kings, and those who are with Him are the called and *chosen* and faithful. G1588: *eklektos* (ek-lek-tos') Select; by implication favorite: - chosen, elect. H972: bâchıyr (baw-kheer') Select: - choose, chosen one, elect. See *Elect: Woman, Wheat, & Offspring* in Chapter 7 for more information.	Isa 45:4 Isa 65:9 Isa 65:22-25 Matt 22:14 Matt 24:22 Matt 24:24 & 31 Mark 13:20 Mark 13:22 & 27 Luke 18:7-8 Luke 23:35 Rom 8:33-35 Rom 16:13 Col 3:11-13 1 Tim 5:21 2 Tim 2:10 Titus 1:1 1 Pet 1:2 1 Pet 2:3-4 & 9 2 John 1:13 Rev 17:14

Key Words/ Phrases	Definition	References
Fall Feasts of the Lord	The last three of the seven feasts of the Lord, all of which are shadows of things to come. Christ fulfilled the first four with His sacrifice on the cross and resurrection during His first coming. He'll fulfill the final three feasts, which are held in the fall, during His second coming. One belief is that Christians will be gathered at the Feast of Trumpets, God's wrath will begin on the Day of Atonement, and Christ will reign for 1,000 years as a type of Feast of Tabernacles – Sukkot. Each fall feast is listed below along with approximate annual dates: 1. THE FEAST OF TRUMPETS (Rosh Hashanah); Tishri 1; starts "Ten Days of Awe" 2. THE DAY OF ATONEMENT; (Yom Kippur) Tishri 10 3. THE FEAST OF TABERNACLES (Sukkot) Tishri 15	Lev 23:24 (Trumpets) Lev 23:28 (Atonement) Lev 23:41-44 (Sukkot)
False Messiah(s)	Many have, and will, come claiming to be the Messiah (the Christ). Jesus seemed to make a distinction between **two groups of imposters**: • Those who'll come *before the end* – part of the birth pangs as represented by the first of broken seals 1-3 (Matt 24:5-6 & Rev 6:2). • One or more that will come *at the time of the Great Tribulation* and deceive the elect through great signs and wonders (Matt 24:21-27). See Chapter Ten of this guide for a more in-depth discussion of this topic.	Matt 24:5-6 & 21-27 Rev 6:2

Key Words/ Phrases	Definition	References
False Prophet	A being that will exercise the power of the Antichrist and do many things on his behalf: • Cause the world's inhabitants to worship the Antichrist (Rev 13:12 & 15). • Do great wonders such as bringing fire down from heaven (Rev 13:13). • Deceive the world's inhabitants (Rev 13:14-15). • Put to death those who refuse to worship the Antichrist or his image (Rev 13:15) • Cause all who will accept it to receive a mark on the right hand or forehead in order to buy or sell in those days (Rev 13:16). In Revelation 13:11-12, we learn that this false prophet of the Antichrist will be something wicked in sheep's clothing and therefore able to deceive mightily. But he'll be destroyed at the end of God's wrath in the same way as the Antichrist – both will be thrown into the lake of fire.	Matt 24:24 Rev 13:11-17 Rev 16:13 Rev 19:20 Rev 20:10

<table>
<tr><th>Key Words/ Phrases</th><th>Definition</th><th>References</th></tr>
<tr><td>God's Wrath</td><td>The Day of the Lord/Day of God destruction against those who remain on earth after the gathering of the dead and alive in Christ. God's wrath is represented in the Revelation by seven trumpet and seven vial judgments as follows:

• Trumpet judgments:
1. Hail and fire; 1/3 trees and all green grass burned up. (Rev 8:7)
2. Great mountain of fire into the sea; 1/3 sea became blood, 1/3 sea creatures and ships destroyed. (Rev 8:8)
3. Star called wormwood fell on 1/3 rivers; men died from the bitter water. (Rev 8:10-11)
4. One-third sun, moon, and stars darkened. (Rev 8:12)
5. Locusts like scorpions released from the pit, with teeth like lions, hair like women, faces of men, and armored. Given power to hurt men (not one of the 144,000 sealed by God) for five months; men seek death but will not find it. (Rev 9:1-12)
6. 200 million "horsemen" kill 1/3 men on earth. Those alive still don't repent! (Rev 9:13-21)
7. Christ gains His kingdom (Rev 11:15)
a. Mystery of God finished (Rev 10:7)
b. Christ's kingdom, ending the 3.5 years since Antichrist entered the temple, and finishing the 70th week of Daniel (Rev 11:2-3; Dan 9:27; Dan 12:7)</td><td>Isa 2:10-22
Isa 24:1-23
Ezek 5:10-17
Ezek 38 & 39
Joel 2:1-32
Joel 3:1-16
Mic 5:10-15
Zeph 1:7-18
Zeph 2
Zeph 3:8-10
1 Thess 5:1-9
2 Thess 1:7-10
Rev 6:12-17
Rev 8-10 (Trumpets)
Rev 11:18
Rev 14:7
Rev 14:9-11
Rev 14:18-20 (Harvest)
Rev 15:1-8
Rev 16:1-21
Rev 19:15</td></tr>
</table>

Key Words/ Phrases	Definition	References
God's Wrath *continued*	• Bowl/vial judgments: 1. Sores on those with the mark of the beast or who worship the beast. (Rev 16:2) 2. Everything remaining in the seas killed. (Rev 16:3) 3. Rivers turned to blood. (Rev 16:4-7) 4. Men scorched by the sun, but none repent. (Rev 16:8-9) 5. Kingdom of antichrist full of darkness and pain, but none repent. (Rev 16:10-11) 6. Euphrates River dried up and men gathered for the battle of Armageddon. (Rev 16:12-16) 7. Terrible earthquake dividing Jerusalem into three parts; great hailstones from heaven. (Rev 16:17-21) The great judgment is also referred to as a time of God's wrath as shown in: • Matt 3:7 • Luke 3:7 • John 3:36 • Rom 1:18 • Rom 2:5-6 • Rom 5:8-9 • Rom 12:19 • Eph 5:6 • Col 3:4-6 • 1 Thess 1:10 Also see *Day of the LORD / Day of God* and Chapter Sixteen of this guide.	Isa 2:10-22 Isa 24:1-23 Ezek 5:10-17 Ezek 38 & 39 Joel 2:1-32 Joel 3:1-16 Mic 5:10-15 Zeph 1:7-18 Zeph 2 Zeph 3:8-10 1 Thess 5:1-9 2 Thess 1:7-10 Rev 6:12-17 Rev 8-10 (Trumpets) Rev 11:18 Rev 14:7 Rev 14:9-11 Rev 14:18-20 (Harvest) Rev 15:1-8 Rev 16:1-21 Rev 19:15

Key Words/ Phrases	Definition	References
Gospel Preached (to all Nations)	One of several actions that will take place within the sequence leading up to the very end. This preaching of the gospel was foretold by Christ in Matthew 24:13-14 and represented by an angel in Revelation 14:6-7. The sequence of events in Matthew 24 and Revelation 14, and the occurrence of the preaching: Matthew 24 1. The events also portrayed in the first 4-5 seals (false Christs, war, famine, and death/persecution) **2. Gospel preached to all nations** 3. The end (rapture and wrath) Revelation 14:6-20 **1. Gospel preached to all nations** 2. Rapture (harvest) 3. Wrath Some believe the preaching of the gospel mentioned here in Scripture is symbolic of our ongoing effort to make disciples of all nations and that Christ can't return until we've reached every soul on the planet. Not only would this be impossible to accomplish, but it's not scripturally sound and is based on allegory. And we're on God's timetable, not ours. See *Two Witnesses* in Chapter Six of this guide for a description of who may be the ones to preach the gospel before the gathering and subsequent wrath (the two harvests in Matthew 13 and Revelation 14).	Matt 24:13-14 Mark 13:9-10 Rev 14:6-7

Key Words/ Phrases	Definition	References
Great Judgment, The	The time at the end of Christ's 1,000-year reign when all who weren't gathered at Christ's appearing will be judged and receive consequences of their actions (or lack thereof). They'll either be found in the Lamb's (Christ's) Book of Life and spared or thrown into the *lake of fire*. Anyone who's accepted Christ – entered into the marriage covenant so-to-speak – and remained His will be gathered and not be subject to this great judgment. Therefore, the New Testament usually presents this judgment from the perspective of those who'll be judged and destroyed at that time. Here are a couple of examples: • Matt 10:14-15 Whoever does not receive you, nor heed your words, as you go out of that house or that city, shake the dust off your feet. Truly I say to you, it will be more tolerable for the land of Sodom and Gomorrah in the day of judgment than for that city. • Matt 11:21-24 Woe to you, Chorazin! Woe to you, Bethsaida! For if the miracles had occurred in Tyre and Sidon which occurred in you, they would have repented long ago in sackcloth and ashes. Nevertheless I say to you, it will be more tolerable for Tyre and Sidon in the day of judgment than for you. And you, Capernaum, will not be exalted to heaven, will you? You will descend to Hades; for if the miracles had occurred in Sodom which occurred in you, it would have remained to this day. Nevertheless I say to you that it will be more tolerable for the land of Sodom in the day of judgment, than for you. See Chapter Sixteen of this guide for additional information.	Dan 12:1-3 Matt 10:15 Matt 11:22 & 24 Matt 12:36 Matt 13:30 Matt 13:40-43 Matt 25:31-46 Luke 10:14 John 5:22 John 5:27-29 Rom 2:2-8 Rom 14:9-10 2 Cor 5:10 2 Pet 2:4 & 9 2 Pet 3:6-13 2 Thess 1:5-10 Heb 9:26-28 1 John 4:17 Jude 1:6-7 Jude 1:14-15 Rev 20:11-15

Key Words/ Phrases	Definition	References

Great Tribulation, The	Represents the 3.5-year authority of the Antichrist and is referred to in Scripture as the time of Jacob's Trouble. Helpful Scripture references:
	
	• Time of Jacob's Trouble:
	    o Jer 30:7
	• Will begin midway through the seven-year agreement with the Antichrist:
	    o Dan 9:27
	    o Matt 24:15
	    o Mark 13:14
	• The 3.5-year persecution of God's people just before the end:
	    o Dan 7:20-25
	    o Dan 12:7
	    o Rev 13:5-7
	• A time like no other – past, present, or future:
	    o Dan 12:1
	    o Matt 24:21
	• Will require patience on the part of the saints during this time:
	    o Rev 13:10
	    o Rev 14:12
	• Antichrist's wrath/authority shortened (stopped before the end of the 3.5-year period) for the sake of the *elect*:
	    o Matt 24:22
	• Ended by the darkening of the sun, moon, and stars and gathering:
	    o Matt 24:29-31
	    o Mark 13:24-27
	    o Rev 6:12-17
	• What those "harvested" at the darkening of the sun, moon, and stars are gathered (raptured) out of:
	    o Matt 24:29-31
	    o Rev 7:9-17
	
	See Chapter Eight of this guide for additional information.
		Deut 4:27-30
		Jer 30:5-7
		Dan 7:20-25
		Dan 12:1
		Dan 12:7
		Matt 24:9
		Matt 24:21
		Matt 24:29-31
		Mark 13:19-20
		Mark 13:24-27
		Luke 21:22-24
		Rev 7:9-17
		Rev 13:5-7

Key Words/ Phrases	Definition	References
New Heaven & Earth	The *world to come* after this era ends. God will reside forever with His people at the creation of the new heaven and earth, which will occur after the great judgment.	Isa 25 & 27 Jer 31:31-40 Joel 3:17 -18 Rev 21:1-27 Rev 22:1-5
One-Hundred-Forty-four Thousand (144,000)	Representatives of Israel in the form of 12,000 from each of the 12 tribes of Israel. The following are key points about this group: • Sealed for protection against God's impending wrath (Rev 7:3-8 & 9:4) • Seen with Christ on Mount Zion during the time of God's wrath, but before the seventh trumpet when Christ will gain His kingdom and enter Jerusalem. They follow Him wherever He goes (Rev 14:1). • There'll be a new song in heaven that no man can learn but the 144,000, which were redeemed from the earth (Rev 14:2-3). • Redeemed from among men, being the first-fruits unto God and to the Lamb (Rev 14:4). • They will be virgins and without fault (Rev 14:4-5). Little is known about this group "redeemed from among men," but God clearly sets them apart and protects them during the time of His wrath. Again, this is most likely part of the remnant God promised to bring back in the last days; they'll be in Jerusalem with Christ. See *144,000 from the 12 Tribes* in Chapter Six for more information.	Zeph 3:13-15 Rev 7:3-8 Rev 14:1-5

Key Words/ Phrases	Definition	References
One-Thousand-Year Reign of Christ	Also known as Christ's kingdom on earth. Events associated with, and surrounding, the reign of Christ: • Prophesied by Daniel and recorded as one of the events to conclude the 70 weeks of years (490 years) period. (Dan 9:24). • Christ will gain His kingdom at the seventh trumpet of God's wrath (Rev 10:7 & 11:15). • Those martyred for their faith by beheading during the wrath/authority of the Antichrist will be resurrected and reign with Him. (Rev 20:4). • Satan will be released near the end of it to again test man only to finally suffer destruction by being thrown into the lake of fire. • The reign and era of this "age" will end with the great judgment of God and creation of a new heaven/earth. See *Christ's Kingdom* and Chapter Sixteen of this guide for additional information.	Rev 20:1-10

Key Words/ Phrases	Definition	References
Rapture	Gathering of Christ's chosen after the darkening of the sun, moon, and stars (e.g. Matt 24:29-31). Although the word *rapture* isn't used in Scripture, it's based on the Latin word *rapio* (caught up) and is a good way to refer to the gathering (harvest) that will happen at Christ's appearing (e.g. Matt 13:30 & 2 Thess 2:1-3). Those gathered out of the Great Tribulation at Christ's appearing are seen in heaven just before God's wrath begins in a vision given to John by Christ (Revelation 7:9-17). Note that this transformation will happen at the darkening of the sun, moon, and stars (cf. Matthew 24:30-31) – the same sign that will also precede the wrath of God (cf. Revelation 6:12-17). **Sequence of the end**: 1. False messiahs and increase in war/ famine (seals 1-3) 2. Persecution and death at the hands of the Antichrist (seals 4-5) 3. Darkening of the sun, moon, and stars (seal 6) **4. Gathering at Christ's appearing - rapture** (seen afterward in Revelation 7:9-17) 5. Short silence (seal 7) 6. God's wrath See *Christ's Coming (Parousia)* for additional information.	Matt 13:30 Matt 24:30-31 Mark 13:26-27 John 14:3 Phil 3:20-21 Col 3:1-6 1 Cor 15:49-52 1 Thess 4:13-17 2 Thess 2:1-3 1 Pet 2:12 Rev 7:9-17 Rev 14:15-16

Key Words/ Phrases	Definition	References
Remnant of Israel	Dispersed descendants of the 12 tribes of Israel brought back to their home in the last days as promised by God. The return was made possible in May 1948 after roughly 1,900 years of Diaspora (dispersion). Christ will reign over them for 1,000 years upon entering Jerusalem and gaining His kingdom at the seventh trumpet judgment. See *Remnant of Israel* in Chapter Six of this guide for more information.	Isa 1:9 Isa 10:17-22 Isa 11:1-16 Jer 23:3-8 Jer 31:6-11 Ezek 6:8-12 Ezek 14:21-22 Joel 2:32 Amos 5:15-20 Amos 9:11-15 Mic 2:12 Mic 4:6-7 Mic 5:3-15 Zeph 2:7-9 Zeph 3:13-14 Zech 8:2-8 Rom 9:27 (Isa 1:9)

Key Words/ Phrases	Definition	References
Restrainer	He who keeps Satan at bay currently. Satan will empower the Antichrist to act wickedly during the 3.5 years of his authority after the restrainer no longer holds him back. Although pre-tribulation rapture proponents claim the restrainer is the Holy Spirit to support an early, secret rapture, several points including scriptural references suggest it's the archangel Michael: 1. The Antichrist (mystery of iniquity) and his works will be revealed at the removal of the "restrainer" (2 Thess 2:7-12). 2. Michael, the protector of Israel, arises at the time of the Great Tribulation (Dan 12:1). His "arising" is probably necessary to war in heaven with Satan at that time (Rev 12:7-13). 3. Michael and his angels will battle Satan and cast him to earth in great wrath toward Jew and Christian at the beginning of a 3.5-year period (Rev 12:7-13). 4. God's Holy Spirit brings wisdom and understanding to believers. He's never mentioned in the same context as restraint, war, etc., as the archangel Michael is (e.g. Acts 9:31, 1 Corinthians 12, & John 14:26).	Dan 12:1 2 Thess 2:7-12

Key Words/ Phrases	Definition	References
Saints	Holy ones as depicted by the Greek word *hagios* (Strong's G40 below) used hundreds of times in the New Testament to depict holy things and people. For example: • *Saint* (or *saints*) is used 61 times in the NT – always for Christian or angel except once for OT saints in Matt 27:52 • *Holy Spirit* (90 times) • *Holy City* (6 times) • *Holy Place* (10 times) Considering context is vital to understanding the intended use and determining whether Scripture is referring to an angel or Christian believer when using the word *saint*! Otherwise, one could erroneously believe *saint* refers to a believer coming back to earth *with* Christ instead of an angel coming to gather believers *unto* Christ as in these verses where *saint* indicates angels: Jude 1:14 And Enoch also, the seventh from Adam, prophesied of these, saying, Behold, the Lord cometh with ten thousands of his *Holy Ones (saints* in King James). The reference in context is to angels, not believers in Christ. 1 Thess 3:13 To the end he may establish your hearts unblameable in holiness before God, even our Father, at the coming of our Lord Jesus Christ with all his *saints*. The reference in context is to angels, not believers in Christ. The following offers additional examples of the use of the word *saint* in the New Testament: *Saints* as **believers** in Christ: • 2 Thess 1:10 When He comes to be glorified in His *saints*. • 1 Cor 1:2 To the church of God which is at Corinth, to those who have been sanctified in Christ Jesus, *saints* by calling, with all who in every place call on the name of our Lord Jesus Christ, their Lord and ours.	Matt 25:31 Matt 27:52-53 Mark 8:38 Luke 9:26 Acts 9:13 Rom 1:6-7 1 Cor 6:2-3 1 Cor 14:33 Eph 1:1 Phil 4:21 Col 1:2 1 Thess 3:13 2 Thess 1:7-10 Jude 1:14-15 Rev 13:7 Rev 14:10 Rev 14:12-15 Rev 16:6-7

Key Words/ Phrases	Definition	References
Saints *continued*	• 1 Cor 14:33 For God is not a God of confusion but of peace, as in all the churches of the *saints*. • Rev 13:7 It was also given to him to make war with the *saints* and to overcome them, and authority over every tribe and people and tongue and nation was given to him. (Compare with Daniel 7.) • Rev 14:12 Here is the patience of the *saints.* *Saints* as those who've died before Christ was crucified and resurrected: • Matt 27:52 The tombs were opened, and many bodies of the *saints* who had fallen asleep were raised. G40: *hagios* (hag'-ee-os) Sacred (physically pure, morally blameless or religious, ceremonially consecrated): - (most) holy (one, thing), saint.	Matt 25:31 Matt 27:52-53 Mark 8:38 Luke 9:26 Acts 9:13 Rom 1:6-7 1 Cor 6:2-3 1 Cor 14:33 Eph 1:1 Phil 4:21 Col 1:2 1 Thess 3:13 2 Thess 1:7-10 Jude 1:14-15 Rev 13:7 Rev 14:10 Rev 14:12-15 Rev 16:6-7
Seal 1	First in a scroll in the Revelation and broken to reveal false messiahs leading up to the end. The false Christ in this display is dressed in white and wears a crown, indicating righteous authority. However, his weapon is a bow, not the weapon of Christ – the sword. Compare the false Christs mentioned in Matthew 24:5 with the representation in Revelation 6:2. Contrary to a popular belief, this doesn't represent *the* Antichrist depicted later in Matthew 24 and whose authority is represented in the fourth and fifth seals below.	Matt 24:5 Rev 6:2
Seal 2	Second in the scroll and broken to reveal an increase in war/violence as the end approaches. Compare this to what Jesus told His disciples about this in Matthew 24:6.	Matt 24:6 Rev 6:4
Seal 3	Third in the scroll and broken to reveal an increase and intensity in famine and earthquakes as the end approaches. Compare this revelation to what Jesus told His disciples in Matthew 24:7.	Matt 24:7 Rev 6:5-6

Key Words/ Phrases	Definition	References
Seals 4 & 5	Fourth and fifth in the scroll, broken to unveil the death and persecution during the authority of the *beast* (the Greek word *therion* is the only "beast" word used to represent the Antichrist or his kingdom). The souls of those killed during this time cry out for an end to the slaughter as seen in the fifth seal and are also identified in Revelation 20:4 as those who'll reign with Christ for 1,000 years after being raised. Compare the events revealed by these broken seals with Matthew 24:9-22.	Matt 24:9-22 Rev 7-11 Rev 20:4
Seal 6	Sixth in the scroll and broken to unveil a complete darkening of the sun, moon, and stars. This event will signify the end of the Great Tribulation and herald Christ's coming, the gathering of believers, and the onslaught of God's Day of the Lord wrath. Also see *Darkening of the Sun, Moon, & Stars.*	Isa 2:19-22 Matt 24:29 Rev 6:12-17
Seal 7	Seventh and last in the scroll, broken to reveal the half-hour of silence that will occur after the darkening revealed in the sixth seal but just before God's wrath begins on the rest of the earth – those not gathered at the darkening of the sun, moon, and stars.	Rev 8:1
Temple (of God)	The third Jewish temple in Jerusalem. Daniel, Jesus, and Paul recorded that the Antichrist will set himself up in the temple during his 3.5-year reign. The temple may be used for this purpose since Scripture also shows us that the Antichrist and his kingdom will exercise authority from Jerusalem at the end. So, contrary to the belief of some, this will be a physical structure and isn't alone symbolic of the body of Christ.	Dan 9:27 Matt 24:15 2 Thess 2:4 Rev 11:1-2

Key Words/ Phrases	Definition	References
Three-and-a-Half Years: Time, Times, and Half a Time	A 3.5-year time period (1 + 2 + .5): Time (not plural) = 1 Times (plural) = 2 Half (or translated as "dividing" of time) = .5 The Hebrew word for time as in Daniel 7:24-25 is *Iddan* (Strong's H5732 below) which suggests a year-long period. The Hebrew word for time in Daniel 12:7 is represented by Strong's H4150 below and also indicates a year. While most Bible scholars seem to agree that this translates to a 3.5-year period, some disagree and argue that "times" may not be "2." Revelation 12:6 and 12:14 appear to be referring to the same period and yet use two different methods of describing the epochs: time, times, and dividing of time, and 1,260 days – both equal 3.5 360-day (Jewish) years. Also, the time of the Antichrist's authority is labeled as time, times, and the dividing of time by Daniel and 42 months (1,260 days) in Revelation 13:5; both describe the same timeframe. H5732 ʽiddân (id-dawn') a set time; technically a year: - time. H4150 môʽêd môʽêd môʽâdâh (mo-ade', mo-ade', mo-aw-daw') properly an appointment, that is, a fixed time or season; specifically a festival; **conventionally a year**; by implication, an assembly (as convened for a definite purpose); technically the congregation; by extension, the place of meeting; also a signal (as appointed beforehand): - appointed (sign, time), (place of, solemn) assembly, congregation, (set, solemn) feast, (appointed, due) season, solemn (-ity), synagogue, (set) time (appointed). Also see *Three-and-a-Half Years: 1,260* days & *Three-and-a-Half Years: 42 months.*	Dan 7:24-25 Dan 12:7 Rev 12:14

Key Words/ Phrases	Definition	References
Three-and-a-Half Years: 1,260 Days	Depicts the last half of the seven-year period that will begin with an agreement between the Antichrist and others – especially Israel. This reference in Scripture is synonymous with other references of 42 months and time, times, and dividing of time. Jewish years were 360 days long; 1,260 days therefore represents 3.5 years. This specific label depicts these events or timeframes: • Time of the two witnesses (Rev 11:3). • Length of Antichrist's wrath + another 30-day period (Dan 12:11). • Israel taken care of in the "desert" (Rev 12:6). See *Three-and-a-Half Years: Time, Times, and Half a Time & Three-and-a-Half Years: 42 months.*	Dan 12:11 Rev 11:3 Rev 12:6
Three-and-a-Half Years: 42 Months	Also a depiction of the last half of the seven-year period Daniel spoke of (Dan 9:27). Since there are 12 months in a calendar year, this timeframe equals 3.5 years. This will be the length of time the Temple Mount will be under gentile control (Rev 11:2) and represents the Antichrist's authority over the saints (Rev 13:5). The fact that 42 months and 1,260 days are in the same context of Revelation 11:2-3 lends credence to the claim that they're the same timeframe. See *Three-and-a-Half Years: Time, Times, and Half a Time & Three-and-a-Half Years: 1,260 days.*	Rev 11:2-3 Rev 13:5
Two Witnesses	Two heavenly hosts sent to earth to prophesy/ witness to the world for 3.5 years (1,260 days) during the authority of the Antichrist. They may be the ones who'll carry out the preaching just before the gathering and subsequent wrath of God (see *Gospel Preached (to all Nations)*). See *Two Witnesses* in Chapter Six of this guide for additional information.	Rev 11:3-10

APPENDIX C

BIBLIOGRAPHY

Anderberg, Roy W. *Post Tribulation Rapture – A Biblical Study of the Return of Christ.* Tucson: Wheatmark, 2008.

Archer, Gleason L. Jr., Paul D. Feinberg, Douglas J. Moo, and Richard Reiter. *Three Views on the Rapture (Pre, Mid-, or Post-Tribulation)*. Grand Rapids: Zondervan, 1996.

Blaising, Craig A., Kenneth L. Gentry Jr., and Robert B. Strimple. *Three Views on the Millennium and Beyond.* Grand Rapids: Zondervan, 1999.

Bright, John. *A History of Israel.* 4th ed. Louisville: Westminster John Knox Press, 2000.

Global University. *Introduction to Hermeneutics: How to Interpret the Bible*. Springfield: Global University, 2006.

Gregg, Steve. *REVELATION, Four Views: A Parallel Commentary.* Nashville: Thomas Nelson Publishers, 1997.

Lindsey, Hal. *The Late Great Planet Earth.* Grand Rapids: Zondervan, 1970.

———. *There's a New World Coming*. Eugene: Harvest House Publishers, 1984.

Miller, Stephen R. *The New American Commentary – Daniel Volume 18.* Nashville: B&H Publishing Group, 1994.

NASB Study Bible. Grand Rapids: Zondervan, 1999.

Price, Randall. *The Stones Cry Out*. Eugene: Harvest House

Publishers, 1977.

Richardson, Joel. *The Islamic Antichrist.* Los Angeles: World Net Daily (WND), 2009.

Skolfield, Ellis H. *The False Prophet.* Fort Myers: Fish House Publishing, 2001.

Van Kampen, Robert. *The Sign.* 5th ed . Wheaton: Crossway Books, 2000.

Whiston, William. *The New Complete Works of Josephus.* Grand Rapids: Kregel Publications, 1999.

APPENDIX D

Answers to Checkup Questions

Chapters One & Two

1. Why is the end-of-the-world topic so important? **Ignorance of what God has shown us about the end of the world and our gathering could allow false teaching to take root. Poor understanding, and therefore weak faith, could pave the way for believing a variety of untruths to include the concept that a gathering (rapture) will happen before the Great Tribulation period. Also, it's probably the single-most talked about topic in Scripture.**

2. According to Christ, what will be some of the signs leading up to the seven-year period at the end**? Increase in righteous imposters (false Christs), war, famine, and earthquakes.**

3. How long, according to Daniel, will the authority we call the Antichrist be in authority and persecute God's chosen? **Three-and-one-half years (you'll later learn that this is also identified as a 42-month and 1,260-day period (3.5 360-day Jewish years).**

4. What sign will precede Christ's appearing in the clouds and our subsequent gathering? **Complete darkening of the sun, moon, and stars.**

5. Who or what will gather all true believers in Christ at His appearing? **Angels coming to earth with Christ.**

6. *Private Challenge / Discussion*: What's your understanding regarding this Bible subject? What had you read, heard, or been taught regarding it before reading Chapters One and Two? What have you done to research, validate, or confirm that information? **Answers will vary.**

CHAPTERS THREE & FOUR

1. Why is it important to understand what an antecedent is and to be able to identify them? **Pronouns refer to subjects already mentioned in Scripture. Being able to recognize them will help you maintain the flow of text and keep your eye on the writer's meaning.**

2. How should you first approach Scripture interpretation – literally or figuratively? Why? **Literally. Assuming the text is figurative and not to be taken at face value opens the door for misinterpretation.**

3. A ________________ is the smallest circle of context for a sentence or verse. **Paragraph.**

4. What resource(s) should you consult to discover the root or meaning of certain words in Scripture? **Concordance or Bible dictionary.**

5. Why is allegorizing Scripture so dangerous? **Doing so increases the risk of masking the writer's true meaning. Again, take all Scripture literally – at face value – unless it's clear you should do otherwise.**

6. *Private Challenge / Discussion*: What are some possible biblical allegories you've heard? Would you take the time to validate them through Scripture research and comparison? **Answers will vary.**

CHAPTERS SIX & SEVEN

1. What two major events are identified in Jeremiah 23:3-6 and Ezekiel 37:21-25? **A remnant of Israel's return home, and the reign of Christ.**

2. The 144,000 will be __________ unto Christ. **First-fruits.**

3. The 144,000 will be sealed against what? **The impending wrath of God.**

4. Why isn't the tribe of Dan mentioned in the list of the 12 tribes to be sealed? Which tribe/leader replaced it? **We don't know for sure, but most likely because of idol worship. The tribe of Manasseh replaced the tribe of Dan.**

5. What will happen to the elect/chosen when Christ appears (according to Matthew 24:31)? **They'll be gathered by Christ's angels.**

6. When will everyone who died before Christ's new covenant, or who refused to enter into Christ's covenant, be judged? **At the great judgment of God following the 1,000-year reign of Christ. The new age/heaven and earth will then begin.**

7. Which two harvests are identified in Matthew 13, John 5:28, and Revelation 14? **The gathering of the elect and destruction of the wicked. In Matthew 13, the harvests are of wheat (good) and tares (the wicked). The harvests are of grapes in Revelation 14; those representing the wicked are put into the winepress of God's wrath.**

8. How long will the two witnesses preach? **1,260 days (3.5 years).**

9. What will happen to the two witnesses at the end of their ministry? **The Antichrist empowered by Satan will kill them, but they'll be resurrected after three days and taken to heaven.**

10. Which seals in the Revelation pertain to persecution and death at the hands of the Antichrist? **Seal 4 (death and persecution) and seal 5 (the souls of those killed are wondering how much more time there will be until God's revenge).**

11. What will happen to those beheaded for their faith during the Antichrist's reign? **They'll be brought back to life during the first resurrection to reign with Christ during His 1,000-year kingdom.**

12. Christ's bride (the church) regularly seals the marriage contract in accordance with which part of a traditional Jewish wedding? **The drinking of wine. Those entering into the covenant with Christ do this through partaking of the communion cup.**

13. List at least one gift Christ as a groom gave the church upon leaving for the betrothal period. **Answers should include righteousness or the Holy Spirit.**

14. Which events will directly precede the gathering of the chosen/elect for the marriage supper? **A darkening of the sun, moon, and stars; trumpet call; shout (Matthew 24:29-31, Mark 13:24-27, and 1 Thessalonians 4:16).**

15. Private Challenge / Discussion: What have you been told in the past regarding the identity of the 144,000 Jews? The two witnesses? Do you believe Jews who accept Jesus and enter into the marriage covenant are called and gathered for the marriage supper at the same time as all other believers who've given their lives to Christ? **Answers will vary, but Romans 10:11-13 and Galatians 3:27-29 can be used to keep a discussion of the latter question on track.**

CHAPTERS EIGHT, NINE, & TEN

1. According to John 8:44, who is the father of lies? **Satan.**

2. When will Satan be permanently removed from heaven and banished to the earth? **After war in heaven (see Isaiah 14:12-15 and Revelation 7-14).**

3. List three different names for the Antichrist based on 2 Thessalonians 2:1-8. **Man of Lawlessness, Son of Destruction, and Lawless One.**

4. Ezekiel 38:2-6 reveals the names of the country of the Antichrist's origin and the seven other countries not subdued by him. What are these eight countries/regions? **Magog (Antichrist's origin), Meshech, Tubal, Persia, Ethiopia, Put, Gomer, and Beth-togarmah. All are Middle Eastern countries or regions surrounding Israel.**

5. The people of what will be the region or kingdom of the Antichrist's origin destroyed Jerusalem and the temple in 70 CE as prophesied by Daniel (Daniel 9:26). Based on accounts by Flavius Josephus and in consideration of the part of the world this happened in, what would've been the most likely ethnic background of those *people*? **Mediterranean and Middle Eastern (e.g. Greek, Syrian, and Arabian).**

6. Scripture such as Daniel 7:25, Revelation 11:12, and Revelation 13:5 indicate the length of time the Antichrist will have authority to persecute and kill God's people. What will be this length of time in days, months, or years? **1,260 days, or 42 months, or 3.5 years. Remember that a Jewish month is 30 days.**

7. The authority of the Antichrist will be a time of great tribulation. Will believers in Christ have to endure this? Helpful Scripture references include Matthew 24:21-22, Revelation 12:13-17, Revelation 14:12-13, and Revelation 13:10. **Yes. And those**

martyred during this time for their faith, testimony, and refusal to accept the beast's mark will earn the right to reign with Christ for 1,000 years.

8. What sign in the heavens will mark the end of the Great Tribulation and precede the gathering of Christian believers? Helpful Scripture references include Matthew 24:29-31 and Mark 13:24-27. **Darkening of the sun, moon, and stars.**

9. Scripture like Ezekiel 16:37-39, Ezekiel 23:28-30, Matthew 23:37-38, and Revelation 17:16-17 hints at who – or what – the harlot of Babylon *could* be. Who or what do you believe the harlot will be? Why? **Answers may vary. Encourage discussion.**

10. Isaiah 1:9-10, Revelation 11:8, and Revelation 16:19 offer clues as to the figurative end-times city Babylon. What city, or location, do you believe this Babylon will represent? **Answers may vary. Encourage discussion.**

11. *Private Challenge / Discussion*: Several theories exist regarding the Antichrist's identity and the makeup of his end-times kingdom. Views also differ as to whether Christians will go through the Great Tribulation. What do you believe about the Antichrist, his kingdom, and whether Christians will go through the Great Tribulation? How has this study affected your beliefs or views of these topics? **Answers will vary.**

CHAPTER TWELVE

1. AccordingtoDaniel2,whatwerethefivepartsofNebuchadnezzar's statue? What empire does each part represent?

   Head of gold:
   Nebuchadnezzar's Babylonian Empire
   Arms and breastplate of silver:
   Mede/Persian Empire
   Belly and thighs of bronze:
   Greek Empire
   Legs of iron:
   Roman Empire
   Feet of iron and clay:
   Latter-days empire (Antichrist's kingdom)

2. What is the "*stone cut out of the mountain without hand*" of Daniel 2:34 & 45? **The messiah, Jesus.**

3. List the three kingdoms depicted in Daniel 7:1-6. **Babylonian, Mede-Persian, and Greek.**

4. Daniel 7:7-8 reveals a fourth beast that will come after the Greek Empire. Which empire does it represent in the near-term? In the far-term? **Near-term: Rome; far-term: Antichrist's empire.**

5. What is the theme of Daniel 7:23-26? **Antichrist's rise to power, time of authority, and destruction.**

6. List at least three similarities between the Antichrist in chapter 7 and Antiochus Epiphanes in chapter 8. **Possible answers:**

   - **Empowered by Satan**
   - **Called a "little horn"**
   - **Enter the temple and stop daily sacrifice**
   - **Magnify themselves as God**
   - **Deceive through a peace agreement**

7. When will the "70 sevens" of years foretold in Daniel 9:24 begin? **With the decree to Ezra to rebuild Jerusalem.**

8. What two major events happened during the first 69 of Daniel's 70 weeks of years? **The rebuilding of Jerusalem and Christ's first coming.**

9. According to Daniel 9:27, what will kick off Daniel's 70th week of years? What will happen in the middle after three and a half years? **A peace agreement will start the last seven-year period (week of years). The Antichrist will dishonor the agreement midway through it.**

10. What will happen in the last half of Daniel's 70th week (based on 11:45-12:2)? **The Antichrist will establish himself in Jerusalem while also flexing his military might. A terrible time of tribulation like never seen on earth will begin then.**

11. Daniel 12:11 tells us of an event or action that will start the 1,260 days (3.5 years) + 30 days for a total of a 1,290-day period. What will it be? **The abolishing of daily sacrifice.**

12. Those who attain a certain number of days from the removing of the daily sacrifice will be blessed according to Daniel 12:12. What is that total number of days? Do we know what the last 45-day period during that time will be used for? **The total number of days will equal 1,335. We know nothing concrete about the last 45 days (after the 1,290 days).**

38. Revelation: Four Views – A Parallel Commentary (edited by Steve Gregg) – page xiv
39. *Three Views on the Millennium and Beyond*, pages 182-192
40. *88 Reasons Why the Rapture will be in 1988; The Final Shout: Rapture Report 1989; 23 Reasons why a pre-tribulation rapture looks like it will occur on Rosh-Hashanah 1993; And now the earth's destruction by fire, nuclear bomb fire* (a 1994 prediction) – all by Edgar C. Whisenant
41. This is from a document downloaded from www.familyradio.com/cross/tract/add/church_add1.htm at 7:58 CST on 02/04/2002.
42. www.familyradio.com
43. See *Christ's Appearing* and *Christ's Coming* in Appendix B for additional information.
44. Matthew 24:30; Luke 21:27; 1 Thessalonians 1:10; 2 Timothy 1:10; Hebrews 9:28 & 10:37; 1 Peter 1:7 & 5:4; 2 Peter 1:16 & 3:10-18; 1 John 3:2; Jude 1:14-15
45. *Three Views on the Millennium and Beyond*, page 21
46. *Three Views on the Millennium and Beyond*, page 21
47. See *Christ's Appearing* and *Christ's Coming* in Appendix B
48. Hal Lindsey – *There's a New World Coming*, pages 73-98
49. *Three Views on the Rapture*, pages 49-58
50. *Three Views on the Rapture*, page 80, and Hal Lindsey – *There's a New World Coming*, page 62
51. *Three Views on the Rapture*, page 37
52. Hal Lindsey – *There's a New World Coming*, page 62
53. *Three Views on the Rapture*, page 32
54. Hal Lindsey – *There's a New World Coming*, page 51
55. *Three Views on the Rapture*, pages 63-68
56. Hal Lindsey – *There's a New World Coming*, page 67
57. *Three Views on the Rapture*, page 18
58. See *Restrainer* in Appendix B
59. *Three Views on the Rapture*, pages 141-143
60. *Three Views on the Rapture*, page 124
61. *Three Views on the Rapture*, page 124
62. *Three Views on the Rapture*, page 139
63. *Three Views on the Rapture*, page 143
64. *The sign*, page 19
65. *The sign*, page 25
66. See Chapter Nine of this guide for scriptural support.
67. *Three Views on the Rapture*, page 175
68. *Three Views on the Rapture, A History of the Development of the Rapture Positions*, page 11
69. *A Biblical Study of the Return of Christ* by Roy W. Anderberg, pages 1-2
70. *Three Views on the Rapture*, pages 201-205
71. endoftheworld@findingrevelation.com
72. endoftheworld@findingrevelation.com

CPSIA information can be obtained at www.ICGtesting.com
260594BV00002B/2/P

9 781613 791448

CHAPTER FOURTEEN

1. What three basic questions did several of Jesus' disciples ask Him on the Mount of Olives?

   a. **When will the temple be destroyed?**
   b. **What will be the sign of Christ's return?**
   c. **What will be the sign of the end of the age?**

2. Which events mentioned in Matthew 24 will, according to Christ, lead to, but not be, the end? **False messiahs, war, famine, and earthquakes.**

3. Christ described the events in question #3 as birth pangs. Why did He call them that? **They'll increase in frequency and intensity as the end draws near.**

4. Who was Christ quoting when He mentioned the "*abomination that causes desolation*" in Matthew 24:15? What will be the "*holy place*" mentioned in the same verse? (NOTE: Scripture we studied from Daniel 9 and 12 and 2 Thessalonians 2:4 may be helpful here.) **Christ was quoting Daniel (cf. 9:27 & 12:11). The "holy place" can be nothing other than a recreated temple of God based on Scripture references listed above.**

5. What event or timeframe will the appearing of the *abomination* in the temple usher in? **The Great Tribulation (authority of the Antichrist).**

6. Why will God cut short the time referenced in question #5 (Matthew 24:22 and Mark 13:20)? **For the sake of God's elect. Otherwise, none would be left alive.**

7. Matthew 24:29, Mark 13:24-25, Luke 21:25-26, and Revelation 6:12-14 describe signs that will appear in the sky when God cuts short the Antichrist's time of authority. Their presence will be seen at the time Christ appears with His angels to gather the

elect. What will these signs be? **Possible answers could include a complete darkening of the sun, moon, and stars, and great earthquakes.**

8. The signs from question #7 and the subsequent gathering will be good news to some (as in Luke 21:28), but not to others. Why do you think the Bible tells us that some will mourn at that time (cf. Matthew 24:30 and Revelation 6:15-17)? **Answers will vary, but the scriptural context seems to indicate that the others not gathered know God's wrath is coming.**

9. What do you think Christ's intent was behind what He said in Matthew 24:28 & 32, Mark 13:28, and Luke 21:29-30? **The parables suggest a theme of "when you see *this*, then you'll see *that*." He gave them several signs and warned them to be watchful. The parables were most likely just tools used to really stress His point.**

10. What are the three major themes portrayed in the parables of Matthew 25?

    a. **Verses 1-13: The parable of the ten virgins waiting for the bridegroom (be ready).**
    b. **Verses14-30: The parable of the talents. Use the time and resources God gave us wisely until the Master's return.**
    c. **Verses 31-40 & 41-45: The great judgment.**

CHAPTER SIXTEEN

1. Who is the author of the Revelation? Who gave it to that author? **Christ, given to Him by God.**

2. What do the seven lampstands of Revelation 1 represent? **The seven churches of Asia Minor at the time of the Revelation (about 90 CE).**

3. What do the seven stars of Revelation 1 represent? **The messengers to the seven churches in Asia Minor.**

4. In His letters to the churches, Christ has nothing against two of them. Which are they? **Smyrna and Philadelphia.**

5. Why is Christ the only one who can break the seals and reveal the end-times events in chapter 5? **Because "*He was slain, and purchased for God with His blood men from every tribe and tongue and people and nation*" (cf. Revelation 5:9).**

6. Which timeframe is unveiled by broken seals 4 and 5 in Revelation 6:7-11? **A three-and-a-half-year reign of the Antichrist allowed by God, the persecution and death it will bring, and the souls of those killed for their faith during that time.**

7. Revelation 6:12-17 covers the breaking of the sixth seal, which outlines the darkening of the sun, moon, and stars that will precede ________________ and ___________ (also check out Matthew 24:29-31). **The gathering of the bride (church) and God's wrath against the rest of the world.**

8. What is the background or nationality of the multitude reflected in Revelation 7:9-17 (seen by John immediately after the darkening of the sixth seal)? **The multitude is made from *every nation and all tribes and peoples and tongues*. In other words, no particular background or nationality.**

9. From what did the multitude in question #8 come out of? **The Great Tribulation during the authority of the Antichrist.**

10. Which trumpet judgment comprised woe #1 of Revelation 9:12? **Five.**

11. Which trumpet judgment or other events comprise woe #2 of Revelation 11:14?
    a. **Trumpet judgment 6 (Revelation 9:13-21).**
    b. **Great earthquake: "*And in that hour there was a great earthquake, and a tenth of the city fell; seven thousand people were killed in the earthquake, and the rest were terrified and gave glory to the God of heaven.*"—Revelation 11:13.**
    c. **You may also wish to add that the seventh trumpet is about to sound (Revelation 11:15).**

12. The seventh trumpet blast (Revelation 11:15) will pinpoint certain apocalyptic events. What will they be?
    a. **Woe #3.**
    b. **The beginning of Christ's kingdom.**
    c. **The official end of the Antichrist's authority given to him by God.**

13. Which two three-and-a-half-year-long scenarios are unveiled in Revelation 11? **Control of the city of Jerusalem by the nations (gentiles) and the testimony of God's two witnesses.**

14. Which three-and-a-half-year-long scenario is unveiled in Revelation 12? **Pursuit and persecution by Satan (through the Antichrist) of a remnant of Israel and of those who hold to the testimony of Jesus Christ. The remnant will be kept safe by God during this period.**

15. What will be happening during the three-and-a-half-year timeframe unveiled in Revelation 13? **This will be the time of authority of the Antichrist. The False Prophet will assist him.**

16. Please summarize what's happening in Revelation 14:2-3 and 15:2-4. Things to consider:
    a. Who's singing the song in heaven? **Those who'll be victorious over the Antichrist by remaining righteous and not accepting his mark or worshipping him.**
    b. What group contains the only earthly beings that can learn the song? **The 144,000.**
    c. What's the context of this vision? **The song being sung after the end of the trumpet judgments and before the bowl judgments. Christ will have just gained His kingdom, and the 144,000 will be with Him on Mount Zion. There is still one woe to go.**

17. What's the theme of Revelation 17 and 18? **Babylon – both as a harlot who will enter into a relationship with the Antichrist and as the location where she and the Antichrist will be. I believe these to be Israel and Jerusalem.**

18. Revelation 17:9-11 gives insight as to the spiritual principality (or principalities) that will be involved with the Antichrist's end-times kingdom. Please describe who the following entities were or will be (when John wrote down the Revelation):
    a. The five that *have fallen*: **Egypt, Assyria, Babylon, Persia, and Greece.**
    b. The one that *is*: **Rome.**
    c. The one that *will come*: **This was probably the Ottoman (Turkish) Empire based on the pattern of conquest.**
    d. The *eighth* ruler: **This will be the Antichrist's kingdom.**

19. What are the primary points or themes of Revelation 19? **The marriage of the bride to Christ, and the destruction of the Antichrist and his armies at the battle of Armageddon.**

20. According to Revelation 20:4-6, who will be with Christ during

His 1,000-year reign? **Those beheaded during the Antichrist's Great Tribulation, which will then be resurrected for this purpose. Also with Him will probably be the 144,000 protected by God during that time and seen with Christ on Mount Zion as He gained His kingdom.**

21. Are hell and the lake of fire the same thing? **Not necessarily. The term 'hell' is often used to refer to three separate locations: Hades, the abyss, and the lake of fire. Hades is a temporary holding place for spirits released from the dead. The abyss will be a holding place for Satan during his 1,000-year incarceration and may be synonymous with hades. The lake of fire is where those not in the Book of Life will be thrown after the great judgment of God. This is also where Satan, the Antichrist, and the False Prophet will end up.**

22. Private Challenge / Discussion: Do you believe the judgment reflected in Revelation 20:11-15 and the "sheep and goat" judgment of Matthew 24 describe the same event? Why? Why not? **Answers may vary.**

23. Private Challenge / Discussion: Revelation 21:8 gives a short list of sinful behavior that will keep us out of God's kingdom and put us into the lake of fire at the great judgment. What do you think someone practicing any of those behaviors could do to become one who "*overcomes*" as in 21:6-7? **Answers may vary but should reflect repentance, which is a change of heart that brings about a change in behavior. Behavior is a repeated pattern that suggests intent. Jesus taught us that intent to sin is just as bad as the act itself (cf. Matthew 5:28). Changing the heart/intent by doing the right things for the right reasons and avoiding sinful behavior because it's the right thing to do would be a great place to start.**

24. Who is the intended audience of the Revelation? **Everyone that hears and heeds the prophecy, although the seven churches of Asia Minor comprised the immediate audience.**

25. *Private Challenge / Discussion*: The word *church* isn't used in Revelation after the seven letters of chapters 2 and 3. A popular theory of those who hold to a pre-tribulation rapture: this is proof that the rapture will happen before any of the events of the Great Tribulation (reign of the Antichrist). What are your thoughts now that you've gone through the entire Revelation? Do you agree? Why? Why not? **Answers may vary.**

26. What consequences await those who modify the Revelation given by Christ (22:18-21)? **Removal from the Book of Life and all that entails to include destruction in the lake of fire after God's great judgment.**

APPENDIX E
NOTES

1. www.globaluniversity.edu
2. Excerpts taken from the Global University's *Introduction to Hermeneutics: How to Interpret the Bible* (page 105)
3. *The New Complete Works of Josephus*
4. www.cais-soas.com/CAIS/Anthropology/Scythian/introduction.htm
5. www.christiananswers.net/dictionary/magog.html
6. www.answersingenesis.org/articles/aid/v4/n1/josephus-and-genesis-chapter-ten
7. www.askelm.com/prophecy/p000201.htm
8. www.wikiislam.net/wiki/Jizyah
9. www.wikiislam.net/wiki
10. www.quranexplorer.com/ & www.muslim.org/english-quran/quran.htm
11. www.answering-islam.org
12. www.islam.tc/prophecies/imam.html
13. While it's true that Antiochus' reign and death conclude an "end-time" period of wrath (indignation), there's no biblical support for an exact period of time (i.e. number of years).
14. The New American Commentary, Volume 18 – Daniel, page 226
15. The New American Commentary, Volume 18 – Daniel, pages 228-229
16. The New American Commentary, Volume 18 – Daniel, pages 234-235
17. The New American Commentary, Volume 18 – Daniel, pages 257 & 265-266
18. See "Fall Feasts of the Lord" in Appendix B.
19. See "Interpretive Concepts & Tools" in Chapter Four of this guide.
20. Revelation: Four Views – A Parallel Commentary (edited by Steve Gregg) – page 38
21. Revelation: Four Views – A Parallel Commentary (edited by Steve Gregg) – page 34
22. Revelation: Four Views – A Parallel Commentary (edited by Steve Gregg) – page 34
23. See "Fall Feasts of the Lord" in Appendix B.
24. See "Fall Feasts of the Lord" in Appendix B.
25. Revelation: Four Views – A Parallel Commentary (edited by Steve Gregg) – page 62
26. Polycarp was a disciple of John's, confirmed by Irenaeus and Tertullian (early church fathers who heard him speak). He was stabbed to death when an attempt to burn him at the stake failed.
27. See "Fall Feasts of the Lord" in Appendix B.
28. www.biblicalastronomy.com and www.watchmanbiblestudy.com/biblestudies/Definitions/Feasts/Def_RoshHashanah
29. Hal Lindsey – *There's a New World Coming*, page 67
30. www.catholic.com/library/Rapture.asp
31. *Three Views on the Millennium and Beyond*, pages 86-99
32. *Three Views on the Millennium and Beyond*, pages 118-127
33. *An Evening of Eschatology* viewed October 5, 2010 (http://vimeo.com/13310674)
34. *Three Views on the Millennium and Beyond*, page 13
35. *An Evening of Eschatology* viewed October 5, 2010 (http://vimeo.com/13310674)
36. *Three Views on the Millennium and Beyond*, pages 36-37
37. *Three Views on the Millennium and Beyond*, pages 50-55